To Bob and Wayne, In the light of Venus! — "Cosmic Ray" Keller Heb. 13:2

Venus Rising:

A Concise History of the Second Planet

Raymond Andrew Keller II

Headline Books, Inc.
Terra Alta, WV

Venus Rising: A Concise History of the Second Planet

by Raymond Andrew Keller II

To order additional copies of this book or for book publishing information, or to contact the author:

Headline Books, Inc.
P.O. Box 52
Terra Alta, WV 26764
www.headlinebooks.com

Tel: 800-570-5951
Email: mybook@headlinebooks.com

ISBN 13: 978-1-882658-31-2

Library of Congress Control Number: 2015944806

PRINTED IN THE UNITED STATES OF AMERICA

This book is dedicated to my beloved wife, Ydalis.
Without her kind assistance, this work would not have been possible.

Foreword

I have known the "Cosmic Ray" and his extensive work in the field of ufology since the mid-1960s and our ventures in organizing various paranormal research groups throughout Northeast Ohio. So I would have to say that I count it a great privilege, both as his colleague and friend, to write the forward for *Venus Rising: A Concise History of the Second Planet*.

Every day the evidence mounts for the existence of intelligent forms of life on other planets. Given the estimated age of our universe since the Big Bang as 14 billion years, and the emergence of humankind on the Earth just 2.5 million years ago, it stands to reason that in the vastness of the cosmos civilizations flourish that are far older and wiser than our own. The findings of the recent European Space Agency's Venus Express probe indicated that intelligent life—as we know it, human beings like ourselves—may have prospered under paradisiacal conditions on Venus for as long as 2 billion years.

In *Venus Rising*, Dr. Raymond Keller explains what happened to the Venusians—that they did not simply go quietly into that good night. In these pages, Dr. Keller reveals that on a personal level we have probably experienced frequent encounters with Venusians, without even realizing it. He blows the cover off the biggest secret that only a handful of powerful individuals know in the highest echelons of officialdom, that space people from Venus look almost exactly like us, but more beautiful/handsome, have infiltrated human society in all nations and have been visiting the Earth since prehistoric times.

Dr. Keller also examines how the inter-dimensionality of the Omniverse impacts our material existence, allowing Venusians and other advanced beings from our solar system and beyond to interact with us. In *Venus Rising,* the professor of world cultures relates some of his more personal encounters with the inhabitants of Venus, both human and otherwise, and points out the Venusians and other extraterrestrials are now increasing their contacts with us because we, as a species, have arrived at a crucial turning point in our cosmic evolution. If you ever had any questions about Venus or Venusians, you will find the answers in this book.

Michael A. LaRiche
Northeast Ohio Coast-to-Coast A.M. Radio Discussion Group
Rootstown, Ohio
23 June 2015

Introduction

Welcome, Dear Reader, to a Big, Beautiful Book.

Published by Headline Books, Inc. and authored by Dr. Raymond Andrew Keller, II, Doctor of Philosophy, the book is well written and scholarly, with detailed attention to various sources of information.

It is Beautiful because it directs the reader to topics and participants who focus not on FEAR; they focus on LOVE.

It is Big because the interpretations and conclusions deal with the past, present and future of planet Earth and humanity, in their relationships with Venus.

The discerning reader will note that there are eight chapters and almost 300 pages of text. The first three chapters average about fifty pages each. Chapter V, Venusians Among Us, contains 80 pages. These later chapters include lovely photographs of lovely people, including actors and actresses, seers, writers and many persons who report their contacts with Venusians.

The discerning reader will note that the focus moves from Venus as a planet to Venus, the Goddess of Love.

Some scholars of ancient scrolls, e.g. Zecharia Sitchin, have claimed that the Earth was settled by various extraterrestrial groups, including Martians and Venusians.

According to that model of human history, Martians established Atlantis in the Atlantic Ocean and Venusians established Lemuria in the Pacific Ocean. When Atlantis collapsed, the remaining inhabitants settled along the American coastline and the Mediterranean areas. When Lemuria collapsed, the inhabitants settled in the Pacific Islands. The Priesthood of Atlantis settled in northern Egypt; the Priesthood of Lemuria settled in southern Egypt.

Thus, the ancient Egyptian culture reflected both the warlike Martians and the peaceful Venusians.

Later, Egyptian pharaohs decided that Jehovah—the male judgmental God—was superior to the gentle female Goddess, Venus.

Moses, with ties to the Royal Family, and leader of the Jews, accepted the message, "Thou shalt have no other gods before Me."

If we humans were created by the ancient gods, to work in the gold mines, by the sweat of our brow, then our history—and our expectation—is to live a short life, while being judged by a fierce god.

However, the author (p. 16) writes about the message from Jesus: Love of God and Love of Humankind. Some scholars claim that Jesus confronted the older priests—with their focus on rules and regulations—and told them there are only these commandments: Love thyself as thy neighbor; and love thy God...."

If this model of human history is correct, then we have a classic question, Who wins the contest, God or Goddess?

There is an ancient story from Native American (American Indian) culture: A grandfather is telling his grandson that every person has two inner wolves struggling for supremacy. One wolf is fearful and angry; the other is gentle and loving. When the grandson asks, "Which wolf wins?" the grandfather replies, "The one you feed."

The author provides more than 50 references to the life and work of Jesus. Further, the author refers to the claim that Jesus (p. 22) came from Venus. If Jesus represents the loving Venus, then we can appreciate the conflict that some Christians experience: Is God a fearful, judgmental God, or a gentle loving Goddess?

Many religious folks have tried to integrate these conflicting philosophies by viewing Jesus as God, who incorporates both the male authority and the female compassion—and ignore the question of whether Jesus and Mary Magdalene were married. These folks also seem to ignore the question of whether Jesus died on the cross or whether he survived the cross.

Several authors have explored the evidence that Jesus survived the cross and continued his mission in India. Dr. James Deardorff, Ph.D., resigned his position as Professor of Atmospheric Sciences, Oregon State University and became a New Testament scholar. He wrote several books on his findings about the authors of the Gospels, as well as the teachings of Jesus about reincarnation. Ida Kannenberg channeled many messages from celestial and extraterrestrial entities. Dr. Joe Lewels, Ph.D., wrote two books on the reports of persons about their previous lifetimes, including experiences during the time of Jesus. Edward T. Martin wrote the book, *King of Travelers*. He described his journey, on foot, as he retraced the route taken by Jesus through India.

In addition to the spiritual mission of Jesus, the author has focused on the scientific mission of another Venusian, Dr. Nicola Tesla.

The work of Dr. Royal Rife, who developed a cancer cure device, has been suppressed for many decades. The work of Dr. Nicola Tesla has been suppressed for many decades.

Many school children are familiar with the work of Thomas Edison, who developed direct current (DC). Many school children have not read about Nicola Tesla, who developed alternating current (AC). The Tesla coil and other technologies create electricity without the need to burn fossil fuels.

Nicola Tesla predicted many scientific and political changes. The author quotes an interview with a correspondent (p. 129), when Tesla stated, "A new sex order is coming—with the female as superior."

That same view is held by another author, Hanna Rosin, in her 2012 book, *The End of Man and the Rise of Women*. Each chapter shows the leadership roles of women in law, medicine, military, academia, business and government activities.

In the United States, women are not yet the leaders in Congress and mega-corporations; however, that shift is occurring. If a woman is elected president of the United States, then everyone will be aware of this shift.

There is another shift that is occurring: Consciousness. According to various authors, there is an increased frequency of energy that is happening—not only on planet Earth—but also throughout the galaxy and the cosmos.

Some authors attribute this shift in consciousness to the "new kids:" Indigo children, children of light, star children, et al. Some authors use the term Star Seed to describe these "new kids:" bright, psychic, aware of their past lifetimes and dedicated to assist Earth and humanity (And two-thirds are female).

If these authors are correct, then humanity is shifting not only in consciousness, but also in contributions: Giving back to Mother Earth, and caring for all creatures on Earth.

In line with these claims, the author provides the reader with a fascinating analysis of the DNA Drama. He cites the work (pp. 237-249) of several scholars on the Human Genome Project. He presents the conclusion of Dr. Sam Chang that the so-called "junk DNA" contains extraterrestrial genes. The author also cites the conclusion of an Armenian cryptographer, Dr. Adnan Mussaelian: the human genetic code was devised by extraterrestrials and produces cancer-related proteins. Two Soviet researchers, V. I. shCherbak and M. A. Makukov, analyzed the human genome, and they concluded that the cove reveals "….an ensemble of arithmetic and ideographical patterns of symbolic language (p. 245)."

The author, Dr. Keller, poses the significant question: What if a radio signal, from Venus to Earth, could activate the human genetic code? What changes might occur within each human on Earth? Would a shift in the human DNA also result in a shift in consciousness?

Perhaps, someday, the reader as well as the author shall know the answers to these questions.

This writer commends the author, Dr. Raymond Andrew Keller, II, Ph.D., for a Big Beautiful Book.

Welcome, Dear Reader! May you enjoy the journey.

In Love and Light,
R. Leo Sprinkle, Ph.D.
Professor Emeritus,
Counseling Services
University of Wyoming

Introduction

While reading *Venus Rising* I was reminded of the famous Shakespeare quote, "There are more things in heaven and earth, Horatio, than are dreamt of in your philosophy." Venus, the second planet from the Sun, associated with the Roman goddess of love and beauty, has fascinated man throughout history. Dr. Keller documents the facts, cultural influence and beliefs regarding this planet from a wide variety of sources: astronomy, space research, mythology, literary history, religion, philosophy, mysticism, the Esoteric Tradition and popular culture.

The really controversial part of the book is the study of Venus in relation to the UFO enigma and contemporary claims of contact with people from other planets, especially Venus. Most mainstream "scientific" ufologists dismiss the first generation 1950s and 60s contactees as frauds and cultists, but my 40+ years of research into contactee cases indicates that some of these individuals actually were in contact with a group of benevolent alien visitors, trying to influence our culture at a critical time in history. There were also, of course, frauds and myth makers and only further research can give us the answer to who of the contactees mentioned by Dr. Keller were genuine. The research presented by Timothy Good in England and Tony Brunt in New Zealand has opened up new vistas indicating there is a deeper mystery involved in the contactee enigma. *Venus Rising* is a comprehensive and exciting scholarly endeavour in the same tradition that can inspire further research into this most fascinating subject.

Scholars and students of Theosophy and the Esoteric Tradition will find much of interest in *Venus Rising*. According to the Esoteric Tradition, Venus harbours an advanced civilisation but in a different part of the multiverse not visible to ordinary physical eyes. The Venusians have a special relation to our planet and have often visited Earth to assist in our cultural development. This was also the information given by several of the early contactees. A conspiracy theory— yes —but a benevolent conspiracy. Our planetary Alcatraz of strife, turmoil and pain can certainly use some outside help. Why not from Venus?

Håkan Blomqvist
Librarian and co-founder of Archives for the Unexplained (AFU), Sweden

Table of Contents

Chapter I:
The Birth of Venus

...For me,
You stand poised
In the blue and buoyant air,
Cinctured by bright winds,
Treading the sunlight.
And the waves which precede you
Ripple and stir
The sands at my feet.
—Amy Lowell, *Venus Transiens*, 1915

In the pantheon of the ancient Roman Empire, Venus was honored as the goddess of love. She reigned over all aspects of love: beauty, fertility, sex, etc. Venus was considered to be the counterpart to the Greek Aphrodite; but she was much more. In the eyes of her ardent Roman devotees, Venus could be counted on to provide divine assistance in battle, help those women seeking to conceive, and even protect those women working in houses of prostitution.[1] According to legends, Venus was born of the churning seas after Saturn[2] castrated his father Uranus,[3] whose blood poured out into the sea, somehow impregnating the waters.[4]

A magnificent depiction of this momentous event is on display at the Uffizi Gallery in Florence, Italy. The "Birth of Venus" or *la Nascita di Venere,* is a beautiful painting completed by the Italian artist Sandro Botticelli in 1486. He was commissioned to render the birth of Venus by Lorenzo di Pierfrancesco of the famous Medici family in Florence. In this masterpiece, we note the goddess Venus emerging from the sea as a fully grown woman, arriving on the shore while standing on a huge half-shell.[5]

---

1   Brittany Garda, "Venus," 27 August 2013, http://www.ancient.eu.com/venus/ (Accessed 19 December 2013) See also Yiannis Papadakis, *Echoes from the Dead Zone: Across the Cyprus Divide* (London: I. B. Tauris, 2005), 67. Some linguistic research indicates that Aphrodite's name did not derive from the Greek *aphros*, signifying foam, but rather from the Egyptian fertility goddess *Pr-Wedyt*. According to the Cypriot cultural historian Papadakis, "There were yet more revealing aspects of Aphrodite. Her cult in Cyprus revolved around sacred prostitution. Before they could marry, women entered Aphrodite's temple and were made available to visitors to the temple. Lively rituals, the Aphrodesia, had been dedicated to the Goddess, during which mass orgies took place under her blessing. Some authors argued that the practice of temple prostitution moved towards the East, all the way to India, as others also pointed out that 'Asia' derived from Al-asia, an ancient name of Cyprus. Somehow, these contributions to world civilization had been left out of our schoolbooks. We never learnt that during the last days of the Aphrodesia, rituals took place during which, as one theory proposed, the emblems of the Goddess- salt and the phallus- were used in certain ways. Our old customs and traditions were said to have so scandalized early Christian writers that they thought that the people of Cyprus descended from demons." The author comments that it seems quite fitting that his homeland's acclaimed Aphrodite should be considered as the "goddess of prostitutes" since Cyprus itself had often been described by many as the "prostitute of the Mediterranean." The island had been conquered and exploited by others throughout history: Arabs, British, Byzantines, Greeks, Ottomans and Turks. See also footnote 101.
2   In Greek he was known as Cronus or Kronos.
3   In Greek he was known as Ouranos.
4   *Theogony of Hesiod* is an epic poem by Hesiod (8ᵗʰ – 7ᵗʰ century B.C.E.), that describes the origins and genealogies of the Greek gods. It was composed sometime around 700 B.C.E. and it was written in the dialect and style of the Homeric Greek. Hesiod's *Theogony* is also the first Greek cosmogony.
5   Guide to Uffizi Gallery Museum, http://www.uffizi.org/artworks/the-birth-of-venus-by-sandro-botticelli/ (Accessed 19 December 2013)

Sandro Botticelli, "Birth of Venus," 1486, now hangs in the Uffizi Gallery. See http://www.google.com/culturalinstitute/asset-viewer/ the-birth-of-venus/MQEeq50LABEBVg?utm_source=google&utm_ medium=kp&hl=en&projectId=art-project.

The cosmogony of the Greeks depicts the birth of the sundry gods and goddesses in a like manner. The initial state of the universe was depicted as one of chaos. There was a dark, indefinite void considered as a primordial condition from which everything else appeared, including the divine beings that came to rule this vast, cosmic realm. Surprisingly, if one cuts through all of Hesiod's Hellenic anthropomorphizing, a more or less accurate cosmology consistent with our contemporary interpretation of astronomical data emerges.

Today it is established that Venus is the second planet out from the Sun. Venus and the other planets of our solar system all formed at the same time, approximately 4.6 billion years ago. Before this time, the region of space that is now occupied by our solar system was filled with a large and diffuse cloud of cold molecular hydrogen. There must have been some celestial event that caused this cloud to collapse, possibly a supernova explosion in our galactic sector or gravitational disturbances generated by a passing star.

The collapsing molecules then broke up into cords of knotting gas. The compression of this material caused it to spin. This was the result of the conservation of momentum from all the particles in the cloud. The cloud's center became evermore dense, eventually forming the star we now know as the Sun. The solar center was then surrounded by a flattened disk of material that coalesced into the planets, to include Venus.

The core of the primitive Sun continued to build up both pressure and temperature until it ignited. The resulting fusion generated the powerful solar winds that cleared out all of the loose material remaining in the solar system, leaving only the planets and their moons. The majority of scientists are in agreement that the planets formed in this manner around the same time because meteorites discovered on Earth, regardless of where they came from within the solar system, can be dated back some 4.6 billion years. Therefore, one can reasonably be assured that Venus shares in the same origins as the other planets, coalescing from the solar nebula in the remotest past.[6]

Astronomers and other scientists continue to discover more information about our solar system and its origins, especially with the advent of space exploration and the dispatch of robotic probes to the Moon, asteroids, comets, other planets and their associated natural satellites. An analysis of the major physical characteristics of the planets reveals two distinct types. The smaller, rocky planets like Mercury, Venus, Earth and Mars, are found nearer the Sun. The

---

6   Fraser Cain, "Origin of Venus," 6 August 2009, http://www.universetoday.com/36884/origin-of-venus/ (Accessed 18 December 2013)

huge, gas planets like Jupiter, Saturn, Uranus and Neptune, are found further out, beyond the asteroid belt. Many of the moons around the gas giants are rocky and solid, however. These moons as well as the smaller, rocky planets closer to the Sun are classified as terrestrial, from the Latin *terra*, because their composition and overall makeup is similar to that of the Earth. Those larger gas planets further out are considered Jovian in nature because their composition and overall makeup is similar to that of Jupiter, the largest planet in the solar system.[7]

Immanuel Velikovsky

The debate over the origins of Venus has somewhat cooled off, even if the planet itself has not. But there have been alternate origin speculations, with the most widely known being that proposed by the Russian-American theorist Immanuel Velikovsky.[8] In his *Worlds in Collision* and other writings, Velikovsky attempts to tie in significant events in ancient history with astronomy and mythology, suggesting that in the relatively recent past, at least in the celestial reckoning of time, Venus had been ejected from the core of Jupiter and had assumed its present orbit sometime around 1,500 B.C.E.[9]

On its journey from Jupiter to position itself as the second planet out from the Sun, Venus wreaked havoc throughout the solar system, especially on the planets Mars and Earth. Velikovsky asserts that many of the "miracles" recorded in the *Old Testament* during the times of Moses and Joshua can be attributed to the near passing of Venus to the Earth on at least two occasions. As Venus skimmed closely the orbit of the Earth, the resulting cataclysms of tidal surges, erupting volcanoes and massively shifting geological plates gave way to earthquakes and plagues that decidedly turned the course of human history.

Critics of Velikovsky are quick to point out that while his theory is interesting, he was not primarily an astronomer but a medical doctor and psychiatrist. Prior to his investigation of celestial phenomena and its impact on history, Velikovsky had written numerous articles on sundry aspects of psychoanalysis that were published in highly respected international journals. Nevertheless, he was not unfamiliar with astronomy, mathematics or physics, for while living in Berlin he worked closely with Albert Einstein in editing and publishing some scientific papers, *Scripta Universitatis Atque Bibliothecae Hierosolymitanarum* (*Writings of the Jerusalem University and Library*).[10]

Critics also point to seeming weaknesses in Velikovsky's theory of cataclysm on the grounds that rocky Venus is so unlike gaseous Jupiter; any changes to the Earth's rotation resulting from the passing of Venus would have been much more severe than detailed by Velikovsky; and the near circular orbit of Venus cannot be accounted for considering the elongated path it took to arrive in its present orbital position.[11]

With respect to the first charge that the debunkers leveled at Velikovsky, that the possibility of a terrestrial and metallic world like Venus being ejected by a gaseous, liquid hydrogen world like Jupiter being at "just about zero,"[12] they do concede that Jupiter does, in fact, have a rocky and metallic core; but they see no way in which a large chunk of that core could have exploded outward beyond all the heavy layers of compressed gases overhead. But how do they account

7   William J. Kaufmann, III. *Discovering the Universe*, 3rd edition (New York: W. H. Freeman and Company, 1993), 92-96
8   Immanuel Velikovsky. *Worlds in Collision* (New York: Doubleday Books, 1950)
9   Isaac Asimov, *Venus, Near Neighbor of the Sun* (New York: Lothrop, Lee and Shepard Books, 1981), 124-126.
10   Albert Einstein, "*Mathematica et Physica*," vol. 1, in H. Lowew and I. Velikovsky, general editors, *Scripta Universitatis Atque Bibliothecae Hierosolymitanarum*, (Jerusalem: 1 January 1923).
11   Asimov, 124-126
12   *Ibid.,* 124

for the many rocky and metallic moons, large and small, already in the Jovian orbit? Perhaps the velocity whence Venus was detached from the Jovian core gave it just enough of a boost to break through the gravitational field that captured the other moons.

As to the second charge, that any slowing down or even momentary stoppage of our planet's rotation would have generated sufficient heat on Earth to create such dire effects like boiling away the oceans,[13] this most likely is an overestimation in itself. If the Earth suddenly stopped spinning due to the close passage of Venus or some other huge celestial object, astronomers believe that there would be drastic consequences, beginning with the planet's very momentum. The Earth moves through space with a rotational velocity of 1,674.4 km/h at the equator. We cannot feel this, however, precisely because of momentum. This can best be explained by relating to the experience of riding in a car. You cannot feel anything unless the car comes to a stop or crashes into something, or hopefully not, someone. Keeping this in mind, consider the following comments from Frasier Cain of the *Universe Today* website:

"And so, if the Earth suddenly stopped spinning, everything on the surface of the Earth at the equator would suddenly be moving at more than 1,600 km/hour sideways. The escape velocity of Earth is about 40,000 km/hour, so that isn't enough to fly off into space; but it would cause some horrible damage as everything flew in a ballistic trajectory sideways. Imagine the oceans sloshing sideways at 1,600 km/hour. The rotational velocity of the Earth decreases as you head away from the equator, towards the poles. So as you got further away from the equator, your speed would decrease. If you were standing right on the North or South Pole, you'd barely even feel it."[14]

So the oceans would not boil away, as Asimov and others conjectured, but they would definitely "slosh" quite a bit and wreak a lot of damage. If the Earth's rotation did not resume, then we would also be looking at a day equivalent to a year with six months in scorching sunlight with the other half year in frozen darkness. Also, the Earth would acquire a perfect spherical shape, with one massive continent occupying the central latitudes and oceans coalescing around the North and South Poles.[15] There would also be no axial tilt, and hence no seasons. But as Velikovsky only stated that a rotational stoppage may have occurred for an hour or less, maybe his theory on this account was not so unreasonable.

As to the critics of Velikovsky and their contention that the near circular orbit of Venus cannot be accounted for with "the rules of celestial mechanics that have proved so useful to astronomers since the time of Kepler,"[16] if Venus was acting like a comet and had originally taken an elongated orbit around the Sun once it was ejected from Jupiter, Velikovsky invokes the role of yet to be detected electromagnetic forces as counteracting agents to gravity and orbital mechanics, serving to stabilize the orbit of Venus as Earth's closest planetary neighbor, gracing an orbit 108 million kilometers (67 million miles) from the Sun. The Earth is approximately 93 million miles from the Sun, so the average distance of Venus from Earth is about 26 million miles, at its closest approach.[17]

---

13 *Ibid.*, 124, 125
14 Fraser Cain, "What Would Happen if the Earth Stopped Turning?," 13 November 2013, http://www.universetoday. com/66570/what-would-happen-if-the-earth-stopped-spinning/ (Accessed 23 December 2013)
15 *Ibid.*
16 Asimov, 124
17 David Talbott, "The Great Comet Venus," 1997, *Ames* website, recovered through *Way Back Machine* website, http:// www.bibliotecapleyades.net/ciencia/ciencia_asteroids_comets63.htm, (Accessed 23 December 2013)

Much to Velikovsky's credit, some of his predictions have actually panned out. As he stated in 1950 that Venus was formed from the seething core of Jupiter then, he reasoned, Venus must still be a very hot planet indeed. Venus proved to be so hot that scientists could not account for its extremely high temperatures even by just supposing a runaway greenhouse effect. In addition, since Velikovsky proposed that Venus has only been around for a relatively short time on the celestial scale, the discovery of unexpectedly high quantities of argon-36 in the Venusian

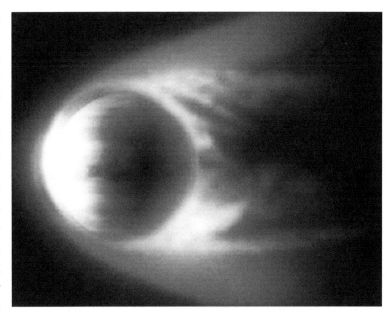

The interaction of the solar wind with the atmosphere creates a comet-like tail on Venus. See www.thunderbolts.info.

atmosphere give some indications that might vindicate his contention that Venus is a young world.[18]

The vitriol strewn in the path of Velikovsky and his adherents by those in the science establishment is totally unnecessary. Pontificating from his own ivory tower, Asimov wrote: "There seems to be no question that Velikovsky's theories, however interesting and dramatic they may be, are quite, quite wrong. There will no doubt continue to be Velikovskians who, for a variety of emotional reasons, will cling to those theories, but if people insist on being foolish, there is no way of stopping them."[19]

Since the 1970s, in various ways both overt and subtle, the scientific establishment has consistently demonstrated an inordinate degree of intolerance, indifference and disdain toward Velikovsky and others advancing knowledge that may lead to significant revelations about our past. Asimov, the late Cornell University astronomer Carl Sagan and others were quick to brand Velikovsky and those willing to even consider his theories as outright "CPs," an acronym for "crackpots." In his vaunted television series, *Cosmos*, Sagan went to great lengths in debunking the idea of a comet-like Venus without regard to photographic evidence from various American and Soviet space probes depicting the long tail of gases that still follows in the orbital path behind the second planet.[20] Sagan even helped to politically organize and direct

---

18 Asimov, 124

19 *Ibid.,* 127

20 "The Tunguska Event, an ongoing mystery," *Bolt from Below,* no author stated, undated, http://para-az.com/let2ed.html (Accessed 27 October 2014). A little more than one hundred years ago in the Tunguska region of Siberia there was a tremendous explosion which some attribute to the myriad but powerful forces at work in our solar system. These forces represented a potential that ancient cultures were well acquainted with, much as Velikovsky maintained, passing on a knowledge of the cosmic calamities these forces engendered in the collective memories of various peoples spanning the globe.

The event of 1908 was an explosion that leveled approximately 400 square miles of the Tunguska river forest and blistered the skin of people hundreds of miles away beyond the immediate impact zone. The event was blamed on the appearance of a bolide, but with advances in science some are beginning to consider other possibilities.

a controlled confrontation with Velikovsky for the purpose of debunking *Worlds in Collision* at the 1974 annual meeting of the American Association for the Advancement of Science, the same group that has consistently tried to squelch information and investigation into UFOs and other unexplained phenomena.[21]

Asimov, Sagan and others of their ilk poignantly demonstrate the difficulties confronting those theorists with truly novel ideas. This is emphasized because these negative approaches and actions by the powers that be and all of their minions toward nontraditional ideas have shown no sign of abating. Like the decrepit leadership of the Inquisition in days gone by, the science establishment of today maintains a vested interest in preventing us from smashing through the wall of illusions that they have constructed for us. Whether all, some, or none of Velikovsky's theories prove correct is not the real issue here. Keeping us from asking the important questions that might change the way we view the solar system, the history of our own world, and even the evolution of humankind, is definitely at the top of the science establishment's agenda.

As a "bolide" is generally believed to be a meteor or meteorite fragment reaching an apparent magnitude of -14 or greater upon entering the Earth's atmosphere- even brighter than a full moon- such objects have generically come to be known as "fireballs." The collision of such a meteor fragment with the Earth, however, often results in the formation of an impact crater. The word bolide is of Greek origin (βολίς, bolis) and simple means "missile."

When ancient peoples would observe such a bright object hurtling through the sky, they would start running for cover to escape the threat of the "terrible goddess with her long flowing hair." And that "hair" was the tail of Venus, which is not visible today unless you have the advanced technology such as that fitted on the Solar and Heliospheric Observatory (SOHO) space probe launched in 1997 by the European Space Agency.

In 1997 the SOHO satellite immediately detected what had not been seen for a long time, the electromagnetic Birkeland current tail structure which extends from Venus and comes very close to the Earth when the two planets are aligned with the Sun. On 30 June 1908, when the Tunguska event occurred, the Earth was actually closing in on the tip of that tail which in former times wrought destruction on the Earth in various forms, including extreme lightning storms.

Earthly lightning provides ample examples of discharge behavior. There are also abundant Earth-space lightning examples, such as the phenomena manifested in sprites, blue jets and elves that occur in the region above intense thunderstorms. Also ground-to-cloud lightning bolts are now well known. A sub-storm could have exploited similar pathways. Sub-storms are electrical discharges within Earth's own tail region. These gravitate toward our planet's polar regions where they are studied as a cause of enhanced aurora displays.

Some scientists have speculated that during the time of the Tunguska event, the Earth was nearly opposite to the position of our departing Moon. It was in eclipse of the Sun, a known factor in the facilitation of altering our planet's geomagnetic condition. And all of this was occurring while a solar maximum was also taking place.

The solar outbursts brought with them the potential for additional activity in our own tail region, a phenomenon observed by numerous observational satellites. Such activity triggers a dramatic intensification of the auroras. On the morning of 30 June, it appears as though the departing Moon, the Earth, and approaching Venus caused an alignment whereby our planet's plasma shield was short circuited, thereby altering the way in which sub-storms behave, magnifying their power and focusing it in the Tunguska region. As other details are introduced, the Venus-induced electric discharge perspective gains increased credibility. Recently, the discovery of Kimberlite pipes and glass beads in the region seems to bolster this theory, as these only occur as the result of an extreme electrical discharge of the mega-lightning variety. The Tunguska region may have been the site of previous discharges.

Such catastrophic interplanetary interactions permeate the texts of ancient legends; and with the discovery of sub-storms we now have several directions which electrical discharges might travel. Earth's plasma sheath is now discharging regularly through the tail; but was that always so? Were the passage of Venus' tail and our Moon's eclipse, synchronized with a solar maximum, contributing factors for a planetary discharge? With future investigations of space plasma behavior we may find new clues to apply to the Tunguska mystery. This is yet another reason for the continued launching of space probes to Venus. By examining its weather patterns, and particularly its tail, we thereby gain significant understanding of our own planetary conditions, environment and evolution. Whether or not Venus emerged from the core of Jupiter, there can be little doubt that Velikovsky was correct in his assumptions that the planet has long and physically interacted with Earth's history, to include its human population.

21   Talbott

Exobiology

Venus and Earth are often considered as "twin planets."
See www.jaxa.jp.

Before the dawn of the space age, Venus was considered to be the most likely abode for the discovery of extraterrestrial life in our solar system. But since the arrival of various probes to Venus, and the discovery of intolerable surface temperatures and high pressures at the lower atmospheric levels, the attention of the scientific community concerned with exobiology, for the most part, has shifted to Mars.

This diversion to Mars may be premature, however, for various reasons. First, Venus is the only Earth-sized terrestrial planet in the solar system, and for the near future, at least, the only Earth-sized world we will have the opportunity to explore. Secondly, as astronomers seek out Earth-size planets in the habitable zones around other stars, the knowledge gained from an extensive survey of Venus could prove useful for future investigations in this emerging area. Third and lastly, Venus provides a contrasting world where we may establish the properties of evolution and the ongoing geochemical processes of our own planet in a wider framework.[22] Excellent examples of this are pointed out by Colorado astronomers Mark A. Bullock and David H. Grinspoon:

"Many geological and meteorological processes otherwise active only on Earth at present are currently active on Venus. Active volcanism most likely affects the climate and equilibrium state of the atmosphere and surface, and maintains the global cloud cover. Further, if we think beyond the specifics of a particular chemical system required to build complexity and heredity, we can ask what general properties a planet must possess in order to be considered a possible candidate for life. The answers might include an atmosphere with signs of flagrant chemical disequilibrium and active, internally driven cycling of volatile elements between the surface, atmosphere and interior. At present, the two planets we know of which posses these characteristics are Earth and Venus."[23]

All indications are that Venus once had warm and habitable oceans and that the evaporation of the Venusian oceans, along with the escape of hydrogen that followed, resulted in an oxygenated atmosphere. Bullock and Grinspoon do admit that the duration of this phase remains "poorly understood," but that throughout this time the terrestrial planets were not isolated, *per se*, adding that, "due to frequent impact transport, they represented a continuous environment for microbial life."[24]

---

22   Mark A. Bullock and David H. Grinspoon, "Astrobiology and Venus Exploration," in *Geophysical Monograph 176: Exploring Venus as a Terrestrial Planet*, eds. L. Esposito, T. Cravens, and E. Stofan (Washington, DC: American Geophysical Union, 2007), 191.

23   *Ibid.*

24   *Ibid.*

The actual timescale for the loss of water on Venus has been suggested to be as low as several hundred million years, but even this low estimate allows for the possibility of the evolution of even more complex organisms than mere microbial life.[25] And more recent studies indicate that the earlier Venusian clouds once served to significantly cool the surface during the moist greenhouse phase. Inasmuch as hydrogen escape rates are linked so tightly to the abundance of water in the upper atmosphere, that are, in turn, strongly dependent on the surface temperature, then it stands to reason that the cloud-albedo feedback significantly extended the lifetime of the early Venusian oceans.[26] Bullock and Grinspoon contend that a current estimate of the situation based on the findings of various space probes, indicate that it is no longer necessary to impose any geological constraints on the longevity of Venus' oceans. They say that, "it is possible that the lifetime of Venus' oceans was measured in billions of years, rather than hundreds of millions." This would necessarily motivate a "much more rigorous calculation of climate during the moist greenhouse phase."[27]

The two scientists also speculate that after billions of years, Venusian ocean life may have migrated to the upper-level clouds which, even on present-day Venus, still constitute a habitable environment.[28] Therefore, at this juncture we still do not understand how and when Venus was

---

25   J. F. Kasting, J. B. Pollack and T. P. Ackerman, "Response of Earth's atmosphere to increases in solar flux and implications for loss of water from Venus," (1984), *Icarus* 57: 335-355

26   Steve Graham, "Clouds and Radiation," (1 March 1999), NASA Earth Observatory, http://earthobservatory.nasa.gov/Features/Clouds/clouds.php (Accessed 20 April 2014) Clouds have some responsibility in both the warming and cooling of planetary atmospheres and surfaces. The low-level clouds tend to cool the planet because they reflect sunlight. The high-level clouds, on the other hand, tend to warm the planet through the entrapment of heat. Therefore, in the earlier warm and moist greenhouse phase of Venus, the clouds would have exercised a cooling effect if there were more low-level clouds or less high-level clouds. Therefore, on an earlier Venus replete with lakes and oceans, the effects on near-surface air temperatures were dependent on the type of then extant cloud cover. If Venus had more low clouds, such as marine stratus clouds, the dominant radiating feature of the clouds would have been manifest in their albedo. In this scenario, any increase in low cloud cover would have acted in much the same way as an increase in surface water/ice cover. In other words, more incoming solar radiation would have been reflected and the Venusian surface would have cooled. On the other hand, high clouds, such as the towering cumulus clouds that extend up to the boundary between the troposphere and stratosphere, would have exercised a much different impact on the surface radiation balance. The tops of cumulus clouds would have reached much higher in the Venusian atmosphere, being much colder than their undersides. Cumulus cloud tops emit much less longwave radiation out to space than their warmer cloud bottoms emit downward toward the surface. Over time, the increase in these higher clouds would have resulted in greater warming at the surface of Venus.

27   Bullock and Grinspoon, "Astrobiology,"195

28   Charles S. Cockell, "Life on Venus," (1999), *Planetary Space Science* 47 (12): 1487–1501: Recognizable life forms could exist in the cloud tops of Venus, much the same way that bacteria have been found living and reproducing in clouds on Earth. Microbes may swarm about in the thick, cloudy Venusian atmosphere, protected from solar radiation by the sulfur compounds in the air. The solar wind may, in fact, provide the medium for the transfer of such *microbiota* from Venus to Earth.

See also Donald Barber, "Invasion by Washing Water," (1963), *Perspective* 5 (4), (London: Focal Press), 201-208; N. C. Wickramasinghe and J. T. Wickramasinghe, "On the possibility of microbiota transfer from Venus to Earth," (2008), *Astrophysics and Space Science* 317 (1–2): 133–137; and Geoffrey A. Landis, "Astrobiology: the Case for Venus," (2003), *Journal of the British Interplanetary Society* 56 (7/8): 250–254. Between the years 1937 to 1961, six waves of ultra-rapid, gelatin-liquifying bacteria showed up in rain-water at the Norman Lockyer Observatory in Sidmouth, United Kingdom. The initial onsets of these bacterial invasions occurred on average 59 ± 17 days following near-dated geomagnetic storms to Venus' inferior conjunctions. Exobiologists have speculated that the bacteria, which had complete tolerance to highly toxic photographic silver salts and demonstrated a strong fluorescence in ultraviolet light, probably originated in the atmosphere of Venus and were transported to Earth by the solar wind. If such microbes transitioned from the Venusian oceans to the upper atmosphere countless millennia ago, then it is not unreasonable to conjecture that all life on Earth owes its very existence to the solar wind and the so-called "comet tail" of Venus. In a certain evolutionary sense, then it is not unreasonable to assert that we are all "Venusians."

See also David Grinspoon, *Venus Revealed: A New Look Below the Clouds of Our Mysterious Twin Planet* (Reading, MA: Addison-Wesley Publishing, 1998); "Venus could be a haven for life," ABC News, 28 September 2002; and Stuart Clark, "Acidic clouds of Venus could harbour life," 26 September 2002, *New Scientist*, http://www.newscientist.com/article/dn2843-acidic-clouds-of-venus-could-harbour-life.html#.VE70fWemUfA (Accessed 27 October 2014): The disequilibrium of the Venusian atmosphere has also pushed scientists to call for further investigation of our sister planet. An analysis of data from the Venera, Pioneer, and Magellan missions has found the chemicals hydrogen sulfide

diverted from a more Earth-like past, or for what duration Venus retained habitable conditions for life as we know it. Most remarkably, the two scientists agree that: "If life begins easily on warm, wet planets (which seems to be the case, judging from Earth), then Venus probably once harbored Venusians. Did they die out as the climate changed?"[29] Clearly, a study of Venus may assist us to comprehend the evolutionary path of habitable, terrestrial planets, no matter where we may find them.

Moderate temperatures in the cloud tops of Venus may allow for the future colonization of the planet by human beings in floating cities such as the one depicted here. See http://www.science20.com/ robert_inventor/will_we_build_colonies_that_float_over_venus_like_ buckminster_fullers_cloud_nine-127573.

(H_2S) and sulfur dioxide (SO_2) together in the upper atmosphere, as well as carbonyl sulfide (OCS). The first two gases are known to react with each other, implying that something must produce them. In addition, it should be noted that OCS is exceptionally difficult to produce through inorganic means. Furthermore, one of the early Soviet Venera probes detected large amounts of chlorine just below the Venusian cloud deck. It has been proposed that microbes at this level may be soaking up ultraviolet light from the Sun as an energy source. This may account for dark patches seen on ultraviolet (UV) images of the planet. Large, non-spherical cloud particles of an unknown composition have also been detected in the cloud decks.

29   Bullock and Grinspoon, "Astrobiology,"196

Chapter II:
Hidden Venus

….When you touch me I die
Just a little inside
I wonder if this could be love
This could be love
Cuz you're out of this world
Galaxy space and time...
—Lady Gaga, *Venus*, 2013

Although contemporary astronomers, for the most part, view Venus as too hot to sustain life as we know it, metaphysicians and mystics throughout the ages have advanced a differing perspective on our sister planet, proffering the notion that there is another Venus existing outside our field of perception. They describe Venus as a spiritual realm. Today we might equate their descriptions with being representative of an inter-dimensional plane. Two accounts of the noted spiritual qualities of this inter-dimensional realm from the thirteenth and the eighteenth century are provided in this chapter. The actual physics of an inter-dimensional Venus are examined later in this book.

Tannhäuser

The first account of an inter-dimensional Venus involves the legend of Tannhäuser (c. 1200-1270), a Teutonic knight who fought valiantly in the Crusade of 1228-1229. Upon his return to central Europe, he became an active courtier in the circles of Austria's Frederick II (1230-1246). Tannhäuser was himself of noble peerage, tracing his lineage to the Lords of Thannhausen. Their family castle and estates were situated between Ellwangen and Dinkelsbühl at Neumarkt in der Oberpfalz, in what is now Bavaria. But more so than his participation in the Crusades or the Court of Frederick II, Tannhäuser received great acclamations as a master of the *leich* (German), *lai* (French), and *lay* (Old English), a lyric and narrative style of poetry written in octosyllabic couplets that often deals with tales of adventure and romance that was so popular in the France and Germany of the thirteenth century.

A collection of Tannhäuser's poetry first appeared in the cited *Codex Manesse*, along with the classic lyric poems of others written in the High German language.[30] Tannhäuser's

---

30 *Codex Manesse* (1340), on display at the Universitätbibliothek Heidelberg: "The *Codex Manesse*, also known as the 'large Heidelberg Lieder Manuscript' (*Cod. Pal. Germ. 848*), was created between 1300 and 1340 in Zurich and is the most comprehensive collection of ballads and epigrammatic poetry in Middle High German language. It consists of 426 parchments leaves, each 35.5 x 25 cm, double-sided, with pagination added in a later scribe's hand. In addition the codex includes 140 blank pages and numerous pages partially blank. The manuscript contains almost 6,000 verses from 140 poets. Its core was formed around 1300 in Zurich. The large collection of Middle High German lyrics compiled by the patrician Rüdiger Manesse of Zurich and his son is considered to be the main source of the *Codex Manesse*. Several addenda were incorporated up to 1340. The manuscript represents the sum total of mediaeval lay songs and with regard to the post-classical *minnesang* (troubadour poetry) it is the main and in some cases the only source." Reference is made to http://www.ub.uni-heidelberg.de/Englisch/allg/benutzung/bereiche/handschriften/codexmanesse.html for additional information. (Accessed 8 January 2014)

contribution to this codex included six lyric poems, a few dance and love songs, as well as a group of *Spüche* (gnomic poems).[31]

Perhaps the most memorable of poems in this important work is his *Bußlied*, for this stroke of master penmanship secured his place in Germanic legend. In this poem, Tannhäuser gives an account of his discovery of the Venusberg, the subterranean home of the goddess Venus. It appears that on his way back from the Crusades, the intrepid poet was enticed by the goddess to pass through a magic gate that instantaneously transported him deep inside an Alpine mountain. There he remained as a lover of the enchanting Venus for one calendar year, helping her out with the many duties in supervising this mysterious city and realm. Despite all the wonders of Venusberg and the beauty of her reigning goddess, at the end of one year our knight is pining to return to his natal land. Venus reluctantly agrees to let him go, assured that his erotic desires for her would eventually lure him back.

"Tannhäuser" enacted in the German Opera House, Berlin (2013). See www.opera-online.com.

Being raised a good Roman Catholic, Tannhäuser started to feel remorse over his sexual escapades with the lovely Venus. He traveled to Rome, the Eternal City, to request an absolution of his sins from Pope Urban IV. Of course, the Pope could not forgive Tannhäuser's sins because he was consorting with a pagan goddess, not just some lusty German girl. The pope told the returning knight that, "forgiveness is as impossible as it would be for his staff to blossom." Then, just three days after Tannhäuser left Rome, the papal staff bloomed with luxuriant flowers. Pope Urban IV sends messengers to find the knight and bring him back to Rome, but he could not be found and was never seen again, having returned to the loving embrace of Queen Venus and her magic realm.

The *Catholic Encyclopedia* points out that while there are other stories in existence where humans encounter enchanting beings and pass through magic portals,

"It is to be noted that in the German version there is a distinct tone of hostility to the papacy, wholly lacking in the Italian variants. In fact the miracle of the blossoming staff is a pointed reproof of the pope's harshness. This can readily be explained if the legend developed in Germany, where antipapal feeling was strong after the days of the Hohenstaufens. The dominant idea of the legend is the glorification of God's infinite mercy to sinners. But this ideal is set forth in a spirit most unfriendly to the Church. The attitude ascribed to the pope by the *Volkslied* (poetic folktale) is wholly contrary to Catholic doctrine."[32]

The Roman Catholic Church dismisses this story and others as too anti-clerical in tone. The ecclesiastical authorities also reasoned that in this formative period of Germanic history,

---

31   "Tannhäuser," *Encyclopedia Britannica*, v. 11 (Chicago: Faculty of the University of Chicago, eds., 1993), 545, 546
32   Arthur F. J. Remy, "Literary or Profane Legends," *Catholic Encyclopedia*, *Vol. 9* (New York: Robert Appleton Company, 1910), http://www.newadvent.org/cathen/09121a.htm (Accessed 8 January 2014)

facts and mythology became inextricably mingled. In the course of the oral transmission, the purely historic narrative simply evolved into legend. Details became emphasized to the point of exaggeration, actions were ascribed to different motives, facts were forgotten or suppressed, chronological and geographical information became confused, and traits and *motifs* from older tales were added. The *Catholic Encyclopedia* described this process in the following manner:

"Gradually this tradition, passing from mouth to mouth, takes on a more definite shape and a more distinct outline, and finally it passes into literature and receives a permanent and fixed form. We are seldom able to give a clear and connected account of the origin and development of a saga or legend. In most cases the literary sources on which we depend for our <u>knowledge</u> are of comparatively late date, and even the earliest of them present the legend in an advanced phase of evolution. Of preceding phases we can form an opinion only through a critical analysis and comparison of the sources. In this process of reconstruction much must be left to conjecture; uncertainty necessarily prevails, and difference of opinion is unavoidable."[33]

Or could it be that the Roman Catholic Church, with its monopoly on religion and spirituality, could brook no interference from any individuals offering a new way of looking at the world and, in so doing, part an ethereal veil and discover another dimension, angelic in its scope? Keeping in mind that troubadour poetry was widely read throughout continental Europe, it has become clear over the centuries that it has greatly influenced Western art in general, but especially the poetry of love. The modern notions of an idealized romantic love can easily be traced to the troubadours of the thirteenth century.

And when one reads the Gospels, it becomes apparent that Jesus' primary message was love, of both God and humankind. Over thirteen centuries, however, the Catholic hierarchy seems to have lost touch with this overarching idea. Troubadours like Tannhäuser were bringing needed illumination to a Europe darkened by a dour and dogmatic priestly class. The following are Ivan M. Granger of *Poetry Chaikhana's* comments on the work of these troubadours:

"The Troubadours lauded love, especially the sweet pain of unattainable love, as embodied by an idealized Lady. They were the poets of the courtly love. Modern commentators often miss the sacred dimension to Troubadour poetry and the path of courtly love. It's a pity that modern audiences tend to read Troubadour poetry as if it was a lot of lovesick romantic poetry. Much of Troubadour poetry, though couched in romantic or even sexual imagery, is truly sacred poetry, emerging from a genuine mystical tradition."[34]

With respect to Tannhäuser and the other troubadours, however, what the *Catholic Encyclopedia* failed to mention was that they were employed as composers, poets and singers in the courts of the Cathar nobles and rulers. Recalling that marriages among the European wealthy of the thirteenth century were brokered affairs between families jockeying for economic and social standing, it is not hard to understand why the younger generation quickly tired of the manipulation. Hence, the troubadour message of courtly love received a warm response. It presented a viable alternative to the church-sponsored marriage monopoly. Courtly love could, therefore, be viewed as a "conscious spiritual practice," as well as an embodiment of the archetypal forces of the "Lover" and the "Beloved."[35]

In Tannhäuser's case, the beloved was Venus while he was the lover. Granger explains that, "the beloved was to embody the ideal of the Divine Feminine, Sophia, Divine Wisdom.

---

33   *Ibid.*
34   Ivan M. Granger, "Poetry Chaikhana: Sacred Poetry from Around the World," P. O. Box 2320, Boulder, CO 80306, <u>http://www.poetry-chaikhana.com/contact.htm</u>, (Accessed 8 January 2014)
35   *Ibid.*

She was to be ever slightly out of reach, but within sight. Her presence was to draw the Lover with her presence, her goodness, her feminine divinity. She was to be a beacon. In striving to embody this for her Lover, she was to merge with the Divine she embodied."[36]

On the other hand, Granger notes that:

"The Lover was usually the man. His was the more active role. He was to seek his Beloved, his idealized Lady. He had to prove himself worthy of her, face great obstacles with humility and perseverance, in her name. In the Lover's intense passion for his Beloved, his constant focusing on her, he was to ultimately become a perfect Lover of the Divine and unite with the divinity he saw embodied in his Beloved."[37]

The goal of courtly love was not primarily one of sexual intimacy. Sex was delayed at first because it would satiate the longing that acted as the spiritual force that drew the man and woman together as Lover and Beloved with the objective of spiritual marriage. Granger believes that while this was the ideal, it is certain that not every couple followed this path, nor did every Troubadour always celebrate the inner sacred meaning of the path. Nevertheless, this was the essence of the relationship in its initial phases; and it was a "pathway taught through societies and particularly passed on through Troubadour poetry and song."[38] Courtly love can, therefore, rightly be seen as a genuine spiritual pathway. In some ways, courtly love approximates the Tantric sexual spirituality that emerged in ancient India.

To a great extent, the Troubadours were also influenced by the great Arab poetry, and especially that of the Sufi that passed into Europe through Moorish Spain, the trade routes of North Africa and Palestine, where the Crusaders interacted with the Muslim world. When the Troubadours speak of the Beloved, she is the same Divine Beloved of the Sufis. Therefore, when reading either Troubadour or Sufi poetry, the Beloved should be understood to represent the sundry aspects of the Divine Feminine.[39]

The Troubadours foresaw our day, when humankind would begin to pass through a very difficult phase. Therefore, they set in motion this "impossible romantic ideal" in a *very few people* as one of the initial processes or steps in obtaining illumination. From their experience and knowledge of Sufism, the Troubadours came to understand that this romantic ideal served to stimulate a chemical correlation in the human brain with a state akin to a bear's hibernation.[40]

Galian, in his exploration of the Divine Feminine in Sufism, comments on the spiritual significance of bears:

"As we know, bears hibernate in caves. They appear almost lifeless. This is an analog of the practice of ancient shamans, and to Sufis who practice the forty-day *halvet* (retreat), in which the Shaman would enter a cave, have an experience of dying, explore the spiritual realms, and then is reborn as the Initiate or Master (just as the bear is reborn each spring as it 'wakes up' and leaves its cave)."[41]

Of course, bears are honored and respected by spiritualists everywhere. Possessing a special relationship to the Moon, bears are known to impart pure and right wisdom. And nothing profane will ever come from the noble Bear. For these reasons, bears are trusted advisors in the spiritual world. The Bear has many animal virtues that are powerful and valuable. Any person

---

36 *Ibid.*
37 *Ibid.*
38 *Ibid.*
39 *Ibid.*
40 Laurence Galian, "Dawning of Light on the Path of Sufism," http://home.earthlink.net/~drmljg/id19.html (Accessed 24 May 2014)
41 *Ibid.*

would be wise to emulate these. One who has the power of the Bear will realize enhanced leadership abilities, wisdom and fearlessness in defense; as well as a better sense of self control

that will allow her or him the ability to use will-power to not speak when angered. Balance, harmony and strength are qualities to be sought for in the Bear.[42]

To the members of the Priory of Sion, obsessed with the Divine Feminine, the Bear was the animal associated with the goddess Diana. Keep in mind that the Merovingian kings, too, from their founder Merovee to Clovis (who converted to Christianity in 496 C.E.), were all worshippers of Diana, whose name literally means "heavenly" or "divine."[43] In Roman mythology, Diana was the goddess of the hunt, the moon and birthing, being associated with wild animals and the woodlands. She possessed the power to talk to and control animals.[44] Like Venus, she was also quite beautiful.

The Bear is closely associated with the goddess Diana. See http://www.sistersofearthsong.com.

And wherever there are bears, they can certainly lead us to the bees, yet another recurring Merovingian symbol. The buzzing or humming sound of these small creatures is likened to the "supersensible sounds" experienced by Sufis as they enter the spirit realms.[45]

Galian writes on the significance of bees:

"There are eleven bees on the Merovingian Coat of Arms because eleven is the number of the *sephirah* on the Tree of Life, called Daath, which *provides an opening into the Abyss or Void.*"[46]

Some may dismiss this as mere coincidence. But there is a law of synchronicity, at least in the eyes of Carl Jung, at work in the Sufi path to illumination. The Sufis assert that there are no coincidences in this world. What we perceive as "coincidences" are merely the manifestations resulting from the ordering of events by Allah.[47]

The industriousness of the bees and the organization of their hives served as a reminder to the Masons, Mormons and others of the pursuit of diligence and labor in bringing about true happiness

Beehive erected outside the Utah state capitol in Salt Lake City. See http://fanaticforjesus. blogspot.com.

---

42 Zahir Karbani, "Bear Totem," *Mani Zone*, 2006, http://www.manizone.co.uk/bear-totem-a-3.html (Accessed 24 May 2014).
43 Galian
44 *Roman Gods and Goddesses*, http://www.crystalinks.com/diana.html (Accessed 24 May 2014).
45 Galian
46 *Ibid.*
47 *Ibid.*

and prosperity in the common good. And like the bear, the bee is a symbol of wisdom. As the bees collect pollen from the flowers, so too can men and women extract wisdom from daily experiences.

Galian explains that the Divine Feminine has always shared a unique relationship to bees. He cites the following statement:

"The bee is sacred to the goddess Venus and, according to mystics, it is one of several forms of life that came to the earth from the planet Venus millions of years ago. Wheat and bananas are said to be of similar origin. This is the reason why the origin of these three forms cannot be traced. The fact that bees are ruled by queens is one reason why this insect is considered a sacred feminine symbol. In India the god Prana- the personification of the universal life force- is sometimes surrounded by a circle of bees. Because of its importance in pollinating flowers, the bee is the accepted symbol of the generative power. At one time, the bee was the emblem of the French kings. The rulers of France wore robes embroidered with bees, and the canopies of their thrones were decorated with gigantic figures of these insects. Of course another 'symbol' used by Napoleon is the bee."[48]

The knowledge of the bee and its Venusian orgin, like other esoteric information passed down from Sufi wisdom to the Cathars, presented a threat to the ecclesiastical hierarchy. So when the Cathars were eventually declared a heretical sect by the Catholic Church and brutally suppressed, the Troubadours were forced to scatter.[49] Nevertheless, in their diaspora their influence of poetic and mystical traditions continued with the emergence of the *Trouveres* in northern France, the *Minnensangers* in Germany (to include Tannhäuser), and the *Fideli di Amore* in Italy (that counted Dante in its ranks). It should also be noted that even St. Francis of Assisi was a great lover of French Troubadour songs and traditions. Commenting on the esteemed saint, Granger pens that,

"Though, he lived and taught within the Catholic Church, elements of Cathar and Troubadour spirituality can be seen in his own radiant ministry: his love of nature (particularly the sun and the moon), his vision of a divine woman, and his relationship with St. Clare (which was very much in the tradition of the chaste Lover-Beloved relationship.)"[50]

In this context, the connection of the Troubadours with the Sufis cannot be overlooked. In the Sufi way, one must consider multiple aspects of any object or situation. This is the first step toward entering a new dimension. It prepares your mind for the journey, so to speak. Since our youth, most of us have desired to travel to other worlds, or even alternate dimensions, at least in our dreams. This yearning also helps to explain the overwhelming interest in UFOs

---

48   Vadge Moore, "Kenneth Grant and the Merovingian Mythos (Dagobert's Revenge 2001)," *Discriminate Media*, 2007, http://www.vadgemoore.com/writings/merovingian_mythos.html (Accessed 24 May 2014)

49   Michael Streeter, *Behind Closed Doors: Power and Influence of Secret Societies* (London, UK: New Holland Publishing, 2008), 49: "The Crusade that tried to wipe out the Cathars was one of the more brutal and appalling episodes in Europe's admittedly long and brutal history. (Some scholars have even spoken of it as the first genocide in modern history.) The reason why the state and Church authorities were determined to obliterate the Cathars was that this secretive movement held 'Christian' beliefs that differed from those of traditional Catholicism, including the belief that Mary Magdalene was the wife of Jesus." Chapter 2 of the book, "Merovingians, Cathars and Knights Templar," pages 40-67, explores the evolution of specific doctrines within these movements related to the Divine Feminine that were the alleged causes of friction with Catholic ecclesiastic authorities. Also of note: In 1025 C.E., there was a group of 30 Cathars practicing an ascetic way of life, tending to their own business and dwelling in the vicinity of the Castle Monteforte near Asti, Italy, who sought to pattern their society after the manner of bees. They preached that one day in the far future all of humankind would be organized as a hive (collective), and even reproduce themselves without conducting a sexual act, like the bees. They also shared many other beliefs similar to those of the early Gnostic Christians. Of a certainty, the bishop of Milan was outraged; so he had all of this group rounded up, trying to force the members to recant. Since none of them would "embrace the cross," the bishop had them all burned in pyres (50).

50   Granger

and other paranormal phenomena manifest in contemporary society. While we no longer have Troubadours to tantalize our imaginations, at least in the traditional sense, we do have various self-described "contactees," individuals who claim to have communicated with extraterrestrials or even ultra-dimensional beings. These latter-day seers have revealed the existence of utopian worlds in our solar system and beyond. The higher councils of light that prevail on these celestial spheres impart light and knowledge to us through the contactees, inspiring and guiding our cosmic evolution.[51]

It seems that from the earliest times there have been "several forms of invisible saints ('friends') corresponding with the general human need for a certain representation of psychic or psychological activity in the whole community."[52]

Hujwiri's *Revelation of the Veiled* reveals that:

"Among them there are four thousand persons who are concealed and who do not know one another and who are not aware of the excellence of their state, but in all circumstances are hidden from themselves and from mankind.[53] Traditions have come down to this effect, and the sayings of the saints proclaim the truth thereof, and I myself- God be praised!-have had ocular experience of this matter."[54]

So who are these hidden Sufis? In Whinfield's translations of *Mathnawi*,[55] the great mystic Rumi asserts that,

"There are always on Earth four thousand persons who are, so to speak, saints without knowing it. These are they who are born with natural goodness, which lifts them without effort to a point that most labor to reach in vain- loyal, gentle, unselfish souls, endowed with a natural intuition of good and a natural inclination to pursue it, the stay and comfort of those who enjoy the blessing of their society, and, when they have passed away, perhaps canonized in the hearts of one or two who loved them.

---

51   Idries Shah, "Hidden Sufis," *Sufis* (Garden City, NY: Doubleday and Company, 1971), 427

52   *Ibid.*

53   In modern psychic parlance, these might be referred to as "walk-ins," A walk-in can be any person whose original soul has departed, but his or her body was replaced with a new soul, either temporarily or on a more permanent basis. In a later chapter, the Earth incarnations of several Venusians will be examined.

54   Ali Al-Hujwiri. *Revelation of the Veiled* (*Kashf al-Muhjub*): *Oldest Persian Treatise on Sufism* (c. 1074) translated by Reynold Alleyne Nicholson, 2nd ed. (London: Luzac, 1936), 213; first Nicholson ed., 1911).

Note: Hujwiri (990-1077) came from Ghazni, now in Afghanistan. He was a Sufi mystic who travelled throughout the Middle East. The *Revelation* was probably written in Lahore, Pakistan, where he was buried, not long before his death in about 1074. It is one of the oldest Sufi works in Persian (Farsi). The *Revelation* is a substantial work aiming to set forth a complete system of Sufism. It contains an elaborate discussion of acts and sayings of the great figures of the past, partly by focusing on features of doctrine and practice, as well as the examination of the different views adopted by sundry Sufi Schools. The author's personal accounts of mystic experiences highlight the treatise.

55   E. H. Whinfield, "Masnaví-i Ma`naví: The Spiritual Couplets of Maulāná Jalálu-'d-dín Muhammad-i Rúmí," Abridged and translated by E. H. Whinfield (London, 1887), xxvii; (Reprinted as "The Teachings of Rumi," Octagon Press, London, 1994)

Note: "The *Masnavi* is Rumi's greatest poetic work, composed during the last years of his life. He began it when he was between the ages of 54-57 [about 1258-1261] and continued composing its verses until he died in 1273 (with the last story remaining incomplete). It is a compendium of Sufi stories, ethical teachings, and mystical teachings. It is deeply permeated with Qur'anic meanings and references. Rumi himself called the *Masnavi* "the roots of the roots of the roots of the (Islamic) Religion.... and the explainer of the Qur'an [*wa huwa uSûlu uSûlu uSûlu 'd-dîn... was kashshâf al-Qur'ân*] (*Masnavi*, Book I, Preface). Its full name is *Mathnawî-yé Ma`navî*, which means 'Rhyming Couplets of Deep Spiritual Meaning.' The name *Mathnawî* (pronounced '*Masnavî*' in Persian) means 'couplets' in Arabic [because the second half of the verse (in Arabic, '*thanî*') rhymes with the first]. It is the name of a type of poetry (called *mathnawî*). The second word, '*Ma`navî*,' means 'significant,' 'real,' 'meaningful,' 'spiritual' in Arabic." See http://www.dar-al-masnavi.org/about_masnavi.html#Translations%20of%20Selections%20from, (Accessed 20 January 2014).

Such spontaneous goodness of this sort is not to be submitted to rules or forms. The inward inclination, not the outward ordinances, is the source of their goodness. 'Against such there is no law.'"[56] They have a standard of thought and character of their own, quite independent of the praise or blame of 'men of externals.'

Sufi teaching, therefore, accords such individuals a place in the overall evolutionary pattern of humankind. Such ones as these walk among us, angels incarnate. But for the most part, they are not even aware of each other's presence. One cannot help but notice the similarity between those select four thousand of old and the contemporary contactees and walk-ins. Even their messages to advance humanity are in a like vein. Are they one and the same? Perhaps, for the Sufi mystic Ghazali has indicated that, "Angels are the higher faculties of man."[57] Where these angels come from and why they were sent among us will be some of the topics to be explored.

As we note from the Sufis, the spiritual pilgrimage through life begins with the quest. It is long and sometimes tiresome, and the travelers must rid themselves of all earthly things, essentially becoming poor, bare and desolate. The seeker awaits the Supernal Light to cast a ray on their desolation. Some have compared this state to Purgatory. What we encounter here is the state of self-stripping and purification that no mystic may omit. The Ray of Supernal Light, upon its shining on the traveler, opens up the door or path to the mystic life. This is the gateway to further illumination.

Emanuel Swedenborg

Rembrandt's drawing of Jacob being visited by an angel (1659). See www. picturingangels.com.

Insofar as continuing contact with ethereal Venus through the ages, we turn to Scandinavia in the eighteenth century and some of the mystic experiences of Emanuel Swedenborg (1688-1772). As early as 1758, this Swedish scientist, philosopher and theologian wrote about his communication with Venusians, who imparted a "powerful influx" to his brain (telepathy). He noted that Venus was inhabited by sundry types of spirits, those of the more primitive realms and the highest order being those of the angelic host. The angels and those spirits with more "humane" dispositions inhabit one side of Venus while the denser, less ethereal, but nevertheless spiritual ones, take up residence on the other side.[58] They come together on occasion when the angelic class provides guidance and instruction for the spiritual advancement of those aspiring to move on to higher planes of existence and illumination.

"The delight of the wisdom of angels is to communicate to others what they know."

—Emanuel Swedenborg

---

56 Apostle Paul to the Galatians 5:22-23 (KJV): "But the fruit of the Spirit is love, joy, peace, forbearance, kindness, goodness, faithfulness, gentleness and self-control. *Against such* things *there is no law.*"
57 Shah, 437
58 Emanuel Swedenborg. *Earths In Our Solar System Which Are Called Planets, and Earths in the Starry Heaven, Their Inhabitants, and the Spirits and Angels There* (1758), 105-110; Library of Light, http://www.universe-people.com/english/svetelna_knihovna/htm/en/en_kniha_earths_in_the_universe.htm (Accessed 4 January 2014)

Swedenborg believed that a being's state of spiritual evolution also determined his or her perception of time and space, indicating levels of inter-dimensionality. Those living in this celestial state can perceive the Sun, stars and other planets dimly. They remain blurred and motionless, as if existing outside of our physical reference to time and space, but constantly sense their exerted power due to their effects. The masters of Venus are those exalted spirits who have completed various incarnations on Earth, overcoming the snares of our planet in the process. The knowledge they gained as avatars on Earth is brought back to Venus to help the more primitive ones prepare for their coming incarnation on the Earth or other spheres. The Venusian masters have delayed their own ascension to yet higher realms to smooth the evolution and transition of spirits on the Earth and Venus, the two planets of our solar system that are inexorably linked. Swedenborg also informs us that Jesus Christ hailed from Venus, and continues his work there today.[59] Interestingly, the writings of Swedenborg concerning the Earth-Venus connection are similar to those of Helena Blavatsky, the founder of modern Theosophy,[60] of which more will be revealed in the next chapter of this book.

The beautiful Princess Duare of Venus defends her newly-arrived lover, the American adventurer Carson Napier, from attack by a ferocious tiger. Scene from the Edgar Rice Burroughs' *Venus* series of books: *Lost on Venus* (1933), *Pirate of Venus* (1934), *Carson of Venus* (1937), *Escape on Venus* (1946) and the *Wizard of Venus* (1970). See http://www.orderofbooks.com/characters/venus/.

To Blavatsky, Swedenborg and Tannhäuser, the notion that Venus or any other world could exist in a spiritual realm unseen by one's physical eyes was not beyond comprehension. For as the Sufis would attest, "all initiatory truths are veiled."[61] But for the more "nuts-and-bolts" scientists, more solid proof was needed. To most nineteenth and a goodly number of twentieth century astronomers, bright but cloud-shrouded Venus remained an enigma. Together with science fiction writers, they let their imaginations get away from them, running wild. Noting the permanent and up-to-that-time never pierced Venusian cloud layer, they speculated about a jungle planet with a wet and warm surface, or perhaps a world of vast oceans, dotted with islands akin to Tahiti or the Hawaiian chain, replete with beautiful maidens.

59   *Ibid.*

60   Helena P. Blavatsky. *Secret Doctrine: The Synthesis of Science, Religion and Philosophy* (London, UK: Theosophical Publishing Company, 1888).

61   Galian: "While almost every reader of Sufism and metaphysics in general, is very familiar with the fact that Allah does not gaze at His friends (*awliya*) directly but cloaks His gaze with a veil (*hijab*), very few students will pause to consider of what these veils may consist. One reads the word 'veil,' and then just quickly forgets it, or just dismisses the concept of 'veiling' with the thought that Allah hides the Mysteries in various ways.

"However, very little thought, or for that matter, information, is given as to how Allah veils His Truths. One way that truth is veiled is through the veil of the fear of appearing or becoming insane or 'crazy.' Other veils include becoming or appearing a fool, the veil of obviousness, the veil of shame, the veil of no longer being concerned with 'stations' on the path, the veil of behaving contrary to Shariah (law), the veil of heresy, and the veil of leaving the Path.

"God is called by many names. She is all the same. However, it *does* matter in this particular age what name human beings use in addressing or thinking of Her. The knowledge of Her Name is related to an individual's special relationship to Her.

"Absolutely nothing can happen without Her Mercy, without Her Grace. The most advanced spiritual techniques in the world are powerless to transform us, unless first She wills it. There are some writers today who want us to believe that if a certain sequence of practices is followed, then enlightenment is guaranteed, somewhat like following a sequence of driving instructions to arrive at a destination. Some of these writers forget completely the necessary ingredients of awe, devotion and love, without which it is not possible to complete the Great Work. The Goddess is not a machine, *astagfirullah. Nor is she a Woman that can be raped and forced to reveal Her Secrets.*"

Chapter III:
Secret Doctrine

I, Jesus, have sent mine angel to testify unto you these things in the churches.
I am the root and the offspring of David, *and* the bright and morning star.
—Jesus, the Christ, in *Revelation* 22:16 (**KJV**)

The planet Venus plays a key role in Theosophy. This chapter explores the origins of Theosophy and the centrality of Venus in its doctrine. Theosophy is not so much a religion, but a philosophy for the so-called New Age, a rediscovery of ancient esoteric knowledge that occupies a central place in the history of emergent spiritual movements. The writings of Helena P. Blavatsky, the co-founder of Theosophy, and some of her followers have exercised a great influence extending far beyond the membership of the Theosophical Society. It has been aptly noted that, "The importance of Theosophy in modern history should not be underestimated. Not only have the writings of Blavatsky and others inspired several generations of occultists, but the movement had a remarkable role in the restoration to the colonial peoples of nineteenth century Asia their own spiritual heritage."[62]

Helena Petrovna Blavatsky (1831-1891) See http://en.wikipedia.org/wiki/Helena_Blavatsky.

Helena Blavatsky certainly grew up under extraordinary circumstances. Born Helena Petrovna von Hahn at Ekaterinoslav, a town on the banks of the Dnieper River in Southern Russia on 12 August 1831, she was the daughter of Colonel Peter von Hahn, and Helena de Fadeyev, a well-known novelist. On the paternal side of her family, she was the granddaughter of the famed botanist and Russian Princess Helena Dolgorukov. After the early death of her mother in 1842, Helena, then only eleven years old, was brought up in her maternal grandparents' house in Saratov. It was there where her grandfather served as the Civil Governor.[63]

Not soon after the death of her mother, the young Helena was aware of being different from those around her. She gradually became cognizant of possessing certain psychic powers; and this puzzled her family and friends. She was impatient with her teachers. She seemed to instinctually know her lessons and wanted to acquire knowledge at a much faster rate than anyone was capable of imparting it to her. She was also quite sensitive and gifted in many areas: linguistics, piano playing, artistry, equestrianism, and the scientific exploration of the natural world. Helena felt that she was wasting her life away in Russia. She wanted to dedicate her life to the service of humankind. She always believed that heavenly avenues were open to her for special guidance and protection. She became determined to tap into these to find a way out of Russia and realize her dreams on higher plateaus of experience and illumination.

62   Robert S. Ellwood and Harry B. Partin, *Religious and Spiritual Groups in Modern America* (Englewood Cliffs, New Jersey: Prentice Hall, 1988), 63

63   Boris de Zirkoff, "Helena Petrovna Blavatsky: A Brief Sketch of Her Life and Work," (Summer 1968), *Theosophia* Vol. XXV, 1(115), Los Angeles, California, 2-3.

When she was almost eighteen, Helena married the middle-aged Nikifor V. Blavatsky, the Vice-Governor of the Province of Yerivan in Armenia. For many years, Helena had been seeking a way out of her dull surroundings, so getting married seemed as good a reason as any to break away. After a few months had passed, she then ran away from her husband and travelled widely in Egypt, Greece, and Turkey on money supplied by her father. Just two years later, she found herself in London. Here she met an individual that she claimed to have previously encountered in some psychic-spiritual visions of her childhood. This gentleman was the Mahatma Morya, a.k.a. "M," a teacher of the Eastern Initiate of royal Indian birth. The teacher did a psychic reading for Helena and informed her of the important work that the Ascended Masters had planned for her. From that moment on, Helena fully accepted M's spiritual authority and guidance.

In the next three years, Helena embarked for Canada, and after adventurous travels in various parts of the United States, Mexico, South America and the West Indies, went via the Cape and Ceylon to India, Mahatma Morya's homeland. She traveled north from India, hoping to traverse the Himalayas and arrive in the fabled land of Tibet. She failed on this first attempt, however, and returned to England via Java. In 1854, Helena went to America again, crossing the Rockies with a caravan of emigrants, probably in a covered wagon.[64]

In the following year, she left for India via Japan. This was the turning point in her life. Boris de Zirkoff writes concerning this period:

"On this trip she succeeded in entering Tibet through Kashmir and Ladakh, undergoing part of her occult training with her Master. In 1858 she was in France and Germany, and returned to Russia in the late Fall of the same year, staying a short time with her sister Vera at Pskov. From 1860 to 1865, she lived and travelled through the Caucasus, experiencing a severe physical and psychic crisis which placed her in complete control over her occult powers. She left Russia again in the Fall of 1865, and travelled extensively through the Balkans, Greece, Egypt, Syria and Italy and various other places.

In 1868 she went via India to Tibet. On this trip H.P.B. met the Master Koot Hoomi (K.H.) for the first time and stayed in his house in Little Tibet. In late 1870 she was back in Cyprus and Greece. Embarking for Egypt, she was shipwrecked near the island of Spetsai on July 4, 1871; saved from drowning, she went to Cairo where she tried to form a *Societe Spirite* which soon failed. After further travels through the Middle East, she returned for a short time to her relatives at Odessa, Russia in July, 1872. In the Spring of 1873, Helena was instructed by her Teacher to go to Paris, and on further direct orders from him, left for New York City where she landed July 7, 1873."[65]

These were the years of intense psychic and spiritual formation for Helena Blavatsky. She was compliant in her total obedience to the teachings of M. This, in turn, endowed her with the spiritual knowledge necessary in a confrontation with a severe physical and psychic crisis; and her overcoming during this time of tribulation permitted her the full control and use of all her occult powers. Being saved from drowning, the sign was given for her to spiritually organize humankind for the receipt of celestial knowledge and illumination to improve conditions for all on Earth.

In October of 1874, Helena was guided by her teachers to Colonel Henry Steel Olcott, a Union veteran of the Civil War who served with distinction as a colonel under the command of General Ambrose Burnside in his campaigns against entrenched Confederate forces in North

---

64   *Ibid.,* 3
65   *Ibid.*

Carolina. When Helena met Olcott for the first time, he was practicing law in the state of New York. In this same year, she also met William Quan Judge, a young Irish lawyer, who was later to play a key role in the Theosophical work.[66]

On 7 September 1875, these three individuals, together with several others, founded an organization which they chose to call the Theosophical Society. The purpose of this new group was to advance the ancient teachings of Theosophy, or the "Wisdom concerning the Divine," which had been the spiritual basis of other great movements of the past such as Neo-Platonism, Gnosticism, and the Mystery-Schools of the Classical world. The inaugural address for the Theosophical Society was given by its President-Founder Colonel Olcott, on 17 November 1875. Starting from a generalized statement of objectives, namely, "to collect and diffuse a knowledge of the laws which govern the Universe," the Founders soon expressed them more specifically. After several minor changes in wording, the *Objects* stand today as follows:

1. To form a nucleus of the Universal Brotherhood of Humanity, without distinction of race, creed, sex, caste or color.
2. To encourage the study of Comparative Religion, Philosophy and Science.
3. To investigate unexplained laws of Nature, and the powers latent in man.[67]

Helena P. Blavatsky continued to build on this philosophy and published her first major work, *Isis Unveiled*, in September 1877.[68] There were only one thousand copies printed with the first edition; but since it sold out in ten days, numerous subsequent editions quickly followed. Basically, *Isis Unveiled* outlines the history, scope and development of the occult sciences, the nature and origin of magic, the roots of Christianity, the errors of Christian theology and the fallacies of established orthodox science. It accomplishes all of this against the backdrop of the secret teachings which run as a "golden thread" through the centuries past that has emerged on occasion in the various mystical movements of the last two thousand years or so.[69]

On 8 July 1878, Helena Petrovna Blavatsky became a naturalized citizen of the United States; and by December, she had left for India via England with Colonel Olcott. They arrived in Bombay in February, 1879, and established the Theosophical Society World Headquarters there. Soon after, they were contacted by Alfred Percy Sinnett, then editor of the colonial government paper, *The Pioneer* of Allahabad. He would prove very helpful to the Theosophical Society in securing the printing of its publications.[70]

After a tour of northwestern India, the founders returned to Bombay and started, in October, 1879, their first Theosophical journal, *The Theosophist*, with H.P. Blavatsky as editor. The society then experienced a rapid growth, and some very remarkable people were attracted to it from around the globe. During the late Spring and early Summer of 1880, the founders spent some time in Ceylon (Sri Lanka). On this island nation, Colonel Olcott laid the foundations for his later work that served to promote a revival of Buddhism in the West. Both Blavatsky and Olcott officially became Buddhists during this period.[71]

In the Fall of 1880, Blavatsky and Olcott visited A.P. Sinnett and his wife Patience at Simla in northern India. From then on, the Sinnetts carried on a continuing correspondence with both Blavatsky and Olcott. What A. P. Sinnett garnered from this imparted wisdom, he wrote

---

66   *Ibid.*, 3, 4, 10
67   *Ibid.*, 3, 4
68   H. P. Blavatsky, *Isis Unveiled* (New York, New York: J. W. Bouton, 1877).
69   Zirkoff, 5
70   *Ibid.*, 4
71   *Ibid.*, 5

in two important books, the *Occult World* (1881)[72] and *Esoteric Buddhism* (1883).[73] Both of these works became immediate bestsellers and generated a worldwide interest in Theosophy. Letters from various Indian teachers to the Sinnetts, providing answers to questions brought up in their 1881 and 1883 works were published in 1923 as *the Mahatma Letters to A.P. Sinnett.*[74] The original letters from these Indian masters to the Sinnets can be viewed in the Department of Rare Manuscripts of the British Museum in London.[75]

In May 1882, representatives for the Theosophical Society purchased a large estate in southern India at Adyar, near Madras; and the Theosophical World Headquarters was moved there in December of the same year. Blavatsky and Olcott engaged in numerous trips to outlying districts where they established branches, received visitors, conducted an enormous amount of correspondence with inquirers, and filled their journal with valuable and scholarly material with the intent of sparking revitalized interest on the part of the Indian people in the spiritual worth of their own ancient scriptures. Two years later, both Blavatsky and Olcott traveled to England to petition for the rights of Indian Buddhists.[76] In the Fall of 1884, Blavatsky was on the European mainland and beginning to write her second monumental work, the *Secret Doctrine.*[77]

By December 1884, Blavatsky found herself back in India, confronting dissention in the ranks of the Theosophical Society. She was in poor health, however, and after a little more than three months of failing to contain the situation, Blavatsky found that the stress was too much for her. She resigned as the Corresponding Secretary of the Theosophical Society and returned to Europe. She never returned to India. History has proven that the accusations made against Helena P. Blavatsky were all false, based on forged and partially forged letters allegedly written by her, charging that she conspired to fabricate "psychic phenomena" in order to deceive the public and promote the sale of her book and literature. These lies were largely fomented by the London-based Society for Psychical Research, an organization whose spies had infiltrated the rival psychic group, the Theosophical Society, being so jealous and threatened by the positive attention and success that Blavatsky had brought to it.[78]

In August 1885, Blavatsky was in Wurzburg, Germany, diligently working on her *magnum opus*, the *Secret Doctrine*. Nearly one year later, she relocated to Ostend, Belgium; and in May 1887, at the invitation of English Theosophists, she moved to a small house in the Upper Norwood section of London. Her very presence here soon spurred Theosophical activities throughout the British Isles. A Blavatsky Lodge was even formed and began to disseminate theosophical ideas.[79]

Blavatsky continued to write her great work; and it was finally completed and published in two large volumes in October-December, 1888.[80] The first volume of the *Secret Doctrine* is mainly concerned with the evolution of the Universe. It also includes an extended elucidation of the fundamental symbols contained in the great religions and mythologies of the world.

---

72   Alfred Percy Sinnett, *Occult World* (London: Trubner and Company, 1881).
73   Alfred Percy Sinnett, *Esoteric Buddhism* (London: Chapman and Hall, Ltd., 1883).
74   Alfred Percy Sinnett, *Mahatma Letters to A. P. Sinnett* (London: T. Fisher Unwin, Ltd., 1923).
75   Zirkoff, 4, 5
76   *Ibid.*
77   H. P. Blavatsky, *Secret Doctrine: The Synthesis of Science, Religion and Philosophy* (London: Theosophical Publishing Company, Ltd., 1888).
78   Zirkoff, 5
79   *Ibid.*, 5
80   *Ibid.*, 6

The second volume, on the other hand, describes the evolution of humankind on this planet.[81] Concerning the importance of the *Secret Doctrine*, Boris de Zirkoff writes:

"In all ages and in all lands, the belief has existed that a divine degree of knowledge is possible to human beings under certain conditions; and, as a corollary to this, the conviction has dwelt in the hearts of people that living men exist who possess this knowledge. In ancient days, some of this higher knowledge was taught in the Mystery Schools, traces of which have been found among the nations of the Earth. In more modern days, its existence has been suspected by intuitive thinkers, who have called it by various names, such as the 'Wisdom Religion,' or the 'Esoteric Philosophy.'"[82]

Helena Petrovna Blavatsky went on to publish numerous other articles and books in her few remaining years. As a flu epidemic was raging through London, she passed away on 8 May 1891 with her remains being cremated at the Working Crematorium in Surrey, England.

It has been said of Helena Petrovna Blavatsky that she,

"...stands out as the fountainhead of modern occult thought, and was either the originator and/or popularizer of many of the ideas and terms which have a century later been assembled within the New Age Movement. The Theosophical Society, which she cofounded, has been the major advocate of occult philosophy in the West and the single most important avenue of Eastern teaching to the West."[83]

Blavatsky used to teach her disciples that Nature is not just "a fortuitous concurrence of atoms."[84] She believed that intelligence permeated the entire universe and that everything and everybody was in their assigned place. Her life mission was to rescue from degradation the archaic truths which are the basis of all religions. She sought to uncover, to some extent, the fundamental unity from which everything and everybody sprang. In addition, Blavatsky was adamant in demonstrating that the occult side of Nature needed to be approached by the science of modern civilization.[85] In fact, it was predicted that Blavatsky would not begin to be recognized for the genius and prophet that she was until the arrival of the twenty-first century. Notes Theosophist I. M. Oderberg:

"HPB's masterpiece, the *Secret Doctrine* (1888), refers to a stream of ancient wisdom that had its origins in a remote antiquity and has survived into our own times. *It contains ideas in seed form that have germinated during the twentieth century, to grow more fully in the twenty-first century when these concepts will be better understood.* The most important of these ideas is the oneness of life, an energy-consciousness that permeates the whole cosmos and is the heart of all the manifestations we perceive around us. All human beings, therefore, share a common humanity, an innate quality that permits no distinctions, such as those raised in the past under the labels race, color, religion, or gender."[86]

---

81   *Ibid.,* 7

82   *Ibid.*

83   J. Gordon Melton, Jerome Clark and Aidan A. Kelly, eds., *New Age Almanac* (Detroit, Michigan: Gale Research Inc., 1991), 16.

84   Zirkoff, 8

85   *Ibid.*

86   I. M. Oderberg, "H. P. Blavatsky's Cultural Impact," *Sunrise* magazine (Pasadena, California: Theosophical University Press), December 1995/January 1996 and February/March 1996. http://www.theosophy-nw.org/theosnw/theos/th-imo.htm (Accessed 22 April 2014)

Venus in Theosophy

This chapter establishes the framework for looking at the planet Venus as both an integral part of the entire universe as well as an object of spiritual discernment in accordance with the new paradigm established by Blavatsky over 125 years ago. Blavatsky herself was quite taken up with the beauty and significance of the second solar planet. From her *History of a Planet*, she writes:

"No star, among the countless myriads that twinkle over the sidereal fields of the night sky, shines so dazzlingly as the planet Venus—not even Sirius-Sothis, the dog-star, beloved by Isis. Venus is the queen among our planets, the crown jewel of our solar system. She is the inspirer of the poet, the guardian and companion of the lonely shepherd, the lovely morning and the evening star. For, Stars teach as well as shine."[87]

Blavatsky also noted that even towards the end of the nineteenth century, the planets and stars remained largely a mystery to astronomers. This was especially so for Venus, because of its thick cloud cover. Blavatsky, however, bemoaned the ignorance that plagued even the so-called "sophisticated" Londoners of her time. Unfortunately, wherever there was a mystery, they generally supposed it to be hiding something evil. "Thus there came to be slandered stars and planets as well as slandered men and women," wrote the seer,[88] with innocent Venus being ravaged in the process.

Blavatsky was well acquainted with the writings of Charlotte M. Yonge that appeared in the *Monthly Packet of Evening Readings for Members of the English Church*, and found a kindred spirit in her. Yonge wrote quite extensively about the religions of the ancient world in the hope of enlightening her English countrymen who looked askance at all belief systems but that officially sanctioned by the Church of England. Naturally, the selection of the name "Lucifer" for a publication of the Theosophical Society was going to raise quite a few eyebrows and generate some degree of hostility toward Blavatsky and her Theosophical endeavors on the part of so-called Christian fundamentalists. So Blavatsky had to be prepared with a reasoned response, and she found it in Yonge, who wrote that:

"Among the ancients, Mercury and Venus each had two names, one as morning, and the other as evening star. When they saw Mercury shining in the dim twilight so favorable to thieves, they called him Mercury; and they considered the special talents of thieves were inspired by a divinity, whom they also called Mercury, and it is doubtful which was named first, the star or the god. Mercury also made men eloquent, and on this account the men of Lystra called St. Paul, Mercurius. But when the planet reached the sun, and passing before him, was lost in his beams for a few days, and then appeared on the other side as a morning star, those old astronomers, not recognizing him, gave him the name of Apollo, the God of the Sun. For the same reasons, Venus was Hesperus, or Vesper, as an evening star, or *Lucifer, the Light-Bearer*, when she was a morning star. When it was known to be the same planet, she was dedicated to Venus."[89]

---

87   H. P. Blavatsky and Mabel Collins, eds., *Lucifer: A Theosophical Magazine* (London, England), V1, September 1887-February 1888, 15.

88   *Ibid.*

89   Charlotte M. Yonge, "Our Evening Outlook," Monthly Packet of Evening Readings for Members of the English Church, 3rd series, V3, Parts XLIII to XLVIII (London, England: Walter Smith, July-December 1884), 383-384.

"For, 'Venus loves the whispers,
Of plighted youth and maid,
In April's ivory moonlight,
Beneath the chestnut shade.'"[90]

"This planet was a special favorite for those who adored the host of Heaven; and the worship of Ashtoreth was an instance of it. She was presented wearing a crescent, and was called the 'two-horned goddess,' so it is nearly certain that the ancients knew of her crescent form, which good observers can see in the clear Eastern sky to this day."[91]

For Helena P. Blavatsky it was abhorrent that this charming goddess of light should be dethroned by the hierarchy of Christian churches over the misunderstanding of a name and function. On the title page of the first edition of *Lucifer*, she quotes another member of the Yonge family on this delicate matter:

"The Light Bearer is the morning star or Lucifer, and 'Lucifer is no profane or Satanic title. It is the Latin *Luciferus*. The Light Bringer, the Morning Star, equivalent to the Greek *Phosphorus*...the name of the pure pale herald of daylight."[92]

Blavatsky became disconcerted over the demotion of Venus. As on the Earth, one's good reputation and fortune may be sacrificed for the benefit of another or party of individuals, Blavatsky reasoned that so it was in the heavens above:

"...and Venus, the sister planet of our Earth, was sacrificed to the ambitions of our little globe to show the latter the 'chosen' planet of the Lord. She became the scapegoat, the *Azaziel* of the starry dome, for the sins of the Earth, or rather for those of a certain class in the human family—the clergy—who slandered the bright orb, in order to prove what their ambition suggested to them as the best means to reach power, and exercise it unswervingly over the superstitious and ignorant masses."[93]

Most of this confusion arose during the so-called "Middle Ages," when this error was successfully raised to the status of a religious dogma in the Roman Catholic Church. Blavatsky succeeds marvelously in explaining the evolution of this corrupt mythology.[94]

Clearly, however, the early Christian church was not so narrow-minded. The Gnostics, centered in Alexandria, Egypt, believed in numerous emanations of God (the One or the Monad), which they called Aeons.[95] In the various Gnostic systems then extant throughout the first through fourth century C.E. Mediterranean world, these Aeons were differently named, classified, and described. The emanation theory, as it has come to be known, was common to all forms of Gnosticism and has its roots in Greek philosophy.[96]

---

90   Horatius, "Battle of Lake Regillus," One of the "Lays of Ancient Rome," sung at the feast of Castor and Pollux on the Ides of Quintilus, 451 A.D. Note: Venus was honored here as the Latin goddess of beauty and love and answered to the Greek Aphrodite. According to Roman tradition, Venus was also the mother of Aeneas, the progenitor of the Roman race. Some sections of this ballad are deemed to be an imitation of the Greek Homer's *Iliad*.
91   C. M. Yonge
92   Charles D. Yonge, quoted by Blavatsky and Collins, eds., in *Lucifer*, see footnote 74. Note: Charles D. Yonge was a Regius Professor of Modern History at Queen's College in Belfast, Northern Ireland and a cousin to Charlotte M. Yonge.
93   Blavatsky and Collins, *Lucifer*, 15
94   *Ibid.*, 15-23
95   John B. Peterson, "_Æons_" in Herbermann, Charles, ed., *Catholic Encyclopedia* (New York: Robert Appleton Company, 1913), 173, 174.
96   Francis E. Peters. *Greek Philosophical Terms: A Historical Lexicon* (New York: New York University Press, 1967), 7, 8.

Aeon derives from the Greek root word *aion*, which in its earliest and non-philosophical sense simple means a "life span." The term is believed to have first been introduced into sixth century B.C.E. philosophical circles by Parmedides of Elea, a Greek colony on the southeast coast of Italy. In a philosophical context, *aion* embodies a "denial of becoming," or a negation of *genesis* (creation) in true being. This, in turn, leads to its corollary of denial in the temporal distinctions of "past" and "future," and the affirmation of *total present simultaneity*. In other words, the Aeons, by their very nature, exist outside of the space-time continuum, at least in the context that we have to negotiate it.[97]

The Aeons, as spiritual emanations, originated as thoughts and spoken intents of the One. They can manifest as either female or male, generally in groups of thirty. Complex hierarchies of Aeons therefore exist and belong to the purely ideal, intelligible but supersensible world. They are immaterial beings associated with hypostatic ideas. Along with the source from which they emanate, the One, they form the *Pleroma* or "region of light", Greek πλήρωμα. The lowest regions of the Pleroma are closest to the material world. In the Alexandrian school, the One was associated with the Sun, while the Aeons were assigned as the guiding spirits of various planets or other celestial objects.[98]

To the Gnostic understanding, the transition of an Aeon from the immaterial to the material, from the noumenal to the sensible, is brought about by acting out one's passions, or in the parlance of general Christian theology, "committing a sin." Here begins humankind's struggle in choosing between the worlds of materiality and spirit. Basilides, a Gnostic teacher who taught in Alexandria from 117 to 138 C.E., claimed that the sin of the last contingent of the Aeons against the Great Archon, or Aeon Creator of the Material Universe, was simply acting on the "desire to know." This rebellion was led by the female Aeon Sophia. As a punishment, the entire Earth was plunged into darkness, losing its place with the other planets of the solar system that still remained in the Pleroma. Teachers from these other worlds in the Pleroma then came to Earth in human form to help those trapped in material existence learn how to overcome it by achieving *gnosis*, or cosmic awareness, and changing their lives in such a way to permit a transition back to the spiritual realm in either this lifetime or future ones.[99]

Aeons are synonymous with angels. They emanate from other worlds in the Pleroma and are here to help humankind return there. Artwork is from www.fanpop.com.

Aeons do indeed bear a number of similar characteristics with Judeo-Christian angels, including their roles as messengers, servants and emanations of God, Angels also exist as beings of light. Many of the Gnostic angels also happen to be Aeons, such as those mentioned in both the *Bible* and the *Book of Enoch*, in addition to others incorporated from other belief systems. The Gnostic *Gospel of Judas*, recently discovered, purchased, held, and translated by the National Geographic Society, also mentions the Aeons and elucidates on Jesus' teachings concerning them. In this gospel, Jesus teaches Judas and

97   *Ibid.*
98   Blavatsky, *Lucifer*, 18.
99   Mead, G.R.S., "Pistis Sophia," in Blavatsky, Helena. *Lucifer* (London: The Theosophical Publishing Society, 1890), 6 (33): 230–239.

the other disciples about his origins as an emanation from the immortal realm of Barbelo. He explains to them that this region consists of a "great cloud of light," so vast that not even the angels have been able to determine the full extent of it. Jesus' mission was to help humankind return to reclaim their place in this exalted kingdom.[100]

Outside of Palestine, the early Christian church blossomed in Alexandria,[101] the Anatolian peninsula (Turkey) and mainland Greece. Naturally, a syncretism with the prevailing Hellenic culture occurred in these areas. This was especially true of the Gnostics. They rapidly embraced the teachings of the Eleatic school of philosophy as espoused by Parmenides and later by his fifth century B.C.E. disciples Zeno of Elea and Melissus of Samos.

Of Zeno little is known, but it is reputed by the eminent historian and philosopher Diogenes Laërtius that he was the son of Teleutagoras and the adopted son of Parmenides. Zeno was "skilled to argue both sides of any question, the universal critic." This may have gotten him arrested and perhaps killed at the hands of the authorities in Elea.[102]

In his early adult life, Melissus was the commander of the famed Samian fleet in the years immediately preceding the Peloponnesian War, helping to greatly expand the influence

---

100 *Gospel of Judas,* Rodolphe Kasser, Marvin Meyer, and Gregor Wurst, eds., (Washington, D.C.: National Geographic Society, 2006), http://www.nationalgeographic.com/lostgospel/_pdf/GospelofJudas.pdf, 1-7 (Accessed 27 April 2014).

101 Alexander the Great, the general-king of Macedonia succumbed to illness (most likely malaria) on 7 June 323 B.C.E. outside Susa, a city of the ancient Persian Empire located in the Lower Zagros Mountains about 160 miles east of the Tigris River. Alexander died at the age of 33 without designating a successor to the Macedonian Empire. Following his death in 323 B.C.E., a struggle for power ensued among his generals. Ultimately, the Macedonian Empire split into four main kingdoms - the one of Seleucus (Asia), Lysimachus (Thrace), Antipater's son Cassander (Macedonia, including Greece) and Ptolemy (Egypt). The rise of Rome put an end to all of these Macedonian kingdoms. Macedonia and Greece were conquered in 167 and 145 B.C.E., respectively. Seleucid Asia fell in 65 B.C.E., and Cleopatra VII, the last Macedonian descendent in the Ptolemy line, committed suicide in 30 B.C.E., after which Egypt was added to the Roman Empire. See "Alexander the Great," http://www.historyofmacedonia.org/AncientMacedonia/AlexandertheGreat. html, 2001-2013 (Accessed 27 April 2014.) While the Greek cult of Aphrodite gained prominence during the reign of the Ptolemy line, there is some evidence that organized devotion to this celestial goddess of love may have originated in Egypt itself. We know, for example, that her name *aphros* traditionally signifies "foam." Hence, this ancient symbolism denotes Aphrodite/Venus as being born upon the churning seas. No indication is given for the meaning of the suffix –*dite*. But the illusion to the foamy seas may be nothing more than a pun or folk etymology, with the true origins of Aphrodite/Venus worship coming from the Egyptian Pr-Wedyt. Wrote Martin G. Bernal (1910-2012), a professor emeritus of Near Eastern Studies at Cornell University: "This name (Pr-Wedyt), given to two cities- one in the Nile Delta, later known to the Greeks as Bouto(s), and the other in Upper Egypt, called Aphroditopolis- demonstrates the identification of Wedyt with Aphrodite. I have already mentioned the Egyptian association of divinities with their dwellings…. In this case, however, the use of Pr-Wedyt as a form of address has been attested (linguistically). ….Semantically, the case for deriving Aphrodite from Pr-Wedyt is very strong indeed." Bernal also points out that Pr-Wedyt was the goddess of fertility associated with new growth after the annual flooding of the Nile, while Aphrodite was linked to the arrival of spring and youthful love. A statue to Pr-Wedyt and her attendant priests and priestesses has also been discovered from the end of Middle Minoan Crete (1700-1600 B.C.E.). This approximately coincides with the Hyksos invasions of Egypt and the adjacent Mediterranean areas sometime around the end of the eighteenth and beginning of the seventeenth century B.C.E. What is significant about this find lies in the associations made of Pr-Wedyt with snakes. In Egypt, the goddess is intimately connected to the emergence of snakes in the annual flooding season; while the Minoan statues show her holding two snakes. See Martin G. Bernal, *Black Athena: Afroasiatic Roots of Classical Civilization, Volume 1: The Fabrication of Ancient Greece, 1785-1985* (New Brunswick, New Jersey: Rutgers University Press, 1987), 65, 66. See footnote 1.

102 Diogenes Laërtius, *Lives and Opinions of Eminent Philosophers*, translated by C.D. Yonge (London: Henry G. Bohn, 1853); See "Zeno" in Chapter IX, http://classicpersuasion.org/pw/diogenes/index.htm (Accessed 27 April 2014).

of Hellenic culture throughout the Mediterranean. Later contribution to philosophy was a treatise of systematic arguments supporting the Eleatic school of thought; and like his mentor Parmenides, he argued that reality is ungenerated, indestructible, indivisible, changeless, and motionless.[103] Melissus also sought to show that reality is wholly without limits and infinitely extended in all directions; and since existence is unlimited, it must also be one.[104] This is what Laërtius wrote about Melissus:

"His doctrine was, that the Universe was infinite, unsusceptible of change, immoveable, and one, being always like to itself, and complete; and that there was no such thing as real motion, but that there only appeared to be such."[105]

In the times that Helena Blavatsky wrote about the ancient world, most of Christendom had only the pages of the *Holy Bible* to go by when it came to the formulation of religious tenets. What was generally thought of concerning the Gnostics of the first through fourth centuries C.E. was that they were the espousers of dangerous and heretical ideas. In fact, until the discovery of the Nag Hammadi codices in Upper Egypt in December 1945, the Gnostic view of early Christianity had largely been forgotten and long ago abandoned. The teachings of Gnostic Christianity were vilified insofar as they were declared heretical by the councils of orthodox Christianity in the fourth century. They had been virtually erased from the pages of history by the early church fathers. The Gnostic gospels were banned and even burned to make room for the prevailing views of traditional Christian theology as culled from the canonical Gospels of Matthew, Mark, Luke and John, and correctly interpreted by the state-religious hierarchy.[106]

More than half a century before the momentous discoveries at Nag Hammadi, Blavatsky grieved over the disparaging remarks from the clergy of her day then being hurled at the Christian Gnostics, who had no way of possibly defending themselves. And concerning the erroneous orthodox Christian association of Venus with the devil, Blavastsky writes:

"The Church believes in the devil, of course, and could not afford to lose him. 'The Devil is the chief pillar of the Church,' confesses unblushingly an advocate of the *Ecclesia Militans* (militant church). 'All the Alexandrian Gnostics speak to us of the fall of the Aeons and their Pleroma, and all attribute that fall to the desire to know,' writes another volunteer in the same army, slandering the Gnostics as usual and identifying *the desire to know* with occultism, magic with Satanism."[107]

Of course, these old rumors, born of unconscionable churchmen of less enlightened eras, persist in sundry conspiracy theories and pop culture, with Hollywood leading the way in creating a very warped image of occult studies. Thereby, many are misled leading into using the word "occult" as synonymous with black magic and demon worship. But in truth, the occult is much more general and much less inherently threatening. The word "occult" literally and simply means "hidden," which is why multiple scientific fields use the term. For example, when a medical test detects something existing in too small of a quantity to be visible, the pathologists aptly describe it as occult.

Blavatsky was aware that an overriding and unsubstantiated fear of the Christian Gnostics

---

103   This quality of motionless, reflective in inter-dimensional environments, was also noted by E. Swedenborg as existing on ethereal Venus. See footnote 47.

104   For a comprehensive analysis of Melissus and the Eleatic philosophy, see Johannes Hubertus Mathias Marie Loenen, *Parmenides, Melissus, Gorgias* (Assen, Netherlands: Royal Van Gorcum, Limited, 1959), 207 pages.

105   Diogenes Laërtius, "Melissus" in Chapter IX.

106   "Issue 200: Ten Top Discoveries," *Biblical Archaeology Review*, Jul/Aug/Sep/Oct 2009, 74-96.

107   Blavatsky and Collins, *Lucifer*, 18.

was based on both historical ignorance and the lack of verifiable information, most of which had been destroyed by either the general persecution of Christians throughout the empire by the Roman authorities or later by the church fathers. But when two Arab peasant boys discovered the Nag Hammadi texts, a thirteen-volume library of Coptic texts hidden beneath a large boulder, Blavatsky and other Theosophists, the latter-day manifestations of the Gnostics, would soon be vindicated. The world was reintroduced to this near-forgotten and much-maligned branch of early Christian thought. The Nag Hammadi codices consist of thirteen leather-bound volumes dated to the mid-fourth century. They contain 52 texts; and some of these were composed as early as the second century.[108]

The Nag Hammadi codices were translated and published by a team of scholars led by James M. Robinson of the Institute for Antiquity and Christianity, Claremont Graduate University in Claremont, California. The ancient documents clearly demonstrated that Gnostic Christianity was not the sinister cult described by orthodox Christian writers. On the contrary, it was a legitimate religious movement that offered an alternate testament to the lives and ministry of Jesus and his disciples.[109]

The Nag Hammadi texts reflect a wide array of attitudes and beliefs in Gnostic Christianity. They include additional gospels and apocalyptic revelations, but they all assert the primacy of spiritual and intellectual knowledge over physical action and material well-being. The *Apocryphon of John*, for example, is a classic revelatory book in the category of second to third century C.E. Sethian Gnosticism.[110] In this text, the risen Jesus reveals to John, the son of Zebedee, the truth about the creation process.

According to this Gnostic mythology,

"...the God of the Hebrew *Bible* is actually a corrupted lower deity. Only through the intervention of Sophia (Wisdom) can *gnosis* be revealed and salvation attained. Thus, while adherents of Gnostic Christianity certainly acknowledged the role of Jesus in their faith, their theology placed greater significance on the intellectual revelation of his message than on his crucifixion and resurrection."[111]

The following list includes whole or fragmentary* Gnostic texts available to us today from the Nag Hammadi and other collections.

Acts of John
*The Hymn of Jesus
Acts of Peter
Acts of Peter and the Twelve
Acts of Thomas
*The Hymn of the Pearl
Allogenes
Apocalypse of Adam
First Apocalypse of James

---

108 Elaine H. Pagels, "From Jesus to Christ: Gnostics and Other Heretics," Public Broadcasting System (April 1998), http://www.pbs.org/wgbh/pages/frontline/shows/religion/story/heretics.html (Accessed 3 May 2014)

109 Biblical Archaeology Staff, "Nag Hammadi Codices and Gnostic Christianity," 29 March 2011, http://www.biblicalarchaeology.org/daily/biblical-topics/post-biblical-period/the-nag-hammadi-codices/ (Accessed 2 May 2014)

110 The Sethians promoted various texts that attributed the passing on of *gnosis* from Seth, the third son of Adam and Eve, and to Norea, the wife of Noah.

111 Biblical Archaeology Staff, see also footnote 86.

Second Apocalypse of James
Apocryphon of James
Apocryphon of John
Coptic Apocalypse of Paul
Coptic Apocalypse of Peter
Books of Jeu
Book of Thomas the Contender
Dialogue of the Saviour
Letter of Peter to Philip
Odes of Solomon
Pistis Sophia
Secret Gospel of Mark
The Sophia of Jesus Christ
Gospel of the Egyptians
Gospel of Judas
Gospel of Mary
Gospel of Philip
Gospel of Thomas
Gospel of Truth
Unknown Berlin Gospel or *Gospel of the Savior*

As noted above, the Nag Hammadi texts contained a fully preserved *Gospel of Thomas*. This text does not follow the canonical gospels of Matthew, Mark, Luke and John in relating the story of Jesus' birth, life, ministry, crucifixion and resurrection. Rather, it presents the reader with an early collection of Jesus' sayings and teachings. Because of its mystical nature, this text was originally classified as Gnostic. However, it now seems to reveal yet another branch of early Christianity with some Gnostic allusions. Like the *Gospel of Truth*, another Nag Hammadi find, the *Gospel of Thomas* offers a symbolic reflection on the life of Jesus as a way of getting the readers or hearers of that text to think about their personal relationship to God and their essential connection with the divine but immaterial worlds of spirit.[112]

One noted Christian radio evangelist writes about the nature of this text:

"Among the most widely read and most popular of the Gnostic Gospels is the *Gospel of Thomas*. Although scholars do not believe it was actually written by the apostle Thomas, it is, nevertheless, composed of one hundred fourteen alleged sayings of Jesus. Some of the teachings attributed to Jesus in the *Gospel of Thomas* are clearly Gnostic in origin, while others closely parallel or even mirror the teachings of Jesus found in the synoptic Gospels. The text begins: 'These are the secret sayings which the living Jesus spoke and which Didymos Judas Thomas wrote down. And he said, 'Whoever finds the interpretation of these sayings will not experience death.' From the very opening words of the *Gospel of Thomas* we find that eternal life does not come through the death, burial and resurrection of Jesus, but rather through the attainment of a special knowledge (*gnosis*) from the secret sayings of Jesus."[113]

---

112   *Ibid.*

113   David Webb, "Gnosticism and the Gnostic Jesus," http://www.searchingthescriptures.net/main_pages/articles/gnosticism_jesus.htm (Accessed 3 May 2014)

So from a historical perspective, the Nag Hammadi codices provide a deeper understanding of the diverse philosophical and theological currents that found expression through early Christianity. Gnosticism and its classically Greek-inspired philosophical ideals permeated not just early Christian thought but also the Jewish and pagan traditions from which Christianity arose. The Nag Hammadi codices are widely regarded as one of the most significant discoveries of the twentieth century. They reveal a complex religious milieu and offer an unparalleled glimpse into alternative visions of early Christianity. Helena P. Blavatsky, the seer that she was, recognized the significance of Gnostic teachings even before the unearthing of the Nag Hammadi documents. Blavatsky and others in her day had only fragments to go on, in addition to obscure references to Gnostic works in the writings of the early traditional church fathers that, unfortunately, were not kindly disposed to the Gnostic point of view.

The early Gnostics probably classified themselves as Christians. Pagels tells us that,

"As far as we can tell, the earliest Christian communities had an enormous variety of viewpoints and attitudes and approach, as we've said. But by the end of the second century, you begin to see hierarchies of bishops, priests and deacons emerge in various communities and claim to speak for the majority. And with that development, there's probably an assertion of leadership against viewpoints that those leaders considered dangerous and heretical. One of the issues that polarized those communities, perhaps the most urgent and pressing issue, was persecution. That is, these people, all Christians, belonged to an illegal movement. It was dangerous to belong to this movement. You could be arrested, if you were charged with being a Christian, you could be put on trial, you could be tortured and executed if you refused to recant. And with that pressure, many said, 'We want to know when a person joins this movement if that person is going to stand with us or is going to pretend they're not with us. So let's clarify who belongs to us....'"[114]

The Gnostic texts offer a different perspective on the lives of Jesus and his disciples, placing more of an emphasis on their message as reflective of the eternal battle between spirit and the material world. Photo of scene from the *Last Temptation of Christ* (1988) with Mary Magdalene, Jesus and Judas (Left to Right). See http://staticmass.net/the-emporium/the-last-temptation-of-christ-movie-1988-review/ .

The church fathers noted that the early Christian congregations were being decimated by a devastating persecution. They witnessed the mass torture and execution of Christians throughout the Roman Empire. Thousands were rounded up and put in prison. In face of this persecution, some of the church leaders believed that some kind of unity needed to be forged. What frustrated them was that the Christians did not all believe the same things. Neither did they all accept the leadership offered them in the times following the era of the original apostles. There were real dangers of fragmentation, and so it would be easy for any rogue community to lose itself in the maelstrom. It was at this point that Pagels stated that,

114 Elaine H. Pagels, "From Jesus to Christ: Gnostics and Other Heretics"

"The sociologist Max Weber has shown that a religious movement, if it doesn't develop a certain institutional structure within a generation of its founder's death, will not survive. So it's likely, I think, that we owe the survival of the Christian movement (as it later evolved) to those forms that Irenaeus and others (church fathers) developed. You know, the list of acceptable books, the list of acceptable teachings, the rituals."[115]

The Catholic Church that ultimately emerged from the ashes of the Roman Empire consolidated what remained of traditional Christianity throughout the Mediterranean world and Western Europe. The Catholic hierarchy could not let any remnants of Gnostic Christianity survive, lest these sects arise to challenge their pontifical authority. In forging a new world order, they needed some degree of unanimity, even if they had to force it on the entire world at the expense of destroying, or at least muting, the Gnostic message. And so even as new Gnostic texts are being discovered today,[116] much is owed to Helena Blavatsky for both an academic and spiritual revival of Gnostic studies.

Insofar as the Christian Gnostics adapted a classic Greek world view in the formulation of their belief systems, the personification of the various "stars"/planets is something that carried over. Aphrodite/Venus was characterized by Pythagoras as the *sol alter*, or second sun, largely because of her unequalled brilliance. Notes Blavatsky:

"Before it began to be called Venus, it was known in pre-Hesiodic theogony as Eosphoros (or Phosphoros) and Hesperos, the children of the dawn and twilight. In Hesiod, moreover, the planet is decomposed into two divine beings, two brothers—Eosphoros (the *Lucifer* of the Latins) the morning, and Hesperos, the evening star. They are the children of Astroeos and Eos, the starry heaven and the dawn, as also of Kephalos and Eos (*Theog*: 381, *Hyg. Poet. Astron.* 11, 42). Preller, quoted by Decharme, shows Paeton identical with Phosphoros or Lucifer (*Grech: Mythol*: I, 365). And on the authority of Hesiod, he also makes Phaeton the son of the latter two divinities—Kephalos and Eos."

"Now Phaeton or Phosphoros, the 'luminous morning orb,' is carried away in his early youth by Aphrodite (Venus) who makes of him the night guardian of her sanctuary (*Theog*: 987-991). He is the 'beautiful morning star' (vide *St. John's Revelation* XXII.16)[117] loved for its radiant light by the Goddess of the Dawn, Aurora, who, while gradually eclipsing the light of her beloved, thus seeming to carry off the star, makes it reappear on the evening horizon where it watches the *gates of heaven*."[118]

In the second through the fourth century, C.E., the mystic Judaic tradition of the Kabbalah, derived from the teachings found in the books of the *Zohar*, ran parallel with that of the Gnostics, wherein the initiates were taught that the,

---

115 *Ibid.*

116 Jonathan Beasley, "Testing Indicates '*Gospel of Jesus's Wife*' Papyrus Fragment to be Ancient," 10 April 2014, Harvard Divinity School, Cambridge, Massachusetts, http://gospelofjesusswife.hds.harvard.edu/testing-indicates-gospel-jesuss-wife-papyrus-fragment-be-ancient (Accessed 8 May 2014). "A wide range of scientific testing indicates that a papyrus fragment containing the words, 'Jesus said to them, my wife' is an ancient document, dating between the sixth to ninth centuries, C.E. Its contents may originally have been composed as early as the second to fourth centuries."

117 Joseph Castro, "When Was Jesus Born?," *Live Science*, 30 January 2014, http://www.livescience.com/42976-when-was-jesus-born.html, (Accessed 10 May 2014). Scholars debate the month of Jesus' birth. In 2008, astronomer Dave Reneke argued that Jesus was born in the summer. The Star of Bethlehem, Reneke states, may have been Venus and Jupiter coming together to form a bright light in the sky. Using computer models, Reneke determined that this rare event occurred on June 17, in the year 2 B.C.E. Hence, another strong Venus connection is established. Interestingly, Venus and Jupiter were in alignment; and Venus is alleged to have been born in the core of Jupiter by I. Velikovsky.

118 Blavatsky and Collins, *Lucifer*, 16. Blavatsky based this statement on the *Theogony* (Greek: Θεογονία, *Theogonia*, pronounced [ᵗʰeogonía] and sundry commentaries concerning it. See footnote 4.

"Creator is infinite and His only will is to do us – all the creatures in the Universe – good. Also it is taught, that our future is determined by the Universal truth of 'cause and effect.' Meaning, a positive act will lead to a positive consequence and vice versa. Hence, we and we alone determine the 'script' of our lives."[119]

The *Zohar* (Hebrew: זֹהַר, lit. *Splendor* or *Radiance*) is considered to be the fundamental work of Jewish mysticism. It was allegedly written by a second century, C.E. rabbi, Shimon bar Yochai, in the midst of Roman persecution. The rabbi, seeking to escape the Romans, hid in a remote cave in Palestine and remained there for thirteen years. Making good use of his time, he began studying the *Torah*. While in the cave, he experienced intermittent visions of the Prophet Elijah who inspired him to write the *Zohar*, a group of books including commentary on the mystical aspects of the *Torah* (the five books of Moses). It also includes sundry scriptural interpretations as well as a plethora of material on mysticism, mythical cosmogony, and mystical psychology. In addition, the *Zohar* contains a discussion of the nature of God, the origin and structure of the universe, the nature of souls, redemption, the relationship of Ego to Darkness and "true self" to *"The Light of God"*, as well as the relationship between "universal energy" and man. It also draws upon much older mystic texts such as the patriarch Abraham's *Sefer Yetsirah* and has come to be classified as an esoteric form of the rabbinic literature known as *Midrash*, which provides yet further illumination on the *Torah*.[120]

As we know from the *New Testament*, Paul and the other apostles first preached to the Diaspora Jewish communities throughout the Mediterranean world, and only later extended their outreach to the wider Gentile world. St. John, directing his message of *Revelation* to these emerging Judeo-Christian communities of the second century, C.E., realized that his reference to Jesus as the "Morning Star" would be readily understood as a clear indicator of his divinity.

For example, from the *Zohar* we learn that every year, in the month of Tishri,[121] we receive an opportunity to recreate ourselves and to receive the infinite abundance offered to us by the Creator:

"The Kabbalists say that in the month of Tishrei (spelling varies) *a gate to a higher dimension*, to the Universal storage of Life Energy is open to us, and allows us to draw blessings and abundance, so we can create and design our lives from the beginning once more. Obviously then, the month of Tishrei is one of the most important months with all of its special holidays. It is during this time that special forces exist in the Universe, to assist us in our process of re-creation, rejuvenation and re-designing our destiny for another year."[122]

This reference to a "higher dimension" is quite significant here. As we noted from Blavatsky, the Christian Gnostics believed that Jesus controlled the gate to this ethereal realm (Barbelo), much as Phaeton/Phosphoros did for the Greeks. And as scientists now assert that harmonics provide the key to opening up new dimensions, it is quite interesting to note that the Kabbalistic *Sefer Yetsirah* (*Book of Formation*), allegedly written by the ancient patriarch Abraham, deals

119 "Tishrei-Libra: Rosh Chodesh Tishrei- The New Moon of Libra," *Live Kabbalah* (Live Kabbalah University website), http://www.livekabbalah.org/index.php/home/gates-in-time/rosh-hodesh/tishrei-libra/, (Accessed 10 May 2014).

120 Isaiah Tishby, ed., *Wisdom of the Zohar: An Anthology of Texts*, 3 vols. translated from the Hebrew by David Goldstein (Oxford: Oxford University Press, 1989).

121 Tracey R. Rich, "Month of Tishri," *Judaism 101*, http://www.jewfaq.org/holiday1.htm (Accessed 14 October 2014): The month of Tishri falls during the months of September and October on the Gregorian calendar. It is probably the busiest time of the year for Jewish holidays. It includes 13 days of special religious significance, seven of them holidays on which work is not permitted; and of this seven, two are considered as "high holidays," the most important of the Jewish year, Rosh Hashanah and Yom Kippur. The month of Tishri roughly corresponds to the Zodiac sign of Libra (23 September through 22 October).

122 "Tishrei-Libra: Rosh Chodesh Tishrei- The New Moon of Libra," *Live Kabbalah*.

with the very structure of the universe, explaining that it was built on twenty-two frequencies which are considered to be its building blocks. These frequencies are represented by the twenty-two Hebrew letters. They can also be employed as conduits for transferring spiritual abundance and energies.[123] More about other dimensions will be discussed later in this book, particularly as they apply to the planet Venus.

In any event, according to the Kabbalah University website:

Venus in Libra will facilitate cosmic awareness and open the gates to other dimensions. See www.star-born.com.

"Each month is controlled by two Hebrew letters; one controls the planet that dominates the month and the other controls the astrological sign of the month. Tishrei's planet is *Nogah* (Venus) and it is controlled by the letter פ (Pe) while the astrological sign of Libra is controlled by the letter ל (Lamed)."[124]

Of course, the zodiac sign of Libra can be visually represented as a scale that symbolizes that special time in the cosmos when our good choices are being measured against our bad choices. Libra is considered as an air sign and it represents central column energy, i.e. the power of balance and thinking. As such, equilibrium and justice are thought of as characteristics typical of an individual born under this sign.[125]

ל – Lamed

The structure of this letter Lamed ultimately controls the month of Libra. *It serves to connect us to the upper spiritual world of Nogah/ Venus.* Please take note that it is the only Hebrew letter that goes above the line, thereby directing us upwards and connecting us to that higher realm – the source of our existence. Additionally, this letter manifests the extraordinary ability to connect us to that world above and beyond, whence we may draw from it both knowledge (*gnosis*) and strength.[126]

Venus, the planet of love, controls Tishrei/Libra. This helps to explain the essence of Tishrei, a month set apart for the bestowal of both love and forgiveness. As Jesus would say, it is a month in which we should "…love thy neighbor as thyself."[127] From this will come the higher state of consciousness, facilitating a connection to the power of "Life" during the month of Tishrei.[128]

The word "*Nogah*" (Venus) in Hebrew also signifies "Light" and has a numerical value of 58. This equates to the Hebrew word "*Ozen*" (ear), which is also used as the root of the word "*Moznaim*" (scales – Libra). And interestingly, the ear is an organ of aural receptivity. Venus is therefore the place in which the power of love and balance of Tishri meet. Unfortunately, this may leave the Libras exposed. Their special connection to Venus and her attendant forces make the Libras overly sensitive to their surroundings. Their ability to listen and to identify

123   A. Kaplan, *Sefer Yetzirah; Book of Creation in Theory and Practice* (San Francisco: Weiser Books, 1997).
124   "Tishrei-Libra: Rosh Chodesh Tishrei"
125   *Ibid.*
126   *Ibid.*
127   Mark 12:31 (KJV)
128   "Tishrei-Libra: Rosh Chodesh Tishrei"

with the thoughts and emotions of other human beings is very powerful and could overwhelm them. If they can learn to use these empathic abilities in a balanced way, they could become great ambassadors or negotiators. They do not do well, however, in a hypocritical, lying and non-harmonic environment, such as is usually found on Earth. Frankly, they love to love and want to be loved; but in order to be in that state they might adapt a chameleon-like behavior of constantly changing their minds. To some, this pattern may be misleading, causing others to think of the Libras as being disingenuous. The special sensitivity that the Libras acquire from their close relationship to the planet Venus gives them an almost supernatural intuition. However, keep in mind that the Kabbalah also relates Libras to the element of air. This means that some Libras may find that their emotions are in conflict with their sense of rationalism. This constant inner dialogue may exhaust them and usually brings them into periods of indecisiveness that can pressure them into making some wrong decisions.[129]

In overcoming this, those born under the sign of Libra need to remember that the secret of success is not always within the boundaries of logic, but in sensation. Being successful is being creative, having inspiration and a devotion to one's inner vision. As one cherishes those things that are seemingly not related and cannot be measured by logic, it soon becomes apparent that these are the items composed of the very spiritual elements that pertain to the upper worlds. So whenever the Libran feels exhausted due to an overabundance of thinking, they should invoke their Venus connection to the spiritual Light, thus turning it over to the Light.[130]

In numerology, both "*Ozen*" (ear) and "*Nogah*" (Venus) equal 58. This number is represented in Hebrew by the letters חנ, signifying *comfort*. If we turn invert these letters, they become נח, meaning *grace*. This implies that Libras generally find favor with others, but may become too comfortable with their positions in life, developing a lazy streak, so to speak. They may require a little nudge to move on their more creative impulses.

Commenting on the Venus connection to Librans, the Kabbalah University website elaborates:

– Pe

"The *Zohar* teaches that the letter פ Pe that created Venus has two faces. As mentioned, Venus is the planet of love, beauty and pleasures. On the outside (the black part) the letter פ looks like a snake hiding its head and poison. The Libra has a tendency to enjoy our world's pleasures, material beauty and living a life of luxury and comfort. There is nothing wrong with this; however, we also have to learn to overcome the illusion of the limited physical world and connect to the power of the soul, to discern evil from good, which is our work on this physical plane. In doing this, we will find within the פ the letter ב – Bet (colored in white). The letter Bet symbolizes the power of blessing. So once again, for Librans and the rest of us, during this month of Tishrei, connecting to the power of balance is the goal."[131]

Libra through Venus can help us connect to the beginning of everything, to the root, the seed, to our source, to the beauty of Creation as manifested in love, supernatural beauty and the harmony of Genesis. Then we will be able to clearly discern that everything is for the best. We can go on to forgive and not to fear the past or the future. This is the kind of "knowing" that will allow us to advance on many fronts in life, having a good conscience and a quiet spirit. Ultimately, the ultra-dimensional Venus force will assist us in getting rid of suffering, pain and

---

129 *Ibid.*
130 *Ibid.*
131 *Ibid.*

chaos in our lives. We will connect to all the abundance that the Cosmos has available for us.[132]

And so it becomes apparent that in Judaic mystic circles, at least, the astrological and spiritual influence of Venus is quite positive. There seems to be no analogy between the positive astral and spiritual personifications of Venus and the negative concept of Lucifer as *Satan*, as he evolved in the minds of later Christian theologians. Blavatsky correctly points out the weaknesses inherent in the arguments advanced by the fundamentalist Christian theologians as "insufficient to justify the building of a theological wall of defense against paganism made up of slander and misrepresentations."[133]

Part of this confusion may have to do with the Christian fundamentalist's literal interpretation of the Gospels versus the Christian Gnostic's esoteric interpretation of them. Mary Baker Eddy, the founder of Christian Science, once penned that the, "one important interpretation of Scripture is the spiritual."[134] As we have noted so far, the esoteric or spiritual interpretation of sacred writings appears to have been the predominant vehicle chosen by the mystics of Judaism, early Christianity and later Islam in its Sufi context. Even Jesus himself once stated that, "I have many things to say to you, but you cannot hear them now. When the Spirit of Truth comes, he will guide you into all the truth."[135] And the Apostle Paul, to whom Jesus appeared in a vision on the road to Damascus, told the Christian congregation at Corinth that:

"I was with you in weakness, in fear, and in much trembling. And my speech and my preaching were not with persuasive words of human wisdom, but in demonstration of the Spirit and of power, that your faith should not be in the wisdom of men but in the power of God. However, *we speak wisdom among those who are mature, yet not the wisdom of this age, nor of the rulers of this age, who are coming to nothing. But we speak the wisdom of God in a mystery, the hidden wisdom which God ordained before the ages for our glory, which none of the rulers of this world knew*; for had they known, they would not have crucified the Lord of glory. But as it is written, '*Eye has not seen, nor ear heard, nor have entered into the heart of man the things which God has prepared for those who love Him (Is. 64:4; 65:17).*' But *God has revealed them to us through His Spirit. For the Spirit searches all things, yes, the deep things of God...* "[136]

As one reads and ponders the words of Christ and his Apostles in the New Testament, there are numerous allusions made to non-worldly knowledge and wisdom, but it does not take center stage. However, this type of *gnosis* appears to be the primary content of the Christian Gnostic writings. Therefore, the severe demotion of Venus by the Christians of later centuries may, in part, be accounted for in its association with the pagan deities attached to that orb, in addition to the planet's unfortunate linkage to Lucifer, which is an incorrect title for Satan or the Devil, taken from *Isaiah* 14:12 (KJV), that states: "How art thou fallen from heaven, O Lucifer, son of the morning! How art thou cut down to the ground, which didst weaken the nations!" Were it not for this quirky transliteration, "Lucifer" would not even exist as a name in the English language and there would be no confusion on the matter. A few leaders in the contemporary Christian church are beginning to catch on:

---

132 *Ibid.*

133 Blavatsky and Collins, *Lucifer*, 17.

134 Rolfe A. Witzche, *Science and Health with Keys to the Scripture in Divine Science,* quote of Mary Baker Eddy in (North Vancouver, British Columbia, Canada: Cygni Communications), 157.

135 *John* 16:12-13 (KJV). The Apostle Paul also wanted to teach deeper spiritual truths to the church at Corinth, but they were not yet ready to receive this further illumination. See *I Corinthians* 3:1-2 (NKJV): "And I, brethren, could not speak to you as to spiritual people but as to carnal, as to babes in Christ. I fed you with milk and not with solid food; for until now you were not able to receive it, and even now you are still not able."

136 *I Corinthians* 2:3-10 (NKJV).

"As it is, we need to be careful, I would suggest, in using the term to describe who the *Bible* calls 'Satan' or 'the Devil'. Most Christians are onto this, yet still the term "Lucifer" persists. In any case, the 'morning star' is the title of Christ throughout the rest of Scripture..."[137]

The pastor, in the above-cited article, then goes on to list the following verses that correctly identify Jesus as the Morning Star:

2 Peter 1:19 (NIV): And we have the word of the prophets made more certain, and you will do well to pay attention to it, as to a light shining in a dark place, until the day dawns and the *morning star* rises in your hearts.

Revelation 2:28 (NIV): I will also give him the *morning star*.

Revelation 22:16 (NIV): I, Jesus, have sent my angel to give you this testimony for the churches. I am the Root and the Offspring of David, and the *bright Morning Star*.

Since it is clear that Jesus is the "Bright Morning Star," even self-identifying himself as such in the last scripture cited above, then how should we understand *Isaiah* 14:12? Blavatsky points out that the original Hebrew text of this scripture verse gives no mention at all of "Lucifer," but only that of *Hillel*, which simply means one who "shines brightly," or perhaps, "one who

"Lucifer" is a name derived from Latin that simply means "Bringer of Light." This name became erroneously synonymous with the rebellious Satan, whose fall is briefly described in Isaiah 14:12 and whose origins appear to be more Zoroastrian than Judaic. See http://thegoldenageofaquarius.com/2014/02/09/the-fallen-angel-a-true-story-about-lucifer/.

howls." Blavatsky ponders, "One can hardly refrain from wondering that educated people should be still ignorant enough at the close of our century to associate a radiant planet- or anything else in nature for the matter of that—with the Devil!"[138]

What Blavatsky does signal, however, is a possible connection of Satan with the ancient Zoroastrian belief system and cosmology.

Before drawing the lines that connect traditional Christian beliefs with the Zoroastrian mythology, however, let us review what Blavatsky taught concerning the fall of the angels and the most beautiful creature of the heavens who supposedly led a third of that supernatural host in a rebellion against God. Blavatsky penned:

"That creature is in theological fancy Venus-Lucifer, or rather the informing Spirit or Regent of that planet. This teaching is based on the following speculation. The three principal heroes of the great sidereal catastrophe mentioned in *Revelation* are, according to the testimony of the Church fathers—'the Verbum, Lucifer his usurper and the grand Archangel who conquered him,' and whose 'palaces' (the 'houses' astrology calls them) are in the Sun, Venus-Lucifer and Mercury. This is quite evident, since the position of these orbs in the solar system correspond in their hierarchal order to that of the 'heroes' in Chapter XII of *Revelation* 'their names and destinies (?) being closely connected in the theological (exoteric) system with three great metaphysical names' (De Mirville's *Memoir to the Academy of France*, on the rapping Spirits and the Demons)."[139]

137 Dean VanDruff, "The Morning Star: Jesus or 'Lucifer?'" *Acts 17:11 Bible Studies* website, http://www.acts17-11.com/dialogs_morningstar.html, (Accessed 10 May 2014)
138 Blavatsky and Collins, *Lucifer*, 22.
139 *Ibid.*, 18, 19

The outcome of this great celestial conflict was that Venus-Lucifer was relegated to the sphere of the fallen archangel, a.k.a. Satan before his apostasy. So how did the Roman Catholic Church apparently reconcile this purported scenario with the fact that the metaphor of the "Morning Star" was also applied to both Jesus and his blessed mother Mary?[140] And how did the seven wandering stars or planetary spirits worshipped by the Romans[141] suddenly become defending angels of the Latin belief system and its attendant dogmas?

Blavatsky answers this by citing De Mirville once again:

"Lucifer, the jealous neighbor of the Sun (Christ) said to himself in his great pride: "I will rise as high as he!" He was thwarted in his design by Mercury, though the brightness of the latter (who is St. Michael) was much lost in the blazing fire of the great Solar orb as his own was, and though, like Lucifer, Mercury is only the assessor, and the guard of honor to the Sun.-(*Ibid.*)"[142]

De Mirville points out that the Archangel Michael, like Mercury, is the friend of the Sun, much like the Zoroastrian Mitra filled a similar role. Blavatsky describes Michael as a "*psychopompic* genius, one who leads the separated souls to their appointed abodes, and like Mitra, he is the well-known adversary of the demons."[143] Blavatsky also points out that in one important chronicle of the Nabatheans, the Zoroastrian Mitra is specifically referred to as the "grand enemy of the planet Venus."[144]

Of course, the vile image we have of Satan today is quite different than the concept of that being held by the ancient Israelites in the *Old Testament*, who simply acknowledged him as a sort of God-appointed prosecuting attorney, as demonstrated in the case of Job. The actual word "satan" is simply the Hebrew word for "adversary." In numerous instances, the fundamentalist Christian Bible translators, both Catholic and Protestant, chose not to render the word as "adversary," but retained the Hebrew word and capitalized the "S" to turn a regular noun into a proper noun. Therefore, those passages that use the reference to "Satan" have only been inferred. This is not because that is what the translation provided us *per se*, but because the Bible translators opted to give us their interpretation of how the word "satan" should ultimately come to be understood.[145] As Blavatsky believed the Christian church needed a devil in order to keep their adherents in line and on the same track with their gospel message, it does not surprise me that the ecclesiastical hierarchy of an emerging religion in the third and fourth centuries C.E. would stoop so slow as to fabricate one.

The nature of God in Judaism is considered by the aforementioned blogger:

---

140 *Ibid.,* 17 Blavatsky elaborates on the evolving syncretism of the Greek, Jewish, Phoenician and Roman conceptions of the goddess Venus with the Roman Catholic formulation of Mary as a personification of the Morning Star.

141 *Ibid.,* 19 Blavatsky informs us of a famous church dedicated to the Seven Angels at Rome. It was completed in 1561 under the direction of Michelango and dedicated as the Church of St. Mary and the Angels. It still stands today. In the missals first utilized in the church in 1563, one may find an *officio* or prayer service directed to the seven angels, beckoning them with their older pagan and occult names as they served as "rectors" or guarding spirits to the planets in the bygone days of the Greek and Roman empires. Of course, in these older times they were honored and worshiped in their own temples. These seven rectors had their prior pagan names abolished by Catholic decree and replaced with the nomenclatures of Jewish angels. Pope Pius V in his Bull to the Spanish Clergy takes note of these angels, stating that, "One cannot exalt too much these seven rectors of the world, figured by the seven planets, as it is consoling to our century to witness by the grace of God the cult of these seven ardent lights, and of these seven stars reassuring all its luster in the Christian Republic." (*Les Sept Esprits et l'Histoire y de leur Cults*; De Mirville's Second Memoir Addressed to the Academy, Vol. II, page 358.)

142 *Ibid.,* 19

143 *Ibid.*

144 *Ibid.,* 19, 20

145 Disappearing Head (blogger's *nom de plume*), in *Religion and Philosophy* Blog, "Evolution of Satan, Part I," 2014, http://disappearinghead.hubpages.com/hub/The-Evolution-of-Satan-Part-1 (Accessed 19 May 2014).

"The many gods of the pagan nations divided the world into many parts and domains, and made it appear as the battle-ground of hostile powers. God however renders Earth and Heaven, light and darkness, life and death as one; a universe ruled by His everlasting wisdom and goodness. It is the work of one great designer and ruler who is the beginning and the end, who arranges everything according to His will. Whereas some sections of the Church have adopted the pagan idea of a god (Satan, Apollyon) ruling over the underworld, this stance has not been accepted by God. In *Psalm* 139:8 David asks where he can hide from the Lord's presence. If he goes to the Heavens He is there, if He goes to the grave, He is there; light and darkness are not hidden by God. There is nowhere that God's influence and rule is absent.

Old Testament scripture insists upon the unity of God and His government of the world, and recognizes alongside of Him no principle of evil in creation. God has no counterpart either in the powers of darkness, as the deities of Egypt and Babylon had, or in the power of evil, such as Ahriman in the Zoroastrian religion."[146]

Now Zoroastrianism was the religion of the Medes and Persians during the time when Israel was in captivity to Babylon. The religion was founded by the Prophet Zoroaster in ancient Persia sometime in the sixth century, B.C.E. Zoroaster merged his monotheistic belief with elements of a prehistoric, polytheistic Indo-Persian religious system that had been in existence at least since 1,200 B.C.E. This, of course, necessitated some drastic adjustments. According

Ahura Mazda and other Zoroastrian deities were depicted with wings for their ability to traverse the skies. Did they serve as the inspiration for angels in the Hebrew Scriptures?

to Zoroastrian tradition, Zoroaster was a reformer who exalted the deity of Wisdom, Ahura Mazda, to the status of the Supreme Being and Creator, while simultaneously demoting various other deities and rejecting other rituals associated with them.[147]

Zoroaster was probably born in Rhages, a city now known as Rayy, a suburb of Tehran, in 628 B.C.E. and died in 551 B.C.E. somewhere in western Afghanistan. At the time of his birth Persia was a Bronze Age culture and the people practiced a polytheistic religion. The religion he was born into was quite similar to an early form of Hinduism as practiced in India. An example is the Zoroastrian-Hindu relationship is found in the Zoroastrian word *Ahura* (Ahura Mazda) and the Vedic word *Asura* (meaning demon). His natal religion included animal sacrifice and the ritual use of intoxicants. But when Zoroaster was 30 years old, he went into the Daiti River to draw water for a Haoma[148] ceremony and when he emerged, he received a vision of Vohu Manah (Good Mind). This vision served to radically transform his world view, and Zoroaster tried to teach this view to others. Zoroaster now believed in only one creator God and he taught that only this one God was worthy of worship. In addition, as some of the deities of the old religion, the Daevas or "heavenly ones," appeared to delight in

146 *Ibid.*

147 Disappearing Head (blogger's *nom de plume*), in *Religion and Philosophy* Blog, "Evolution of Satan, Part 2," 2014, http://disappearinghead.hubpages.com/hub/The-Evolution-of-Satan-Part-2 (Accessed 19 May 2014).

148 Haoma is a plant that grows on the mountain sides in Afghanistan and Iran. Its consumption stimulates alertness and awareness. The use of psychoactive plants was a key factor in the formation of many ancient and contemporary religions and plays a sacramental part in the conduct of many religious observances.

war and strife, Zoroaster concluded that these were evil spirits and workers of Angra Mainyu or Ahriman, God's adversary.[149]

Zoroaster or Zarathustra, noted prophet, was born in 628 B.C.E. in Persia and died in 551 B.C.E. in the area comprising present-day Afghanistan. See https://sites.google.com/site/amazingworldsproject/zorastrianism.

In the Zoroastrian belief system, the Creator Ahura Mazda is all good, and no evil originates from Him. Also, good and evil have distinct sources, with evil (Ahriman) trying to destroy the creation of Mazda, and the good trying to sustain it. Mazda does not dwell on this world, and His creation is represented by the Amesha Spentas and the host of other Yazatas (angels), through whom the works of God are evident to humanity, and also through whom the worship of Ahura Mazda is ultimately directed.[150]

Here the Zoroastrians have much in common with the Gnostics, for they view the Amesha Spentas as the "divine sparks," or the first six emanations (Greek *Aeons*) of the Creator, through whom all subsequent creation was accomplished. As an emanation of the Creator, a Yazata is a divine being that is considered worthy of worship. Ahura Mazda is the beginning and the end, the creator of everything that *can and cannot be seen*, the Eternal, the Pure and the only Truth.[151]

Angra Mainyu, on the other hand, is the evil spirit or evil mind and is identified with the daevas that deceive humankind and themselves. While in later Zoroastrianism, the daevas are demons, Zoroaster's formative view was that the daevas are simply "wrong gods" or "false gods" that are to be rejected, but not yet demons. These daevas were identified as the offspring, not of Angra Mainyu, but of *akem manah* or the manifestations of "evil thinking". Angra Mainyu induced the daevas to choose *achistem manah*, or "worst thinking". Thus the concept emerged that Ahriman deceived some of the "heavenly ones" and led them into evil.[152]

Zoroastrianism states that active participation in life through good thoughts, good words, and good deeds is necessary to ensure happiness and to keep chaos at bay. This active participation is the central element in sustaining Zoroaster's concept of free will. Ahura Mazda will ultimately prevail over the evil Angra Mainyu or Ahriman, and *at that time the universe will undergo a cosmic renovation and time as we know it will cease to exist.*[153]

The blogger explains this happy period:

"In the final renovation, all of creation, even the souls of the dead that were initially banished to "darkness", will be reunited in Ahura Mazda, returning to life in the undead form. At the end of time, a savior-figure (a Saoshyant) will bring about a final renovation of the world, in which the dead will be revived."[154]

Judaism does not, however, support the idea of an evil spirit independent of and in opposition to God, whether this being is called Ahriman or Satan. On Judaic and Zoroastrian syncretism, the blogger relates:

149 Disappearing Head, "Evolution of Satan, Part 2"
150 *Ibid.*
151 *Ibid.*
152 *Ibid.*
153 *Ibid.*
154 *Ibid.*

"Whether Cyrus II was a Zoroastrian is subject to debate. It did, however, influence him to the extent that it became the non-imposing religion of his empire, and its beliefs later allowed Cyrus to free the Jews and allow them to return to Judea when the emperor took Babylon in 539 BC. Darius I was a devotee of Ahura Mazda. However, whether he was a follower of Zoroaster has not been conclusively established, since devotion to Ahura Mazda was at the time not necessarily an indication of an adherence to Zoroaster's teaching.

Due to the similarities between the two religions, it is not hard to see how ideas and beliefs were shared between the followers of both. According some scholars it is believed that key concepts of Zoroastrian have had influence on the Abrahamic religions. Thus they hold that Judaism refined its concept of monotheism and adopted features such as its eschatology (death, judgment, heaven and hell), angelology and demonology through contacts with Zoroastrianism."[155]

Before Israel's exile to Babylon, Satan was only considered as an accuser of God's people whose place was still in the Heavenly Council. But after the exile, with the influence of Ahriman on Israel's concept of Satan, he had now acquired the ability to lead people astray from God. We also have the beginnings of the idea of Satan deceiving a third of the angels which can be seen to be derived from the belief that Angra Mainyu induced the daevas to choose "worst thinking" and follow a path leading to destruction. In the 400 year period between the *Old Testament* and Jesus' ministry on Earth, the concept of Satan was even further developed. Influenced by apocryphal writings, such as the *New Testament* books of *Jude* and *Revelation*, the concept of Satan as a fallen angel was introduced. Additionally the new ideas of Zoroastrian demonology, previously unknown to Judaism, were also enhanced under the influence of these writings, and demons also became elevated to the status of angels, albeit fallen ones. The Zoroastrian Amesha Spentas, in turn, became the good angels enlisted on the side of Jesus in the ongoing battle with Lucifer/Satan and his minions. And much as the Amesha Spenta known as Mitra/Mithra conquered the planet Venus in the name of Ahura Mazda, according to the Zoroastrian chronicles, Michael defeated Lucifer and took control of the sphere in the name of Jesus, according to Roman Catholic hierarchy.

Blavatsky sustains this, declaring of the Jesuit cleric De Mirville's writings,

"A candid confession, for once, of perfect identity of celestial personages and of borrowing from every pagan source. It is curious, if unblushing. While in the oldest Mazdean allegories, Mitra conquers the planet Venus, in Christian tradition Michael defeats Lucifer, and both receive, as war spoils, the planet of the vanquished deity."[156]

According to ancient Zoroastrian legend, Venus was conquered by Mitra (a.k.a. Mithra), the corresponding guardian spirit to the Christian archangel Michael, who defeated Lucifer. See http://apranik.blogspot.com/2009/10/zoroastrianism.html.

Furthermore, in *Lucifer*, Blavatsky and Collins quote the learned German Marquis J. J. I. Dollinger:

---

155 *Ibid.*
156 Blavatsky and Collins, *Lucifer*, 20.

"Mitra possessed, in days of old, the star of Mercury, placed between the sun and the moon, but he was given the planet of the conquered, and ever since his victory he is identified with Venus (*Paganisme et Judaïsme*, Bruxelles, Belgium: Goemaere, 1858; Vol. II, page 109, French translation)."[157]

Zoroaster's reforms cannot be understood without an accurate knowledge of the teachings and traditions into which he was born and inculcated. His family was of modest means, but his forefathers served as valiant knights in the Persian Empire. There were three classes in ancient Persian society: the chiefs, priests and warriors. Consequently, it should not be surprising that the Zoroastrian religion reflects a similar stratification among the divine beings. As there could only be one Ahura Mazda to preside over the heavens, however, the lesser lords such as Mitra and Varuna had to be reassigned to rule over other celestial realms. Hence Blavatsky notes that Mitra led the conquest of Venus.

Blavatsky and Collins further cite the Marquis Dollinger that,

"In the Christian tradition, St. Michael is apportioned in Heaven the throne and the palace of the foe he has vanquished. Moreover, like Mercury, during the palmy days of paganism, which made sacred to this demon-god all the promontories of the earth, the Archangel is the patron of the same in our religion.

Blavatsky and Collins offer the following commentary on this: "This means, if it does mean anything, that now, at any rate, *Lucifer-Venus is a sacred planet*, and no synonym of Satan, since St. Michael has become his legal heir?" They point out many carryovers and the syncretism of Mitra to Michael in the Christian tradition through various artifacts and cultural elements. From this it becomes evident that the so-called "pagans" of the ancient world understood the role of planetary spirits (perceived as *divine councilors*) and the Sun itself (*perceived as God*).

Therefore, the question arises concerning the identity of Michael. Here the canon of Christian scriptures provides some clues. With only five references to Michael in the pages of the *Bible*, it is understandable that so much room has been left for rampant speculation. From the *Old Testament* book of *Daniel*, however, we come to learn that Michael was "one of the chief princes" in the Kingdom of God (*Daniel* 10:13 NIV). In fact, at the time that Daniel, as a prophet, was penning his revelatory book, Michael was specifically charged with watching over and protecting the Jews of the Babylonian Diaspora (*Daniel* 12:1)."[158]

But most significantly, in the ninth verse of *Jude* in the *New Testament*, Michael was designated as "*the* archangel." Note that the *Bible* makes no references to the existence of other archangels. Also of great importance is the meaning of the name Michael as the "One Who Is Like God." We also receive further light and knowledge concerning the identity of Michael in the *New Testament* book of *1 Thessalonians* 4:16 (RSV), whence we discover that the command of the Lord Jesus Christ for the commencement of the resurrection in the latter days is described as "the archangel's call." Since the term "archangel" is never used in a plural sense in the Christian or Jewish cannon of scriptures, one can logically infer that there is only one archangel in the heavenly hierarchy; and Jesus is He. Therefore, the *Bible* provides us with enough scriptural evidence to support a linkage of the identities of Michael and Jesus. As the Son of God, Jesus Christ was known as Michael in the period before he arrived on Earth to

---

157 *Ibid.*
158 Editorial Board, Watchtower Bible and Tract Society, *Reasoning from the Scriptures* (New York: Watchtower, 1985), 218

accomplish his ministry in Judea and the subsequent redemption of humankind.[159]

But what do we know about Jesus in the period before his Earthly ministry, when he acted in the full power of the mighty archangel? The Apostle John, in exile on the Greek island of Patmos at the end of the first century C.E., specifically provides us with that information, or at least the early Christian interpretation of the events. In *Revelation* 12:7-12, we learn that Michael and his angels (those who remained faithful to Yahweh), fought against Satan and the rebellious angels, a contingent that amounted to about a third of the angelic host. Michael was victorious and the vanquished legions of Satan were cast out of the heavenly/spiritual realms. That both Jesus and Lucifer/Satan have come to be equated with the planet Venus as the "Morning Star" serves to strengthen the assertions made by some Biblical scholars that Gnostic and Zoroastrian influences affected early Christianity to a greater extent than was previously imagined.

So where did these fallen spirit beings end up? Right here on Earth, on the physical plane of existence. In *Revelation* 19:11-16, the Apostle John, the "Beloved of Christ," further states that in the latter days another battle would take place between the same parties of angels, where Jesus would lead the armies of heaven against the united nations of Earth, under the power of Satan, who is now described as the "prince of this world" (*John* 12:31).[160] These latter-day events were also foretold by Daniel, who associated the "standing up of Michael" in a "time of trouble such as never has been since there was a nation till that time" (*Daniel* 12:1, ESV). These will be great days of tribulation whence every individual will have to decide on whose side they will stand.

However, as a Christian with some Gnostic inclinations, I must add here that, in my opinion, the status of Jesus Christ as the archangel Michael in no way diminishes his divinity. Attentive *Bible* readers will note that creaturely angels, whether in human or other forms, are not hard to come by. After all, even up to and including our modern era, the Apostle Paul revealed that "some have entertained angels unawares" (*Hebrews* 13:2, KJV). However, careful readers of the *Old Testament* will encounter a unique and startling double identification; for in some passages they will meet with a party called the "Angel of the LORD," who is also revealed to be the LORD. When this angel speaks, there is none of the prophet's "Thus saith the Lord," nor any other indication that He is speaking for another, and not Himself. *Therefore, when the Angel of the LORD speaks, it is God Himself Who is speaking.*

The division of the *Bible* into an *Old* and *New Testament* is an artifice of theologians to separate the Hebrew from the Greek scriptures. But to Yahweh, the *Bible* is one complete revelation to humankind that should not be added to or subtracted from. The Angel of the LORD is known in Judaism as being the "Theophanic Angel," or God Angel.[161] In the Hebrew Scriptures, the Theophanic Angel appears on many occasions. Here are a few examples:

Exodus 3:2-14 (KJV) may be the most poignant, for the Theophanic Angel directly informs Moses that He is God.

And the Angel of the LORD appeared to him in a flame of fire from the midst of a bush. So he looked, and behold, the bush was burning with fire, but the bush was not consumed. Then Moses said, "I will now turn aside and see this great sight, why the bush does not burn."...

159 *Ibid.*

160 2 Corinthians 4:4 (New Living Translation): "*Satan, who is the god of this world*, has blinded the minds of those who don't believe. They are unable to see the glorious light of the Good News. They don't understand this message about *the glory of Christ, who is the exact likeness of God.*"

161 "The Angel of the Lord," *Holy, Holy, Holy*, author not stated, undated, http://thriceholy.net/theophanicf.html (Accessed 28 October 2014).

Moreover He said, "I am the God of your father — the God of Abraham, the God of Isaac, and the God of Jacob." And Moses hid his face, for he was afraid to look upon God...Then Moses said to God, "Indeed, when I come to the children of Israel and say to them, 'The God of your fathers has sent me to you,' and they say to me, 'What is His name?' what shall I say to them?" *And God said to Moses, "I AM WHO I AM." And He said, "Thus you shall say to the children of Israel, 'I AM has sent me to you.'"*

In *Judges* 6:1-18, He appears to Gideon, who builds an altar and worships him as Jehovah. To this, the Theophanic Angel does not object; whereas the lesser angels specifically forbade their being worshipped by human beings, as with the angel who appeared to John the Beloved in *Revelation* 22:8-9 (KJV): "And I John saw these things, and heard them. And when I had heard and seen, I fell down to worship before the feet of the angel which shewed me these things. Then saith he unto me, See thou do it not: for I am thy fellowservant, and of thy brethren the prophets, and of them which keep the sayings of this book: worship God."

The Angel of the LORD also appeared to Joshua before the battle of Jericho was to take place:

Joshua 5:13-15 (KJV): And it came to pass, when Joshua was by Jericho, that he lifted up his eyes and looked, and, behold, there stood a man over against him with his sword drawn in his hand: and Joshua went unto him, and said unto him, Art thou for us, or for our adversaries? And he said, Nay; but as captain of the host of the LORD am I now come. And Joshua fell on his face to the earth, and did worship, and said unto him, What saith my lord unto his servant? And the captain of the LORD'S host said unto Joshua, Loose thy shoe from off thy foot; for the place whereon thou standest is holy. And Joshua did so.

Once again, the Captain of the LORD's Host did not object to receiving the worship of Joshua or declaring the ground where he appeared to be holy, or sanctified. Only Jehovah/Yahweh is entitled to such homage. Note the objections of the Apostle Paul to the priests of Jupiter/Zeus at Lycoania who wanted to worship him and his companion, Barnabas, as gods:

Acts 14:11-16 (KJV): And when the people saw what Paul had done, they lifted up their voices, saying in the speech of Lycaonia, *The gods are come down to us in the likeness of men.* And they called Barnabas, Jupiter; and Paul, Mercurius, because he was the chief speaker. Then the priest of Jupiter, which was before their city, brought oxen and garlands unto the gates, and would have done sacrifice with the people. Which when the apostles, Barnabas and Paul, heard of, they rent their clothes, and ran in among the people, crying out, And saying, *Sirs, why do ye these things? We also are men of like passions with you, and preach unto you that ye should turn from these vanities unto the living God, which made heaven, and earth, and the sea, and all things that are therein*: Who in times past suffered all nations to walk in their own ways.

The worship of any created being is forbidden in the scriptures: "Who changed the truth of God into a lie, and worshipped and served the creature more than the Creator, who is blessed for ever. Amen." (Romans 1:25). There is only One God who may lawfully be worshipped: "Then saith Jesus unto him, Get thee hence, Satan: for it is written, Thou shalt worship the Lord thy God, and him only shalt thou serve" (Matthew 4:10). Yes, there are many angels of God who are created beings, including human beings. But good angels and men of God will not allow a man or woman to worship them: "And I fell at his feet to worship him. And he said unto me, See thou do it not: I am thy fellow-servant, and of thy brethren that have the testimony of Jesus: worship God: for the testimony of Jesus is the spirit of prophecy" (*Revelation* 19:10).

And so it becomes clear that there is something different going on when the Captain of the Lord's Host accepts Joshua's act of worship.

In *Judges* 13:7, He also appears to the future parents of Samson, announcing to Manoah and his barren wife that she will soon conceive and give birth to a mighty son in Zion.

In addition, the Angel of the LORD led Hagar and her son Ishmael out of the desert, to make of Ishmael the father of many nations (*Genesis* 17:1-20). He also appeared to Abraham, preventing the sacrifice of Isaac (*Genesis* 22:11-12), wrestled with Jacob (*Genesis* 32:24-30 and *Hosea* 12:3-5), and saving Shadrach, Meshach, and Abednego in the midst of King Nebuchadnezzar's fiery furnace (*Daniel* Chapter 3).

So when we arrive at the Greek Scriptures of the New Testament, we see that Yahweh has continued to intervene in human history in the form of a Theophanic Angel, revealed to us as *Jesus Christ*. Taking into consideration what we learn from *Exodus* 33:20 (NLT), where God states that, "*But you may not look directly at my face, for no one may see me and live,*" we come to understand why Yahweh would need to assume such an appearance. That is why *John* 1:18 states that, "No one has ever seen God, but the *One and Only Son, Who is Himself God* and is in closest relationship with the Father, has made Him known." So it is through the medium of the Theophanic Angel that Yahweh relates to humankind, and ultimately redeems us from our lower selves, or original sin, as some wish to categorize our fallen nature.

Also, keep in mind that the word "angel" derives from the Hebrew *mal'ak*, which signifies a *messenger, envoy or ambassador*, i.e. one sent. This word could even apply to an ordinary human being, such as indicated in *Genesis* 32:3 (ESV): "Then Jacob sent *messengers* before him to Esau his brother in the land of Seir, the country of Edom." In its most literal meaning, the word does not specify any order of created heavenly beings, though God does maintain a hierarchy of created, ministering spirits to fill various tasks.

John the Baptist served in the capacity of a human *mal'ak* as pointed out by Jesus in *Matthew* 11:10-11(KJV): "For this is he of whom it is written: 'Behold, I send My messenger before Your face, Who will prepare Your way before You.' Assuredly, I say to you, among those born of women there has not risen one greater than John the Baptist; but he who is least in the kingdom of heaven is greater than he." The second angel or "messenger of the covenant," is God Himself, God incarnate in the Lord Jesus Christ.

Of course, the planets visible from Earth with the naked eye, and particularly Venus, the brightest among these, have played a significant role in the development of all the world's major religions. But in the context of Western culture, dating from the *Pax Romana* until the current age, our focus rests on the transitional period between the paganism of the Roman pantheon and the emergence of Christianity in the first few centuries of the Common Era. The discovery of newly discovered Gnostic texts is shining a much-needed light on this subject. And although Blavatsky was perhaps unnecessarily harsh in her criticism of the early Church Founders, it seems that a type of syncretism between Roman paganism and Christianity managed to survive well into the Middle Ages and beyond, whence it is experiencing a sort of revival in the so-called "New Age" of the twentieth and twenty-first centuries.

What we know of the ancient religion was that all of the planets, except for Earth, were named after Greek and Roman gods and goddesses. Mercury, Venus, Mars, Jupiter and Saturn received their names thousands of years ago, being discovered as "wandering stars" versus those that seemed to move in fixed positions. Because of this special characteristic, they were endowed by ancient priests and kings with anthropomorphic as well as divine qualities. In the latter sense, each planet was deemed to possess a *guiding spirit*. It was only much later- after telescopes were invented- that the other planets were discovered, with the tradition of naming them after Greek and Roman gods and goddesses being continued.

The Romans designated Mercury as the messenger of the gods, since he appeared to move so fast through the starry vault of the heavens and so close to the Sun. Due to her brilliance, Venus was named as the supreme goddess of love and beauty. Mars, with its blood-red tinge, was recognized as the god of war. Jupiter supplanted the Greek Zeus as the king of the gods; and Saturn ruled as the god of agriculture. The synthesis came about with Christianity reassigning the guiding spirits of the known planets as angels of the Judeo-Christian pantheon.

Concerning Jesus and his attachment to the planet Venus, *2 Peter* 1:19 (NIV) states, "*We also have the prophetic message as something completely reliable, and you will do well to pay attention to it, as to a light shining in a dark place, until the day dawns and the Morning Star rises in your hearts.*" In other words, the light of Christ is manifest in the planet Venus, and it is given to all who heed the prophetic message and absorb the knowledge that leads to eternal life provided to us by the Master Himself. All are afforded such an opportunity to become one with Jesus Christ and rule with him in celestial glory. In *Hebrews* 12:23 (KJV), for example, the Apostle Paul writes: "To the General Assembly and Church of the Firstborn, which are written in heaven, and to God the Judge of all, and to the spirits of just men made perfect,...." From this scripture we gather that Jesus Christ, as the head of the mystical body of believers, is the *Firstborn of the Spirit in the Fullness of Time* and all of those who heed his doctrine and teachings will have their names written in heaven and a glorious residence there prepared for them by the Master Himself. Note the words of Jesus as recorded in *John* 14:2 (KJV): "In my Father's house are many mansions: if it were not so, I would have told you. *I go to prepare a place for you.*" Are those who are reborn, that is born in the Spirit, going to have their souls whisked away to a new ethereal home on Venus? Is Venus Heaven?

Insofar as Jesus Christ being the *Firstborn among many brethren*, the Gnostics as well as the early Christians with independent bodies centered in Alexandria, Antioch, Jerusalem and Rome, interpreted this scripture as a reference to Jesus Christ as proceeding from the *Logos*,[162] being the first to emerge from the *Pleroma* or the Heavenly Realm to which the ethereal planet Venus certainly plays an integral part.

A contemporary Gnostic would identify the *Pleroma* as a universal field of consciousness, a spiritual realm of the universe, and the dwelling place of the Monad, the singularity of intelligence or Divine Mind (*Logos*) that the Platonic Greeks referred to as the Demiurge. This entity was understood by the philosophers of old to be an artisan-like figure responsible for the fashioning and maintenance of the physical universe. But despite the Demiurge's role as Grand

162 David T. Runia, Philo in *Early Christian Literature: A Survey* (Minneapolis, MN: Fortress Press, 1993): The noted Alexandrian Greek philosopher of the first century, Philo (25 B.C.E. – 50 C.E.), posited in his writings that the Logos was known by various names: the *Chief of Angels*, the *Shadow of God* and the *Son of God*. Within a few decades of his death, it is apparent that the early Christian community adopted Philo's theology and applied it to Jesus Christ. This is evidenced in the first chapter of the *Gospel of John*, the last and most mystical of the four accounts of the life of Christ, where the Logos is introduced as the *Word*. In this gospel, John informs us that this very Logos has assumed the form of Jesus Christ, for he writes that, "the Word (Logos) became flesh and lived among us, and we have seen his glory, the glory as of a father's only son, full of grace and truth (John 1:14)." Among the Jewish community of the first century, C.E., the Logos was also equated with wisdom. The *Wisdom of Solomon*, for example, depicts the Logos as a *force of divine origin* that exercises an enlightening effect, imparting wisdom to all who come within its immediate vicinity. Therefore, that John would describe Jesus as the "True light, which enlightens everyone (John 1:4-5, 9)" makes perfect sense. See also Robert Wright, *Evolution of God* (New York, New York: Little Brown and Company, 2009), 240, 241.

Architect of all that we perceive in this reality, He is not necessarily thought of as being the same as the creator figure in the familiar monotheistic sense insofar as both the Demiurge plus the material from which He fashions the universe are considered as uncreated and eternal.[163] Some Gnostic schools, however, believe that once the Demiurge emerged from the *Pleroma*, He fashioned the physical universe out of already-existent materials, the product of some other higher dimensional being that had long since moved on.[164]

The philosophical usage of the term Demiurge as a proper noun derives from Plato's *Timaeus*, written about 360 B.C.E., in which the being is presented as the creator of the universe. This is the generally accepted definition of the Demiurge in the Platonic (c. 310–90 B.C.E.) and Middle Platonic (c. 90 B.C.E. – 300 C.E.) philosophical traditions. In the various branches of the Neo-Platonic school of the third century C.E. onwards, the Demiurge is the fashioner of the real, perceptible world after the model of thought constructs, but in most Neo-Platonic systems) is still not itself "Monad," or "The One." In the arch-dualist ideology of some Gnostic schools, the material universe is inherently evil, while the non-material world is good. Therefore, to their way of reasoning, the Demiurge is malevolent insofar as being linked so intimately to the material world.[165]

When we look at the *New Testament Gospel of John*, however, we encounter what is perhaps the most Gnostic and Hellenized of the four presented accounts of the life of Jesus. The very text begins with an identification of Jesus' divine origins: *John* 1:1-5 (KJV) reads: "In the beginning was the Word, and the Word was with God, and the Word was God. The same was in the beginning with God. All things were made by him; and without him was not any thing made that was made. In him was life; and the life was the light of men. And the light shineth in darkness; and the darkness comprehended it not."

From this scripture we come to gather that Jesus was an emanation of the Word (*Logos*) or Divine Mind that exists as an uncreated being through all eternity. We also learn that Jesus is the Grand Architect of all we perceive in this reality and that through his life on Earth humankind receives the light and knowledge it needs to transcend the darkness. In other words, Jesus is God. And through His efforts on our behalf, all may be saved.

During the middle ages, as Blavatsky points out, the Roman Catholic Church supplanted Mercury with Michael, assigning him the role as Prince and Protector of the Church, but detaching him from direct identification with Jesus. Nevertheless, the planet Venus which Michael conquered, was still equated with Heaven, albeit the third of seven celestial levels.[166] The

163 On the complexity of Gnosticism, see Larry W. Hurtado, *Lord Jesus Christ: Devotion to Jesus in Earliest Christianity* (Grand Rapids, MI: William B. Eerdmans Publishing, 2005), 519–561.

164 Matthew Johnson, "Is the Universe a Bubble? Let's Check," 17 July 2014, Perimeter Institute for Theoretical Physics, http://www.perimeterinstitute.ca/news/universe-bubble-lets-check (Accessed 28 October 2014). Theoretical physicists now posit that in the beginning was a vacuum that simmered with energy (variously called dark energy, vacuum energy, the inflation field, or the Higgs field). Much like water in a pot, this high energy began to evaporate; and as it did so, it began forming bubbles in the process, with each bubble containing yet another vacuum, whose energy was lower, but still not zero. This energy, in turn, drove the bubbles to expand; and inevitably, some bubbles bumped into each other. It was at this point that the theorists claim that it was possible that some of these bubbles produced secondary bubbles. Maybe these bubbles were rare and far apart; but maybe they were packed as close as foam. But here is the beauty of this theory: Each of these bubbles was a universe unto itself. In this scenario, our universe is one bubble in a frothy sea of bubble universes. Hence, one could equate the high energy Higgs field that existed in the beginning with the Monad, or the One, having manifested archangels in each of the bubble universes. That's the multiverse hypothesis-Theosophy syncretism in a bubbly nutshell.

165 John Sallis, *Chorology: On Beginning in Plato's Timaeus* (Bloomington, IN: Indiana University Press), 86.

166 Michael Ward, "The Seven Heavens," 2007, *Planet Narnia* website, http://www.planetnarnia.com/planet-narnia/the-seven-heavens (Accessed 28 October 2014). In the pre-Copernican world, a geocentric view of the cosmos prevailed. The universe was believed to be divided into seven heavens, each ruled over by a particular sphere with an

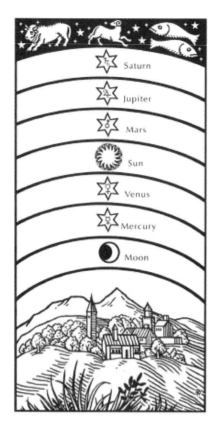

Before the sixteenth century, when Renaissance Polish astronomer Nicolaus Copernicus verified the heliocentric nature of the solar system, the planet Venus was considered to dominate the third of seven celestial levels, with each one being thought of as a heavenly realm. See http://www.planetnarnia.com/planet-narnia/the-seven-heavens/venus.

concept of Seven Heavens is a part of religious cosmology found in many major religions such as Catholicism, Hinduism, Islam, Judaism and Gnosticism, with the Throne of God said to be above the Seventh Heaven, at least in some Abrahamic religions.

Hermeticism is identified as a branch of Gnostic religion, being closely related to Christian Gnosticism. Together they are often viewed as sister religions, with both flourishing in Alexandria, Egypt, around the same time and in the same spiritual climate. Both of these Gnostic branches share the goal of the soul escaping from the material realm through true understanding gained by placing an emphasis on the acquisition of a personal knowledge of God. For the Christian Gnostics, this could be accomplished through establishing a personal relationship with Jesus Christ gained by consistent scriptural readings and the practice of various spiritual disciplines. Both of these traditions are firmly rooted in Western culture; representing a balance between Greek rationality, Biblical faith and a Gnostic application, such as was employed by the Cathars of the twelfth through fourteenth centuries in various parts of Southern France and Italy. Both groups saw the fundamental relationship between God and man as defined through obtaining a *gnosis* sufficient to be able to "see" God; and in some instances become one with God. Both of these belief systems accepted the concept of the *Pleroma* as being divided into seven realms or levels.

The Catholic/Christian conception of a seven-tiered heaven derives from Judaic traditions. Consider the following entry in the 1906 edition of the *Jewish Encyclopedia*:

"The Seven Heavens in the Talmud. (see Ps. lxviii. 5)"

"There are seven heavens one above the other: (1) Velon [Latin, *velum*, "curtain"]," which is rolled up and down to enable the sun to go in and out; according to Isa. xl. 22, "He stretched out the heavens as a curtain"; (2) Raḳi'a, the place where the sun, moon, and stars are fixed [Gen. i. 17]; (3)

attendant guardian angel/spirit. The seven planets included the Sun (Sol) and the Moon (Luna), which we now don't regard as planets at all. The other five were Mercury, Venus, Mars, Jupiter, and Saturn. Copernicus, a 16th century Polish astronomer, would soon overturn this entire cosmic structure. He argued that, rather than the Sun going round the Earth, as everyone had previously thought, it was actually the case that the Earth orbited Sol. His epoch-making work, *On the Revolutions of the Heavenly Bodies* (1543), ushered in modern astronomy and a 'heliocentric' or Sun-centered understanding of the universe. The Sun was no longer viewed as a planet, but as a star, the star of our solar system. The Moon also lost its status as a planet and was now demoted to a satellite of planet Earth. And as astronomical knowledge increased, new planets were added to the list. Uranus was discovered in 1781, Neptune in 1845, and Pluto in 1930; although it was relegated to the category of 'dwarf planet' in 2006, much to the dismay of many. Although only five of the traditional seven planets are still viewed as planets, they continue to govern our lives in at least one sense. In the English-speaking world, we still refer to the planets all the time, because they give us the names of the days of the week. Saturday is named after Saturn; Sunday is named after Sol (the Sun); Monday is named after Luna (the Moon); and so on. Venus was equated with Friday. In Old English *Frīgedæg* signifies the "day of Frigga," named after the Germanic goddess Frigga, the wife of the supreme god Odin. She was considered to be the goddess of married love. Hence, with the translation of the Late Latin *Veneris dies* or "day of Venus," Frigga became equated with the Roman goddess of love, Venus; and this compares with the Dutch *vrijdag* and German *Freitag*.

Shehakim, in which are the millstones to grind [*shahak*] manna for the righteous [Ps. lxxviii. 23; comp. Midr. Teh. to Ps. xix. 7]; (4) Zebul, the upper Jerusalem, with its Temple, in which Michael offers the sacrifice at the altar [Isa. lxiii. 15; I Kings, viii. 13]; (5) Ma'on. in which dwell the classes of ministering angels who sing by night and are silent by day, for the honor of Israel who serve the Lord in daytime [Deut. xxvi. 15, Ps. xlii. 9]; (6) Makon, in which are the treasuries of snow and hail, the chambers of dew, rain, and mist behind doors of fire [1 Kings, vii. 30; Deut. xxviii. 12]; (7) "Arabot, where justice and righteousness, the treasures of life and of blessing, the souls of the righteous and the dew of resurrection are to be found. There are the ofanim, the seraphim, and the hayyot of holiness, the ministering angels and the throne of glory; and over them is enthroned the great King."[167]

In the New Testament, the Apostle Paul at one point speaks of being taken up to "the third heaven" (*2 Cor.* 12:2), where he is escorted into the presence of the Most High. And Dante Alighieri, in his *Divine Comedy*[168] describes his journey through three distinct regions: Hell (*Inferno*), Purgatory (*Purgatorio*) and Paradise (*Paradiso*), being guided first by the Roman poet Virgil and then by Beatrice, the subject of his love and of another of his works, *La Vita Nuova*. Interestingly, it is in Paradise that Dante finds himself on the planet Venus, representative of the third level of Heaven, that wondrous and celestial domain.

While modern readers, so acquainted with Hell through the Halloween machinations of Hollywood, can easily grasp Dante's *Inferno*, the theological nuances presented in the other books require a certain amount of patience and knowledge to appreciate. *Purgatorio,* for example, is considered the most lyrical and human of the three. Interestingly, this transitional realm also serves as the abode for the most poets. *Paradiso,* on the other hand, is by far the realm imbued with the most theological overtones with so many beautiful and ecstatically mystic passages in which Dante tries to describe what he confesses he is unable to convey. At one point, Dante looks into the face of God Himself and declares, "*all'alta fantasia qui mancò possa*" — "at this high moment, ability failed my capacity to describe," (*Paradiso* XXXIII, 142).

With its seriousness of intention, literary stature, stylistic range and wide array of subjects and content, the *Divine Comedy* has come to be recognized as the benchmark in the emergence of Italian as an established literary language. In pushing beyond the limits of Latin writing imposed during his time, Dante is considered as a forerunner of the Renaissance. Dante's in-depth knowledge of Roman antiquity, coupled with his evident admiration

Dante Alighieri, born in Florence, Italy, 1265; and died 14 September 1321 at 56 years of age, depicted in this painting created by Sandro Botticelli on 31 December 1494. The *Birth of Venus*, depicted earlier in this book, was another of Botticelli's artistic accomplishments. See http://en.wikipedia.org/wiki/Dante_Alighieri#mediaviewer/File:Portrait_de_Dante.jpg.

---

167 Cyrus Adler, et al., "Angelology," *Jewish Encyclopedia*, 1906, (online edition), http://www.jewishencyclopedia.com/articles/1521-angelology#4364 (Accessed 19 October 2014)

168 Dante Alighieri, *Divine Comedy*, written between 1308 and his death in 1321. See translation by Henry Wadsworth Longfellow, 2nd edition (London: George Routledge and Sons, 1886).

for some aspects of pagan Rome, also point forward to the more illumined fifteenth century. By the nineteenth century, Dante's reputation had grown and solidified substantially; so much so that by 1865- on the 600th anniversary of his birth- he had become firmly established as one of the greatest literary icons of the Western world.

Dante introduces us to the wondrous sphere of Venus in *Paradiso, Canto* VIII: 1-30, which follows:

"The Third Sphere: Venus and Earthly Love"

"In its Pagan days the world used to believe that lovely Cyprian Venus beamed down fond love, turning in the third epicycle, so that those ancient peoples, in ancient error, not only did her the honour of sacrifice and the votive cry, but honoured Dione as well, and Cupid, one as her mother, the other as her son, and told how Cupid sat in Dido's lap: and from her, from whom I take my start, they took the name of the planet, that courts the Sun, now setting in front, and now behind."

"I had no sense of rising into her sphere, but my Lady's aspect gave me faith that I was there, because I saw her grow more beautiful. And as we see a spark in a flame, and as a voice can be distinguished from a voice, if one remains fixed and the other comes and goes, so, in that light itself, I saw other lamps, moving in circles, faster or slower, in accord, I believe, with the nature of their eternal vision."

"Blasts never blew from a chill cold, visibly or invisibly, so rapidly that that they would not seem slow and hindered, to whoever had seen those divine lights coming towards us, leaving the circling that has its first conception in the exalted Seraphim. And among those who appeared most in advance, Hosanna sounded, in such a manner that ever since I have not been free of the desire to hear it again."[169]

Dante encounters angels on Venus. See http://paintingandframe.com/prints/gustave_dore angels_in_heaven_dante%27s_divine_comedy_illustration-12907.html.

The following is a summary of Dante's incredible journey to Venus from *Paradiso*, "Paradise Canto IX: Third Heaven, Sphere of Venus:"

Dante invokes Charles Martel's wife, Clemence, telling her how their bloodline is headed for bad luck. Dante claims that Charles told him to "be silent" about this; in other words, Dante has been sworn to secrecy, but vaguely tells Clemence that her family's wrongs will be avenged.

Then Charles turns towards the Sun and Dante praises him for doing so.

Now another soul approaches Dante, growing brighter to show that she wants to talk to him, and Dante secures Beatrice's permission.

Dante asks her to speak.

She talks about her birthplace. She comes from the hills of Romano where a "firebrand descended" and brought a lot of grief to the land.

---

169 A. S. Kline (translator), *Divine Comedy, Paradiso, Cantos VIII-XIV*, 2000, http://www.poetryintranslation.com/PITBR/Italian/DantPar8to14.htm#_Toc64099863 (Accessed 29 October 2014).

She reveals that this firebrand is her kin, saying that she and he came from one root. *She names herself as Cunizza and identifies herself as a lover, which is why she's here on Venus. She isn't bitter about being this low in Heaven because she has turned her love towards God. She then introduces the shining soul beside her as a man who is and will remain famous for centuries to come.*

But now Cunizza turns away from her shiny friend to convey an ominous prophecy about the people of March of Treviso whom she calls "rabble" and the Paduan Guelphs who refused to listen to the crown. She talks about the murder of despots, and about the ransom of the King's men. She foreshadows that these people will spill so much blood that it would take a huge vat to contain all of it.

She justifies her words by invoking the judgment of the Angelic Intelligences that rule Venus, called the Thrones. She claims that since they shine down with the judgment of God, it is her right to speak such truths. She joins the dance of the spirits again while her shiny friend comes towards Dante.

Dante says that it's obvious the soul knows what he (Dante) is thinking because the soul is one of God's blessed.

The soul answers, starting with his birthplace. He details the geography of his home city, Marseilles France). Finally, he identifies himself as Folco. He was also lover. In his life, he was so "impressed with [Venus'] rays" that he was rivaled by famous lovers like Dido (who was in love with Aeneas), Phyllis (who committed suicide when she thought Demophoön was cheating on her), or even Hercules (abductor of Iole).

But Folco says he's grateful that God put him here.

But enough about me, says Folco. I know you're curious about this brilliant soul beside me.

Folco names his really bright neighbor as Rahab and says she has the "highest rank" in Venus. Since she lived before Christ, she went to Hell upon death, but was the first one taken up to Heaven when Christ harrowed Hell. This was a just act because she was always sympathetic to Christ.

(Note: According to the *Book of Joshua* in the Bible, Rahab was a prostitute. When Joshua sent two messengers to spy on the city of Jericho, Rahab aided them by hiding them in her house and helping them escape. As thanks for her help, Rahab's family was spared when the Israelites destroyed Jericho.)

Then Folco discusses Dante's city, Florence. He claims Florence's founder was Lucifer himself and the golden lilies, its emblem, turn good priests into greedy men. Because of that, the Church no longer studies the Gospels but only its own decrees.

But don't worry, Folco says grinning, Florence will soon be rid of those corrupt priests.[170]

Many parallels to later descriptions of the planet Venus and its inhabitants, such as those found in the writings of Emanuel Swedenborg, are found here in Dante's *Canto IX*. Among those depictions are of Venus as a heavenly realm, albeit a lower one; the rulers of the planet being angelic intelligences, or Thrones, responsible for watching over the Earth and intervening when and where they deem it necessary to do so; and lastly, that love is the most potent force on Venus, capable of redeeming sinners in all stages of iniquity, as aptly shown in the cases of the spirits dwelling there and interviewed by Dante, of Cunizza, Folco and Rahab. And in the case of the latter, Rahab, a former prostitute who assisted Joshua and the Israelites breach the

---

170 "*Paradiso Canto IX….,*" summary of, *Schmoop University*, 2014, http://www.shmoop.com/paradiso/canto-ix-summary.html (Accessed 19 October 2014)

walls of Jericho, she found herself in Hell in the afterlife. But after Jesus had resurrected from the dead and descended down into the Inferno, she was the first one to find herself liberated from that sorry place…. and all because her heart was in the right place. Jesus had prepared a wonderful new home for her on the planet Venus. Rahab is also mentioned in the *Gospel of Matthew* 1:5 as one of the ancestors of Jesus.

In any event, the key insight to be gained behind the depictions of multi-layered heavens is that Heaven is not a single state in which all saints and angels are equal and all people receive the same reward. Of course, Heaven is to be experienced differently by various individuals, based not so much by what they did or did not manage to accomplish in this life, but on how much they opened themselves up to the Infinite Love of God, for "*God is Love;*"[171] and the beautiful planet Venus is definitely a part of the Divine Plan and Celestial Kingdom.

While not directly connected to Christian Gnosticism, contemporary Neo-Paganism eventually adopted some of the theology embedded in Hermeticism and other beliefs grounded in the Western Mystery Tradition. Wicca, for example, is regarded as one of the earliest and more famous of the Neo-Pagan religions. The practitioners of these sects honor both a Goddess and a God, considering both of these entities as "aspects" of a single, yet greater being. Silver Ravenwolf expresses the importance of such a cosmological balance in terms of the Qabalistic Tree of Life:

"Down we go then, to the first two branches of the tree, right below the All. Each branch is exactly the same, one on the right side of the tree and one on the left. Totally balanced in every respect to each other. They represent the God and the Goddess, or the Lord and the Lady. Separate yet equal, together they combine into the essence of the All."[172]

The Neo-Paganists contend that the God and Goddess are merely the masculine and feminine aspects of *The All*. Both of these cosmic entities express themselves through sub-aspects as the gods and goddesses of the various pantheons.[173] In this sense, Neo-Paganism is much like Hermeticism where archangels, angels, and demons are all seen as embodying aspects of God. The use of animal imagery, herbs, signs and stones to draw down the powers of planetary spirits are part and parcel of both Hermetic and Neo-Pagan belief systems. In the latter, such sympathetic magic practices are often identified, rightly or wrongly, as "witchcraft." The Goddess Venus is highly honored among contemporary Neo-Paganists; and her planetary sign has been co-opted by the global feminist movement and the cause of women's equality and rights.

An astute celestial observer might well detect that the heavens themselves proclaim the divine role of the planet Venus in human affairs. About 4.6 billion years ago, in the plasma disc that would eventually coalesce into our solar system, the planets formed in orbits spaced approximately at right angles along a Golden Spiral. In this process of early formation, the emerging planets and their attendant moons began to exhibit resonant and vibratory properties. The clearest indication of this was found in the resonant orbit of Venus to the Earth.[174]

In the case of the formation of Venus and Earth so long ago, gravity acted as a damping well in space around these sister planets, forming spherical bubbles around each orb within

---

171 *1 John* 4:8 (Holman Christian Standard): "The one who does not love does not know God, because God is love."

172 Silver Ravenwolf, *To Ride a Silver Broomstick: New Generation Witchcraft* (St. Paul, MN: Llewellyn Publications, 1993), 44.

173 *Ibid.,* 45

174 Richard Merrick, "Harmonic Patterns," *Token Rock Sound Center,* undated, http://www.tokenrock.com/harmonic_nature/harmonic_patterns.php (Accessed 22 October 2014).

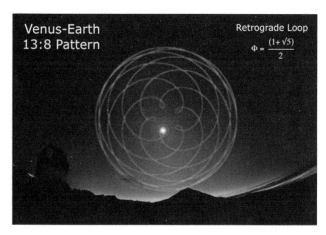

Venus-Earth 13:8 Pattern

Retrograde Loop

$$\Phi = \frac{(1+\sqrt{5})}{2}$$

The orbits of Venus and Earth are in near-perfect harmony, creating beautiful resonant patterns corresponding to the Fibonacci spiral number sequence. See http://www. tokenrock.com/harmonic_nature/harmonic_patterns.php.

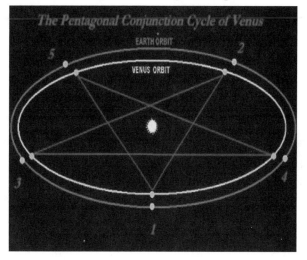

The orbit of Venus, when bringing the planet in close conjunction with the Earth, creates the pattern of a pentagram. For this reason, among many others, the ancients considered Venus to be a divine orb. This has to do with the sacred geometry inherent in the Earth-Venus orbital relationship, based on the five conjunctions in eight Venus year cycles. This orbital correspondence to the Fibonacci number series is quite significant and further explored in later chapters. See www.abovetopsecret.com.

which waves reflected and formed stable patterns.[175]

Richard Merrick, a noted expert in harmonic resonance patterns, stated that:

"In the heliospheric current sheet of the sun, a Phi-damping well once existed in the plasma between Earth and Venus. At one edge of the well was the planet node Venus and at the other Earth. For every 13 orbits that Venus travels around the Sun, Earth travels almost exactly eight, creating the resonant proportion 13:8. Since 13 / 8 = 1.625, the two orbits straddle the stabilizing Phi-damping eigenvector in the space between, forming the geometry of a pentagonal star in the two planet's conjunctions."[176]

Among the Gnostics and many others in ancient times, this star cymatic pattern was better known as the Star in the East, the Morning Star, the Babylonian Star and the Star of Bethlehem. Since Venus appeared in the sky before the Sun, it was called the "Light Bringer," or in Latin "Lucifer," as Blavatsky pointed out. Nevertheless, this orbital star pattern exhibited by Venus played a prominent role in the development of many early religions and associated the orb with the sacred feminine presence of God. This included Aphrodite, Ashtoreth, Astarte, Demeter, Eastre, Hathor, Innana, Ishtar, Isis, Kali, Ostara, Semiramis, the Hindu Vena (a.k.a. Shukra), and Venus.[177]

Surely then, the light of Venus has maintained its brilliance throughout the ages. Her light, like that of the Moon, is reflective of the glory of the Sun. It is a light that shines in the darkness; but by sheer contrast with the darkness Venus is highly accentuated. Venus is not only a celestial light that teaches and shines. She inspires!

---

175 *Ibid.*
176 *Ibid.*
177 *Ibid.*

Chapter IV:
The Contactees

"Your understanding of life and the Universe is very limited. As a result, you have many false concepts about other worlds and the composition of the Universe; and so little knowledge of yourselves! But it also is true that there is a growing desire on the part of many on Earth who seek sincerely for greater understanding. We who have traveled the path you now are treading are willing to help and to give of our knowledge to all who will accept it."
—Venusian Master to George Adamski, ***Inside the Space Ships*** (1955)

Venus outshines all but the Sun and nearby Moon. See www.greek-mythology-pantheon.com.

UFO contactees are those individuals who claim, or claimed, to have met and conversed in person with beings from beyond our world. Some of these contactees even claim to have taken trips on extraterrestrial craft; while others have demonstrated the extrasensory ability to channel communications from their new-found extraterrestrial friends. There are also a minority among the contactees who have been inspired and have gone on to establish quasi-religious sects. There appears to be a great degree of overlap among these contactees and some of the groups which promote their assertions. Nearly all of the contactees that have come forth publicly bring us important messages from the extraterrestrials they have communed with, messages that offer guidance for the improvement of life upon the Earth through the promotion of peace and understanding among all of humankind.[178] In this chapter we will examine some of the contactees who have claimed contact with Venusians, or have even claimed to be Venusians, and their important messages to augment our spiritual advancement.

Of the Venusians, it has been said that they are, "perhaps one of the most, if not the most, benevolent alien races in this galaxy," noted one ufologist (UFO researcher), adding that,

"Pure Venusians are very trusting beings, always trying to reach out to help those whom they feel are suffering terribly, never thinking about being rewarded or commended for their kind deeds. Earth residents take unfair advantage of a Venusian's innate capacity to openly embrace and reach out to their planet, but our friends still choose to return to this plane of conflicts, assisting in its slow but progressive spiritual evolution, regardless of the negative response to

---

178   Hierophant's Apprentice, "Contactees: Making Friends with the Space Brothers," Fortean Times, February 2011, http://www.forteantimes.com/features/articles/5062/random_dictionary_of_the_damned.html (Accessed 22 May 2014).

their gestures. This planet is indeed fortunate to feel the unconditional Love vibrations that can only emanate from Venus!"[179]

One of the most interesting in this group of contactees claiming contact with Venusians was Tuesday[180] Lobsang Rampa. Born into a working class family, the son of a plumber, as Cyril Henry Hoskin on 8 April 1910, at Plympton, Devon, in the United Kingdom, he dropped out of high school and was apprenticed by his father. He eventually became a plumber himself and married, adopting one child. But Hoskin's life was routine, at best, and he frequently complained of having to work so hard in such a class system that only favored the wealthy. He literally despised the capitalist England of the late 1940s and yearned for something better for himself and his family. He

This is a depiction of a beautiful Venusian woman's appearance to Howard Menger as a ten-year-old boy in the woods not far from his home in New Jersey. Painting appears in Howard Menger's *From Outer Space to You* (1959).[184]

avidly read books from the Theosophical Society as well as anything he could find on the Far East- Tibet in particular.[181]

Then one day in 1949 he climbed up into a fir tree in his backyard, attempting to photograph an owl. No sooner had he snapped a picture of the bird, then some branches snapped from under him and he fell to the ground and suffered a concussion. After being out for several minutes, he finally came to, aided to his feet by his wife. He then related to her the strangest account. He said that he had somehow been transported to the astral plane, where he was approached by a Tibetan Buddhist monk by the name of Tuesday Lobsang Rampa. Rampa said that he had been injured in an automobile accident and that his Earthly life was nearly over. Since Hoskin was unhappy with his life on the terrestrial plane, Rampa wondered if Hoskin would not mind letting him utilize his body so that Hoskin's spirit could go onto higher realms.[182]

Rampa told Hoskin that this was actually the Thirteenth Dalai Lama's idea. The Inmost One, as the Dalai Lama is known, explained to Rampa:

"We have located a body in the land of England, the owner of which is most anxious to leave. His aura has a fundamental harmonic of yours. Later, if conditions necessitate it, you can take over his body." He cautioned his disciple: "You will return to hardship, misunderstanding, disbelief, and actual hatred, for there is a force of evil which tries to prevent all that is good in

---

179 "Alien Races on Earth," http://www.angelfire.com/md/aliencounsel/alienraces.html (Accessed 22 May 2014)
180 In Tibet, persons are named in accordance to the day they on which they are born.
181 Phil Hine, "One from the Vaults: The Fantastic World of Lobsang Rampa," 2014, http://enfolding.org/one-from-the-vaults-the-fantastic-world-of-lobsang-rampa-i/ (Accessed 22 May 2014).
182 *Ibid.*
184 Howard Menger, *From Outer Space to You* (Clarksburg, West Virginia: Saucerian Books, 1959): Howard Menger (February 17, 1922 – February 25, 2009) was an American contactee who claimed to have met various extraterrestrials from throughout our solar system in the course of his life. He chronicled these encounters, some which led to actual flights aboard the space ships, in two books, *From Outer Space to You* and the self-published *High Bridge Incident* in 1991, which was co-authored by his wife Connie. Menger, like George Adamski, described the Space Brothers as being "angelic" in nature. This contactee rose to prominence in the 1950s, being second to Adamski in popularity on the lecture circuit among UFO devotees. Menger's books also contained timely advice and information on religion, new sources of energy and agriculture that he gleaned from his contacts with friendly aliens.

connection with human evolution."[183]

Hoskin apparently agreed to this deal. With great difficulty, Rampa entered the Westerner's body, rose to his feet, and was helped inside by Hoskin's wife. Suffice it to say when Hoskin regained consciousness, he was not himself. His memories of his life as an Englishman began to fade until eventually they were completely gone, replaced by the full memories of the life of a Tibetan from babyhood onward.[184]

When he had recovered sufficiently, he took various free-lance jobs to support his new wife and a cat named Fifi Greywiskers, to whom he attributed uncanny psychic powers. When he inquired about a job as a ghostwriter, however, he was encouraged by a literary agent to write his own book. To this he reluctantly agreed, for he preferred to conduct research on the human aura.[185] So he undertook the arduous task of writing his first book, the *Third Eye*.[186]

Many believe that Tuesday Lobsang Rampa was a recognized incarnated Tibetan abbot and fully qualified medical lama with a special task in life. Rampa did not return to this planet to just write books or even to attempt to disseminate occult knowledge. He came to this world in order to do a special task, and that was to clarify the faults of human beings to others in the astral planes. They wanted to know why we humans have continually gone wrong, why human beings are a failed species. They wanted to know this in order to develop a plan that can help us. Other avatars have come before for the same purpose. Some have met with limited success, but many failed in the attempt. It can be said of Rampa that he at least enjoyed a moderate degree of success.[187]

He wrote nineteen books to make money to carry out his research work, the work he was sent here for. So while these books have helped millions of people in various ways, that was not his primary purpose in writing them. But through his writings, he managed to inform the Earth's inhabitants about their real selves, why they are here, what they should and shouldn't be doing and finally, how to progress spiritually as we all must.

His books were devoted to such esoteric subjects as the nature of auras, extraterrestrials, future wars, the lost years of Jesus, and expositions of the Law of Karma. Two of his most unusual works were a volume entitled *Living with the Lama*,[188] which was dictated telepathically to him by his cat, Fifi Greywhiskers, and *My Trip to Venus*,[189] from which ten percent of the royalties were to be sent to the Save a Cat League of New York. His books have sold more than four million copies to date, and sales have continued to skyrocket since his death at the age of 70 on 25 January 1981 in Calgary, Alberta, Canada.[190]

What gives credence to Rampa's assertions is their ready acceptance by those in the academies of Buddhist and Tibetan studies. In fact, many entered these fields precisely because they were inspired in their readings of Tuesday Lobsang Rampa. Noted Lopez, "For some it was a fascination with the world Rampa described that had led them to become professional

---

183 David S. Lopez, Jr., "Lobsang Rampa: Mystery of the Three-Eyed Lama," Tricycle Magazine, Winter 1998, http://www.tricycle.com/feature/lobsang-rampa-mystery-three-eyed-lama (Accessed 22 May 2014).

184 *Ibid.*

185 *Ibid.*

186 Tuesday Lobsang Rampa, *Third Eye* (London, UK: Secker and Warburg, 1956)

187 "Tuesday Lobsang Rampa," updated 2 June 2013, http://www.lobsangrampa.org (Accessed 22 May 2014)

188 Tuesday Lobsang Rampa, *Living with the Lama* (London, UK: Corgi, 1964)

189 Tuesday Lobsang Rampa, *My Trip to Venus* (Clarksburg, West Virginia: Saucerian Books, 1966)

190 Lopez, "….Mystery of the Three-Eyed Lama"

scholars of Tibet."[191] And when Lopez presented classes on Tibet at the University of Michigan, he would require his students to read Rampa's *Third Eye* without telling them anything of the purported lama's background. Of this, Lopez notes that the "students were unanimous in their praise of the book, and despite six prior weeks of lectures on Tibetan history and religion, they found it entirely credible and compelling, judging it more realistic than anything they had previously read about Tibet."[192] Even the Dalai Lama credited Rampa with generating a positive image and publicity for Tibet.[193]

On the subject of flying saucers, Rampa stated that sightings of these craft were quite common throughout the Himalayas and that he had taken a trip in one from the Chang Tang Highlands of Tibet to Venus. As to why his homeland should receive so much attention from extraterrestrials, Rampa pens:

"It is remote from the bustle of the everyday world, and is peopled by those who place religion and scientific principles before material gain. Throughout the centuries the people of Tibet have known the truth about flying saucers, what they are, why they are, how they work, and the purpose behind it all. We know of the flying saucer people as the gods in the sky in their fiery chariots."[194]

Rampa was not the only lama to be chosen for the trip to Venus. Six others, all of high lama rank, had also received telepathic communications from the Venusians that they were to ascend above the cloud bank toward the mountain peaks, where they would be met by an interplanetary delegation and escorted onboard a scout ship. At a certain point they arrived at a vast mesa, perhaps five miles across, encompassed on one side by a massive glacial ice sheet. They also found the remnants of a ruined city, although some buildings appeared to have remained intact. And yet others looked almost new. Of course, nearby the lamas encountered the scout ship. Rampa wrote that "in a spacious courtyard, there was an immense metal structure which reminded me of two of our temple dishes, clamped together, and it was clearly a vehicle of some sort."[195] Rampa estimated that the craft was approximately 50 to 60 feet in diameter.[196]

T. Lobsang Rampa enjoys an intimate moment with his psychic cat, Fifi Greywhiskers.
See www.examiner.com.

The lamas were met by beings who telepathically communicated instructions to them, helping them board the ship and seating them in what seemed to be a movie theater of some sort. Here they watched images from Earth's distant past, highlighting the interactions of Venusians

191   David S. Lopez, Jr., *Prisoners of Shangra-La: Tibetan Buddhism and the West* (Chicago: University of Chicago Press, 1998), 112.
192   *Ibid.*
193   Karen Mutton, *T. Lobsang Rampa: New Age Trailblazer* (Frankston, Texas: TGS Publishing, 2006), 166, 167.
194   Rampa, *My Trip to Venus*, 2.
195   *Ibid.*, 3
196   *Ibid.*, 4

and other extraterrestrials in Earth's history, during which time the craft had whisked them quickly and silently above the Earth's atmosphere. When the documentary/orientation was over, they found themselves docking with a yet larger ship in a stationary orbit on the far side of the Moon. Here they witnessed maintenance personnel servicing various spacecraft in a massive hangar. They also noted that spacecraft were continually arriving and departing and that there were many different types of people onboard, "ranging from those about fifteen feet tall to some about five feet tall."[197]

Of course, these were not all Venusians. Rampa explains:

"We learned that there was an Association, a Brotherhood composed of incarnate and disincarnate entities. Those who were incarnate came from many different planets, and they had as their one aim the safeguarding of life. Man, we were told, was certainly not the highest form of evolution, and these people, these guardians, worked for creatures of all kinds, not merely for man."[198]

Rampa's observations confirmed what Blavatsky, Swedenborg and others had taught, that the whole Omniverse is a habitable zone. The lamas learned that the entirety of the Earth was a colony of the Brotherhood, and that various extraterrestrial races were patrolling the Earth to do what they can to "mitigate the effects of atomic radiation and, it was hoped, save the people of Earth from blowing their world to pieces."[199]

A Venusian explained to Rampa that the Brotherhood maintained a base on the far side of the Moon, beyond detection of Earth's sensory instruments. For added security, the base was constructed deep under the lunar surface. The Venusian remarked that:

"Yet, upon Earth, people are taught that we do not exist. They have to be taught so because of the religious teaching that Man is made in the image of God, and the people of Earth think that Man is the Earth human. Today to admit the possibility of Man on other planets would be to prove the various religions wrong. Again, those who hold the power of life and death over nations dare not let it be known that there is even a greater power, for to do so would be to lessen their hold upon their enslaved people."[200]

Rampa and the others were sent down to the Moon on a levitation platform. After resting for about the equivalent of half an Earth day at the lunar base, the Venusian approached the lamas and said, "My brothers, you have endured much according to any standards. This night we are going to take you far away from your own Earth, we are going to take you to a planet which you call Venus. Take you there just to show that *there are civilizations beyond anything that you know on Earth, take you so that your days of life upon Earth may be brightened by the knowledge of what is, and what can be.*"[201]

The Venusian escort provided some details on the electromagnetic propulsion system utilized on scout ships in the vicinity of planets, as well as the more complex quantum energies employed in propelling their larger carrier ships at faster-than-light speeds in interplanetary and intergalactic space. Rampa, in his account, goes on to explain the "deranged" shifting of colored light patterns that he and the others saw through a portal as the ship zipped speedily on to Venus in what seemed to be only minutes:

"...but on we sped without feeling any sensation, outstripping light itself... We were

197 *Ibid.*, 4, 5
198 *Ibid.*, 5
199 *Ibid.*
200 *Ibid.*, 11
201 *Ibid.*, 13, 14

spellbound in our seats watching outside. Instead of pinpoints of light we saw streaks as is some clumsy artist had daubed a black wall with glowing colors which changed as we looked at them. At last the colors began to appear more normal. The black gave way to purple, the purple to red-brown, and then to scarlet-red, and then behind us again we saw pinpoints of light. Stars, though behind us were green and blue, while ahead of us they were red and yellow. As we slowed down still more the stars ahead turned to their normal colors, as did those at the back."[202]

With our present understanding of physics, this might be described as some sort of inter-dimensional flux. And perhaps this might be the only means by which people of the material world can transition to a planet like Venus, which exists in a spiritual realm beyond the range of most human perception. In any event, Rampa and the others continued to watch in awe as the ship orbited Venus maybe three or five times. Rampa was not really sure because the planet was entirely covered in white, fleecy clouds, "a ball which reminded me of thistledown floating against a black sky."[203]

The lamas descended through the cloud layer down to the Venusian surface in a scout craft. As they passed under the clouds, they were astounded by the view:

"The clouds by some magic of the Gods had been made invisible, and beneath us we saw this glittering world, this world filled by superior beings. As we sank lower and lower we saw fairy cities reaching up into the sky, immense structures, ethereal, almost unbelievable in the delicate tracing of their buildings. Tall spires and bulbous cupolas, and from tower to tower stretched bridges like spiders' webs, and like spiders' webs they gleamed with living colors, reds and blues, mauves and purples, and gold, and yet what a curious thought, there was no sunlight. This whole world was covered in cloud. I looked about me as we flashed over city after city, and it seemed to me that the whole atmosphere was luminous, everything in the sky gave light, there was no shadow, but also there was no central point of light. It seemed as if the whole cloud structure radiated light evenly, unobtrusively, a light of such a quality as I had never believe existed. It was pure and clean."[204]

The scout ship landed without even a mild jerk or tremor. When they disembarked they were led into a great hall where they were met by a Venusian delegation, the members of which were described as being "tall, grave faced, but with a dignity and presence not known upon the turbulent Earth."[205] Of the Venusian appearance, generally, Rampa notes that throughout his stay on Venus, he "saw no one who by Earth standards was not startlingly beautiful."[206] And this beauty even extended to their vast minds, where ugliness was unknown. The lamas surely felt calm in the presence of such angelic beings, who greeted them telepathically in floods of welcoming thoughts. Telepathic entities such as these do not require the use of translators or translation devices insofar as telepathy employs the universal language of thought.

The Earthmen were directed to take seats in a remote-controlled air car. It was about thirty feet long and floated some two or three inches above the ground. The air car whisked them from the reception hall at the spaceport to the great Hall of Knowledge. Their Venusian escort continued to accompany them in the air car. The air car glided into a docking bay and a group of younger Venusians, perhaps students, flocked around the monks as they disembarked from

---

202 *Ibid.*, 15
203 *Ibid.*
204 *Ibid.*, 16
205 *Ibid.*, 17
206 *Ibid.*, 16

the vehicle. If there was such a thing as a "super star" on Venus, Rampa and the others felt like they were treated as one, being bombarded by all kinds of questions about life in Tibet from the enthusiastic Venusian youth.[207]

After this brief interlude with the young ones, the lamas were escorted into the chamber of the Lords of Venus. Here they received telepathic transmissions concerning the history of Earth, from its primeval origins to the evolution of humankind and the rise and fall of great civilizations and empires, all the way to the present age and up to the year 3,000 C.E. Rampa writes, "It was wonderful the things we saw and heard. We seemed to be upon the Earth, as if we were standing beside, or even slightly behind, the principal actors. We could see all, hear all, but we could not touch, nor be touched. But eventually these wondrous impressions faded into the year 3,000 and something."[208]

The Lords of Venus explained that the past, present and future are all illusions. The Earth they saw in the year 3,000 C.E. was very much like the Venus the lamas were visiting. However,

Rampa and the lamas see cities beyond imagination on Venus. See www.science20.com.

without constant vigilance on the part of the inhabitants of Earth, it might not turn out so pleasant. One of the Lords communicated frankly with Rampa:

"Now you see, my brother, why it is that we guard the Earth, for if man's folly is allowed to go unchecked terrible things will happen to the race of men.. There are powers upon the Earth, human powers, who oppose all thought of our ships, who say that there is nothing greater than the human upon the Earth so there cannot be ships from other worlds. You and your brothers have been shown and told, and have experienced this so that you through your telepathic knowledge, can contact others so that you can bring influence to bear."[209]

None of the monks, including Rampa, were aware of the passing of time on Venus. None of them were sure just how long they were there. Rampa estimated that it could have been days, or maybe even weeks. Rampa also noted that the Earth now "seemed a tawdry place" that "paled into insignificance against the glory of Venus." The lama also leaves us in suspense, for he states that he has visited our Sister Planet many times since.[210] And as we will see in the case of other contactees, there is more than the mere fate of Earth at stake in the outcome of human affairs.

George Adamski, "First Ambassador to Outer Space"

Interestingly enough, George Adamski was another contactee with ties to Tibet. He was actually born in Poland in 1891(His father was Polish and mother Egyptian.), but he and his family immigrated to the United States two years later, settling in the bustling metropolis of New York City. Like Cyril Hoskin (Rampa) in his youth, the young Adamski was an avid reader,

---

207 *Ibid.*, 18
208 *Ibid.*, 19
209 *Ibid.*
210 *Ibid.*

with a particular interest in astronomy, science fiction, Theosophy and Tibetan Buddhism.[211]

But unlike Hoskin, Adamski was satisfied with his life in the Western world, i.e. America, and pleased that his parents saw fit to bring him to this land that offered such exciting possibilities. At the age of 22, he even enlisted in the Army, where he served in K Troop of the 13th Cavalry Regiment under the command of General John J. Pershing (1913-1916) at the Mexican border. Adamski was part of the unit that took part in the expeditionary force sent to track down Francisco "Pancho" Villa after he and his band of revolutionaries had raided an arsenal in Columbus, New Mexico.[212] General Pershing pursued Villa for nine months until the United States became involved in World War I. This facilitated the general's summons back to Washington, D.C., for reassignment. The chase for Villa was called off. Clearly, at this point America had "bigger fish to fry."

One year after his honorable discharge from the Army, Adamski was married and took a temporary job with the government doing maintenance work in Yellowstone National Park.[213] The Adamskis then moved up to Oregon where he worked at a flour mill.[214] George continued to carry out odd jobs throughout the western states; but he knew deep in his heart that he was destined for a higher purpose than performing itinerant labor.

By the mid-1930s, Adamski found himself drawn to Laguna Beach, California. It was here that he became aware that many of his friends were intrigued with his vast knowledge of Tibetan Buddhism and wanted to know more. So he established a religious society known as the Royal Order of Tibet that held weekly meetings in a Temple of Scientific Philosophy and even began lecturing on "universal law" before live audiences as well as on radio programs. By 1940, Adamski set up a 20-acre ashram on the slopes of Mt. Palomar where he and his growing contingent of disciples could farm and study. He built a home known as Palomar Gardens as well as a restaurant, the Palomar Gardens Café, where interested individuals could come to chat with and learn from wisdom proffered by the amiable guru.[215]

Adamski adjusts reflector telescope at his ashram on the slopes of Mt. Palomar, California, in 1952. See http://www.utexas.edu/its/webspace/.

Even though the mystic Adamski lacked any formal education, his ardent disciples referred to him as "professor." They took everything he said to be the gospel truth and were willing to follow him to the ends of the universe, quite literally. And then one day, on 20 November 1952, a day which was to change *ufology*, or the study of UFOs, forever, Adamski drove six of his

---

211 Michael Scott-Blair, "Palomar Campground Expanding its Universe," *Union-Tribune*, San Diego, California, 13 August 2003

212 *Ibid.*

213 *Santa Fe Ghost and History Tours*, "George Adamski- UFO Contactee or Hustler?," http://www.santafeghostandhistorytours.com/GEORGE-ADAMSKI.html (Accessed 28 May 2014). From the period of 1916-1919, Adamski was no longer on active duty, but continued with the National Guard. It was during this time that he married Mary A. Shimbersky on December 25, 1917. She passed away in 1954.

214 Scott-Blair

215 Leonard Solomon and Steve Solomon, *How to Make the Most of a Flying Saucer Experience* (Baltimore, Maryland: Top Hat Press, 1998), 54-56

associates out to Desert Center, California, with the anticipation of at least obtaining a sighting of one of the elusive objects that had been so numerously reported in the press.[216] But what they saw more than exceeded all of their expectations. First, a massive cigar shaped object, a mother ship, ascended from behind a range of mountains in the distance; and then a smaller, bell-shaped craft appeared in the sky, encompassed by an unparalleled brilliance as the Sun reflected off its shiny metallic body. Adamski then instructed those in his party to wait at the observation point, for he set off alone on foot behind a hill where the scout ship had nestled. Adamski sensed telepathic instructions from the pilot of the ship; and he was acting on them. He knew that he would soon be meeting a being from another world.[217]

Soon Adamski caught sight of an individual waving at him. As he approached, Adamski took note that the extraterrestrial *appeared* as a human male. Adamski estimated his height to be about five feet, six inches. He had long blond hair and probably weighed around 135 pounds. The alien was wearing a glossy-light chocolate colored one-piece uniform (jumpsuit) and seemed to be in his late twenties. Adamski was awed by the sheer beauty of his form, thinking that it surpassed anything he had seen before in the people of Earth.[218] He later noted that, "I felt like a child in the presence of one with great wisdom and much love, and I became very humble within myself... from him was radiating a feeling of infinite understanding and kindness, with supreme humility."[219]

On Adamski's encounter with Orthon, Thompson writes:

"Through a combination of sign language and telepathy, *Adamski learned that the spaceman had come from Venus to warn Earthlings away from their warlike ways, in particular to encourage a halt to nuclear testing, a practice that the Nordic-looking starman said was upsetting the harmony of the universe.* Many Venusians already lived in disguise among humans from various walks of life, Adamski learned from this genial traveler, who allowed the 'professor' to tour and photograph the landed spacecraft so long as he refrained from taking photographs of the Venusian."[220]

At the very dawn of the space age, Adamski proved to be a huge success on the lecture circuit. In his talks, he would also elaborate on some of the information he had previously presented in his books on esoteric wisdom as well as the flying saucer phenomenon.[221] And following the publication of his first two flying saucer books, his schedule filled up completely as he was making the customary promotional rounds on both radio and television talk shows. In addition, he did not hesitate to pass on to those in his growing audiences the crucial concern

---

216 *Santa Fe Ghost and History Tours*: The six people that went with Adamski were George Williamson, who went back to the landing site after the craft took off and made plaster casts of Orthon's boot prints, Betty Williamson, Lucy McGiness, Alice K. Wells, as well as Al and Betty Bailey.

217 Keith Thompson, *Angels and Aliens* (New York, New York: Fawcett Columbine, 1991), 29

218 *Ibid.*

219 Collin Bennett, *Looking for Orthon* (New York, New York: Paraview Press, 2001), 35.

220 Thompson, 29

221 George Adamski, *Questions and Answers: Wisdom of the Masters of the Far East* (Laguna Beach, California: Royal Order of Tibet, 1936).

_____, *Pioneers of Space: A Trip to the Moon, Mars and Venus* (Los Angeles, California: Leonard-Freefield, 1949)

George Adamski and Desmond Leslie, *Flying Saucers Have Landed* (New York. New York: British Book Centre, 1953)

George Adamski, *Inside the Space Ships* (New York, New York: Abelard-Schuman,1955)

_____, *Flying Saucers Farewell* (New York, New York: Abelard-Schuman, 1961)

_____, *Cosmic Philosophy* (Freeman, South Dakota: Pine Hill Press, 1961)

that the "Space Brothers"- as he liked to call them- had concerning the dangers of nuclear proliferation and the future of planet Earth. Adamski related that he continued to enjoy a series of clandestine meetings with extraterrestrials walking among us that he would encounter at various bars and cafes throughout the Greater Los Angeles area.[222] Keeping in mind that Orthon explained to Adamski that Venusians live among us, trying as best they can to blend into our society, then it goes to reason that such contacts with the Space Brothers would take place. And so far as we know, after his meeting in the California desert with Orthon, Adamski did experience contacts with the extraterrestrials on the following dates: 18 February 1953, 12 April 1953 and 24 April 1955.[223]

Perhaps this hurried pace and all of the publicity it generated was worth it to Adamski, especially in light of the mission he had been charged with by the extraterrestrials to serve as Earth's first ambassador to outer space.

Adamski stands with portrait of Orthon, the Venusian saucer pilot. See http://forgetomori. com/2009/aliens/uma-alienigena-como-dolores-barrios/.

It seems that the Venusians had been preparing Adamski for some time to serve in his high calling as their emissary to the inhabitants of the Earth. Perhaps his keen psychic awareness developed through years of study of Eastern philosophy and Theosophy uniquely equipped him for the big responsibilities he would later have to shoulder. In any event, Adamski's first sightings of a UFO took place on 8 and 9 October 1946 at his ashram in Palomar Gardens, California. Adamski felt an overpowering urge to set up his six-inch reflecting telescope on those nights. While conducting astronomical observations, he spotted a large cigar shaped craft in the middle of a meteor swarm, which he would later to come to understand was a huge *mothership*.[224] At first, some skeptics dismissed Adamski's claim to have seen a spaceship beyond the Earth's atmosphere as pure "nonsense" or perhaps a "hallucination." However, when other people in San Diego also reported seeing an unusual object in the sky over the same nights, the doubters were hard pressed to deny that Adamski, the amateur astronomer, had seen a real, physical craft of some sort. While they quickly dismissed it as an ordinary "blimp" sighting, Adamski knew that a blimp could not reach the altitude he was observing the object, nor

---

222 Thompson, *Angels and Aliens*, 29
223 *Santa Fe Ghost History Tours*
224 The term has achieved prominence in science fiction and in UFO lore, which extend the idea to apply to spaceships serving as the heart of a fleet. The concept of *mothership* (almost always spelled as a single word) clearly implies that the other ships in the fleet are dependent on the mothership for at least some services. Motherships are essentially the sci-fi equivalent to modern flagships. Typically, a mothership will take up station in an area and remain there for long periods, while smaller ships sortie to interesting destinations. Sometimes a mothership is large enough to operate alone, or is so huge that it contains a fleet in its body. *South Antelope Valley Press*, Palmdale, California, 10 July 1947: A variant of the term *mother ship* can be traced to the hundreds of claimed UFO sightings in the United States during the summer of 1947, when a woman in Palmdale, California, was quoted by the contemporary press as describing a "mother saucer (with a) bunch of little saucers playing around it" when referring to the objects she witnessed on 7 July. The term was further popularized in UFO lore through the UFO sightings of George Adamski in the 1950s, who claimed to sometimes see large cigar-shaped Venusian motherships, out of which flew smaller sized flying saucers.

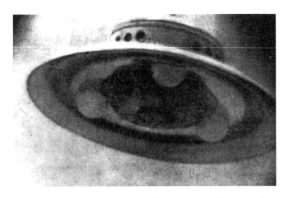

Orthon permitted Adamski to take a photograph of his Venusian scout craft as it was taking off, but forbade him to snap a photograph of his person. Technical difficulties with Adamski's camera caused the picture to become blurry. See www.kmatthews.org.

if it could, survive the impact of a meteorite collision.[225]

This was the first of numerous sightings leading up to his ultimate encounters with Orthon and other Space Brothers and Sisters. During this interim period, his sighting with the largest number of UFOs took place in 1947, when he claimed that he saw 184 flying saucers passing over in formation in the night sky over Mt. Palomar. These craft were segmented into 32 saucers per wave. Of course, Adamski's interest in all things "outer space" multiplied exponentially with each passing observation of extraterrestrial craft, so much so that by 1949 he authored a book about what he imagined it would be like to travel on a spaceship between the planets. The book, titled *Pioneers of Space*, was presented as a science fiction account of what it would be like for an Earthling to meet aliens and go with them on a ride in their spacecraft to visit Venus, Mars and the Moon.[226] Insofar as the Venusians have telepathic abilities, it would not surprise me if much of the information found in the pages of *Pioneers of Space* was directly channeled into Adamski's conscious mind by them, thereby preparing his mind for what he would actually come to experience firsthand.

Adamski claimed that he was taken into outer space as a guest of the extraterrestrials on several occasions. His meetings with advanced souls are described in detail in his second and third flying saucer books; and much of what he writes about conditions on Venus, Mars, the Moon and other bodies in our solar system

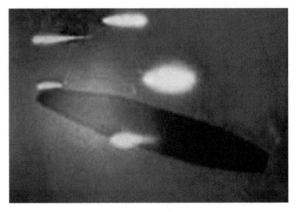

Photograph of mothership taken by Adamski with camera attachment to his six-inch reflector telescope at Palomar Gardens, California, on 29 May 1950. Note the intense ionization fields around the smaller scout craft. See www.exopolitics.org.

jives with the accounts provided by Rampa and other contactees, albeit with a slightly more technical aspect with detailed drawings of the interior of various spacecraft and more precise descriptions of propulsion systems. And according to Adamski, all planets and any natural satellites they may have, throughout the solar system, are inhabited by beings whose spiritual and technological achievements far surpass our own. Adamski remained faithful to the message he was called to preach by the celestial hierarchy: precisely that the universe is a big place that serves as a cosmic school and every soul is an enrolled student.[227] So if you get things right here on Earth, when you die you will reincarnate on another planet, a higher sphere in the heavens-much like in a commencement/graduation.[228]

225 *Santa Fe Ghost and History Tours*
226 *Ibid.*
227 *Ibid.*
228 *1 Corinthians* 15:39-49 (NKJV): "All flesh is not the same flesh, but there one kind of flesh of men, another flesh of

The purpose of every form of life in the universe is to acquire knowledge and wisdom, and thereby grow into the full measure of their being. The Space Brothers also confirmed something that Adamski had suspected from his study of Theosophy: that Jesus Christ was a Venusian master who had incarnated on Earth in order to try and help humanity, guiding us by the pure light of his excellent example.[229] Other great teachers and ascended masters from Venus and other worlds have also graced our planet, but many have not paid them sufficient heed, or even failed to recognize them as spiritual leaders in any capacity.

The planet Earth is considered the most problematic world in our star sector. Adamski and other contactees have been permitted to view the rise and fall of many civilizations on Earth before our own, taking note that these had destroyed themselves in senseless warfare. Humanity seems to have been stuck in a fruitless pattern of growth-war-destruction-start all over, growth-war-destruction-start all over, *ad infinitum*. It seems as though humanity is trapped in a cycle of destruction, and will never break into a realm of harmony that would serve to enable all the people of Earth to reach a new level of wisdom.[230] For this reason, the Hierarchy of Light will continue to send us sundry celestial avatars and messengers until such a time as humanity is deemed ready to join the cosmic brotherhood that anxiously awaits us.

In 1962, Adamski disappeared for a few weeks, causing some degree of worry among his followers. When he reappeared, he claimed that he had been transported to Saturn aboard one of the motherships to attend a conference with delegates from all the planets in our solar system. At this conference he was given certain instructions for the work to be carried out here on Earth. It should be pointed out that Adamski stuck to his extraterrestrial accounts even unto death. He suffered a fatal heart attack on 23 April 1965 while visiting friends in Silver Springs, Maryland. Earlier in the morning, on the very day that he was to die, Adamski assured those friends gathering around him that the Space Brothers were going to come and visit with him at the house in just a few hours.[231] I am sure they did.

Setting the Stage

The decade of the 1950s was also considered to be the golden age of science fiction. And at the outset, there were two high quality motion pictures that would play a role in setting the stage for the public's emerging perceptions of the UFO phenomenon: the *War of the Worlds*[232]

---

animals, another of fish, and another of birds. *There are also celestial bodies and terrestrial bodies; but the glory of the celestial is one, and the glory of the terrestrial is another. There is one glory of the sun, another glory of the moon, and another glory of the stars, for one star differs from another in glory.* So also is the resurrection of the dead. The body is sown in corruption, it is raised in incorruption. It is sown in dishonor, it is raised in glory. It is sown in weakness, it is raised in power. *It is sown a natural body, it is raised a spiritual body. There is a natural body, and there is a spiritual body.* And so it is written, 'The first man Adam became a living being.' The last Adam became a life-giving spirit. *However, the spiritual is not first, but the natural, and afterward the spiritual. The first man was of the earth, made of dust; the second Man is the Lord from heaven. As was the man of dust, so also are those who are made of dust; and as is the heavenly Man, so also are those who are heavenly.* And as we have borne the image of the man of dust, *we shall also bear the image of the heavenly Man.*" The Apostle Paul is imparting accurate knowledge contrasting the inferior and temporal material world with the superior and eternal spiritual realms. Humans go from a corruptible material body to an indestructible ethereal body following death. The kernel of this immortal spirit lies in each human being. It is sometimes referred to as an "oversoul" or "higher self." If one desires to pass through this veil while yet alive in the flesh, he or she must rid themselves of all material concerns. Thus they will be able to successfully transition to a spiritual realm through conscious unification with their higher self, thereby attaining some degree of Christ consciousness.

229 *Santa Fe Ghost and History Tours*
230 *Ibid.*
231 *Ibid.*
232 *H. G. Wells' War of the Worlds* (Paramount Pictures, 1953): George Pal, Producer; Bob Haskin, Director; Starring Gene Barry and Ann Robinson.

and the *Day the Earth Stood Still*.[233] These films also facilitated the branching of ufology into two camps, with the *War of the Worlds* representing the "nuts and bolts" crowd and the *Day the Earth Stood Still* indicative of the more spiritual adherents of the contactee movement.

It is generally conceded that the book upon which the movie *War of the Worlds* was based, written by the Fabian socialist H. G. Wells, was, in truth, a commentary against imperialism. First published in 1898, at the height of the Victorian age and British global expansion, it gave Her Majesty's subjects pause to think over the path the Empire was taking. In Wells' own words from the first chapter of the book. "Eve of the War," we find the following statement:

"And before we judge them [the Martians] too harshly, we must remember what ruthless and utter destruction our own species has wrought, not only upon animals, such as the vanished Bison and the Dodo, but upon its own inferior races. The Tasmanians, in spite of their human likeness, were entirely swept out of existence in a war of extermination waged by European immigrants, in the space of fifty years. Are we such apostles of mercy as to complain if the Martians warred in the same spirit?"[234]

Until Wells' invasion novel, British subjects could not conceive of any foreign race conquering their precious island homeland. The British also took pride in their sophisticated technology, for it aided them in carrying out the "White Man's Burden" of spreading the blessings of Anglo-Saxon "civilization" to all of the so-called "inferior" colored races that peopled the planet.[235] After all, they reasoned, it was for their own but ultimate good. But Wells' *War of the Worlds* neatly turns the table on the haughty imperialists, for the Martian invaders he conceives are so vastly superior to the British in weapons technology that they easily conquer the very heart of the Empire in quick time. In writing this fantastic story, Wells turns his readers' heads to reconsider the very nature of imperialism itself.[236]

Another science fiction theme incorporated into the *War of the Worlds* is a warning for the future of humankind against overvaluing intelligence against more human qualities. Wells describes the Martians as having evolved overdeveloped brains. And while this species possesses increased intelligence, they are totally lacking in emotion. Wells, through the voice of the Narrator, refers to an 1893 publication suggesting that the evolution of the human brain might outstrip the development of the body. For the Martians, organs such as the stomach, nose, teeth and hair had withered away over time. If this same scenario were to occur in human evolution, it would leave us as thinking machines, but totally dependent upon drastically augmented technology just to continue to interact with the environment.[237]

On the other end of the spectrum, we turn our attention to the *Day the Earth Stood Still*, a film that epitomizes the alien envoy or enlightened alien scenario. This movie was based on a short story by Harry Bates[238] and envisions the arrival of a wise visitor from another planet

233 *Day the Earth Stood Still* (Twentieth Century Fox, 1951): Julian Blaustein, Producer; Robert Wise, Director; Starring Michael Rennie and Patricia Neal. Note: Patricia Neal co-starred with Helmut Dantine in what some consider a sequel to *Day the Earth Stood Still*, titled *Stranger from Venus* (Lobby Card Princess Pictures, United Kingdom, 1954): Burt Balaban, Gene Martel and Roy Rich, Producers; Burt Balaban, Director. The movie was based on a story provided by Desmond Leslie, who co-authored *Flying Saucers Have Landed* (1952) with George Adamski, and written by Hans Jacoby. Movie description: "Tonight, first contact will be made!- A beautifully-crafted tale of a superior being from Venus who has the power of life and death at his touch;" *IMDb* review, http://www.imdb.com/title/tt0047529/ (Accessed 2 June 2014).

234 Herbert George Wells, *War of the Worlds* (London, UK: William Heinemann, 1898), 2.

235 Rudyard Kipling, "White Man's Burden," poem in *McClure's Magazine* 12, New York, New York, February 1899.

236 George Zebrowski, "Fear of the Worlds," in Glenn Yeffeth. *War of the Worlds: fresh perspectives on the H.G. Wells classic/ edited by Glenn Yeffeth* (Dallas, Texas: BenBalla, 2005), 235–41.

237 H. G. Wells, "Man of the Year Million," *Pall Mall Gazette*, London, UK, 6 November 1893: Wells' novel may be alluding to this article that he himself had written.

238 Harry Bates, "Farewell to the Master, "*Astounding Science Fiction* (magazine), Dell Publishing, New York, New York,

The Martians launch an attack on the Earth in the George Pal production of *War of the Worlds* (1953). See http://filmes.film-cine.com/the_war_of_the_worlds-m4464.

by the name of Klaatu, outstandingly played by Michael Rennie. From the dialogue, it is insinuated that Klaatu comes from a nearby planet in our solar system, most likely Venus. The alien in this movie is not like the grotesque creatures found in *War of the Worlds*, but rather appears much as we do. Klaatu lands his flying saucer just a few blocks from the White House, steps out and announces that he is here on a mission of peace from the Federation of Planets. The storyline continues in a manner much reminiscent of the gospels of Christ, culminating with Klaatu's death, resurrection and ascension back into the heavens.

And just as with Christ, the authorities are unable to accept either this savior figure or his message. Nevertheless, while Klaatu escapes from an Army hospital and makes his way into Washington, D.C., he assumes the identity of a one "John Carpenter," whence he takes up residence in a boarding house where he finds that most of the common people living there are accepting and kind. Note the initials of his assumed identity- J. C. - yet another Christological allusion.

Also, the more time that Klaatu spends with humans, the more he begins to appreciate them. He finds a reason for hope in the best sentiments and aspirations of humankind when he takes his landlady's son to the Lincoln Memorial and reads aloud the words of the Gettysburg Address inscribed on the wall there. And he is impressed with the scientific humanism made manifest to him in the Albert Einstein-like astrophysicist he decides to confide in, Professor Jacob Barnhardt.

In order to understand the historical significance of both *War of the Worlds* and the *Day the Earth Stood Still*, it becomes necessary to frame them in both a political and religious context. A review of the film in the *Decent Films Guide* does this nicely:

"...War of the Worlds is widely described as a Cold War paranoia fable, thus a 'conservative' movie, while the Day the Earth Stood Still is often interpreted as a critique of Cold War paranoia and a plea for global unity (specifically on behalf of the United Nations), and thus a 'liberal' film. On a religious level, War of the Worlds expressly credits divine providence rather than military preparedness for human survival, while the Day the Earth Stood Still holds mankind answerable to a higher power for its barbarism and cupidity. Each of the two films explores and develops a basic existential insight: that we are privileged people in a world of darkness, unable to sustain ourselves, dependent on a higher benevolence; that we are a lawless and wayward people, weighed in the balance of a larger moral order and found wanting."[239]

As with the American body politic, the divergence of opinion concerning these two films and their respective outlooks also split the UFO community right down the middle. The "conservative" wing, represented by retired Marine Corps aviator, Major Donald E. Keyhoe, believed that UFOs were physical, extraterrestrial craft, but asserted that the contactees' claims

---

October 1940.

239   Steven D. Greydanus (film critic for *National Catholic Register*) in *Decent Films Guide*, "Day the Earth Stood Still (1951)," movie review, 2010, http://decentfilms.com/reviews/daytheearthstoodstill1951 (Accessed 29 May 2014).

Patricia Neal and Michael Rennie starred in the *Day the Earth Stood Still* (1951). See http://www.imdb.com/title/tt0043456/.

were all fraudulent.[240]

Donald E. Keyhoe was born in Iowa on 20 June 1897. He graduated with a Bachelor of Science degree from the Annapolis Naval Academy, Class of 1920, and piloting both balloons and airplanes in the period between the World Wars. After a night crash at Guam, however, he retired from active duty with the rank of major and began a career in freelance writing. Throughout the 1930s and early 1940s, Keyhoe wrote fictional aviation adventure stories for various pulp magazines, in addition to factual articles for major newsstand magazines such as the *American, Cosmopolitan, Redbook,* the *Saturday Evening Post* and *True.* And then during the late 1940s and early 1950s, Keyhoe personally test-flew a wide variety of aircraft, evaluating their features and performance for a series of articles in *True* magazine.[241]

When the first "flying saucers" were reported by the civilian pilot Kenneth Arnold as soaring over Mt. Rainier in Washington State in June of 1947, Keyhoe, as an experienced aviator was skeptical. But when *True* asked him to investigate the numerous UFO sightings that plagued the entire country in 1949, Keyhoe interviewed many fliers as well as military officers in the Pentagon, whence he discovered that expert observers had seen the real metal discs, some at close range. His first article on the subject, "Flying Saucers Are Real," in the January 1950 issue of *True,* caused quite a national sensation, becoming one of the most widely read and discussed articles in publishing history. The popularity of the UFO articles in *True* allowed Keyhoe to expand them into a paperback book that also met with tremendous success.[242] In January 1957, Keyhoe became Director of the newly formed National Investigations Committee on Aerial Phenomena (NICAP), with headquarters in Washington, D.C. With his Marine Corps background, Keyhoe provided the needed leadership for the new UFO organization that encouraged a "serious study" of the UFO evidence and pressed the members of Congress to hold hearings on the subject.[243]

Keyhoe was clearly of the opinion that UFOs presented a threat to humankind, not a boon to the advancement of our species' cosmic evolution, as the contactees professed. He believed that the extraterrestrials were conducting a reconnaissance of our planet, biding their time and preparing for an invasion. Keyhoe's second book, *Flying Saucers from Outer Space,*[244] was even mentioned in the screen credits as being the inspiration for Columbia Picture's epic 1956 science fiction film, *Earth vs. the Flying Saucers.*[245] Keyhoe's vivid descriptions of the mysterious objects, culled from UFO reports on file with NICAP and Air Force investigations, were used to give a realistic background to the fictional movie. Of particular note are Keyhoe's

---

240 Thompson, 31

241 "Donald E. Keyhoe: Brief Biography from NICAP," *UFO Evidence,* http://www.ufoevidence.org/researchers/detail3.htm (Accessed 29 May 2014)

242 Donald E. Keyhoe, *Flying Saucers Are Real* (New York, New York: Fawcett Publications, 1950)

243 "Donald E. Keyhoe: Brief Biography from NICAP"

244 Donald E. Keyhoe, *Flying Saucers from Outer Space* (New York, New York: Holt, 1953).

245 *Earth Versus the Flying Saucers* (Columbia Pictures, 1956): Sam Katzman and Charles Schneer, Producers; Fred F. Sears, Director; Starring Michael Hugh Marlowe and Joan Taylor. Note: Marlowe also played the role of the Judas, Tom Stevens, to Rennie's Christ-like Klaatu in *Day the Earth Stood Still.*

descriptions of UFOs with a stationary central cabin and rotating slotted outer disc. Recorded sightings of such UFOs facilitated the design of the deadly saucers in the movie.

But Keyhoe, for his part, met with limited success in debunking the contactees. In the public's eye, it made no sense that aliens in their ships could traverse the vast distances of space to arrive on our world, yet never land their craft, get out and communicate with the local inhabitants. Additionally, all of the contactees, as well as Keyhoe and his NICAP organization, were claiming that the United States government, and in particular the newly created Air Force, were hiding the truth about UFOs from the American people in a massive cover-up operation for which Project Bluebook was just a front. While the UFO community could make the clear distinction between the "nuts and bolts" ufologists, as they came to be called, and the contactees, the public could not. The reason for this was that, "in the public mind, at least, there were parallels between the extreme claims of government conspiracy put forward by Keyhoe's UFO research group,…., and the extreme behavior of groups such as George Van Tassel's Giant Rock Spacecraft Convention, an annual southern California gathering where the faithful gathered to hear interplanetary gospel…."[246]

The "Doomsday Clock"

Keyhoe's books inspired the design of the saucer in *Earth Versus the Flying Saucers* (1956). See http://www.smithsonianmag.com/ist/?next=/smithsonian-institution/earth-vs-the-flying-saucers-the-hirshhorn-23999283/.

The contactees, like the atomic scientists, were prophetic in their warnings of the dangers inherent in nuclear proliferation from the very start of the Atomic Age. The atomic scientists were concerned that the Earth itself would no longer sustain any forms of life, let alone human, following an all-out nuclear war between the Union of Soviet Socialist Republics and the United States. The contactees also echoed these sentiments, and added that the Space Brothers were working behind the scenes throughout the world, doing all they could to push back the hands of the Doomsday Clock.

The Doomsday Clock is internationally recognized by concerned individuals everywhere. The position of the clock's hands in proximity to midnight denotes just how close some of the leaders of the world's scientific community believe that the human race has come in approaching the destruction of civilization on Earth. Here the scientists are in agreement with the contactees, for the first and foremost danger sign that can advance the clock is the proliferation of nuclear weapons. As of 2007,[247] however, the scientists on the editorial board of the *Bulletin* also decided that the setting of the Doomsday Clock should reflect climate changes and new developments in the life sciences and cyber-technology that could inflict irrevocable harm to humanity.[248] The clock was most

246 Thompson, 31-32
247 Dawn Stover, "How many Hiroshimas does it take to describe climate change?," *Bulletin of the Atomic Scientists*, Chicago, Illinois, 26 September 2013.
248 Even as I am writing this, I notice two articles in the morning newspaper, *Dominion Post*, Morgantown, West Virginia, 30 May 2014: "Study: Species extinct faster than before" and the "Rise of the Supercomputers: Era of co-evolution with machines will be the reality soon." The first article states that, "Species of plants and animals are becoming

recently reset to five minutes to midnight on 14 January 2014.[249]

That the contactees came forth in the late 1940s and early 1950s is symptomatic of the events taking place in Cold War America. In 1949, for example, the Doomsday Clock was set at only three minutes to midnight. In the fall of that year, President Harry S. Truman informed the American public that the Soviets tested their first nuclear device, thereby officially starting the arms race. The atomic scientists at the *Bulletin* advised, "We do not advise Americans that doomsday is near and that they can expect atomic bombs to start falling on their heads a month or year from now, but we think they have reason to be deeply alarmed and to be prepared for grave decisions."[250] Of course, the Soviets denied everything.

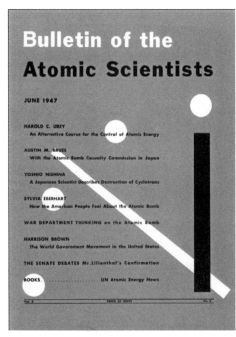

Since June of 1947, the Science and Security Board of the *Bulletin of the Atomic Scientists* has maintained the Doomsday Clock on a wall of its editorial office on the campus of the University of Chicago. See http://restraint.org/design/3192/badass-of-the-month-martyl-and-the-doomsday-clock/.

And the situation did not get any better by 1953, when the *Bulletin* staff moved the clock to an unprecedented two minutes before midnight. After much debate, the United States decided to dedicate its scientific resources to the creation of the hydrogen bomb, a weapon far more powerful than any mere atomic bomb. In October 1952, the United States tested its first thermonuclear device on a small atoll in the Pacific Ocean, totally obliterating it.[251]

Naturally, the Soviet Union could not let this stand; and in just nine months they had tested an H-bomb of their own design. Now "the hands of the Clock of Doom have moved again," the *Bulletin* announced, adding that "only a few more swings of the pendulum and, from Moscow to Chicago, atomic explosions will strike midnight for Western civilization."[252] To the contactees, this was a sure sign of the paramount importance of their mission. Putting aside any differences they may have had in the past, they came together at the Giant Rock Airport near Landers in Southern California on 1 March 1954 for what would be the first of many important "Spacecraft Conventions."

---

extinct at least ten times faster than they did before humans arrived on the scene" and that this did not bode well for the future of humankind. The article attributes this species loss to global climate change. The second article deals with the implanting of *neuromorphic* chip technology into human beings, augmenting a co-dependency on machines. This implantation will facilitate computer and mechanical interface with the human nervous system. But the author, Peter Goldmark, notes that the day may soon arrive when the machines will no longer "need us to design, update and maintain them" since gradually supercomputers and super-robots can assume this responsibility. But as humans become outmoded technology, who, or should I say what, will see fit to redesign, update and maintain us?

249 Stephanie Pappas, "Doomsday Clock Set at Five to Midnight," Live Science, Tech Media Network, 15 January 2014, http://www.foxnews.com/science/2014/01/15/doomsday-clock-set-at-5-til-midnight/ (Accessed 31 May 2014).

250 "Timeline," referring to the 1949 Cold War situation when the Doomsday Clock was reset at three minutes to midnight, in *Bulletin of the Atomic Scientists* website, http://thebulletin.org/timeline (Accessed 31 May 2014).

251 *Ibid*: continuing to clock reset in 1953 and attendant events.

252 *Ibid.*

Gatherings at Giant Rock

To UFO enthusiasts and the spiritually inclined throughout the world, Giant Rock holds great significance. To begin with, it was the home and workplace of the mysterious George Van Tassel, simply known as "Van" to his friends. Van Tassel, like Adamski, claims to have made contact with extraterrestrials in the 1950s and to have been tutored by them on a variety of subjects. These extraterrestrials also gave him instructions on how to build a structure known as the "Integratron," which could assist in the process of human cellular rejuvenation as well as well as accomplish many other important functions necessary for the survival of humankind on this planet, such as *time travel*.[253]

Van Tassel, a young pilot and engineer from Ohio, moved to Southern California in 1930 where he lived with an uncle who owned an automobile repair shop. One day while working in his uncle's garage, he met Frank Critzer, a down-and-out prospector who needed to have his car repaired. Van Tassle found the prospector to be an amiable and engaging gentleman, and the two soon became close friends. Because of Critzer's financial difficulties, Van Tassel fixed his car for free. Critzer was even allowed to sleep in the garage while Van Tassel made the necessary repairs to his vehicle. Van Tassel felt that he should do something more for Critzer, and so he gave him a trunk full of canned goods along with $30, which was a substantial amount of money back then in the first year of the Great Depression. In return for Van Tassel's kindness, Critzer promised to include Van and the uncle in any mining claims he might stake out in the future.[254]

Sure enough, just one year later Critzer mailed a map to Van Tassel, showing him how to get to Giant Rock, a massive boulder surrounded by a dry lake bed sacred to the Native Americans. For uncounted centuries, the indigenous peoples of California called it the "Great Stone," which is the place where Critzer was living. Van Tassel followed Critzer's map and when he arrived at the destination, he was surprised to find that Critzer had dug under the massive boulder in order to carve out a dwelling place. Critzer fabricated an alcove within the cavity of the rock to set up house. The rooms that Critzer went on to dig out under the rock were no more than a total of 400 sq. ft. The rock itself stands seven stories high and weighs slightly over 100,000 tons.[255]

By all accounts, Critzer was a squatter insofar as he was living on government land. Nevertheless, the idea of carving out a cave under the rock was a good one. Kathy Doore, a researcher of Giant Rock history, notes that,

This is the structure housing George Van Tassel's "Integratron" at Landers, California. See http://www.labyrinthina.com/rock.htm.

"In the summer the maximum temperature under the Rock is 80 degrees F. In the winter, the temperature is a minimum of 50 degrees F. In contrast, the temperature outside the cave swings

253 Kathy Doore, "George Van Tassel's Amazing Integratron at Giant Rock," *Labyrinthina, the Official Blog of Kathy Doore*, http://www.labyrinthina.com/rock.htm (Accessed 31 May 2014)
254 *Ibid.*
255 *Ibid.*

between 25 degrees F to 115 degrees F." To improve the property, Critzer made an airstrip, and five straight roads leading up to Giant Rock. This inspired the locals in nearby Landers to affectionately call him "Straight Road Critzer." He died in August 1942 in an unfortunate altercation with the police, standing his ground rather than vacate his home.[256]

In the years that followed, however, Van Tassel went on to acquire employment as an aeronautical engineer, flight inspector and test pilot. (The pilot's license he acquired as a teenager in Ohio was still valid.) He also worked for Douglas Aircraft throughout the 1930s and alongside Howard Hughes in the 1940s with Hughes Aviation, where he was Hughes' personal flight inspector for testing experimental aircraft. All though this time, Van Tassel continued to visit Giant Rock, taking his wife with him there on short vacations. He felt such an attraction to this rock that in 1945, he made an application to the Bureau of Land Management to lease the property. Knowing how slow it sometimes takes a bureaucracy to work, in two years this request was approved; whence he quit his job at Lockheed Aviation and moved his wife and three daughters to the Mojave Desert near Landers, occupying the four square miles of land surrounding Giant Rock that the government had allowed him to develop as an airport.

This is an artist's conception of typical Venusian scout ship, modeled after descriptions provided by Adamski and other contactees. See http:// projectswordtoys.blogspot.com/2011_04_01_ archive.html.

The area was covered with decomposed granite, thus making it an ideal site for such an endeavor. Before the year was out, Van Tassel opened the Giant Rock Airport and Café, which remained in operation until 1975. Howard Hughes himself was noted to be a frequent guest who flew in just for the delicious pies that were the specialty of Van Tassel's wife at the café.[257]

Van Tassel believed that the rock's crystalline structure possessed the piezo-electric characteristics necessary to augment human thought waves into signals strong enough to traverse the distances of outer space. In 1953, he began a series of experiments to test this theory, conducting weekly meditations in the rooms under the boulder in the anticipation that this would lead to contact with extraterrestrial beings. He was not disappointed, for on 21 August 1953 a scout ship from Venus landed and a man wearing a jumpsuit stood at the foot of his sleeping bag, announcing, "I am Solganda; and I would be pleased to show you my craft." Van Tassel was then led to a hovering scout craft, similar to the saucer that carried Orthon in the Adamski encounter, after which he stepped into a "butter-colored" light emanating from the underside of Solganda's transport. The Venusian then escorted Van Tassel on a tour of the ship and told that him that he had been chosen to bring a message of peace and interplanetary brotherhood to all of the inhabitants of Earth. Solganda also explained the principles of cell rejuvenation, whereby the human cell structure is exposed to powerful *negative ionization fields*.[258] This revelation formed the basis by which

---

256 *Ibid.*
257 *Ibid.*
258 National Institutes of Health, abstract for article, T. Ryushi, I. Kita, et al., "Effect of exposure to negative air ions on the recovery of physiological responses after moderate endurance exercise," *International Journal of Biometeorology*, February 1998; 41(3): 132-136. See http://www.ncbi.nlm. nih.gov/pubmed/9531858 (Accessed 31 May 2014). Abstract reads as follows: "This study examined the effects of negative air ion exposure on the human cardiovascular and endocrine systems during rest

Van Tassel would later go on to develop the Integratron device. Unfortunately, Van Tassel died before he could complete the structure; but what was left behind continues to focus and amplify powerful geomagnetic forces running through its unique location, i.e. it was built over a large underground aquifer. Its all-wood construction also facilitates the set up of a resonant sound field.[259]

Following Van Tassel's contact with the Venusian, he went on to meet other extraterrestrial and ultra-dimensional beings and wrote several books about his encounters with them.[260] Like Adamski, Van Tassel learned that "all planets are inhabited." Much as NASA (acronym: <u>N</u>ever <u>A</u> <u>S</u>traight <u>A</u>nswer) scientists would like to think- and have us believe- that there are nothing but lifeless rocks and balls of fiery gases out there, the contactees affirm what Blavatsky and the Theosophists have been saying all along: That all the omniverse is a habitable zone; and that everything in it is alive, emanations from a field of consciousness without beginning or end of days and having no limitations as far as either space or time itself is concerned. This is what Jesus, the Christ, referred to as the realm of *Barbelo* and the Gnostics as the *Pleroma*.

This photo of Giant Rock near Landers, California, aptly demonstrates its immensity. It has long served as one of the "special centers" around the world where, historically, people have been drawn to it for spiritual energy. Strange electromagnetic forces have created a vortex near the rock that has drawn scientists, UFO specialists and countless tourists to this remote location. See http://www.lucernevalley.net/giantrock/.

The First Spacecraft Convention

In the contemporary world, UFO conventions are fairly common and well-attended events, taking place in cities of varied sizes around the world at almost any given moment. But in the early

---

and during the recovery period following moderate endurance exercise. Ten healthy adult men were studied in the presence (8,000-10,000 cm-3) or absence (200-400 cm-3) of negative air ions (25 degrees C, 50% humidity) after 1 h of exercise. The level of exercise was adjusted to represent a 50-60% load compared with the subjects' maximal oxygen uptake, which was determined using a bicycle ergometer in an unmodified environment (22-23 degrees C, 30-35% humidity, 200-400 negative air ions.cm-3). The diastolic blood pressure (DBP) values during the recovery period were significantly lower in the presence of negative ions than in their absence. The plasma levels of serotonin (5-HT) and dopamine (DA) were significantly lower in the presence of negative ions than in their absence. These results demonstrated that exposure to negative air ions produced a slow recovery of DBP and decreases in the levels of 5-HT and DA in the recovery period after moderate endurance exercise. 5-HT is thought to have contributed to the slow recovery of DBP." Additionally, UFO researcher Brad Steiger notes that extraterrestrials, their hybrid star children and any extraterrestrial or ultra-dimensional "walk-ins" on Earth, all share an "attraction to powerful things in nature, such as thunderstorms, lightning, waterfalls, and surf, with all of these significantly generating higher atmospheric negative ion counts. In the case of thunderstorms, the greatest amount of negative ionization occurs in the period as the storm is building up a charge, right before the rain starts to fall. See *Ashtar Command Crew*, http://www.ashtarcommandcrew.net/forum/topics/are-you-a-starseed-find-out-more-about-yourself?xg_source=activity#ixzz33KRIe99M (Accessed 31 May 2014).

259   Kathy Doore

260   George W. Van Tassel, *I Rode a Flying Saucer* (Los Angeles, California: New Age, 1952)

_____ *Into this World and Out Again* (Los Angeles, California: De Vouss, 1956)

_____ *Council of Seven Lights* (Los Angeles, California: De Vouss, 1958)

_____ *When Stars Look Down* (Los Angeles, California: Kruckeberg Press, 1976)

George Van Tassel (1910-1978), UFO contactee. See www.ancient-code.com.

to mid-1950s, they could definitely be described as a novel invention. On 4 April 1954, George Van Tassel held the first of what we would refer to in our time as a "UFO convention," but to the contactees and their largely California-based flock of that era was known as an "Interplanetary Spacecraft Convention;" it being convened at Van Tassel's own Giant Rock airport facility in the blistering heat of the Mojave Desert.[261] Despite its remote location, thousands of pilgrims would make their way to the rock to participate in annual Spacecraft Conventions for the next 23 years. Speakers at the conventions included the contactees, of course, with them being the main draw, but also international scientists from numerous fields of research and leaders from various religious backgrounds would ascend the dais. Booths were set up by various vendors that displayed hundreds of books on the extraterrestrials, their craft and most importantly their civilizations and what we have to learn from their cosmic evolution and our future on this planet, as well as in space.[262] Speakers at the first convention included contactees Orfeo Angelucci, who would go on to author the *Secret of the Saucers*;[263] Truman Bethurum, Daniel Fry and George Van Tassel; as well as investigative journalist Frank Scully,

who wrote one of the first UFO books dealing with crashed saucers in New Mexico;[264] and George Hunt Williamson, one of the witnesses to Adamski's Desert Center meeting with Orthon, who went on to write several books, one on UFOs[265] and two others on mysticism.[266] He was also an early proponent of the ancient astronaut theory long before Erich von Daniken and his *Chariots of the Gods* arrived on the scene.[267]

The common thread in all the presentations made that day, however, was the escalating arms race between the Americans and the Soviets. In order to understand the motives

This comic humorously depicts Van Tassel's first encounter with the Venusian saucer pilot Solganda. The cartoonist misspelled the pilot's name as "Solgonda." See www.comicjuanochoa.co.

261 Jerome Clark, *Alien Worlds: Social and Religious Dimensions of Extraterrestrial Contact* (Syracuse, New York: Syracuse University Press, 2007), 27.

262 Kathy Doore

263 Orfeo M. Angelucci, *Secret of the Saucers* (Amherst, Wisconsin: Amherst Press, 1955)

264 Frank Scully, *Behind the Flying Saucers* (New York: Holt, 1950)

265 Alfred C. Bailey and George Hunt Williamson, *Saucers Speak* (Los Angeles, California: New Age, 1954)

266 George Hunt Williamson, *Other Tongues, Other Flesh* (Amherst, Wisconsin: Amherst Press, 1953); and *Secret Places of the Lion: Alien Influences on Earth's History* (London, UK: Futura Publications, 1958): The last-cited book provides Williamson's views on the rise of Mormonism as a modern-day religion and the historical significance of its founding prophets, Joseph Smith and Brigham Young.

267 Eric von Däniken, *Chariots of the Gods* (New York, New York: G. P. Putnam's Sons, 1968).

of the contactees and their followers, it is important to place the agenda of the Spacecraft Convention in its proper historical perspective. Van Tassel did just that in reiterating the concerns of the Venusian hierarchy. As the host of the convention, Van Tassel opened the proceedings by quoting a revelation that he received less than two years ago, on 18 July 1952, from a being calling himself "Ashtar," a Venusian space station commander patrolling that sector of space between his planet and Mars, with a focus on Earth, or "Shan," as our planet is known by the inhabitants of Venus.[268] Through a "cone of receptivity," here is the telepathic communication that passed through Van Tassel's mind and was later relayed to the conventioneers:

"Hail to you beings of Shan, I greet you in love and peace, my identity is Ashtar, commandant, Quadra Sector, patrol station Schare, all projections, all waves. Greetings, through the Council of Seven Lights; you have been brought here inspired with the inner light to help your

Dana Howard was one of the lesser known contactees in the United States in the 1950s. In this photo she is seen at the first Giant Rock Spacecraft Convention in 1954, selling some self-published booklets in which she claimed that she flew to Venus on several occasions, sometimes in a physical craft and other times psychically. Howard claimed that she eventually married a Venusian and raised a family on Venus; and that at such a time when Earthlings achieve a "higher spiritual level," they will all be able to migrate to Venus as well. She first began encountering Venusians in 1939 near her home in California. Interestingly, she was a long time member of the Theosophical Society long before her first contact. In her estimation, the spiritual teachings of the Venusians paralleled those of Blavatsky. Who knows, maybe Blavatsky was one of them. See http://ufologie.patrickgross.org/ce3/1939-06-usa-california.htm

fellow man. You are mortals and other mortals can only understand that which their fellow man can understand. The purpose of this organization is, in a sense, to save mankind from itself. Some years ago, *in your time*, your nuclear physicists penetrated the "Book of Knowledge;" they discovered how to explode the atom.

Disgusting as the results have been, that this force should be used for destruction, it is not compared to that which can be. We have not been concerned with their explosion of plutonium and UR 235, the Uranium mother element; this atom is an inert element. We are concerned, however, with their attempt to explode the hydrogen element. This element is life giving along with five other elements in the air you breathe, in the water you drink, in the composition of your physical substance, hydrogen. Their efforts in the field of science have been successful to the extent that they are not content to rest on the laurels of a power beyond their use, *not content with the entire destruction of an entire deity at a time.* They must have something more destructive, they've got it.

When they explode the hydrogen atom, they shall extinguish life on this planet. They are

---

268 Kathy Doore

tinkering with a formula they do not comprehend. They are destroying a life giving element of the Creative Intelligence. Our message to you is this: you shall advance to your government all information we have transmitted to you. You shall request that your government shall immediately contact all other earth nations regardless of political feelings. Many of your physicists, with an inner perception development have refused to have anything to do with the explosion of the hydrogen atom. The explosion of an atom of inert substances and that of a living substance are two different things. We are not concerned with their deliberate determination to extinguish humanity and turn this planet into a cinder. Your materialism will disagree with our attempt to warn mankind. Rest assured, they shall cease to explode life giving atoms, or we shall eliminate all projects connected with such. Our missions are peaceful, but this condition occurred before in this solar system and the planet, *Lucifer*, was torn to bits."[269] We are determined that it shall not happen again.

"The governments on the planet Shan have conceded that we are of a higher intelligence, they must concede also that we are of a higher authority. It is so not necessary to have to enter their buildings to know what they are doing. We have the formula they would like to use. It is not meant for destruction. Your purpose here has been to build a receptivity that we could communicate with your planet, for by the attraction of light substances-atoms, we patrol your universe. To your government and to your people and through them to all governments and all people on the planet of Shan, accept the warning as a blessing that mankind may survive. My light, we shall remain in touch here at this cone of receptivity. My love, I am Ashtar."[270]

UFOs as Archetypes of the Apocalypse

Carl Gustav Jung, the famous Swiss psychiatrist and psychoanalist, was paying close attention to the activities of the contactees and ufology in general. He asked his family and friends to save all of the information they could gather on UFO sightings and encounters,[271] as he planned to write a book on the psychic and spiritual significance of the flying saucer phenomenon, which he ultimately accomplished at the age of 83.[272] Of course, this was indicative of his intuitive nature, especially when it comes to sensing shifts in the collective consciousness long before outer changes made these shifts obvious to others. Being in his later years, Jung began to focus his energies and research into a study of cosmic archetypes, to include those of the apocalypse and the sudden spurt of UFO activity of all types since the dawn of the atomic age.

The first of these shifts that Jung noted was the approach of the end time, at least as we know it, and the activation of what he called the "archetype of the apocalypse." Even as the conventioneers were gathering at Big Rock, Jung was in tune with the *zeitgeist*, or "spirit

---

269 Ashtar may be alluding here to a distant time in Venus' own history. Blavatsky noted that a war in outer space was fought over control of the planet Venus (*Lucifer*), where Michael and his forces prevailed. Adamski also pointed out the great devastation he saw throughout the solar system, and attributed this to the Biblical "war in the heavens" (*Revelation* 12:7, KJV). This theme was placed in a more contemporary and scientific context in the East German-Polish produced science fiction movie, *First Spaceship on Venus* (1960), where the only Venusians who survived a thermonuclear interplanetary war were those who had built vast cities underground and downloaded their intelligence into small machines that looked like floating ping-pong balls sprouting antenna arrays. Scientists on a politically united Earth discover an ancient but small metallic disc near a meteor crash site in Siberia that contains an audio recording from Venus, a planet from which no life had previously been detected, and dispatch a mission to search for the source of the message.
270 Kathy Doore
271 Deidre Bair, *Jung: A Biography* (New York, New York: Little, Brown and Company, 2003), 568-569, 830.
272 Carl G. Jung, *Flying Saucers: A Modern Myth of Things Seen in the Sky* (Brooklyn, New York: Harcourt, Brace, 1959). This book was based on his previous writings regarding the subject of UFOs.

of the age," and realized that this long prophesized "end time" was drawing near. Jung deeply felt that it was important for people to know about this archetype as he recognized the power inherent in each individual to change the future. He knew that if enough people become aware of the impending apocalypse as an archetype, then they could understand its intentions and internalize its meaning in their own lives, and *perhaps alter the fate of the world by moving the planetary consciousness in a more positive direction.*[273] Clearly the contactees and their followers were in tune with this same *zeitgeist.*

Because UFOs were seen in many different places around the world, in widely different cultures, by different types of people, and by both genders, young and old, Jung believed that there were both physical and psychic realities manifest in the phenomenon. Coupled with the messages of universal peace emanating from the contactees, most

First Spaceship on Venus (1961): Director: Kurt Maetzig; Producers: Hans Mahlich and Edward Zajicek for Deutsche Film (DEFA of East Germany) and Zespol Filmowy "Iluzjon" of Poland, respectively. The film is based on the novel, the *Astronauts* (1951) by Stanislav Lem. Starring in the feature is Yoko Tani as the alluring but mysterious Doctor Omigura (left) and Oldrich Lukes as Professor Hawling (right). In this scene Doctor Omigura is giving her old friend Professor Hawling a pre-flight physical before blasting off for an unparalleled experience above and below the surface of war-torn Venus. See http://capricornio-uno.blogspot.com/2010/03/first-spaceship-on-venus-1960-vose-der.html.

people sincerely wished that there were such concerned and exalted beings inhabiting other planets and visiting the Earth in their flying saucers. As a trained psychologist, Jung found it very interesting that a shared response to similar occurring UFO events that transcended cultures and personal differences bespoke of some sort of "eruption" from the collective unconscious.[274]

Jung was not using the term "eruption" in any sense that would reflect negatively upon the sanity of the UFO observers or even the contactees. An explanation of this term is provided in a Jungian website:

"By 'eruption' Jung meant 'projection.' Projection—the 'expulsion of a subjective content into an object' —or seeing outside oneself something that actually lies within—is how Jung interpreted the UFO phenomenon. The "something" here could be our 'collective but unacknowledged fear of death,' an unconscious desire for salvation or deliverance from the anxieties of outer reality, an unrecognized capacity for wholeness, or one's individuation. The round, oval or cylindrical shapes of the UFOs, mentioned earlier, would be perfect carriers of such projections."[275]

273 Susan Mehrtens, "Jung and the Archetype of the Apocalypse," blog of, posted 17 April 2013, *Jungian Center for the Spiritual Sciences*, http://jungiancenter.org/essay/jung-and-archetype-apocalypse (Accessed 2 June 2014)
274 Carl G. Jung, "Civilization in Transition," Collected Works, Volume 10, (Princeton, New Jersey: Princeton University Press), 609.
275 Susan Mehrtens, "Signs in the Skies: A Jungian Perspective on UFOs," blog of, posted 17 April 2013, *Jungian Center for the Spiritual Sciences*, http://jungiancenter.org/essay/signs-skies-jungian-perspective-ufos (Accessed 2 June 2014)

To be sure, the average UFO observer or contactee would deny that he or she was doing any kind of "projecting." But the very nature of projection is involuntary and unconscious. In other words, projection can be viewed as more of a spontaneous answer of the unconscious to the present conscious situation. Therefore, in consideration of the tendency of the psyche to strive for balance, such projections would be compensatory, i.e. they would try to balance the fears and anxieties people feel by offering an experience that was inspiring, uplifting and numinous.[276] And what better way to assuage a public in panic with the Doomsday Clock so near to the hour of Armageddon than to offer them salvation brought to humankind aboard a flying saucer from Venus. In a prior age, those imparting such "revelations" would be considered as holy individuals, shamans of a high order, or even prophets of God.

In the words of Jung:

"In the threatening situation of the world today, when people are beginning to see that everything is at stake, the projection-creating fantasy soars beyond the realm of earthly organizations and powers into the heavens, into interstellar space, where the rulers of human fate, the gods, once had their abode in the planets."[277]

In terms of an archetypal symbol, Jung saw UFOs as "carriers of the gods," a phenomenon that had become an "impressive legend" and "living myth."[278] That Jung in no way depreciated the claims of the contactees is evident in the following analysis advanced by Dr. Susan Mehrtens, President of the Jungian Center for the Spiritual Sciences: "By 'myth' Jung did *not* mean 'a false story,' which is how our culture often defines 'myth.' To Jung myths were 'original revelations of the preconscious psyche,' and carriers of great depth and vital meaning. So he put great store in UFOs. They were a *very* important feature of our time, a feature that certainly had psychological reality."[279]

But to Jung's mind, did the flying saucers manifest a *physical* reality? To answer this question, Mehrtens notes that, "Perhaps because he recognized them as so important, this aspect of the UFO phenomenon bedeviled Jung, and he admitted that, because of the physical evidence—the photos and radar reports—UFOs could not be 'disposed of' simply as psychological artifacts."[280] Jung himself cites the case of the contactee Orfeo Angelucci, one of the speakers at the first Spacecraft Convention. While Jung feels that Angelucci was probably "naïve" in believing that his efforts to spread the word about the inspirational experience he had in his meeting with extraterrestrials in the California desert would actually affect immediate political change in Washington, he nevertheless applauds him for his attempts to try and make a difference in directing the public's consciousness toward the need to reassess America's nuclear buildup.[281] Nevertheless, the sage psychologist placed Angelucci's experience in the context of a projection.[282]

Said the professor for the Jungian Center with respect to Angelucci's encounters being viewed as a projection:

"OK. *Maybe it was, but does that mean it could not also have been something that*

---

276 *Ibid.*
277 Carl G. Jung, *Collected Works*, Volume 10, 610.
278 *Ibid*: "carriers of the gods," 622; "impressive legend," 625; "living myth," 614.
279 Susan Mehrtens
280 *Ibid.*
281 Carl G. Jung, *Collected Works*, Volume 10, 791-802 (his analysis of the Angelucci case)
282 *Ibid.*, 795

really happened to the man? It certainly transformed his life. Jung alludes to this fact in his reference to Angelucci experiencing the 'individuation process,' albeit in an unconscious way. Angelucci is not an isolated case. Reports of UFOs have grown in number in the decades since Jung's death in 1961, and *in many of these reports, the witnesses speak of how the experience was life-changing, in positive, spiritually-meaningful ways.* I think *the UFO phenomenon is offering all of us (even those who have not personally seen a UFO) the opportunity to expand our vision of reality and of what is possible.* It does not have to be a negative experience or cripple our imagination."[283]

Jung was reminding us of our need to understand what is going on in the world around us. He realized the crucial nature of the transitional time that the Cold War era represented, a period of time when it was possible for the superpowers of the United States and the Soviet Union to engage in

Flying Objects Real, Psychiatrist Insists

ALAMOGORDO, N. M., July 29 (UPI)—Dr. Carl Jung, the father of analytical psychology, said today that so-called unidentified flying objects "are not mere rumor" and the U. S. Air Force was "creating panic" by withholding information about them.

Jung's statements were printed in the monthly bulletin of the Aerial Phenomena Research Organization, UFO filter center. Jung serves as chief psychologist for the center.

"In the course of years, I gathered a considerable mass of observations," Jung wrote. "However, I can only say for certain these things are not mere rumor. Something has been seen.

"A purely sychological explanation is ruled out by the

DR. CARL JUNG
"... something has been seen"

Associated Press Photo

Dr. Carl Jung believed that some UFOs were real, physical objects, while others were projections of the unconscious mind.
See www.organizedreligion.me.

warfare at such a massive thermonuclear level that it would literally reduce our planet to a smoldering, radioactive cinder. Therefore, it became all the more important for individuals to seize the numerous opportunities available to them in that unique time, embracing what "healing effects" these may have offered in assisting them in the extension of their capacity to change and help us all to develop into an awareness of our true power and ability. Clearly then, the phenomenon offered hope to humankind on many levels. Mahrtens summed this up nicely:

"We can use the visions of UFOs as indications of inner realities so as to take back these projections we are putting 'out there,' in physical reality and in outer space, and integrate them into our 'inner space.' Jung knew we have both the ability and the need 'to reach a new physical as well as spiritual basis beyond our actual conscious world…,'but *we have to make the choice to do so.*"[284]

Mahrtens believes that humankind alone possesses the wisdom, capacity and power to remain free, become whole and achieve the individuation necessary to rescue our planet. She suggests that, "We need only to look in the mirror and do our inner work."[285] The possibility exists, however, that many of

Jung was obsessed with the case of California contactee Orfeo Angelucci.
See www.erenouvelle.fr.

283   Mehrtens
284   *Ibid.*
285   *Ibid.*

these UFO visions are not originating from the individual human subconscious mind, but are actually implanted there by intelligences foreign to this world, guiding humankind in their evolution of art, the emergence of new cultural norms, religious ideas, scientific theory and application, as well as societal thought and the new, corresponding institutions emplaced to administer our affairs.

The "Space Intelligences" (SIs)

Adamski, Van Tassel and other contactees purportedly maintained telepathic communications with the Venusians and other extraterrestrials. At the very least, they could predict when the flying saucers would appear overhead. Hence they would call for sky watches that permitted their followers to see firsthand the existence of alien spacecraft.

But what about actually seeing into the future? Or performing miracles? Could the Space Brothers provide such information and powers to those psychically attuned and adept here on Earth? There were many who claimed to channel revelations from the extraterrestrials; but perhaps the most remarkable contactee case on record, in this regard, is that of Ted Owens, sometimes known as the "PK Man," insofar as he manifested psychokinetic abilities, i.e. the ability to manipulate matter with the sheer force of his mind.

Ted Owens (1920-1987) maintained that he had established contacts with multi-dimensional, extremely advanced beings called Space Intelligences (SIs). As a young man, Owens suffered a series of head injuries. Despite these injuries, or perhaps because of them, Owens developed a very high intelligence quotient and became a member of Mensa. He also developed skills in several trades and began to manifest extraordinary talents. In adulthood, Owens claimed to have encountered a UFO, whose occupants initiated telepathic communications with him. Owens soon gathered a loyal contingent who wanted to know more about these multi-dimensional beings. The UFO prophet said that these aliens could best be described as Space Intelligences, as they were invisible beings of pure energy. Some of the beings did manifest a physical form, or what appeared to be a physical form, to him, and these he described as something akin to insects. Owens also believed that his head injuries facilitated effective two-way communications with the SIs, and may have been caused by them for just that very purpose. He recognized that the information and powers granted to him by the SIs were substantial and that very few in Earth's history had manifested such abilities. Like other contactees, he understood from the SIs that his mission was to warn of the dangers in nuclear testing and experimenting, and also of the need for the peoples of all nations to work together and take good care of the environment for future generations.

The following is only a small portion from a question and answer session conducted with Ted Owens:

Q. Have the SIs been among us on the earth?

A. Yes, *the SIs have been among us on the earth.*

Q. You say they like children... and they work with children... what kind of work are they doing?

A. If you were going to sow a crop, as a farmer, what would you take out in the fields to plant - half-grown corn cobs? Jay interjects: I would take what I wanted to grow.

A. Yes, you would take seeds. *Children are seeds. If the U.S. can survive for the next year or two, the children that have grown up by that time, and which the SIs have reached, will be important to the SIs, in their work with humans on earth.* Now, I'll give you a beautiful illustration of this. Yesterday afternoon I came home from work, fell into my chair, hot and tired, took off my shoes, and the downstairs door-buzzer buzzed. I put on my shoes and went downstairs, and there was a long-distance phone call for me from New Jersey.

It was a 13-year-old boy who had heard me over a local radio program in 1965, two years ago, and he had been trying to find me ever since. That boy was brilliant, absolutely brilliant. He asked me questions that were a lot better than any questions that have been asked of me on any of the many radio and TV interview programs I have been on. This boy said he had an old box full of UFO material in his home, everything he could lay his hands on which dealt with UFOs. He said that he and his mother and father had been in their car, driving on the New Jersey Turnpike one evening when suddenly they saw a flying saucer right over them. They pulled to the side of the road, and the UFO was 50 feet directly over them. Ever since that day he has been doing nothing but thinking about and studying about UFOs. Do you see what I mean about their working with children?

Q. So *they are making the children interested in them?*

A. *You bet they are! They are establishing a contact with them. But the problem is, they can contact the minds of children but the children cannot communicate back with the SIs. It is not a two-way proposition. That is where I come in. I have written a book, giving my exact method of communicating with the SIs. Complete. This is for the purpose of children being able to get in touch with the SIs.*

Q. Do the SIs have any influence on the "prophets" of our day?

A. Prophets? Yes, a great deal of influence. *Of course, you have to bear in mind that SIs monitor the thinking of our key people in high places, as well as other people in low places that we would not suspect they would be interested in - and they influence their thinking, certainly they do. They also influence the masses of people through television.*

Q. The "prophets" don't know of this, do they? I mean, they don't know their thinking is being influenced.

A. *That's right - they don't know it - they think their thoughts and predictions are their own; but in many cases they are simply reflecting what the SIs are putting into their minds.*

Q. Then the SIs are having the "prophets" do certain work?

A. Yes. You see, *the SIs are interested in the entire human race as a whole - not the black race, the white race, the yellow race, etc., as such. They aren't interested in our race problems, or our politics. They are interested only in making the surface of the world healthy and happy and productive, growing and creative. So they influence key people toward certain things, like chess pieces on a board, and these people do not realize they are being manipulated, but they are, according to the SIs' wishes - to bring about results among the masses of people.*

The SIs even bring about revolutions…. They are interested primarily in the healthy condition of the surface of the earth, and all that lives on that surface.

Q. Is it possible that we can ever reach the SIs' level of intelligence? You know, like being able to move things with our minds, and so forth.

A. Absolutely impossible. *They have different powers than we. They have different laws of nature. You see, the SIs are in a different world entirely. They are in another dimension. But they have discovered how to switch from their dimension into our dimension. Thus they have access both to their world and our world, while we are limited to our world.* So we could never do what the SIs can do.

Q. In other words, we are completely different, then, from the SIs.

A. Yes, completely different.

Q. Is there a wall between our dimension and their dimension? Couldn't we, some way, get into their dimension?

A. *We don't know how to do this, but they do know how. Just suppose, for a moment, we were SIs. We could make ourselves invisible, then appear right out in a field, or inside Cape Kennedy, or inside a crowded city - in the earth dimension. We would see these strange creatures (humans, us), yet the strange creatures (humans, us) couldn't see us (SIs) unless we wanted them to, at which time we could make ourselves visible, or in some form we wanted to made visible. But if we remained invisible then we could observe the earth creatures at their work and at their play.*

Q. You mean, then, that there could be a "SI or SIs right here, right now, watching us?

A. Absolutely. *Now suppose we, as SIs, switch ourselves into this other dimension, this earth dimension, to observe these earth creatures performing all sorts of actions - and we wish to experiment with these earth creatures, to get some results with them. We can do one of two things: we can go into the earth dimension, and work with the earth creatures, unbeknownst to them, or we can switch ourselves back into our own SI world, or dimension, we can cause ship wrecks and plane wrecks or submarine wrecks in the earth world, or dimension. In other words, we, as SIs while in the SI world, or dimension, can produce effects across other worlds or dimensions.*[286]

For the remainder of the interview, Owens describes how the SIs have protected him over the years from physical harm, some of the healings and other miracles he accomplished with the aid of the SIs, as well as some of the accurate predictions he has made with information channeled to his mind directly by the SIs, especially involving weather and climate change. But most significant, his remarks concerning the children and their importance to the SIs in carrying out their agenda here on Earth need to be carefully considered.

That the government itself was concerned about the impact that ufology was having on the young people of the turbulent 60s was evidenced in the final document of the University of Colorado scientists commissioned by the Air Force to investigate UFO reports across the United States from 1966 to 1968. It was chaired by University of Colorado astrophysicist, Dr. Edward U. Condon, and titled, *Scientific Study of Unidentified Flying Objects.*[287] While it could not explain some cases, the report concluded that the government should close Project Bluebook, the on-going Air Force UFO investigation headquartered at Wright-Patterson Air Force Base in Dayton, Ohio, established in March 1952, insofar as UFOs presented no discernible threat to national security. And this it did in December 1969, the year following the issuance of the Condon Committee report. The report concluded that most UFOs were misinterpretations of natural or astronomical phenomena, like viewing the planet Venus through a cloud inversion layer or watching balls of ionized swamp gas dance along power lines. Clearly, the Condon Committee had its own agenda with regard to debunking the entire UFO phenomenon, and it heartily recommended that the scientific community as well discontinue investigating UFO reports, as it was essentially a waste of time. In this same vein, Condon himself recommended that teachers refrain from giving credits to students doing reports on UFOs and related

---

286   Ted Owens with questions by Chuck Jay, "Questions and Answers," extracted from *How to Contact Space People* (Clarksburg, West Virginia: Saucerian Books, 1969), republished in *Jinn* website, http://www.thejinn.net/questions_and_answers.htm (Accessed 4 June 2014).

287   Edward U. Condon, chair, *Scientific Study of Unidentified Flying Objects* (Boulder, Colorado: Board of Regents, University of Colorado, 1968), 965 pages, including index, subsequently republished by Bantam Books, New York, 1969.

subjects and that they actively redirect the children's curiosity into other avenues of scientific investigation.

Concluded Condon:

"The subject of UFOs has been widely misrepresented to the public by a small number of individuals who have given sensationalized presentations in writings and public lectures. So far as we can judge, not many people have been misled by such irresponsible behavior, but whatever effect there has been has been bad.

A related problem to which we wish to direct public attention is the miseducation in our schools which arises from the fact that many children are being allowed, if not actively encouraged, to devote their science study time to the reading of UFO books and magazine articles of the type referred to in the preceding paragraph. We feel that children are educationally harmed by absorbing unsound and erroneous material as if it were scientifically well founded. Such study is harmful not merely because of the erroneous nature of the material itself, but also because such study retards the development of a critical faculty with regard to scientific evidence, which to some degree ought to be part of the education of every American.

Therefore *we strongly recommend that teachers refrain from giving students credit for school work based on their reading of the presently available UFO books and magazine articles.* Teachers who find their students strongly motivated in this direction should attempt to channel their interests in the direction of serious study of astronomy and meteorology, and in the direction of critical analysis of arguments for fantastic propositions that are being supported by appeals to fallacious reasoning or false data."[288]

Oddly enough, while Dr. J. Allen Hynek, an astronomy professor from Northwestern University and long-time consultant to the Air Force under three UFO projects: Sign, 1947-1949; Grudge, 1949-1952; and Bluebook, harshly criticized most of the findings of the Condon report with respect to the reality of the UFO phenomena, on a scientific basis,[289] he agreed with Condon's assessment regarding children and any possible involvement they may have with ufology.

Wrote Professor Hynek:

"There is, however, one area in which the reviewer is in accord with Dr. Condon, and that is in his recommendation that science credit not be given in elementary schools for term papers and projects on UFOs. School children are too lacking in critical faculties to be turned loose in UFO land. Present material available to them is apt to be pulp 'literature,' itself written sensationally and unscientifically, cases undocumented, with no attention whatever to analysis; a mere collection of sensational anecdotes."[290]

---

288 *Ibid.,* 8

289 J. Allen Hynek, *UFO Experience: A Scientific Inquiry* (Chicago, Illinois: Henry Regnery Company, 1972), 192-244. Hynek did not believe that the Condon Report had settled anything with respect to the UFO question. He criticized the report for its highly slanted approach and its inability to furnish satisfactory scientific explanations for at least a quarter of the reports it selected to investigate. Hynek did not believe that Condon properly understood the nature and scope of the UFO phenomenon; and he objected to the notion that only extraterrestrial life could explain genuine UFO activity. By focusing solely on trying to disprove the extraterrestrial hypothesis in his report, Condon and the other University of Colorado scientists overlooked any serious attempt to validate UFOs as a problem worthy for scientific inquiry, whether physical or social. The existence of UFO reports dating back from antiquity at least merited investigation on the basis of scientific reason.

290 _____,"Condon Report and UFOs," *Bulletin of the Atomic Scientists*, Volume XXV, Number 4, Chicago, Illinois, April

As noted in Owens' answers to Chuck Jay, the SIs managed to wield significant influence over the "prophets," or trend setters, in contemporary society, at least insofar as affecting our children's perceptions about life beyond the Earth. In fact, he specifically mentions the SIs' control of television during the 1960s, when new science fiction programs were constantly popping up each season, like *Lost in Space, Outer Limits, Star Trek*, etc.

Later on in the interview, Chuck Jay asked an additional question concerning the SIs and television, to which Owens replied that,

"...*the SIs influence the minds of masses of people through TV sets.* They can broadcast from their space ship, and it comes through your TV set into your mind, on a subliminal level, while you are watching *Gunsmoke*, for instance. Incidentally, *the SIs have told me that they gave us humans the idea of TV, just for this purpose, so that they could broadcast thoughts and ideas to humans through the TV sets.* "[291]

If Owens is correct, then it becomes imperative to examine the motivations of the SIs in manipulating media, especially those aimed at children. So far, the only possible rationale for the SI manipulation, that I can see, is the preparation of humankind for a future in space, culminating with extraterrestrial or multi-dimensional contact. George Hunt Williamson and other ufologists have claimed that various alien species have long exercised influence in the cosmic evolution of humankind, preparing us for just such a time. And Rampa foretold that we would have a glorious future beyond all imagination if we could somehow survive as a species until the year 3,000 C.E. In the television of the 1960s, for example, the *Outer Limits* presented an episode where a benign but inquisitive being from another dimension of time and space slid down a laser beam and ended up in the studio of a California radio station. For the first time, millions of young viewers considered the

Does the exposure of UFO literature, tales of close encounters, movies and television programs negatively impact the children? Or does it inspire them?
See www.manojspace.worldpress.com.

possibility that life did not necessarily have to exist "as we know it," and might even exist in realms we have never before conceived of. And in *Star Trek*, the premise offered by its creator Gene Rodenberry was that the Earth would enjoy a splendid future following its acceptance into the *United Federation of Planets*, a concept that certainly echoes much of the lore circulated in the contactee circles about what is really going on in outer space, with all of its "infinite diversity in infinite combinations."

1969, 42.
291 Ted Owens

As a species, however, the human race has always been wary about what its children are exposed to. In the previous decade, much of the same criticism that was directed against ufology in the 1960s was being aimed at the producers of comic books. In 1953, with an estimated 70 million copies of various comic book titles appearing every month, and being rapidly snapped up by millions of American youth, parents and government authorities began to express some concern over the content of these magazines.[292]

In 1954, Dr. Fredric Wertham, a Freudian-trained German psychiatrist and immigrant to the United States, published a book on the "unwholesome" influence that comic books were exerting on young people, titled *Seduction of the Innocent*.[293] Wertham supposedly based his book on the observations he made of juvenile delinquents while working on the staff at the Bellevue Mental Hygiene Clinic in conjunction with the New York Court of General Sessions. As far as superheroes went, the psychiatrist was particularly miffed at Superman, both in his comic books and television persona. Wrote Wertham:

"Actually Superman (with the big S on his uniform-we should, I suppose, be thankful that it is not an S.S.) needs an endless stream of ever new submen, criminals and 'foreign-looking' people not only to justify his existence but even to make it possible. Superman has long been recognized as a symbol of violent race superiority. The television Superman, looking like a mixture of an operatic tenor without his armor and an amateur athlete out of a health-magazine advertisement, does not only have 'superhuman powers,' but explicitly belongs to a "super-race.""[294]

Even Lex Luthor could not prove to be such a diabolical foe to Superman as the mad doctor Wertham. In his effort to smear the comic book industry, Wertham was later found guilty of manipulating, overstating, compromising, and fabricating evidence in support of the contentions expressed in *Seduction of the Innocent*.[295] In addition, he intentionally mis-projected both the sample size and substance of his research, thereby making it appear to be more objective and less anecdotal than it truly was.[296] And for the most part, he did not adhere to standards worthy of scientific research, opting to use questionable evidence as rhetorical ammunition for his argument that comics were a symptom of cultural failure.[297] Despite these underhanded measures, however, Wertham did succeed in pressuring the United States Senate in open hearings to push for the creation of a self-censoring body within the comic book industry. However, as a result of Wertham's testimony and as an alternative to government regulation, in 1954 the Comics Code Authority was formed by the Comics Magazine Association of America with the purpose of allowing the comic book publishers to self-regulate the content of their material.[298] The "Comics Code" that they created appeared as a logo on every comic book for sale in the United States well into the beginning of the twenty-first century.

With all of the pressures generated by this controversy, the sales of comic books took a drastic plunge. Daniels notes in *Superman: Complete History*, that even though the Comics Code was created,

---

292 Les Daniels, *Superman: Complete History* (San Francisco, California: Chronicle Books, 1998), 131.

293 Fredric Werthham, *Seduction of the Innocent: Influence of Comic Books on Today's Youth* (New York, New York: Rinehart and Company, 1954).

294 Daniels, 31: Quotes Wertham in regard to the persona of the Superman character.

295 Carol L. Tilley, "Seducing the Innocent: Fredric Wertham and the Falsifications that Helped Condemn Comics," *Information and Culture: A Journal of History* (2012), 47 (4), 383–413.

296 Jeet Heer, "Frederic Wertham and the Campaign against Comic Books," *Slate*, http://www.slate.com/articles/arts/culturebox/2008/04/the_caped_crusader.html (Accessed 4 June 2014)

297 Tilley, 403-405

298 "The Press: Horror on the Newsstands," *Time*, 27 September 1954.

"...the damage was already done. Distribution dried up, publishers went bankrupt, and by the time parental indignation was redirected toward rock 'n' roll a few months later, the comic book industry appeared to be on its last legs. "We were really suffering," said Julius Schwartz (at DC Comics). Still, DC was one of the few publishers still standing, and it fell to Schwartz to pump some new blood into the business."[299]

Beginning in 1956, Schwartz introduced new versions of some of DC's older Golden Age characters such as the Flash, Green Lantern and the Atom. This revamp became known as the Silver Age of comics, and also led to the creation of yet totally new superheroes by the end of the decade.[300] But probably unknown to Schwartz, this new vanguard may have found its inspiration directly from the SIs.

Comic Books and the Ted Owens Connection

As noted previously, *Ted Owens said that one of the more important missions of the SIs was to instill a thirst for knowledge about life beyond the Earth in the minds of the children.* Then it should come as no big surprise that *one of Owens' biggest adherents, Otto O. Binder, was involved as a mover and shaker in the comic book industry,* and is credited with creating all of the following characters:[301]

A
- Alura

B
- Beppo (comics)
- Bizarro
- Black Adam
- Black Zero
- Brainiac (comics)

C
- Cosmic Boy

I
- Ibac

J
- Jax-Ur

K
- King Kull (DC Comics)
- Krypto

L
- Lucy Lane
- Legion of Super-Heroes

M
- Marvel Family
- Mary Marvel
- Miss America (Marvel Comics)
- Mister Atom
- Mister Mind and the Monster Society of Evil

O
- Oggar

R
- Garth Ranzz

S
- Saturn Girl
- Space Cabbie
- Streaky the Supercat
- Supergirl (Kara Zor-El)

T
- Tawky Tawny
- Thom Kallor

U
- Uncle Marvel

Z
- Zor-El

Otto Oscar Binder was born in Bessemer, Michigan on 26 August 1911. He was noted as one of the more prolific American authors of science fiction and non-fiction books- especially concerning UFOs and space exploration; but his major forte was comic books. At the time of his death on 13 August 1974 at his home in Chestertown, New York, Binder left behind almost 50,000 pages of comics comprising over 1,300 scripts for Fawcett Publications and more than 2,000 for 20 other publishers, including some 93 heroes in 198 magazines.[302]

His first published piece- that he co-wrote with his older brother Earl (born 4 October 1904)- was a science fiction novelette, the *First Martian,* appearing in the October 1932 issue of *Amazing Stories,* whose editor, Ray Palmer, later went on to become one of the leading

---

299 Les Daniels, *Superman,* 131.

300 *Ibid.,* 132

301 "Category: Characters created by Otto Binder," *Wikipedia,* updated 27 March 2013, http://en.wikipedia.org/wiki/Category:Characters_created_by_Otto_Binder (Accessed 11 June 2014).

302 Nelson E. Bridwell, "In Memorium: Otto Oscar Binder," *Amazing World of DC Comics, #3* (New York, New York: DC Comics, November 1974), 30.

Scene from *Superman and the Mole Men* (1951), where the Man of Steel (played by George Reeves), himself an immigrant to planet Earth, stands *with* the mysterious visitors, defending them against a xenophobic mob that wants to kill them in a small mining town. Contrary to Wertham's allegations, Superman has always used his Kryptonian powers for good: fighting for the oppressed, the weak and minorities. See www.wikia.com.

lights of the international UFO community and a huge proponent for the contactees. Many of the contactees' books would never have been published had it not been for the careful oversight of Ray Palmer, who saw that their works were properly edited, printed and distributed through his own publishing house, the Amherst Press in Wisconsin. Binder would go on to write many more science fiction novelettes for *Amazing Stories*, including the "Adam Link" series.[303] Adam Link was a robot created in the image of a man who attained sentience and *tried to blend in as inconspicuously as possible into human society.*

Binder entered the comic book universe in 1939, only one year after Superman premiered in the June 1938 issue of National Periodical Publications' (later DC Comics) *Action Comics* #1. Later in life, Binder would do much to reshape not only Superman, but the entire cadre of characters surrounding him. But in 1939, Binder waded into the pool of comicdom, providing outsourced content for various publishers from the studios of Harry A. Chesler in New York City; and in the following year, he was hired by Fawcett Publications' comic book division, where his creative impulse was given full reign.[304]

At Fawcett, Binder created a slew of new characters. Although the idea of Captain Marvel did not originate with him, he greatly added to his legacy through the development of his entourage in many story arcs in *Captain Marvel* and later in separate spin-off comic books.[305] And much as Stan Lee would like to take credit for the creation of the "Friendly Neighborhood Spider-Man," a similar web slinging character was created by Binder in Fawcett's *Whiz Comics* #89, September 1947 issue, albeit this Spider-Man was a nemesis of Captain Marvel. Binder stayed with Fawcett until 1953, when the comic book division of the company shut down due to the public's fickle Wertham-inspired outcries.

Even while working full-time for Fawcett, Binder was writing stories for other comic book companies as well, to include Timely Comics (that eventually became the Marvel Comics franchise we all know so well today),

Otto O. Binder, 1911-1974

303 "Binder, Eando," entry in *Encyclopedia of Science Fiction*, 19 April 2014, http://www.sf-encyclopedia. com/entry/binder_eando (Accessed 11 June 2014): "Eando" was the he most famous of the joint pseudonyms used by the brothers Earl Andrew Binder (1904-1966), who was born in Austria-Hungary and came to the United States in 1910, and Otto Oscar Binder in early collaborative science fiction writing ventures.
304 Bridwell, 30
305 David Baugher, "Otto Binder: Famous Author of Comic Books," *Answers*, http://weird.answers.com/news/otto-binder-famous-author-of-comic-books (Accessed 11 June 2014)

Quality Comics, EC Comics and National Periodical Publications.[306]

Binder began writing some stories for National Periodical Publications in 1948, introducing readers to Merry, the Star-Spangled Girl. By 1956, however, Binder was working full time on the staff of National, where he was totally focused on building up the new DC universe through a near-total transformation of the Superman legacy and franchise, breathing new life into the publisher's main storylines.[307] His best known works included the introduction of the *Legion of Super-Heroes, a strange assembly of extraterrestrials with super powers guarding the Earth and its star sector in the thirty-first century.*[308] (Shades of T. Lobsang Rampa!). Interestingly, *the Legion could travel through the time barrier to whisk the young Clark Kent as Superboy from his farm in Smallville, Kansas, back in the 1950s, to help them do battle with the monstrous powers that threaten the universe in their own time frame.*

And in 1959, together with artist Al Plastino, Otto Binder created Supergirl.[309] Binder informed us in the pages of various Superman titles that Supergirl was born as Kara Zor-El, the daughter of Alura In-Ze and Zor-El, members of the planet Krypton's ruling Science Council. Zor-El was the younger brother of Jor-El, the father of Superman (Kal-El). Zor-El believed his brother's warnings that the core of Krypton was unstable and would soon explode and destroy the planet. He was prudent, however, and made preparations to save his community, Argo City, by fabricating a bio-dome around it and plating it with lead shielding to protect its residents from any lethal kryptonite radiation they might encounter in space. As Krypton blows up, Argo City survives on one of the larger fragments and assumes a stable orbit around their solar system's red sun until one day, some thirteen years later (as measured in Earth time), it is bombarded by a massive kryptonite meteor storm that breaks through the shielding. Zor-El and Alura place their now teenage daughter Kara into a space pod similar to the one that carried Kal-El to Earth some thirteen Earth years previously, launching her into the void with the coordinates preset for a promising world circling a yellow sun in a distant sector of the galaxy that were previously provided by Jor-El.

Legionnaires in the 31st century: Lightning Lad, Saturn Girl, Superboy and Cosmic Boy. See www.legionofsuperheroes.marianobayona.com.

The space pod sustains the young Kara on her long journey to Earth. Along the way, she is instructed with everything she will supposedly need to adapt apart from a Kryptonian environment, such as how to use and develop the amazing superpowers she will acquire under the invigorating rays of a yellow sun. Well, Kara was prepared for almost everything, except the idiosyncrasies of Earth's human population.

Upon her arrival on Earth, she is met by her cousin, now known as Superman, who detects the pod's approach with his telescopic vision as it enters our solar system. Kal-El is delighted to discover that he has a cousin and takes Kara under his wings, but warns her that *she must always use her newly acquired superpowers for the betterment of humankind.* In his identity as Clark Kent, Superman enrolls Kara in the Midvale Orphanage, on the outskirts of Metropolis, under the name of "Linda Lee." With Kara at the orphanage, he can keep an eye out for her

306 "Otto Binder," *Comic Vine*, http://www.comicvine.com/otto-binder/4040-42374/ (Accessed 11 June 2014)

307 Nelson E. Bridwell, "In Memorium: Otto Oscar Binder," 30.

308 Otto Binder and Al Plastino (writers); Stan Kaye and Curt Swan (artists), "Legion of Super-Heroes," *Adventure Comics* #247 (New York, New York: DC Comics, April 1958)

309 Otto Binder (writer) and Al Plastino (artist), "Supergirl from Krypton," *Action Comics* #252 (New York, New York: DC Comics, May 1959)

between missions, helping her along until her identity as Supergirl could be revealed to the entire world and she can join him in the never-ending battle for truth, justice and the American way. So in the early phases of Supergirl's time on Earth, we observe her in the pages of various Superman titles, most notably *Action Comics*, as she tries to fit in as an advanced, super-powered alien living as a proverbial "stranger in a strange land" on such a backward planet. In 1972, Supergirl finally got her own comic book and has since passed through five series of *Supergirl* titles with varied incarnations.

With artistic collaborators on the pencils and inks, Binder also went on to co-create the super villain Brainiac (<u>Bra</u>in <u>I</u>nter-<u>A</u>ctive <u>C</u>onstruct), *a meta-humanoid whose brain was upgraded by integration with a microcomputer*; the Phantom Zone, *another dimension where Krypton's most ruthless criminals could be banished to, rather than executed*; and the supporting characters of Lucy Lane (the younger sister of Lois Lane), Beppo the Super Monkey, Titano the Super Ape, and Krypto the Super Dog. In addition, the first issue of *Superman's Pal, Jimmy Olsen*, saw Binder presenting us with Jimmy's signal-watch, a gift from Superman that when activated transmitted an emergency signal that only a Kryptonian could hear, whereby Superman could quickly hone in on Jimmy's location and rescue him from whatever predicament the ambitious cub reporter found himself in.[310] It presaged the appearance of personal cell phones with "beeper" apps. And in *Jimmy Olsen #31*, Jimmy's Elastic Lad identity was revealed.[311] Jimmy

Kara Zor-El and cousin Kal-El fly together. See www.theages.ac.

exhibited the same abilities that Dr. Reed Richards of the Fantastic Four would demonstrate in Marvel Comics many years later. Binder was also responsible for creating the ever-strange Bizarro World, a square planet peopled by disfigured caricatures of Superman, his family and friends.

Each episode of the popular *Superman* television series, starring George Reeves as the Man of Steel, opened with Superman standing in a starry field speckled with mysterious worlds, announcing his arrival as a "*strange visitor from another planet with powers and abilities far beyond those of mortal men.*" Naturally, to many children watching this at the time, this was their first exposure to science fiction, and it got them thinking about what might be awaiting us "out there," *that there might be advanced beings like Superman who could lend us a hand and lift up our dire civilization*, if you can call it such, out of the muck. Of course, many of the questions that the young people had about Superman and his origins could not be answered in a thirty-minute television broadcast, minus the commercials, so they had to pick up various DC titles at the newsstands each month in search of the answers.

310 Otto Binder (writer); with Curt Swan and Ray Burnley (artists), "Boy of 100 Faces," *Superman's Pal, Jimmy Olse*n #1 (New York, New York: DC Comics, September-October 1954)

311 _____; with Ray Burnley, Stan Kaye, Curt Swan (artists), "Boy Who Hoaxed Superman," *Superman's Pal, Jimmy Olsen* #31 (New York, New York: DC Comics, September 1958)

Binder, the author of superior science fiction, tried his best to satisfy this desire among the youth. One of the greatest Superman stories in this regard was Binder's three-part story in *Superman* #132 that detailed what Kal-El's life would have been like had the planet Krypton not exploded.[312] In it, we are allowed to explore the mysterious planet in all of its glories and scientific advances. Interestingly, the expansive version of Krypton presented in Superman #132 parallels the accounts given by the contactees of the civilization they encountered on the planet Venus, from the way the Venusians dress, the kinds of schools they attend, their socio-economic-political structure, the type of architecture noted in the majestic cities, with beautiful spires, flowing arches, green belt eco-zones and parks, levitation tracks for hover cars, etc. *This is extremely important because at a subconscious level the youngsters were being prepared for the eventual transformation of the Earth and even the other planets of the solar system, through the process of terra-forming, into just such gardens of Eden- a process that they would lay the groundwork for and begin its initial stages.*

The latest incarnation of Supergirl believes that Zor-El's space pod dropped her off at the wrong stop. See www.comicvine.com.

Binder's *Superman* #132 was also credited as the inspiration for Superman co-creator Jerry Siegel's "Superman's Return to Krypton" arc that first appearing in *Superman* #141.[313] A fellow DC staffer, writer-editor E. Nelson Bridwell, referred to this tale as the "classic Superman storyline." By developing the theme of *time travel and quantum shifts through space*, Superman returns to the planet of his birth- *making sure it was in a time before he was born*- where without revealing his true identity he meets his parents, makes many new friends and experiences the joys of exploring his long lost natal world.

Of course, the existence of meta-humans, super-powered extraterrestrials and supernatural beings operating on Earth is a given in contemporary science fiction. But the concept is nothing new and may be based in actual fact. A good example can be found in the first issue of *Shazam*,[314] a DC Comics 1970's title reviving the original *Captain Marvel* series. To commemorate the life of the prolific comic book and science fiction writer, this issue features an appearance by Otto Binder as a character who meets a young Billy Batson and is astonished that the lad, who was reported missing twenty years ago, is still a boy. There is a true spiritual quality associated with this ability in projecting an appearance of perpetual youth.

While we are all familiar with the many apparitions of Mary, the mother of Jesus, as a young girl, it is interesting to note that this power was also ascribed to her dearly beloved son, the Savior Himself. In the Gnostic *Gospel of Judas*, for example, we find the following concerning the Earthly ministry of Jesus:

"When Jesus appeared on earth, he performed miracles and great wonders for the salvation

312   Otto Binder (writer); Wayne Boring, Stan Kaye, Curt Swan (artists), "Superman's Other Life," *Superman* #132 (New York, New York, DC Comics, October 1959)

313   Jerry Siegel (writer); Curt Swan (cover artist); Wayne Boring (pencils) and Stan Kaye (inks), *Superman* #141 (New York, New York: DC Comics, November 1960)

314   Denny O'Neil (writer) and C. C. Beck (artist), *Shazam!*, (New York, New York: DC Comics, February 1973)

of humanity. And since some [walked] in the way of righteousness while others walked in their transgressions, the twelve disciples were called.

He began to speak with them about the mysteries beyond the world and what would take place at the end. *Often he did not appear to his disciples as himself, but he was found among them as a child.* "[315]

Apart from always remaining young, other meta-humans from the pages of comic books and science fiction novels have demonstrated the ability to fly. And while we are all familiar with sundry accounts of people, animals or objects being levitated aboard alien spacecraft, there is yet another strange phenomenon to consider, i.e. the extraordinary ability manifested by some human-appearing entities of flying, some under their own power and others with the aid of an apparatus. Consider the case of Spain's "Wingless Angel," as related by paranormal researcher Stephen Wagner:

"It's easy to dismiss such sightings as misidentified birds or alcohol-induced illusions when one or two people report them. When as many as 240 people, however, attest to seeing the same thing, the reports are far more difficult to discount. Such a sighting took place over several of days in June, 1905 in Voltana, Spain. The accounts consistently described a woman dressed in white flying through the air - without the aid of wings. The woman sometimes flew against the wind, and one woman said she might have heard it singing as it passed overhead."[316]

Wagner provides many more contemporary examples of flying humanoids. Interestingly, the vast majority of this these types of

"Superman's Other Life" allows the reader to explore the wonders of Krypton. See http://dc.wikia.com/wiki/Superman_Vol_1_132.

The descriptions of Krypton in DC Comics parallel those of Venus as given by the UFO contactees. See http://dc.wikia.com/wiki/Superman_Vol_1_141.

---

315   *Gospel of Judas*, Rudolphe Kasser, et al., editors. It should also be pointed out that Sanat Kumara, briefly introduced to the Western world by Blavatsky, belonged to a group of ascended entities from Venus known as the "Lords of the Flame," whom some fundamentalist Christians have misunderstood as being Lucifer and the fallen angels, respectively. Sanat Kumara gained yet greater prominence when Blavatsky's close-friend and colleague Charles W. Leadbeater wrote that this exalted being was the "King" or *Lord of the World*, and the head of the Great Brotherhood of Mahatmas (Teachers) who had first revealed the principles of Theosophy countless millennia ago. Later Theosophical authors such as Alice Bailey and Elizabeth Clare Prophet have revealed yet further details about Sanat Kumara and his consort Lady Master Venus. When they materialize to seekers on the physical plane, they are usually depicted as taking on the appearance of a 16-year-old boy and 16-year-old girl, respectively. They are ascended masters, hence immortal beings with celestial and indestructible, etheric bodies. See Blavatsky's *Secret Doctrine: The Synthesis of Science, Religion, and Philosophy*, Vol. 1 (London, UK: Theosophical Publishing House, 1888), 457-458; and Vol. 2:106, 140, 319, 584. Also see C. W. Leadbeater, *The Masters and the Path* (Adyar, India: Theosophical Publishing House, 1925), 296–299 and Elizabeth and Mark Clare Prophet, *The Masters and Their Retreats* (Corwin Springs, Montana: Summit University Press, 2003), 339–341.

316 Stephen Wagner, "Unsolved: Flying Humanoids," *about entertainment*, undated, http://paranormal.about.com/cs/humanenigmas/a/aa082503.htm (Accessed 15 October 2014).

sightings occurred during the late 1940s and first half of the 1950s, during the height of the so-called "Contactee Era." Here is a brief summation of some of these flying humanoid reports from that crucial era:[317]

16 January 1948, Chehalis, Washington: Bernice Zaikowski, along with some children returning home from school that joined her in her garden, were privileged to witness a flying man who came to hover some 20 feet above her barn. Zaikowski and the young observers claimed that the being deployed a set of long silver wings that appeared to be attached to his body. These seemed to help keep him aloft. He was also seen adjusting some kind of controls on a chest harness. A distinct "whizzing" sound was also noted along with this sighting.

April 1948, Longview, Washington: Two witnesses observed three helmeted men flying with no motors or propellers in view. Nevertheless, some "motor-like" sounds were heard in conjunction with the flight.

Early 1950s, Pelotas, Brazil: A couple was taking an evening stroll when two fast-moving shadows crossed their path. They looked up and noticed two flying humans passing overhead at an approximate altitude of 30 feet. The couple's eyes remained transfixed on the fliers. They noticed that they had descended vertically, landing some short distance away. The couple observed that each of the fliers was about six feet tall. When the flying pair noticed that they were being observed, they squatted close to the ground, attempting to hide. At the woman's insistence, the couple finally opted to get out of the area, lest the flying humanoids would give them chase.

Sometime in 1952, Camp Okubu on the outskirts of Kyoto, Japan: One evening, Private Sinclair Taylor, a young soldier on guard duty at the base, saw what he first thought was an extremely large bird off in the distance. But as it came closer and hovered above him, he noticed that the entity had the appearance of being a man. Private Sinclair estimated that the being was nearly seven feet tall. The flying man also deployed a set of wings, the span of which the Sinclair estimated to also be about seven feet. Naturally, Private Sinclair was frightened and fired his rifle at the flying man; but in his nervousness the soldier missed and the being just flew away. The guard had some trepidation about reporting the incident, as he thought that his superiors might think he was drunk on duty. But in the interests of security, he went ahead and reported the sighting to his immediate superior, a platoon sergeant. Surprisingly, the sergeant accepted his report without making any accusations against Private Sinclair, noting that another guard had previously made a similar report to him last year.

18 June 1953, Houston, Texas: Three individuals were out on their veranda, relaxing on a hot summer night. Suddenly, they sighted a winged creature that alit on a nearby pecan tree. One of the witnesses described the entity as having, "the figure of man with wings like a bat. He was dressed in gray or black tight-fitting clothes," and added that, "He stood there for about 30 seconds, swaying on the branch of an old pecan tree." All three of the witnesses agreed that the flying man was wearing a cape and quarter-length boots, looking like a real-life Batman from DC Comics-fame. Most remarkably, one of the observers claimed that the Batman was enveloped in a "halo of light."

Autumn of 1956, Falls City, Nebraska: One afternoon, a man preferring to identify himself simply by the name of "John Hanks," saw a winged creature flying only about 15 feet above the ground. These wings were like shiny aluminum and had multi-colored lights running along their underside. In this case, the wings, spanning 15 feet, were clearly attached to the man by

---

317 *Ibid.*

means of a shoulder harness. As with some of the other reports, this flying man also had some kind of control panel affixed to his chest, and he manipulated the dials as he flew. While it is apparent that this man flew with the aid of an apparatus, we have to keep in mind that hang gliding did not become a sport until the mid-1960s and ultra-light aircraft did not make their appearance until the early 1970s. Therefore, this sighting, taking place in 1956, might easily be attributed to some remarkable human invention. But what distinguishes this case, however, is the witness' description of the flying man himself: leathery wrinkled skin, large watery blue eyes and a face that was "very frightening, almost demonic." Mr. Hanks, fearing the unknown, also attested that he was paralyzed with fear as this "man" flew over.

Wagner asks, "How can we account for such sightings?" And he concludes, "Men and women flying with bat's wings are hard to explain. Even the cases in which the people seem to be flying by some mechanical means appear to be out of time, using technology that hadn't been invented yet... or if it had been invented by these 'pilots,' is entirely unknown."[318]

However, one would logically have to assume that those reports describing a harness, metal wings and some kind of controlling apparatus were clearly indicative of an advanced technology operative within our own laws of physics. Those of beings flying under their own power may have had access to anti-gravity belts or some type of technology far beyond anything we have the capability to fabricate in our own time. Yet other cases of flying beings may be indicative of manifestations from an angelic/spiritual or ultra-dimensional realm existing outside our own space-time reference. Consider the following incident that took place at the height of the United States' involvement in Vietnam:

Sometime in 1969, Vietnam: Three U.S. Marines were standing guard one night at the United States military base in Da Nang when they were approached by a winged creature. But this one was extraordinarily different than the others we have looked at. As it flew closer and closer, the Marines could see that it had the *form of a naked black woman.* Her wings were enormous and bat-like. The Marines also noted that she glowed from head to

Superheroes always seem to show up right when we need them. Superhero stories, like that of the Batman, inspire us and provide models of coping with adversity, finding meaning in loss and trauma, discovering our strengths and using them toward achieving good purposes. See http://www.gamesradar.com/batman-arkham-knight-review/.

toe with an "eerie greenish light."[319]

Of course, monsters and unusual creatures of almost every description have been reported over the centuries. From ghosts to crypto-zoological anomalies like the Chupacabra, there seems to no limit to the variety of unexplained entities that people claim to have seen/witnessed. But of all of these reports, one of the most curious types of sightings - and quite rare - are those of human-like beings that fly. We can only say "human-like," however, because in most respects they look like us, except that many have wings. But because we live in a so-called "modern age," most of these odd creatures are not assumed to be either angels, devils or gods (as traditional depictions have them as human-like beings with wings), but as something else;

318 *Ibid.*
319 *Ibid.*

and that "something" is definitely quite unusual.

Paranormal investigators are quick to note that the appearance of mysterious entities seems to change over time, just as the appearance of UFOs. Contactees like Ted Owens believe that the Saucer Intelligences are non-human beings, ethereal in nature, and that they can manifest in any form in our physical universe. Whether beings or ships, they always seem to be one step ahead of our current technology.

Concerning the appearance of strange humanoids and UFOs noted throughout the annals of history, Dr. J. Allen Hynek asked, "Do humanoids and UFOs alike bespeak a parallel 'reality' that for some reason manifests itself to some of us for very limited periods? But what would this reality be? Is there a philosopher in the house?"[320] Perhaps if there were, he or she would speculate that the humanoids, from whatever reality they came from, are leading the way by providing the inspiration for what we can do, and more importantly, what we can become.

Besides flying, another sought after power since the beginning of recorded history has been that of super strength and near invulnerability, like that of Achilles, Hercules and Samson of old. In the case of Superman, his Jewish creators Joe Shuster and Jerry Siegel may have taken some inspiration from the centuries-old legend of the Golem of Prague. Jewish historian Marie Southard Ospina writes, "Then there is the Golem. In a sense, the late 16th century Golem was very much to the Jewish community what Superman was to Americans in the 1930s."[321] Both of these characters, although fictitious, were created to give people strength and hope. The Golem and Superman were created to fight for truth and justice; and both were created in a time of crisis for the Jewish community. Back in the Cleveland, Ohio, of 1932, and the imaginations of Shuster and Siegel, Superman was their vision for an American Golem.

Southard relates that..."when Rabbi Loew created the legend in Prague, there had been a claim by an anti-Semitic priest that Jews killed Christian children to use their blood in Passover rituals. Supposedly, Loew's Golem guarded Jews during the most dangerous season for these attacks, Easter time. Anti-Semitism in Prague was high at this time, and Jews were being accused of a variety of crimes, one of the worst being murdering children. The entire Jewish population was in need of comfort and hope that they would not always be chastised, rejected and oppressed; thus the creation of the Golem. Grossman put it perfectly, saying that like superheroes, the Golem's goal was to 'confront a world of evil.' The Jews needed that; they needed to know someone would save them from the evil being thrown their way."[322]

When we look at Superman, the extraterrestrial who employs his mighty strength for the benefit of the oppressed and downtrodden, we cannot help but draw comparisons with the Golem of the 16th century. When the two Cleveland lads first came up with the idea of Superman, the United States was facing the lowest point of the Great Depression. It was of the highest unemployment, poverty, deflation, plunging farm incomes, and low profits that turned the "American Dream" into a complete nightmare. It was such a terrible time that Americans did whatever they could to escape this reality, leading to immense popularity of movies, board games, Yankee baseball fanaticism, and, of course, superheroes. At such a time when families could barely support their children, it comes as no surprise that a figure whose main goal was to save people from any kind of harm was created. Anti-Semitic totalitarianism was also a real specter haunting the American political scene. Superman was rapidly embraced because he

---

320   J. Allen Hynek, *UFO Experience: A Scientific Inquiry* (Chicago: Henry Regnery Company, 1972), 139.

321   Maria Southard Ospina, "What Jesus, the Golem and Superman Have in Common," 13 April 2013, blog, http://mariesouthard.com/ (Accessed 17 October 2014)

322   *Ibid.*

was the ultimate rescuer, and this was especially so for the American Jewish community.

But do some extraterrestrials have such powers; and do they use them for the good of humankind? Apart from the accounts of angelic intervention on behalf of various mortals caught up in dangerous predicaments, there is some evidence that alien beings do possess such remarkable traits. Paul M. Vest, a theosophist and esoteric researcher of the 1950s and early 1960s who wrote extensively on the contactee movement for such publications as *Mystic* and *Fate*, noted that Venusians were bequeathed with super-strength and near invulnerability while operating in the Earth's environment.

One pleasant summer day in 1953, Vest received a phone call at his Los Angeles residence from a man who simply identified himself as "Bill." The gentleman asked Vest for a meeting to discuss some of his more recent articles on various aspects of the flying saucer movement, all the while assuring Vest that he had some information to pass on to him that would help bolster and advance the claims of the contactees in the eyes of the public, particularly those being made by Orfeo Angelucci, mentioned previously. Bill wanted Vest to specifically write an article extolling Angelucci and promoting the important messages delivered to him by advanced extraterrestrials in our solar system. After chatting for about an hour, Vest agreed to meet Bill, with their rendezvous taking place a few days later outside a bus station in Santa Monica. Bill had to travel down to Los Angeles from his home on the outskirts of Seattle. While Vest told Bill that such a long trip would not be necessary, Bill insisted that it would be more secure to pass on certain information to him in person, to avoid the risk of tapped telephone conversations.

Bill was about six-feet tall and had dark, almost black eyes, black hair and high cheekbones, giving him a somewhat oriental look. His skin was unusually white with a slight blue tinge and his fingers were very long and tapering, even seeming to be without joints. Like Adamski's Venusian contact, Orthon, Bill's hands demonstrated a tender and rare feminine quality, for a man. But what made Paul Vest so intrigued was that Bill's hand felt like it had no bone structure beneath his skin. Vest also took note that Bill's ears were oddly-pointed, appearing more delicate and complex than any he had seen before.

When Bill spoke, his voice had a peculiar resonant quality. He took great care in choosing his words, speaking slowly and clearly with no trace of an accent. He sounded like a typical mid-Westerner, the sort of individual the networks might choose to host a radio or television newscast. His grammar was flawless. Of the enigmatic Bill, Vest wrote the following:

Superman carries out a never-ending battle for truth and justice. See http://content.time.com/time/arts/article/0,8599,1679961,00.html.

"I have met swamis, yogis, mediums, clairvoyants, mystics and self-styled messiahs by the score, but I have never been duped by any of them, even those who were sincere and self-deceived. Also, I have met several persons whom I know without any doubt to be true spiritual adepts even as I have known several sensitives, or mediums, who are honest, sincere and able to produce authentic paranormal phenomena. From years of research and experience in occult and psychic phenomena I now can usually discern the true from the false at a glance."

"But my strange visitor had me deeply puzzled from the moment I first met him. *He was like no person I had ever encountered before*! Perhaps ESP entered into my awareness of his strange psychic and spiritual qualities. *In his presence I was immediately acutely conscious of a completely foreign and heretofore unknown vibration. I didn't know who he was, but I did know my visitor was no ordinary man.*"

Usually, Vest would meet with individuals at a neutral location, such as a coffee shop. But trusting that Bill was an extraordinary soul with whom he could trust, he invited him to his nearby apartment where they continued their conversation in the living room, being seated in comfortable lounge chairs. At first they discussed the case of Orfeo Angelucci, but later moved on to the topic of Venusians and other Etherics living among us.

Vest's article about his meeting with Bill and the information he received concerning the Venusians' agenda on Earth, was published in the August 1954, issue #5 of *Mystic* magazine (Evanston, Illinois). Its editor, Ray Palmer, an associate of Otto Binder and publisher of other esoteric and science fiction literature, was an early promoter of the "flying saucer phenomenon" and the emerging contactee movement.

In the preface to Vest's article, Palmer wrote that, "this story is labeled on our contents page as true…. What we want to caution you, however, is that sometimes everything is not exactly what it seems to be. If Venusians actually are walking our city streets, *Mystic* intends to do its level best to prove it. Thus we ask that anyone who can add to Mr. Vest's story come forward now with any evidence they may possess. It may be extremely important! *The identity of the 'flying saucer men' may be absolutely vital to our national safety!*"

Over the course of *Mystic* magazine's run, numerous accounts of Venusian activity on Earth were indeed published, further augmenting the tremendous claims asserted by Vest in the important August 1954 edition. For in it we discover that not only are Venusians and other extraterrestrials walking around unencumbered on the streets of our cities, but that they can appear much as ourselves, blending in with our populations due to a familiarity with our customs, languages and manners. They dress as we do and can easily pass for one of us. But going beyond mere assimilation, these aliens among us demonstrate amazing powers of extra-sensory perception as well as super strength.

The following is an account of two Venusians in a Los Angeles newspaper office that was related to Vest by the ever so mysterious Bill:

There was a pause as I pondered his words. Then he abruptly changed the subject. "After I leave you, you may begin to doubt much of what has passed between us," he continued. "Therefore I want you to contact the persons whose names and addresses I have given you. In particular I want you to get in touch with a newspaper reporter on a large Los Angeles daily (he gave me the name of the newspaper reporter, the name of his newspaper and two telephone numbers where he might be reached. But as the reporter has since requested that I not use his name or the name of his newspaper, I will refer to him as Max Morton and his newspaper as the Los Angeles World). "This reporter, Max Morton," he went on, "has been contacted by two Venusians and from an earthly factual standpoint his contact is highly significant."

"But, I don't quite understand," I remonstrated. "Why didn't the

Los Angeles World print Morton's story? I'd think it would rate headlines around the world."

"Bill" smiled. "The reporter and his associates still can't quite convince themselves that the whole thing isn't a big hoax of some sort. They have factual proof of something highly extraordinary in the metal plate, but they're still dubious as the idea of space visitors is a rather touchy subject now."

I promised to phone Max Morton the following day.

At about 10:30 that night I drove "Bill" to the bus stop and watched him board a Los Angeles bound bus. He said he was leaving the following day for the North, but promised to see me again after my story of Angelucci's experiences appeared in print.

Later, I contacted Max Morton at the Los Angeles World as I was eager to hear what he had to say about the two Venusians. In brief, here is the fantastic, but true story he gave me:

In February, 1953, a strange-appearing man, dressed in a tweed suit, came into the newspaper office. He told the receptionist that he was from the planet Venus and stated that he wished to see the City Editor. She, of course, thinking it was a gag, rang the City

Editor and quipped, "A man just dropped in from the planet Venus to see you."

"Oh yeah," remarked the harassed editor. "I'm busy. Let Max Morton talk to him. He's interested in characters."

The receptionist, still certain it all was a huge joke, sent the "character" into the press room to see Max Morton.

I asked Max for a description of the person, and the minute description he gave tallied in every detail with the mysterious "Bill" who had visited me.

Max said the fellow had looked at him with a serious face and stated in a forthright and direct manner that he was from the planet

Venus. But as a more or less hard-boiled reporter, Max was familiar with screw-balls and was not too

The mysterious "Bill" revealed much of the Venusian agenda for the early "contactee movement" in California of the 1950s to esoteric researcher and writer Paul Vest. See http://ufoarchives. blogspot.com/2013/12/who-was-paul-m-vest.html.

surprised-as he frequently met "Napoleons," "Peter the Greats," etc. In reply he made some wise-crack.

With that the Venusian ran his thumb nail lightly across Morton's desk. Genuinely startled, Max saw that the glazed, hard surface of his desk was gashed to the depth of about half an inch.

He began to wonder about the fellow and attempted to duplicate the feat. But, he declared, he couldn't even make a slight dent in the desk top. He was puzzled, but still thought it was just some trick the odd-ball had learned.

With slight urging the fellow commenced talking about himself.

Briefly, his story was that he and a companion had arrived on this planet in a flying saucer. They landed their craft in the desert near Barstow, California and concealed it there. In Barstow they were able to get some old clothes and hitch-hiked into Los Angeles.

Max, still sure it was all a hoax being perpetrated on him, jokingly asked them how they learned our language. The Venusian replied that the inhabitants of his planet monitored our radio and television broadcasts and thus had easily learned our, languages and customs. He said that he and his companion had come here specifically to study earthlings at close range and to gain a better understanding of our minds and thought processes.

The reporter was by no means convinced that the fellow was anything but a crackpot, but he was getting curious. When he had to leave for an appointment at the Court House, he agreed to see the "Venusian" and his companion the following day.

When the fellow arrived the following afternoon he had his companion with him. Max said the second one appeared to be almost an identical twin of the first.

In the meantime, Max had procured a heavy plate of the hardest alloyed steel. He suggested that the Venusian attempt to mark the metal as he had the desk surface. With apparently no effort the fellow ran his thumb lightly across the steel. Dumbfounded, Max saw that the metal was gouged across its entire surface in a streak over half an inch deep.

Max was beginning to feel rather uneasy, but was certainly not convinced the fellows actually were "Venusians".

Both of them stuck firmly to their story, however, and later requested Max to help them get jobs in Los Angeles. They said they were without funds and found they couldn't get around here without money.

Max skeptically agreed to see what he could do.

Through a friend in the newspaper's Department of Investigation he was able to get the first one a job in that department. But he made the fellow promise to keep his identity secret. Hence only three persons on the newspaper's staff knew who the Venusian really was-or claimed to be!

The fellow worked for several weeks in the Missing Persons office and succeeded in astounding all of his co-workers with his baffling and amazing abilities. Max declared the so-called Venusian could locate missing persons within an hour in cases that had baffled their best investigators for months.

In fact Max was beginning seriously to wonder if the Venusian might actually be telling the truth. For it was obvious to everyone that the fellow possessed incredible extra-sensory perception. Max talked with him and asked the Venusian for permission to write an article about him for publication in a magazine. But the Venusian steadfastly refused; in fact he said he and his companion wanted no publicity whatsoever as it would negate the true purpose of their visit here.

Nevertheless Max went to work on an article about them. But before it was completed the Venusian and his companion suddenly disappeared. Investigators have not been able to find any trace of them since.

Max provided a full report to the Federal Bureau of Investigation (FBI), along with an analysis report of the gouged steel plate. The metal analysis was conducted by one of the foremost laboratories in the Greater Los Angeles area and indicated that the mark pressed into the steel plate would require an exerted pressure of over 1,700 pounds to have produced it. The report further stated that, "such pressure exerted by any known force would shatter that particular type of metal before marking it." Yet even more incredible, *an analysis of the indentation itself revealed the presence of over a dozen elements not present in the rest of the metal.*

All of this was certainly enough to convince Max that the two strangers who were working at the *World* newspaper were truly Venusians. Max also mentioned that most of the "worldly knowledge" demonstrated by the Venusians appeared to come largely from what could be gleaned from radio and television broadcasts. He also informed Vest that he had his permission to write about the two strangers, provided that he did not reveal anything about Max's real identity or the name of the newspaper. Ray Palmer, editor of *Mystic*, apparently conducted some independent investigations of his own and verified the names of both the editor and newspaper involved, thus confirming the story in his mind, at least.

Vest was also certain that "Bill" was a Venusian, despite the fact that the Washington State visitor only intimated that he was originally from another planet, without letting Vest know which one. Vest assumed that Bill must be a Venusian because the physical description given by Max of the two mysterious newsmen matched in nearly every detail that of "Bill." In addition, Bill stated that he was not of the same order of Etherics, the ultra-dimensional guardians in the space sector surrounding the planet Neptune in communication with Orfeo Angelucci.

So there we have it: Aliens with a wide assortment of super-powers are operating right here on Earth. These accounts of tremendous feats parallel those stories of ancient mythologies like the gods of Mount Olympus, or to be more contemporary, those found in the pages of comic books or in Hollywood superhero movies. It is clear that comic book and science fiction writers like Otto Binder, fascinated as they were by the UFO phenomenon and the amazing tales of the contactees, fused a specific knowledge of ufology into their artistic endeavors.

Otto Binder's daughter and only child, Mary, died in 1967. She had been on her way to school one morning when a car jumped the curb, veering into the driveway in front of the school and killing her. As film producer and comic book historian Michael Uslan, a family friend, recalled, "Otto never recovered. His wife never recovered. She had a breakdown, and Otto started drinking, and eventually he dropped dead of a heart attack. And the three of them were gone, like in a flash."[323]

Uslan grew up in Englewood, New Jersey, knew the Binders well, and went to school with Mary. Uslan further commented on this period:

"When you consider at that point in time (when a dispute over the rights to Captain Marvel was taking place in the courts between various comic book publishers) all of these must be discussed in the context of their times, the majority of the readers were eight-to-12-year-old boys.

Bobby Klein and I, we probably felt like kids sitting around a campfire and having a camp counselor just pull us in with the greatest stories ever. It was like being at the feet of your grandfather as he told stories of the family.

And the greatest advantage for me at age 13 or 14 [laughs] was that here was a guy who had the most beautiful blonde of a daughter in the world, who was about my age, though she seemed a lot older, who didn't look at Bobby and me as geeky comic book nerds! His daughter was Mary, and she was named after Mary Marvel.

Her dad and her uncle were in the comic book business, and she even corrected me once, when I said Otto wrote *Captain Marvel*. She said, 'No, it was *Captain Marvel Adventures*. [She laughs.] I remember saying, "Oh, boy, this is the girl I'm going to marry! A girl who knows comics! This is great!'

It was a wonderful family. His wife, Ione, was a wonderful, warm hospitable woman as well. Mary and I never dated. I was too shy, too in awe of her to ask her out, are you kidding?

323 Recollection of Michael Uslan in Zack Smith, "An Oral History of Captain Marvel: The Lost Years: 1954-1973, Part 3," 30 December 2010, *Newsarama*, http://www.newsarama.com/6759-an-oral-history-of-captain-marvel-the-lost-years-pt-3.html (Accessed 2 November 2014).

By the time we were 16, there was a terrible, terrible tragedy. Mary was getting ready to go into school one morning, and a car jumped the curb, and went into the driveway in front of the school and killed her."[324]

Binder had become disheartened with Mary's death, but somehow managed to soldier on for another seven years. Being raised as a traditional Lutheran, Binder sought answers in religion, but failed to find any. He was unable to rationalize faith and science; but perhaps he found some comfort in the esoteric teachings of Owens and other contactees that some advanced souls, like Mary surely was, reincarnated on Venus or an alternate celestial sphere. In any event, Binder returned to his primary love of science and science fiction, writing numerous books and articles in both genres, particularly focusing on the theme of UFOs.[325] Of this period, Binder commented:

"We finally made up our minds to "start a new life." When we moved to upstate New York (from Englewood, New Jersey) in 1969, I quit DC and comics entirely and went back into the sci-fi paperback field. Curtis Books bought seven of my books in a row, including a few oldies, and Belmont issued another half a dozen. I began selling "gothics" besides a batch of flying saucer books and articles for *Saga* magazine."[326]

Binder was, in fact, a huge proponent of the so-called "ancient astronaut theory." He believed that at some time in the remote past, an extraterrestrial intelligence began to interact with the course of human evolution. Binder theorized that human beings are "homo-hybrids," an "interstellar crossbreed," so to speak. In other words, our genetic makeup is half-human and half-extraterrestrial. He first presented this theory in his book, *Unsolved Mysteries of the Past* (1970). He also wrote *Mankind: Child of the Stars* with Max Flindt (1974), discussing the concept of "astroevolution." The most famous ancient astronaut proponent, Eric von Däniken, wrote the foreword for this book, which was revised and reprinted in 1999. Binder also wrote extensively on ufology in magazines, including articles detailing the experiences of noted UFO contactee Ted Owens, mentioned previously in this chapter.

Ancient Astronauts

Long before Binder and von Däniken popularized the ancient astronaut theory, however, credit should be given to Helena P. Blavatsky and her ardent band of Theosophists. Within the pages of Blavatsky's *Secret Doctrine*, the reader encounters a translation of the 20,000 year-old sacred text of the *Book of Dyzan*, a sacred text written in the ancient pre-Sanskrit Senzar language that she managed to uncover while studying with Buddhist masters at a monastery

---

324 *Ibid.*
325 Otto O. Binder, *Flying Saucers Are Watching Us* (New York, New York: Belmont, 1968)

_____ *What We Really Know About Flying Saucers* (New York, New York: Fawcett, 1968)

_____ *Ted Owens, Flying Saucer Spokesman: Incredible Truth Behind the UFO's Mission to* Earth (Clarksburg, West Virginia: Saucerian Books, 1970)

_____ *Unsolved Mysteries of the Past* (New York, New York: Tower Publications, 1970)

_____ and Max H. Flindt, *Mankind: Child of the Stars* (New York, New York: Fawcett, 1974)

Note: Binder wrote many other books and articles about space, which included numerous references to UFOs but were not specific to the subject.
326 Jim Steranko, *Steranko History of Comics 2* (Reading, Pennsylvania: Supergraphics, 1972), 21.

in Tibet. Douglas M. Baker, a medical doctor and leading light in Theosophical circles in the United Kingdom, comments on Blavatsky's extraordinary find:

"It told how 18,000,000 years ago, great beings from Venus, perfected intelligences which had been once human themselves, applied their stimulatory forces to the Earth and provided the neo-evolutionary spurt which changed animal-Man of the Earth into a being capable of abstract thought in an act which is referred to in occultism as individualization."[327]

Mary Binder (1953-1967), daughter of comic book author and ufologist Otto O. Binder, was named after one of Otto's greatest comic book character creations, "Mary Marvel." Bill Schelly, a biographer of Binder, writes that, "Binder knew great heights of professional success, and devastating personal tragedy. When his 14 year old daughter Mary was killed in a freak car accident in 1967, Otto left the comics field completely, moving to the Adirondacks, and turned his attention to writing science fiction and UFO books." See http://www.newsarama.com/6759-an-oral-history-of-captain-marvel-the-lost-years-pt-3.html and Bill Schelly, *Words of Wonder: Life and Times of Otto Binder* (Seattle, WA: Hamster Press, 2003).

The ancient text conveys the story of how the Lords of Flame arrived on Earth from our sister planet Venus at a time when the inner planets of our solar system were in a perfect alignment with the Sun, a fortunate astrological configuration, to be sure. The Lords of Flame took advantage of the close proximity of both Mars and Venus with the Earth, resulting from the close conjunctions of these orbs, to transplant an abundant array of both Martian and Venusian life forms to our world for the benefit of nascent humankind. Among the Venusian life forms brought to Earth were ants, bees, some domesticated animals and wheat.[328]

Mary Marvel, one of the earlier creations of Otto Binder, and the precursor to Supergirl. See http://www.comicvine.com/forums/battles-7/mary-marvel-vs-gladiator-138229/.

But whereas the contemporary ancient astronaut theorists propose that the aliens who colonized our world had carbon-based physical structures that conformed to environmental conditions here on Earth (life as we know it), the Theosophists maintain that the Lords of Flame

---

327   Douglas M. Baker, *Occult Significance of UFOs* (Essendon, UK: Little Elephant), 1979, e-book edition, 2011, http://www.amazon.com/Occult-Significance-UFOS-Douglas-Baker-ebook/dp/B006V7X5VW (Accessed 3 November 2014).

328   *Ibid*: Because Venus may have existed for over two billion years as an Earth-like planet teeming with carbon and water-based "life as we know it," it is not unreasonable to assume that third dimensional life forms (physical to our senses) were maintained off-world when atmospheric and surface conditions began to rapidly deteriorate. If the Venusians were still in their third dimensional form, as we are today, they may have transported indigenous Venusian life forms to Earth, thereby establishing, as it were, a garden colony. However, if the Venusian civilization reached a fourth or fifth dimensional level, whereby they could travel backward or forward through time, then it would not be out of their technological range to go back in time to an earlier Venus, secure the plants and animals they needed, and transport them to Earth. And once the Venusians transitioned to a sixth dimensional level or higher of existence, converting to spiritual or ultra-dimensional beings, they could have created the life they would place on Earth first in the form of thought constructs, then going on to speak them into physical existence upon their arrival here. In this sense, one can define the Venusians as "gods," with a small g, insofar as they are like the gods of ancient mythology, capable of carrying out what appear to be supernatural or miraculous feats of magic. But we must keep in mind that there is nothing magic or supernatural about these feats, for the Venusian Lords of Flame are merely applying the higher applications and manifestations of natural principles that we yet have not come to understand. These powers still remain latent in humankind. The Venusian masters are cosmically advanced beings that can help us return to the Divine Source (the Monad) from which we all originated. See "God and the Gods," *Aetherius Society*, 2014, http://www.aetherius.org/god-and-the-gods/ (Accessed 3 November 2014).

were spiritual entities (ultra-dimensional beings) that could thrive on any planet, regardless of its atmosphere (or lack of), gravity, temperature or any other factor. The Aetherius Society, a New Age UFO religion that incorporates some tenets of Theosophy and maintains its American headquarters in Los Angeles, California, offers the following explanation:

"There is intelligent life on other planets within this Solar System, but it exists at a frequency of vibration which is higher than the frequency of vibration of the plane that we inhabit on Earth.

If, for example, NASA were to send astronauts to Venus, they would not discover any signs of Venusian civilization unless the intelligences on Venus chose in some way to make their existence known to them. If, however, a great adept of yoga were to consciously leave the body and project to a plane of Venus that is inhabited, he or she would be able to see that Venus is in fact teeming with life. Such a plane would be physical – but a higher form of physicality than our physical senses or science as we know it is currently able to detect."[329]

Occult masters assert that given enough time, humankind can adjust to the conditions found on almost any planet, even going to the extent of discarding the physical body but retaining consciousness in a subtler, more etheric body. Rather than having an individual distorted in their form, outline or shape to conform to the ever-changing conditions of any given planet, Divine Providence has come up with a more than suitable alternative. The ancient sages well understood that Man is as old as the universe itself; and is as much a "principle" of the universe as its most fundamental aspect of light. And as there is light to be found on the physical plane with its color and other inherent qualities, there is also the glorious light of the so-called Buddha plane.[330] In a like manner there exist various manifestations of humankind at sundry levels of density and quality.

Therefore, apart from the visible stars and planets of our universe, we have to keep in mind the Theosophical point of view that there are billions upon billions of etheric planets filling the immensity of outer space. Although these are not visible to the human eye, they nevertheless transmit radio waves. In our solar system alone, occult masters estimate that there are some 60 planets composed of subtle substances whereon numerous alien species make their homes.

Baker claims that some of the radio emanations from these extraterrestrial civilizations have been recorded by the personnel at select radio telescope facilities, such as the one at Jodrell Bank, but that the transcripts of these transmissions have been classified as top secret by the governments of Earth in the interest of respective national security interests. Of these hidden worlds, Baker notes that, "there is subtle life, the forms of which consist of aether bodies similar to the aether parts of our own bodies photographed by radionic cameras in the de la Warr Laboratories at Oxford and seen through the *screens of Kilner* (aural detection devices employed by psychic researchers)."[331]

Ergo, it is according to the structure of a planet that both its qualities and degree of development along the scale of spiritual evolution are determined; and thus will the corresponding structure

---

329 "UFOs and Extraterrestrial Life," *Aetherius Society*, 2014, http://www.aetherius.org/ufos-and-extraterrestrial-life/, (Accessed 3 November 2014)

330 *Ocean Light Zen Center*, Buddhist Temple in Seattle, Washington, 26 October 2012, https://www.facebook.com/OceanLightZen?fref=nf, (Accessed 3 November 2014): When Buddha sat under the bodhi tree, he saw the morning star (Venus) and contemplating its serene beauty and magnitude thereby attained enlightenment.

331 Baker

of its inhabitants be dictated. However, all of the human forms that are resident on the planet are essentially "man-like" in their shape, and for the most part as symmetrical as we are.[332]

Just as ufology is divided between the two camps of those who welcome the benevolent space brothers and those who fear any possible invaders, it is also divided over the issue of ancient astronauts. In the first faction are those who subscribe to the more "esoteric" theories of inter-dimensionality, as outlined in the previous paragraphs; and in the second are those adherents of the more concrete, "nuts and bolts" philosophy that extraterrestrials have to originate from a planet very much akin to our own in its environmental and geological conditions. In other words, aliens cannot exist if they do not conform in any degree to "life as we know it." This means that it must at least be carbon-based, require water for its survival and function within a limited and moderate temperature range no more or less suitable for the maintenance of extremophile organisms, much as might be found in the vicinity of thermal vents on the ocean floor or trapped under glaciers in the polar regions.

Both camps have already answered the question, "Are we alone in the universe?" As they already believe that ancient astronauts have played at least some small part in determining the

course of Earth's history, the disagreement they haggle over is the nature of that ancient and/or continuing alien presence. In a more remote time, the hearer of such a question might assume that you were asking them if God or angels existed. But when one asks that question today, it is generally thought that the questioner wants to know whether or not you believe that intelligent life exists on a planet other than the Earth.

"Are we alone in the universe?" is the question that persists and will not go away quietly into that good night. Just a few short decades ago, those in the "nuts and bolts" camp believed that there might be intelligent life on Mars or Venus, since both of these planets at least share some of the outward appearances of being similar to Earth. But with the advent of unmanned space vehicles/probes, subsequent scientific discoveries have reduced NASA and other exploratory agencies to merely looking for the evidence of liquid water on various space bodies throughout our solar system, and beyond when we include the Kepler mission.

As for Mars, there appears to be some water frozen beneath its surface, but there are no signs of intelligent life forms currently present. And as for Venus, there are no indications of any life as we know it, except for the possibility of microbial organisms flourishing in the upper cloud decks, where the air is much more rarified and temperatures are quite balmy. But certainly no life as we know it can exist on the Venusian surface, with temperatures hot enough to melt lead and massive atmospheric pressure at more than 90 times that of Earth being a constant

The ancient Egyptians recognized that the emanations of light from various celestial bodies were "living intelligences." Here the great Pharaoh Akhenaten and his family prepare to receive further light and knowledge from the One God, Aten (the Sun). See http://en.wikipedia.org/wiki/Aten. In a revelation received by the Mormon prophet Joseph Smith in Kirtland, Ohio, on 6 May 1833, he related to those assembled at the temple constructed there that the "Glory of God is Intelligence."

332 *Ibid.*

there. For the rest of the solar system, there does appear to be liquid oceans under the ice of Jupiter's large moon of Europa and Saturn's small moon of Enceladus. Nevertheless, there are no surface indications of life on either of those distant satellites.

In the mid-1990s, beginning with Vega, astronomers began to detect planets orbiting around stars in our galactic neighborhood. What they learned was that other planetary systems lacked any form of consistency. From the start of such astronomical exploration, we came to discover that the composition of our own solar system seemed to be unique. As to the 2,000 plus exoplanets later discovered by Kepler, only a few hold out the most meager possibilities of containing liquid water. And so far as the general public knows, radio telescopes have continued to scan the skies for the telltale signals of intelligent life coming from other yet distant star systems, but have turned up nothing.

So with the overwhelming lack of evidence, why do the "nuts and bolts" people continue to search for "life as we know" in the seeming cosmic void? They do this because they cling to a materialistic world view. They assume that there is nothing special about the Earth. Hence, whatever happened here by way of the evolutionary process must have occurred countless times on other worlds scattered throughout the universe, replicating the emergence of life as we have come to understand it.

But in order for more complex forms of life to exist on the physical plane, a rocky, terrestrial planet is required. This planet must also have, as the Earth does, plate tectonics, the right atmospheric mix and a large, well placed moon to facilitate tides and stabilize the tilt of its axis. The planet must also be situated at the correct distance from a certain type of single star and orbit around that star on a nearly circular path in order to maintain the water on its surface in a liquid form for most of the year. Astronomers refer to this optimal orbital placement as the "Goldilocks Zone," where conditions are just right for the emergence and maintenance of life as we know it.

Yet even this is not enough. Our habitable planet also needs a home within a stable planetary system that includes some outlying giant planets to protect the inner system from too many deadly comet impacts. This planetary system must also be situated in a safe neighborhood within just the right type of galaxy. In other words, the galaxy needs to contain enough heavy elements to allow for the stellar formation of terrestrial planets within it. Our planet should also have formed during the narrow window of cosmic history allowing for planetary formation. And then in what is essentially an omniverse, our planet must be located within a universe with a fine-tuned set of constants and physical laws that make stars, planets and human beings a possibility.

Dr. Jay W. Richards, a noted Christian philosopher and theologian, wrote the following concerning the conditions requisite for the emergence of more complex forms of life elsewhere in the universe:

"Initially, you might think that such a precise configuration of life-friendly factors suggests that Earth is part of some cosmic design. But some scientists familiar with this evidence now argue that while the conditions that allow for complex life may be highly improbable, perhaps even unique to Earth, these conditions are still nothing more than a fluke. The universe, after all, is a big place, with some 10^{22} stars in the part we can see. With so many opportunities, maybe at least one habitable planet will turn up just by chance.

Notice that even though the *evidence contradicts* the Copernican Principle, the materialist assumptions that inspired it remain in place."[333]

333 Jay W. Richards, Ph.D., "Search for Extraterrestrial Life," *Christian Worldview Journal*, 19 May 2010, http://www.

Richards argues that our very existence is the result of a conspiracy rather than a coincidence. As it turns out, the same rare, finely tuned conditions that allow for the emergence of intelligent life on Earth also make it strangely well suited for viewing, analyzing and discovering the rest of the universe around us. On these conditions, Richards elaborates:

"The fact that we inhabit a terrestrial planet with a clear atmosphere and water on its surface; that our moon is just the right size and distance from Earth to stabilize the tilt of Earth's rotation axis; that the size and shape of the moon and sun match in our sky; that our position in our large spiral galaxy is just so; that our sun is its precise mass and composition: all of these and many more are not only necessary for Earth's habitability; they also have been surprisingly crucial for scientists to discover the universe."[334]

Fortunately for all of us, the Earth rests in one of the universe's rare pockets of habitability, providing us with one of the best locations for scientific discoveries to be realized. Richards notes that this is surprising, because "there is no reason to assume that the very same *rare properties* that allow for observers would also provide the best overall setting for observing the world around them."[335] Such a correlation between life and discovery forms a pervasive and telling pattern. It not only contradicts the Copernican Principle, but it additionally suggests that the very *universe itself was designed for discovery.*

The search for physical yet advanced alien life forms will continue, despite the poor showing of the materialist philosophy upon which it is based. It will go on because scientists are now fully aware of just how difficult it would be for life on Earth to have emerged spontaneously from some pre-biotic, primordial soup. The chasm between the chemistry of the early Earth and a reproducing cell is too deep and wide for the scientists to bridge, so many now seek evidence that life originally came from somewhere else and found a friendly environment here in which it could flourish and propagate.[336]

And then there are those with more anti-religious motivations. These are the advocates of the Search for Extraterrestrial Intelligence (SETI) who wrongly assert that finding life elsewhere in the universe will deal a decisive blow to traditional religious beliefs. Of course, God is free to create a universe which is teeming with physical life or a universe in which it is quite rare. No matter where SETI investigations lead the scientist, the findings will in no way demote the status of God as either the Prime Cause or the Sovereign of the Universe.[337]

Whether the searchers for advanced alien life realize it or not, the motivation for their quest is more than a materialist philosophy, but rather a spiritual one. Since they reject the idea of a Heaven, they hope that knowledge, moral guidance and immortality may come to us from some extraterrestrial civilization millions or billions of years in advance of our own. Then in the quest for ancient astronauts, it may be that "nuts and bolts" researchers would be better off in not so quickly dismissing the contactee adherents. They may find that the esoteric philosophies will provide some crucial answers, much as they did for our ancestors in prior ages who first recorded encounters with angels, demons, gods and other celestial beings.

Regardless of our personal conceptions about the extraterrestrial interlopers, the proponents of the ancient astronaut theory believe that the first alien explorers came to Earth countless

---

colsoncenter.org/the-center/columns/call-response/15227-the-search-for-extraterrestrial-life (Accessed 4 November 2014): The journal is published by the Chuck Colson Center for Christian Worldview, Lansdowne, MA. Jay W. Richards received his doctorate in philosophy and theology from the Princeton Theological Seminary and writes articles and books on many subjects in these areas, including the themes of God and evolution.

334 *Ibid.*
335 *Ibid.*
336 *Ibid.*
337 *Ibid.*

millennia ago. And falling in the "nuts and bolts" category, most proclaim that these aliens were beings whose biology was similar to that of modern humans. They created the progenitors of modern humankind by mixing their genetic makeup with that of sub-humans. Allegedly, the purpose of humankind was to serve as a slave race for the ancient astronauts, principally by providing food, mining precious ores and carrying out construction labor. To get our ancestors to submit to the authority of the ancient astronauts to rule over them, the extraterrestrials did not allow the humans to view them face-to-face, but only their figurative representations in the form of symbols (idols), suggesting that their visages were both divine and frightening. Nevertheless, some select humans (prophets and shamans) were occasionally permitted to see their emissaries; and these often appeared as "angels." The aliens would bar the humans from approaching them, except priests and others who had cleansed and covered themselves appropriately. Perhaps these were precautions taken by the extraterrestrials to prevent the spread of germs, thereby suggesting their susceptibility to earthly diseases.

According to these "nuts and bolts" theorists, the ancient astronauts apparently moved about the Earth in spacecraft using a chemically combustible fuel, landing only in safe zones on mountaintops or other rocky outcroppings. This reduced their exposure to dust and provided physical protection from the majority of humans, serving both as a disease control measure and perimeter security. Ancient astronaut theorist William L. Saylor, commenting on the interaction of ancient astronauts with early humanity, writes that:

"The earliest sites had a cave under the rock that protected the priests during the coming and going of the spacecraft. Later they built, or provided humans with tools to build, cyclopean structures – huge earthen, baked brick, or stone ceremonial platforms and pyramids, which served as landmarks and as landing and feeding sites. Since they had little defense against earthly bacteria, they developed methods to nourish themselves with the vapors emanating from food and drink which humans provided and burned for them. The food and drink was provided through the custom of sacrifice, the burning of the meat and blood of animals, and sometimes humans, which the Ancient Astronauts demanded. These ceremonial and feeding sites were located all over the world, most on or near the current equator or near earlier pole-shifted equators. They taught humans agriculture, astronomy, engineering, and provided the first laws. They then departed from the face of Mankind."[338]

In the movie *Contact*, Jodie Foster as an atheist SETI researcher encounters an advanced alien intelligence that has assumed the identity of her deceased father. The aliens materialize in human form allowing us to relate to them and listen to their important message. See http://media.gunaxin.com/the-least-intimidating-movie-aliens/88089.

Superficially the ancient astronaut theory sounds plausible, but its "nuts and bolts" theorists make many assumptions about the aliens and their origin that, in the light of what we now understand about the universe, do not make much sense. For example, why do the aliens have to be "life as we know it?"

338 William L. Saylor, "Ancient Alien Astronaut Theory," *World Mysteries*, 2000-2002, http://www.world-mysteries.com/aa.htm (Accessed 4 November 2014): After a military tour at the Walter Reed Institute of Research, Saylor joined the faculty of the University of North Carolina at Chapel Hill where he developed software for medical imaging applications. He holds a Master of Science degree in Physics from the Naval Postgraduate School and his lifelong hobby is the study of ancient mysteries.

If they are billions of years beyond us or based on an entirely different chemistry or physics, then this condition could easily be precluded. And if their technology was so advanced, they would have no need for human construction brigades of any type. They could easily device machines to do this type of work; or if they were extremely advanced, manipulate matter with their minds. Additionally, for a civilization with the technological capability to traverse the galaxy at ultra-light speeds or pass through man-made wormholes in space, why would they resort to the use of primitive combustible fuel vehicles either within our atmosphere or outside it? And after traveling through the vast distances of outer space, why would the aliens suddenly just "depart from the face of Mankind?" Wouldn't it make more sense for a contingent of the aliens to remain on Earth, or at least in the vicinity of our planet, to monitor our progress, or lack thereof?

Much thought was given, however, to the idea of ancient astronauts in the initial development phases of the space program in the Union of Soviet Socialist Republics (USSR), where in 1964, noted astronomer Nikoli Kardashev developed a scale to distinguish extraterrestrial civilizations that might be encountered as the cosmonauts ventured out into the heavens. Called the Kardashev Scale, it serves to categorize alien civilizations based on their respective abilities to harness varied types of energy at a macro scale.

For example, a Type I civilization harnesses energy at a planetary level. A Type II civilization employs energy at a solar level; and a Type III civilization uses galactic level energies.[339] As a species, humankind is still in the process of attempting to utilize energy on a planetary scale; therefore we are so far not even classified as a Type I civilization. Nevertheless, if humankind can hold things together here on Earth and arrive at the Type I level, then it is not unrealistic to think that we may be invited, as an emergent space-faring species, to join in some kind of solar or even galactic federation.

While most of the scientific community initially scoffed at the idea of ancient astronauts, in their 1966 book, *Intelligent Life in the Universe*,[340] noted American astronomer Carl Sagan and Soviet astrophysicist I. S. Shklovski devoted an entire chapter to arguments that scientists and historians should seriously begin to consider the possibility that extraterrestrial contact occurred at some point during our recorded history.[341] Nevertheless, Sagan and Shklovski stressed that at this juncture the very notion of ancient astronauts was at best speculative and unproven.

Both the American and Soviet scientist argued that at sub-light speeds interstellar travel by extraterrestrial life was a certainty, even when considering technologies that were established or feasible in the late 1960s, pointing out that, "...civilizations, *aeons* more advanced than ours,

---

339   Michael Salla, "Moon-size UFO near Sun may be evidence of Type II alien civilization," *Honolulu Exopolitics Examiner*, 3 November 2014, http://www.examiner.com/article/moon-size-ufo-near-sun-may-be-evidence-of-type-ii-alien-civilization (Accessed 5 November 2014): A moon-sized object of unknown origin appeared near the sun and was caught on film on 2 November 2014 by the Solar Dynamics Observatory as it began recording an increase in solar flare activity as of 28 October 2014. The object displayed unusual geometry, comprising right angles. This led some astronomers to conclude that the object was of alien origin and serves as a dramatic example of a Type II extraterrestrial civilization on the Kardashev Scale since it was apparently manipulating solar energy and leaving in its wake a long trail of solar particles. The 2 November 2014 video of the Moon-sized object so near the Sun provides ample evidence for the presence of a very advanced extraterrestrial civilization within our own solar system. The uncloaking of the Sun-orbiting artificial moon may have been the result of its passing so close or through a massive solar flare, creating an ionization effect in addition to the solar comet-like tail.

340   Carl Sagan and I. S. Shklovski, *Intelligent Life in the Universe* (San Francisco: Holden-Day, 1966)

341   Sagan is credited with writing most of the chapter on the "Possible Consequences of Direct Contact," that scientifically examines the issues raised when considering the possibility of extraterrestrial contact with humans in the remote past.

must be plying the spaces between stars..."[342] Also, Sagan and Shklovski noted that repeated instances of extraterrestrial visitation to Earth were plausible, but would be extremely rare;[343] and pre-scientific narratives can provide a potentially reliable means of describing contact with "alien" civilizations.

To help illustrate this hypothesis, Sagan cites the 1786 expedition of French explorer Jean-François de Galaup, comte de La Pérouse. The Frenchman established the earliest known contact between European and Tlingit cultures. Fortunately, the contact story was preserved as an oral tradition by the preliterate Tlingit. Over a century after its occurrence, the Native American account was recorded by United States Navy anthropologist George T. Emmons. And although it is framed in a Tlingit cultural and spiritual context, the story remained an accurate telling of the 1786 encounter. According to Sagan, this bolsters the assertion that "under certain circumstances, a brief contact with an alien civilization will be recorded in a re-constructible manner." He further states that the reconstruction effort will be greatly aided if, "1) the account is committed to a written record soon after the event; 2) a major change is effected in the contacted society; and 3) no attempt is made by the contacting civilization to disguise its exogenous nature."[344]

Sagan and Shklovski's book forages through ancient history and arrives at a few examples that might be construed as representative of alien contact with humankind. Nevertheless, it should be pointed out that while both of these scientists considered contact with extraterrestrials as possible, it still remained improbable. In his 1979 book, *Broca's Brain*, Sagan suggested that he and his Soviet counterpart might have inspired the wave of ancient astronaut books that flooded the "astounding science" publishing market in the 1970s.[345] He also expressed disapproval of "von Däniken and other uncritical writers" who seemingly built on these ideas not as guarded speculations, but as "valid evidence of extraterrestrial contact." Sagan argued that while many legends and purported out-of-place artifacts were cited in support of ancient astronaut hypotheses, "very few require more than passing mention" and could be easily explained within a more conventional academic framework of history and science. Sagan also took the opportunity to once again reiterate his earlier conclusion that extraterrestrial visits to Earth were possible but unproven, and highly improbable. But he did note that it was not unreasonable to assume that perhaps the Earth has been visited at least a few times down through the ages by the emissaries of an extraterrestrial civilization.

So if extraterrestrial contact is at least probable, has it transpired in our modern age? Of course, many contactees and the new UFO religious movements that have arisen around them assert that contacts are a lot more frequent than Sagan and Shklovski would like us to believe. Some of these new faiths include Raëlism, Scientology, various branches of Theosophy and the Unarius Society, to name but a few; and all of these maintain that in both ancient times and the present-day, contact with extremely advanced extraterrestrial intelligences has taken place. Many of these faiths see both ancient scriptures and recent revelations as connected with the actions of aliens from other planets in our solar system and beyond. Sociologists and psychologists have found that the numerous contactee groups have many similarities, whereby the respective members of these UFO organizations apparently identify their attachment to

342 Carl Sagan and I. S. Shklovski, *Intelligent Life*, 464
343 *Ibid.,* 461
344 *Ibid.*, 453
345 Carl Sagan, *Broca's Brain* (New York, New York: Random House, Inc., 1979), 67.

particular belief systems and the contactees who proffer them with the memes of science fiction.[346]

Dr. J. Allen Hynek, Director of the Lindheimer Astronomical Research Center at Northwestern University in Evanston, Illinois, was clearly fascinated with various reports of humanoids attendant to UFO landings. Of the humanoid cases he investigated, Hynek noted that:

"They seem to come in two sizes, large and small, with the former predominating. The Hopkinsville humanoids and many of those recounted in *Passport to Magonia*[347] are much akin in appearance to the "little folk" of legend and story- elves, brownies, etc. Large heads, spindly feet, and, generally, a head that sits squat on the shoulders without much evidence of neck are often described. *The larger humanoids are reported to be human size or a little larger and are generally well formed. Sometimes they have been termed beautiful.* The smaller ones generally are described as about three and a half feet tall."[348]

Upon hearing banter and jokes about "little green men," Hynek's common sense approach to the UFO phenomenon would cause him to recoil. For most people, humanoid reports tended to throw the whole UFO concept into disrepute. Sure, they reasoned, *unidentified flying objects* might exist, but humanoids were "something else." Hynek recognized that humanoid reports deserved serious, scientific attention. There were many questions that needed to be answered concerning the humanoid reports and any possible contacts they made with humans, whether abductees or contactees. Hynek was cognizant that the UFO occupant reports were becoming too numerous to ignore, but he doubted that the humanoids were of extraterrestrial origin, at least in the sense that the "nuts and bolts" ancient astronaut theorists and ufologists posited this hypothesis in the early 1970s.

Hynek concurred with W. T. Powers, a fellow scientist who wrote a scathing critique of the University of Colorado *Condon Report*. Powers reserved some of his harshest words for Dr. Edward U. Condon, the director of the Air Force-contracted Colorado report. Wrote Powers:

"If Condon really wanted to take a physical science approach, why did he not investigate whether or not an unknown physical phenomenon was responsible for some well-chosen class of UFO reports? Why did he waste his time and our money chasing after lights-in-the-sky reports and reports of Venus, and, especially, why did he set up that straw-man ETI hypothesis? If we don't even know whether a phenomenon exists, how can we possibly test any wild guess about its cause?"[349]

Hynek resented that the Condon Committee chose to test the Extraterrestrial Intelligence (ETI) hypothesis, for this

The core beliefs of the contactee community serve as the outline for creating a wondrous future beyond imagination. See www.pinterest.com.

346   See Christopher H. Partridge, *UFO Religions* (London, UK: Routledge, 2003) for an excellent anthology covering the growth and spiritual implications of the contactee movement.

347   Jacques Vallee, *Passport to Magonia: On UFOs, Folklore and Parallel Worlds* (Chicago: H. Regnery Company, 1969): This book relates over 900 UFO sightings over the past 100 years, linking them to multi-dimensional manifestations versus the dominating extraterrestrial hypothesis, so common at the time it was written. The more "nuts and bolts" crowd went into a tizzy after this book was published, although it prompted Dr. J. Allen Hynek to move closer toward Vallee's positions and later work with him on many UFO and paranormal investigations and projects.

348   J. Allen Hynek, *UFO Experience*, 161,

349   W. T. Powers, "A Critique of the Condon Report," refused publication in *Science* magazine, 1969, but reviewed by Hynek and lauded by him. Excerpts appear in Hynek, *UFO Experience,* 207-210.

theory posits that UFOs are *solid* evidence of extraterrestrial visitations. The Northwestern University scientists wondered how the ETI hypothesis could possibly be shown to be false. Yes, elaborate observational networks might be set up around the United States; but what if no UFOs showed up? Hynek asked rhetorically, "Is that negative proof?" And he answered the question with a resounding "No." After all, the professor reasoned, one can always say that the intelligently guided alien spaceships *knew* that they were expected, and simply avoided the trap.[350]

And insofar as the Condon Committee was unable to find even a partially valid explanation for almost a third of the cases they looked at (swamp gas, Venus seen under unusual atmospheric conditions, unconventional military aircraft, etc.), Hynek pondered what this might possibly say about the ETI hypothesis. In the professor's estimation, it signified nothing. Because there is no salient evidence for the existence of intelligent life in the universe on the physical plane, one could easily postulate worlds existing outside our dimension in the astral or etheric planes that would easily satisfy and explain virtually all of the reported antics of any UFO. In other words, there was no way for the Condon Committee to establish that the ETI hypothesis was true or false since its members had devised no operational method for accomplishing this feat. Therefore, the Condon Committee could hardly be considered to be conducting a "scientific investigation" into the reality of the UFO phenomenon. Since accepted scientific procedure requires that any hypothesis be put to a test, then it is more or less an "If this happens, then the following will ensue...." type of scenario. If the "then" in this hypothesis is testable, it may thus be demonstrated to be either false or true. Hynek asked, "Is there some crucial experiment that can be performed or some observation made that will prove the hypothesis false? If not, how can one distinguish between one hypothesis and another?" Such hypotheses would forever remain in limbo, with warring sects haggling over them. Hynek wrote that, "Even if the Condon Committee had had orders of magnitude more data, they tackled a hopeless task. *The only hypothesis the committee could have productively tested was: There exists a phenomenon, described by the content of UFO reports, a phenomenon which presently is not physically explainable.*"[351] Not surprisingly, this corresponds nicely to the hypothesis arrived at by the psychologist Carl Jung, as previously explained in this chapter.[352]

To Hynek, the old paradigms for the analysis of various UFO phenomena were no longer applicable since it was "something" that apparently existed in some level but could not be readily classified as *physically explainable* in the context of our current degree of scientific sophistication and understanding. An exemplary and noted astronomer like Hynek came early to the conclusion that UFOs did not fit nicely within the accepted Newtonian macroscopic view of the universe. But in the quantum *omniverse* of dark matter, alternate dimensions, parallel worlds and temporal distortions like wormholes (space and time tunnels), perhaps a place for these illusory objects might be found.

In the early 1970s, it began to look like Hynek was coming out of his "nuts and bolts" box to look at the UFO phenomenon from a new perspective, one he would come to share with the great French ufologist Jacques Vallee- that the UFOs and their occupants hailed from other dimensions, other realities.

Hynek was distinguishing himself as a bold scientist, versus a mere technician. Gary Zukav, a New Age theoretician who incorporates cutting-edge physics into his paranormal

---

350 Hynek, *UFO Experience*, 201.
351 *Ibid.,* 200-201
352 Carl G. Jung, *Collected Works*

investigations, examined the qualities that constitute a true scientist:

"When most people say 'scientist' they mean 'technician.' A technician is a highly trained person whose job is to apply known techniques and principles. He deals with the known. *A scientist is a person who seeks to know the true nature of physical reality. He deals with the unknown.*

In short, *scientists discover* and *technicians apply*. However, it is no longer evident whether scientists really discover new things or whether they *create* them. Many people believe that 'discovery' is actually an act of creation. *If this is so then the distinctions between scientists, poets, painters and writers is not clear.* In fact, it is possible that scientists, poets, painters and writers are all members of the same family of people whose gift it is by nature to take those things which we call commonplace and *re-present* them to us in such ways that our self-imposed limitations are expanded. *Those people in whom this gift is especially pronounced, we call geniuses.*

The fact is that most "scientists" are technicians. They are not interested in the essentially new. Their field of vision is relatively narrow; their energies are directed toward applying what is already known. *Because their noses often are buried in the bark of a particular tree, it is difficult to speak meaningfully to them of forests.*"[353]

Therefore, in regard to ancient astronauts, it is much more likely that they were perceived as "gods" or other supernatural beings, precisely because they were much more than physical beings or humanoids akin to us, even though they presented the appearance of being such. They were probably multidimensional, and hailing from some other reality. We must keep in mind, as Zukav has affirmed, that *"Commonplace contradictions, in fact, are at the heart of the new physics. They tell us again and again that the world* (or the universe to which it belongs) *may not be what we think it is. It may be much, much more."*[354] The god and angel-like qualities ascribed to some current UFO occupants by the contactees may also fit within this same paradigm.

Analysis of the Contactee Movement

The contactees are those special individuals who are convinced that they encountered alien "space intelligences." In many cases, ufologists have observed that there does seem to be a heightening of what one would normally consider manifestations of extrasensory perception (ESP) or other psychic powers after the contact experience with an allegedly benevolent space being. Therefore, some contactees maintain that they remain in direct communication with these entities through telepathic thought transference. Along with these newly-acquired abilities, the contactee is often left with a timetable of certain predictions for future events.

Like Ted Owens, many of the contactees continue to be instilled with an almost religious fervor to spread the message that was given to them by these exalted beings. According to an entry in the *Encyclopedia of the Unusual and Unexplained*, a distillation of such messages would reveal concepts such as the following:

"Humankind is not alone in the solar system and now brothers and sisters from outer space have come to Earth to help those humans who will listen to their promise of a larger universe.

The space beings want humankind to become eligible to join an intergalactic spiritual federation.

353 Gary Zukav, *Dancing Wu Li Masters: An Overview of the New Physics* (New York, New York: William Morrow, 1979), 9, 10.
354 *Ibid.,* 27

The space beings are to assist the people of Earth to lift their spiritual vibratory rate so they may enter new dimensions. (According to the space beings, Jesus, Krishna, Confucius, and many of the other leaders of the great religions came to Earth to teach humanity these same abilities.)

The citizens of Earth stand now in the transitional period before the dawn of a New Age of peace, love, and understanding.

If the Earthlings should not raise their vibratory rate within a set period of time, severe Earth changes and major cataclysms will take place."[355]

As to how the flying-saucer contactees encounter these remarkable entities, a synthesis of such experiences reveals the following:

They first saw a UFO on the ground, hovering low overhead, or heard a slight humming sound above them that drew their attention to a mysterious craft.

Next, a warm ray of "light" emanated from the craft and touched the contactees on the neck, the crown of the head, or the middle of the forehead. They may have lost consciousness at this point and, upon awakening, may have discovered that they could not account for anywhere from a minute or two to an hour or two of their time. Those contactees who later claim direct communication with space beings generally state that they have no recollection of any period of unconsciousness, but they maintain that they "heard" a voice speaking to them from inside their own heads.[356]

Many of the contactees are also told that they were selected precisely because they are aliens themselves, planted on Earth as very small children to carry out important missions for the "space brothers" later in life, thus fulfilling their destinies. It should also be noted that after the initial contact experience, nearly all seem to suffer through several days of restlessness, irritability and sleeplessness. And when they finally do get some sleep, they report having unusual dreams or even nightmares.[357]

After a period lasting anywhere from one week to several months, the contactee who received a message from the space beings feels prepared to go forth and share it with others, with none feeling any fear of their space brothers and sisters. In fact, most look forward to a return visit from these exalted beings. However, family and friends of the contactees do report that they are different and changed persons after their alleged experience with these entities.[358]

The *Encyclopedia* entry also notes that:

"Most UFO contactees agree that the space beings' most prominent characteristic is wisdom, and they seem to take their scientific knowledge for granted. After all, contactees reason, if they have traveled through space from other worlds to Earth, then they must be extremely intelligent."[359]

Of course, the "nuts and bolts" scientists remain singularly unimpressed with the specific technical information that has been relayed by the contactees. On the other hand, those sympathetic to the contactees recognize the ethereal nature of their experiences and might argue that the alien science is just too incomprehensible to humankind at this point in our

355 "UFO Contactees and Abductees," *Encyclopedia of the Unusual and Unexplained*, author not stated, on-line edition, 2008, http://www.unexplainedstuff.com/Invaders-from-Outer-Space/UFO-Contactees-and-Abductees.html (Accessed 7 October 2014)
356 *Ibid.*
357 *Ibid.*
358 *Ibid.*
359 *Ibid.*

cosmic evolution as a species, so there is no use in trying to distinguish it from our own, as theirs will always come across as "magic." Yet other theorists suggest that the contactees are not communicating with alien entities at all, but rather, with a higher aspect of their own psyches, or "oversouls," to borrow from the parlance of the psychics.

Many other UFO researchers and theologians have noted that the extraterrestrials, or whatever they are, appear to function as the angels of more conventional religions. Both classifications of beings are concerned about Earth and its future and seem to be actively trying to protect it and its inhabitants. Both the angels and the space beings manifest as powerful entities that appear to transcend our own space-time continuum, exerting control over the physical limitations of our own reality—yet they are benevolent in their actions toward bumbling, ineffectual humankind. It also seems that these entities have deliberately placed themselves in the role of being the messengers of God or some other celestial authority, like the Lords of the Flame on Venus. Most of us sincerely want to believe that such beings exist and that they can help us extricate ourselves from any emergent disasters of our own making. Many of the contactees have also been known to employ some of the techniques of Spiritualism, whereby following the initial contact, they act as sensitives in channeling information from the entity after its departure from the Earth plane. The late British contactee George King, founder of the Aetherius Society, provides us with an excellent example of this. His channeled messages from various entities from other planets in our solar system and beyond have provided significant spiritual guidance in the lives of thousands worldwide. Many of the contactees in this psychic category also share backgrounds in the study of Theosophy and are or were at one time active members of the Theosophical Society or other psychic development groups.

While it is impossible to estimate how many individuals claim to receive messages from such entities, contactee groups continue to emerge and coalesce around them. Some provide new spins on previously given revelations and others generate new food for thought. There is also a group of the so-called "silent contactees"—men and women who have not gathered groups about them but who have established contact with what they feel are entities from other worlds or levels of existence. For better or worse, these contactees have directed their lives according to the dictates of those entities. These men and women come from all walks of life. They confide their experiences only to close associates and family members, so we will probably never know how many there truly are.

Apart from Helena Blavatsky and the Theosophical Society, Venusian contacts with select humans continued to play a significant role in the formation of many esoteric religions well into the twentieth century. In 1934, an American couple, Guy and Edna Ballard, formed the so-called I AM sect, which drew heavily on Theosophy and featured Venusian elements. The Ballards claimed that Venusians were operating inside a complex deep under Mt. Shasta in Northern California. And in 1943, Britain's noted Christian fantasy writer, C.S. Lewis, restaged the tale of the Garden of Eden on Venus in his mystical novel, *Perelandra*.[360] And two years later, it was John Whiteside Parsons, a ubiquitous figure who linked the worlds of rocketry, science fiction, and the supernatural, who reportedly had a vision in the Mojave Desert involving a Venusian. As it turned out, Parsons was a close associate of L. Ron Hubbard, the founder of Scientology, who later claimed his own Venusian experience. In the early 1970s, however, after the Mariner and Venera space probes relayed unfavorable information about the Venusian surface back to awaiting scientists in the United States and Soviet Union, respectively, Scientology officials

---

360 C. S. Lewis, *Perelandra* (London, UK: Bodley Head, 1943).

Christian mystic C. S. Lewis wrote about the planet Venus as the site of the Garden of Eden, humankind's original home. He referred to the planet's true name as *Perelandra*. See http://dkmz.net/perelandra-c-s-lewis-anti-gospel/.

downplayed Hubbard's Venusian contact claims and tried to erase such from the official history of their church. Other religious groups sprang up related to Venus, such as the previously mentioned Aetherius Society, founded in 1956, and Eckankar, established in 1965, with its focus on the ancient art of astral travel.[361]

Of course, Venus has always had the advantage of its brightness, which has caused countless mistaken reports of flying saucers. Such prominent figures as J. Allen Hynek, Jacques Vallee, and Frank Salisbury[362] all conceded that the planet caused a lot of false UFO sightings. Additionally, at the height of the contactee movement in the 1950s, Venus was so influential that it outdid Mars and all other planets. It was during this decade that the majority of the visible contactees were reporting contacts with Venusians.[363] Notes *Canadian National Post* correspondent Scott Van Wynsberghe: " In a 1977 survey by J. Gordon Melton, a sampling of 35 of these early 'contactees' featured 13 cases of Venusians and only 11 with Martians."[364] And suspecting that something other than "spacemen" were at work here, UFO investigators Jerome Clark and Loren Coleman have commented: "The Venusian claims usually contain the strongest religious overtones."[365]

---

361 Scott Van Wynsberghe, "I'm Your Venus: Our Weird, Nasty Sister," 4 September 2012, *National Post*, Toronto, Ontario.

362 Frank B. Salisbury, space biologist at Utah State University, *Utah UFO Display: A Scientist's Report* (Old Greenwich, Connecticut: Devin-Adair Publishers, 1972): Dr. Salisbury analyzed over 400 UFO reports from Utah's Uintah Basin.

363 Van Wynsberghe

364 *Ibid.*

365 *Ibid:* Direct quote taken from *National Post* article.

Chapter V:
Venusians Among Us

Why do I love the sound of children's voices in unknown games
So much on a summer's night,
Lightning bugs lifting heavily out of the dry grass
Like alien spacecraft looking for higher ground,
Darkness beginning to sift like coffee grains over the neighborhood?
Whunk of a ball being kicked,
Surf-suck and surf-spill from traffic along the by-pass,
American twilight, Venus just lit in the third heaven,
Time-tick between "Okay, let's go," and "This earth is not my home."
Why do I care about this? Whatever happens will happen
With or without us, with or without these verbal amulets….

—Charles Wright, "American Twilight"
in *Negative Blue: Selected Later Poems* (2000)

From the earliest antiquities, the Venusians have been looking out for us. Here some winged "Venus girls" swoop down to save Wonder Woman. See http://thanley.wordpress.com/tag/venus/.

In American poet laureate Charles Wright's "American Twilight," one senses nostalgia for the pre-Vietnam War era in the United States. There was, and still is, a perception that this was a care-free time. Wright highlights suburban children playing kickball outside right before sunset, when the fireflies are first coming out for the night. But it's also a "twilight" season, to be sure, for there is a darkness rolling in. Newly constructed freeways, with their arteries and by-passes sated with automobiles, are clogging the landscape; and the political leaders ponder what should be done about stemming communism around the world.

The 1950s and early 1960s marked the dawn of the Space Age, and with it the so-called "Space Craze." Sparked by massive waves of flying saucer sightings, Hollywood generated movies like *The Day the Earth Stood Still* (1951), *The War of the Worlds* (1953) and *This Island Earth* (1955).[366] These dramatic presentations captured both the attention and interest of most Americans. But the so-called Space Age really went into high gear when the Soviets launched the Sputnik I satellite in October 1957. After that, Americans lives would change forever.

---

366 *This Island Earth* (Universal International Pictures, 1955): William Alland, Producer; Joseph M. Newman, Jack Arnold, Directors; Starring Jeff Morrow, Faith Domergue and Rex Reason.

Naturally, the presence of a Soviet satellite in orbit around the Earth caused an instant media sensation. It also sparked an overwhelming sense of fear in the hearts of many Americans. And when the Soviets launched Sputnik II, many more Americans became obsessed with the idea that our country was lagging behind the Soviets and that the more we delayed getting into space, the harder it was going to be to catch up.

The Space Craze even impacted children's education in public schools. Just one year after the first Sputnik launch, Congress passed the National Defense Education Act. This supplied educators with one billion dollars over seven years to develop skills that were essential to augmenting national defense. By passing the act, the Congress hoped to ensure that America would have enough scientists and engineers to develop and sustain our own space program well into the future. Even the young Senator John F. Kennedy of Massachusetts successfully picked up on the Space Race as a talking point in his 1960 presidential bid.

And just as the Space Craze infiltrated both America's news and entertainment, it also influenced the development of numerous consumer products. Throughout the Space Craze, children eagerly played with space-themed toys and new forms of playground equipment that emulated Space Race artifacts like helmets, ray guns and rockets. The Space Craze even impacted the development of adult consumer products such as tailfins on cars, inspired by rockets, and new futuristic, Space Age-designed appliances such as those originally modeled in Disneyland's flying saucer-shaped Home of Tomorrow exhibit. Even fashion and household decorative items were tailored to meet the huge Space Craze demands.

But even more so than the fear generated by the Soviet presence in space, Americans were intrigued by the possibility of intelligent life existing on other planets, especially nearby in our solar system. The rash of UFO sightings since the late 1940s had convinced the majority of Americans that the so-called "flying saucers" were real. Despite official denials from the Air Force and other government agencies, the majority of Americans came to believe that these objects were interplanetary spacecraft. Many critics of the government cover-up summed it up best with the following slogan: "Flying Saucers Are Real, The Air Force is an Illusion." And if the UFO occupants looked anything like us, it was not unreasonable to assume that they could blend in with our population, much as the alien Klaatu, when posing as "Mr. Carpenter," did in the movie, *The Day the Earth Stood Still.*

Easy Rider and the Venusians

While the findings of the United States Mariner and the Soviet Venera probes certainly put a damper on finding any extant Venusians, at least in the estimations of the scientific community, some of the popular notions about the Venusian "space brothers" managed to carry over from the contactees of the 1950s and into the collective consciousness of Americans in the late1960s. For example, in the 1969 cult classic, *Easy Rider,*[367] two counterculture bikers, Wyatt (Peter Fonda) and Billy (Dennis Hopper), travel from Los Angeles to New Orleans, hoping to discover the real America, whence they pick up a hitchhiker, George Hanson (Jack Nicholson), along the way in the California desert. From the following dialogue, we come to understand that Hanson was familiar with the writings of George Adamski, who addressed many of the same aspects of Venusians here on Earth in his numerous flying saucer books:

---

367 *Easy Rider* (Columbia Pictures, 1969): Peter Fonda, William L. Hayward, Bob Rafelson and Bert Schneider, Producers; Dennis Hopper, Director; Peter Fonda, Dennis Hopper and Terry Southern, Writers; Starring Peter Fonda as Wyatt, Dennis Hopper as Billy and Jack Nicholson as George Hanson.

Campfire Chat from *Easy Rider*, "The Venusians"

Wyatt explains how George should smoke the joint: You've got to hold it in your lungs longer.

Billy: What…. was that, man? What the hell was that?

Wyatt: I don't know, man.

Billy: I was watching this object…. like the satellite we saw. And it went right across the sky. And then…. I mean, it just suddenly…. It just changed direction and went whizzing off. It flashed and—

Wyatt: You're stoned out of your mind.

Billy: Oh, yeah. I'm stoned, man. But, like, I saw a satellite. And it was going across the sky, and it flashed three times at me and zigzagged and whizzed off. And l saw it.

George: *That was a UFO beaming back at you. Me and Eric Heisman was down in Mexico two weeks ago. We seen forty of them flying in formation. They've got bases all over the world now. They've been coming here ever since 1946, when scientists started bouncing radar beams off the moon. And they've been living and working among us ever since. The government knows all about them.*

"Miss Flying Saucer" by Bill Randall (1959) epitomizes the upbeat spirit of the Space Age. See www.tumblr.com.

Billy: What are you talking, man?

George: You just seen one of them, didn't you?

Billy: I saw something, but l didn't see it working here.

George: *Well, they are people, just like us from within our own solar system. Except that their society is more highly evolved. They don't have no wars. They got no monetary system. They don't have any leaders, because each man is a leader. Because of their technology they're able to feed, clothe, house and transport themselves equally and with no effort.*

Billy: You know something? You want to know what I think? I think this is a crackpot idea. That's what I think. How about that? Think it's a crackpot idea. If they're so smart, why don't they reveal themselves and get it over with?

George: *Why don't they reveal themselves is because if they did it'd cause a general panic. Now, we still have leaders upon whom we rely to release this information. These leaders have decided to repress this information because of the shock that it would cause to our antiquated systems. Now, the result has been that the Venusians have contacted people at all walks of life…. all walks of life. It would be a devastating blow to our antiquated systems. Now Venusians are meeting with people in all walks of life in an advisory capacity. For once, man will have a god-like control over his own destiny. He'll have a chance to transcend and to evolve with some equality for all.*

Wyatt: How's your joint, George?

George: I believe it went out. I got to talking so much, I clean forgot about…. It went out.

Wyatt: Save it and we'll do it tomorrow morning. *It gives you a new way of looking at the day.*

In the above dialogue, a true sense of the *Zeitgeist* was captured. The counterculture was in full swing, with protests raging against the so-called "Establishment" that bogged us down into a seemingly endless conflict in Vietnam. Americans were looking for alternatives; and it was nice to know that a Shangri-La that we could strive to emulate existed somewhere, even if in the Venus of imagination. At least it provided some with a "new way of looking at the day."

George Hanson (left, Jack Nicholson), smoking his first joint, pontificates on the Venusian presence on Earth with Wyatt (right, Peter Fonda) and Billy (not shown, Dennis Hopper). See www.standbyformindcontrol.com.

David Bowie, a.k.a. the "Space Oddity"

Even across the "Pond," so to speak, the Venusians were not lost to the public's awareness of their presence on Earth. Here are some of the lyrics from David Bowie's single, "Memory of a Free Festival,"[368] that later made it into his *Space Oddity* album in 1969:

> *We scanned the skies with rainbow eyes and saw machines of every shape and size*
> *We talked with tall Venusians passing through*
> *And Peter tried to climb aboard but the Captain shook his head*
> *And away they soared*
> *Climbing through*
> *the ivory vibrant cloud*
> *Someone passed some bliss among the crowd*
> *And We walked back to the road, unchained*

The alien motif is so prominent in the lyrics of nearly all of David Bowie's songs that some have begun to speculate that the glam rocker may himself be of extraterrestrial origin. Notes entertainment correspondent Jamie Lees of the St. Louis, Missouri, *Riverfront Times*:

"I think this is a case of hiding in plain sight. Since the very beginning of his career, Bowie has presented himself as a space age being from another universe, a star from the stars. There is scarcely a Bowie song or piece of art that does not reference space or aliens: *Space Oddity, Starman, The Rise and Fall of Ziggy Stardust* and the *Spiders from Mars, The Man Who Fell to Earth, Moonage Daydream, Hallo Spaceboy, Earthling, Life on Mars, Loving the Alien...* the list could go on and on. (And if you can show me that *Oh, You Pretty Things!* is about any subject other than the impending extraterrestrial colonization of Earth, then I'm all ears.)"[369]

In his Ziggy Stardust[370] persona, David Bowie presents himself to us as an alien assuming the form of a rock star; while in the movie, *The Man Who Fell to Earth*,[371] he depicts an

368   *Space Oddity* (RCA, 11 July 1969), David Bowie, artist
369   Jamie Lees, "David Bowie Releases *The Next Day*, is Real-Life Space Alien. No, Seriously," 13 March 2013, St. Louis, Missouri.
370   *Ziggy Stardust and the Spiders from Mars* (RCA single, 6 June 1972), David Bowie, artist
371   *The Man Who Fell to Earth* (British Lion Film Corporation and Cinema 5, 1976), Michael Deeley, Si Letvinoff, John

extraterrestrial who crash lands on Earth and then becomes extremely wealthy through the sale of various inventions in the hopes of finding some way to return to his home planet and help the inhabitants there solve a severe water shortage. In his album, *The Next Day*,[372] the rock icon continues with the space theme throughout. Of his work on *Next Day*, Lees further notes that:

"Bowie's recent role on Earth is to act as an internationally successful music icon with unprecedented staying power. The job of "rock star" really is the perfect cover for an alien: he can easily influence the masses, any odd or outrageous behavior is expected and he has the ability to freely spread his alien seed among unsuspicious females (Groupies).

Glam rock, specifically, helped Bowie to blend in. Seen as a fashion trailblazer, he could appear weird and shiny and futuristic and he was just seen as a leader among the glittered masses. Aliens must be able to see the future, too, because they seem to have set Bowie's human time clock improperly. He's always been a little bit ahead of the trends, be it through embracing glam, utilizing electronica or pushing new genres and styles. Recently when he's caught by paparazzi on the streets, he seems to always be wearing a version of an all gray outfit-- is it the uniform of the future? I guess we'll find out.

Even now, his health, productivity and good looks just don't make any sense. He's aged very well–a little too well, if you ask me. In his work, he's always shown a unique ability to collaborate with the unique, the talented, the odd and the unexplainable. His long-time bass goddess, Gail Ann Dorsey, is too amazing to be real and what's up with his alien twin sister, Tilda Swinton? He finally broke down and featured her in his new music video. Again, putting the obvious right in our faces as to avoid suspicion."[373]

Bowie is currently married to Iman Mohamed Abdulmajid, the Somali supermodel, actress and entrepreneur, who with her big head and long limbs, Lees describes as the "closest thing we have on this planet to an alien-looking female." Iman, however, has so far withheld any comments on Bowie's alien nature; but his former wife Angela had quite a bit to say about it:

"And now I have to tell you something important, crucial really. Although I am uncertain about it these days, I must confess that as I watched David committing his art to tape in that studio, a feeling inside me became a conviction. *David was one of the Light People.*

This belief was an integral component of my attraction to him, and a powerful factor in the loyalty and trust I (mis)placed in him. So I'll tell you about the Light People, and you can scoff all you want or maybe, if you were there in the sixties (and I mean there, not just catching the whole strange trip on TV), you will understand.

The Light People, in my scheme of things, were aliens: extraterrestrials, inhabitants of some other planet or space or dimension. They were infinitely more advanced, intelligent and powerful than Earth people, and indeed, we may have been their creation; it was possible, I theorized, that Earth was a science project of sorts for the Light People, and human

David Bowie portrays an extraterrestrial in *The Man Who Fell to Earth*, British Lion Film Corporation and Cinema 5 (1976). See http://www.blu-raydefinition.com/reviews/the-man-who-fell-to-earth-uk-release-blu-ray-review.html.

Perverall and Barry Spikings, Producers; Nicholas Roeg, Director; Starring David Bowie, Rip Torn and Candy Clark.
372 *Next Day* (Columbia single, 8 March 2013), David Bowie, artist
373 Jamie Lees, "David Bowie Releases *The Next Day*"

society the equivalent of an elaborate ant colony they could observe and manipulate at will. They did this chiefly by monitoring crucial junctures in human development, and sending in entities to influence events toward the course they desired. Such entities were spirits, basically, which could dwell and operate within otherwise entirely human beings."[374]

So in Angela's estimation, an alien spirit just walked into David's body. Nevertheless, it did not seem to do the rocker any harm, for he found himself in good company. Angela further explains:

"My theory posited that many of the great individuals in human history, those who advanced our progress far beyond contemporary reason or pulled our fat from the fire when all seemed lost- Leonardo, Galileo, Newton, Gandhi, Churchill- were hosts to Light People spirits. So as I lived and breathed and went about my business in the cosmic atmosphere of sixties alternative London, it made perfect sense to me that David, along with a handful of other unique voices- Bob Dylan, John Lennon, Jimi Hendrix- was Lit from within.

Thus there were in my rationale the very best reasons for my long devotion to David. I was serving the Light.

Ultimately, the Light People philosophy served my purposes very well. It was like a good pair of shades and a particularly effective set of earplugs all in one: it kept the sunlight out of my eyes as I focused dead ahead on my goals, and it diminished the din of reality as I moved resolutely forward. *Reality is fine, you know, but it can really get in your way when you're chasing a dream."*[375]

Throughout his career, Bowie has made numerous references to UFOs and extraterrestrials in interviews spanning multi-media. For example, in a December 1974 appearance on Dick Cavett's *Wide World of Entertainment* television program, Bowie acted out the shaky take-off of a conventional aircraft, and then demonstrated the vertical take-off of a "flying saucer" in response to Cavett's questioning as to why he refused to fly with any commercial carrier. The implication was that he had previously been a passenger on a flying saucer and preferred the way it flew over a traditional airplane or jet.

And in an interview with a correspondent from *Creem* magazine,[376] Bowie described seeing a fleet of UFOs fly over an English observatory on a regular basis, in addition to his distrust in handing over information about UFOs to the media, in general, that he accused of "cultural manipulation" to obscure the truth about alien visitations. Also, during a radio interview in the British Isles, Bowie was asked what he thought UFOs might be, to which he responded, "A friend and I were travelling in the English countryside when we both noticed a strange object hovering above a field. From then on I have come to take this phenomenon seriously. *I believe that what I saw was not an object, but a projection of my own mind trying to make sense of this quantum topological doorway into dimensions beyond our own. It's as if our dimension is but one among an infinite number of others."*[377]

An additional incident of note took place at the 34th annual edition of the Brit Awards held in London on 19 February 2014, where Kate Moss received the British phonographic industry's Best Male Artist award on behalf of David Bowie for the release of his *Next Day*

---

374 Angela Bowie with Patrick Carr, *Backstage Passes: Life on the Wild Side with David Bowie* (New York, New York: Cooper Square Press, 1993), 56.

375 *Ibid.,* 57

376 Bruno Stein, "David Bowie: An Exclusive Interview," *Creem* magazine, February 1975, Vol. 6, No. 9.

377 Peter R. Koenig, "The Laughing Gnostic: David Bowie and the Occult," 1996, http://www.parareligion.ch/bowie.htm (Accessed 11 November 2014).

album. Noel Gallagher, the emcee at the proceedings, announced that, "David Bowie is sending his representative on Earth, which is the one and only Kate Moss, who is going to accept this award on his behalf." When Moss took to the stage, she was attired in Bowie's original Ziggy Stardust outfit.

Said Moss, "Good evening, ladies and gentlemen; David has asked me to say this." She then held up a card and went on to read it, continuing: "In Japanese myth, the rabbits on my old costume (of Ziggy Stardust), that Kate's wearing, live on the moon. *Kate comes from Venus, and I from Mars*. So that's nice. I'm completely delighted to have a Brit for being Best Male, and I am – aren't I, Kate?" Moss nodded and Gallagher joined in with a resounding, "Yes."[378]

Besides being called out as a Venusian by David Bowie, in 2007 *Time* magazine listed Moss, a supermodel, music and cultural icon, as one of the 100 most influential people in the world.[379] What we can gather from this is that if Bowie's ex-wife, Angela, is correct, and Bowie was telling the truth about being a Martian and Kate Moss a Venusian, then aliens from the multi-dimensional aspects of various planets in our solar system have influenced the development of our society throughout history down to the present time, especially proving to be a significant force in the entertainment industry.

Nikola Tesla

If Venus does harbor any kind of life, physical or ultra-dimensional, its discovery will mark one of the greatest achievements in human history. And who could have guessed that Venusians were living among us through countless millennia? When the idea first pops into one's mind, it almost seems impossible. In the next few pages, however, we will examine some of the more audacious claims made by the great inventor, Nikola Tesla (1856-1943), concerning his own Venusian origins and the Venusians' glorious long-range plans for us and our planet. And of all the Venusians that have contributed to the development of civilization and advanced technology here on Earth, Nikola Tesla would have to rate a place somewhere near the top of the list.

For Tesla, often referred to as a "wizard" and the "patron saint of modern electricity," is credited with being the inspiration for radio, radar and even robotics. Among his creations and inventions are counted the channeling of alternating current, fluorescent and neon lighting, wireless telegraphy and the giant hydroelectric turbines still in use harnessing energy at Niagara Falls. These turbines are known for generating some of the least expensive electricity anywhere on the planet.[380] And concerning the recent installation of power outlets to recharge electric cars in New York State and neighboring Ontario Province, Niagara Falls Mayor Paul Dyster said:

"It was in Niagara Falls that Nikola Tesla, father of the electrical age and early advocate for Niagara hydropower, first demonstrated the superiority of AC power transmission, helping to light the world at the end of the 19th and beginning of the 20th centuries. Now, we're entering the second great age of electricity, as we seek new sources of clean, green electrical power to light our homes, power our factories, and fuel our all-American passion for automobiles with

378 Ashley Lee, George Szalai, BRIT Awards: David Bowie Accepts Best Male Artist Award through Kate Moss," *Hollywood Reporter*, California, 19 February 2014.

379 Belinda Luscombe, "Artists and Entertainers: Kate Moss," *Time* magazine, 3 May 2007.

380 "Niagara Power Plant," *New York Power Authority*, http://www.nypa.gov/facilities/niagara.htm (Accessed 16 November 2014).

the advent of the electric car. How fitting that we have gathered here in Niagara to celebrate Gov. Andrew Cuomo and NYPA's determination to move our state to the vanguard in providing vital logistic support for the future development of the electric car industry."[381]

Incidentally, before proceeding to the life of Nikola Tesla, it should be pointed out that David Bowie played the role of Tesla in the film, *The Prestige*.[382] Also remember that Bowie played an *alien who became a prolific inventor* in the film, *The Man Who Fell to Earth*, previously referenced. The original title of the "Man Who Fell to Earth" has aptly been applied to only one authentic super-genius and his love for humanity; a great gift that fell from Venus-Nikola Tesla.

The assertion that Tesla claimed to be a Venusian comes from Arthur Matthews**,** the last man to have worked side-by-side with the great scientist on a plethora of ground-breaking experiments and projects. Tesla is alleged to have passed on all of his secrets to his young apprentice, Matthews, who generally kept a low profile, keeping out of the public eye. He lived in a modest home tucked away on the shores of rural and rustic Lake Beauport, Quebec, Canada. Long after Tesla's death, thousands of inquiring individuals, such as curiosity-seekers, would-be inventors and the agents of various governments, made the trek to Canada to tap Matthews for information. They would ask him about Tesla's work on sundry projects and seek help in building some kind of apparatus or another, but Matthews would always say that the "answers are in Tesla's patents, lectures and articles." If the seeker was diligent enough, he or she was near certain to find the answer so ardently sought for.[383]

In the early 1940s, Matthews co-authored a book with Tesla, the *Wall of Light*;[384] but it was not copyrighted until 1971. The book represents the only known writings of Tesla that were not of a solely technical nature. Part I was written by Tesla and Part II by Matthews. Tesla writes passionately about his boyhood experiences, feelings, research and strange life amongst Earth's human population. In Part II, Matthews writes about his and Tesla's work on the construction of an impenetrable force field device that they called the "Wall of Light." He also provides an account of the landing of a saucer-shaped scout craft on his property, whence two occupants disembarked, identified themselves as Venusians, and spent the remainder of the day filling him in on the missing details of Tesla's remarkable life.

Matthews acknowledged that, "…Tesla had strange ideas," adding that, "*He always thought he came from the planet Venus. He said as much to me, and the crew of a Venus spaceship said in one of their first messages, that a male child was 'born' onboard their ship during its trip from Venus to Earth in July, 1856*… He arrived in Smiljan, near Gospic in Lika, Croatia. (This is why he claimed that he was *not born*)."[385] Of course, whether Tesla was an Earthling or a Venusian, he had to be born at some place and at some specific time. So what we can infer from this is that in the last statement, Matthews meant to say that he was *not born on Earth, in the traditional sense that Earthlings are born, but born on Venus through another birthing process we have yet to comprehend.*

381 Maura Balaban and Doug Hartmayer, "New Electric Vehicle Charging Stations Installed at Niagara Falls International Airport to Mark National Drive Electric Week: EV Infrastructure Part of Charge NY Initiative to Meet Growing Demand for Plug-Ins," *New York Power Authority* press release, *19 September 2014,* http://www.nypa.gov/Press/2014/091914.html *(Accessed 16 November 2014).*

382 *The Prestige* (Warner Brothers, 17 October 2006): Christopher Nolan, et al., Producers; Christopher Nolan, Director; Starring Hugh Jackman, Christian Bale, Michael Caine, David Bowie.

383 Doug Yurcher, "Son of Tesla," *World Mysteries Blog*, 31 August 2013, http://blog.world-mysteries.com/guest_authors/doug-yurchey/son-of-tesla/ (Accessed 13 November 2014).

384 Arthur Hugh Matthews, Nikola Tesla, *Wall of Light* (Lake Beauport, Quebec, Canada: Self-published, 1971).

385 *Ibid.*

In the revealing *Wall of Light*, Matthews reported that the Venusians informed him that Tesla was born on one of their spaceships at midnight on 9 July 1856; although his birth was later reported as taking place on 10 July 1856. The Venusians entrusted the infant to a suitable couple of "Earth parents," the Rev. Milutin (Serbian Orthodox Church) and Djuka (Mandic) Tesla (the daughter of a Serbian Orthodox priest),[386] who would raise the young boy as if he were their own son. The child was named Nikola by the Venusians, which is the name of his family town, in reverse, on Venus, called *Alokin*.[387] In later years, but before Jerry Siegel and Joe Shuster came up with their comic book creation, Tesla was referred to as the "*Superman of the Industrial Age*."[388] One cannot help but noticing the parallels in Tesla's arrival on Earth with that of the Kyptonian infant, Kal-El, who was found and raised by the goodly Kansas farm couple, Jonathan and Martha Kent. We should also keep in mind that before their character evolved into the moral American champion of freedom and justice beloved by all, Jerry Siegel and Joe Shuster's original "Superman" was not operating under the guise of the mild-mannered reporter Clark Kent, but openly challenging the powers-that-be as Bill Dunn, a megalomaniacal, mad scientist who first appeared in the January 1933 issue of *Science Fiction*, the Cleveland boys' locally produced mimeographed sci-fi genre fanzine. Bill Dunn was more in line with Nietzsche's concept of the *ubermensch* and certainly conformed to early twentieth century Americans' ideas of what constituted a "mad scientist."[389] Many of these Americans, viewing Tesla with all of his so-called "eccentricities," along with the lethal weapons potential in many of his strange inventions, also came to see him as this shadowy figure, a "Superman" to be respected, for sure, but possibly a deranged one that should also be feared.

Contrary to popular belief, the great financier J. P. Morgan and Tesla were always fast friends. Matthews affirmed that Morgan never removed his funding for Tesla's 187-foot Wardenclyffe, Long Island, New York, power station. Tesla was already wealthy in his own right and his so-called "magnetic transmitter" did not depend on continued funds from Morgan to remain operational. But Tesla did change the purpose of Wardenclyffe from being a world radio-broadcast tower to that of a world electrical-power tower. Nevertheless, it was

Arthur Matthews (left), Canadian associate of the great scientist and inventor, Nikola Tesla (right), and the book they co-authored, *The Wall of Light* (center). See http://blog.world-mysteries.com/guest_authors/doug-yurchey/son-of-tesla/.

386   Margaret Storm, *Return of the Dove* (Baltimore, Maryland: self-published, 1959), 72. Also see John Sanidopoulos, "Nikola Tesla's Father- Fr. Milutin Tesla," 14 May 2010, *Mystagogy*, http://www.johnsanidopoulos.com/2010/05/nikola-teslas-father-fr-milutin-tesla.html (Accessed 13 November 2014).

387   Matthews. Also of note, in the science fiction cult classic, *Venus on the Half-Shell* (New York, New York: Dell Publishing, 1975), a novel by Philip José Farmer, writing under the alias of "Kilgore Trout," a fictional recurring character in many of the writings of Kurt Vonnegut, a common element found therein is the origin of many of the characters' and locations' names whereby Farmer put in a lot of references to literature and fictional authors. In *Venus*, Farmer formed most of the alien names by transposing the letters of English or non-English words. It may be that Farmer got the idea to do this from reading Tesla's account in the Matthews' *Wall of Light*.

388   *Ibid.*

389   Les Daniels, *Superman: The Complete History*, 13-15.

Tesla himself who dismantled the tower- his life's work and ultimate achievement of giving the planet free power and all the energy it could possibly ever use. He realized that people had not matured to the point that they could be trusted to use this new power toward the achievement of peaceful objectives. He especially feared that German scientists could misapply his technology to intensify the electro-magnetic pulse of the transmitter and split the Earth in two, much like a glass shatters at a certain pitch.[390] It did not escape the attention of many in the media, either, that since such a device to power global cities could be turned into a doomsday weapon, its inventor must himself be some sort of mad scientist whose plans were nefarious from their inception. Basically, it was the ultimate power interjected at the wrong time.

"This was the Venusian, the 'Superman' who arrived on this Earth in a spaceship, as a tiny baby, and who grew to maturity to fulfill his great mission.... that of assisting Ascended Master Saint Germain to set up the machinery for the new scientific civilization that will lift the Aquarian Age to heights of glory." -Margaret Storm, *Return of the Dove* (1959), page 244. Sketch reprinted from 1894 newspaper article appearing in http://hello-earth.com/nikolatesla/nikolatesla.html.

As the Venusians have told numerous contactees, the people of all lands must arrive at the conclusion that they are finished with their respective countries' military-industrial complexes. Once they have applied the admonition found in *Isaiah* 2:4 (NIV), such wonderful technologies can exist here on Earth for the benefit of all humankind: "....*They will beat their swords into plowshares and their spears into pruning hooks. Nation will not take up sword against nation, nor will they train for war anymore.*" As Tesla knew only too well, we will never be on the road to Utopia so long as military governments and secret operations remain hold sway over our planet.

From the pages of the *Wall of Light*, Matthews informs us that the Venusian spaceship that landed on his Quebec property on numerous occasions was a scout craft that only required two people to guide it. He also noted that there did not appear to be any visible piloting mechanisms since the Venusians were able to accomplish all of their maneuvering by means of thought projection. The craft seemed to be composed of metal and looked like two huge saucers put together rim-to-rim. Circling these rims about twenty feet away from the ship's main body was an unsupported band of material that the Venusians referred to as the "guide ring." This was most remarkable, as it had the

appearance of being suspended in mid-air, as if held in place by some magnetic force. There was also a mothership in orbit around the Earth that carried twenty-four smaller spacecraft, ground vehicles, crew, gardens, a recreation area, study rooms and a meeting hall. The Venusians told Matthews that, "We are amazed and saddened to find how much of your lives is devoted to inventing and using destructive machines with which you murder each other. We see you spending vast sums of money pretending to bring peace on earth, when you should know that

---

390 Doug Yurcher, "Son of Tesla"

the only way of obtaining peace is free - through Christ- Love. There is no other way, so why waste your money?"[391]

In addition, Tesla allegedly communicated with Venusians by means of the so-called Tesla-Scope, which he built in 1898. Then, with Matthews, he rebuilt it in 1938, incorporating various modifications that made it smaller and more streamlined. The Tesla-Scope reportedly would emit a loud *"buzzing sound,"* reminiscent of a beehive, whenever contact with the Venusians was established.[392] And according to Tesla's esoteric biographer, Margaret Storm, "to Arthur Matthews, he (Tesla) gave a design for an interplanetary communications set. He left to Matthews the task of getting the public interested in communicating with the inhabitants of other planets."[393] Nevertheless, Tesla, the great inventor, mentioned many times during his career that he thought his inventions such as his Tesla coil, used as a "resonant receiver", could communicate with other planets. He even noted the reception of repetitive signals on his devices of what he believed were extraterrestrial radio communications coming from Mars and Venus, beginning in 1899.

Of course, contemporary radio astronomers are quick to dismiss Tesla's intercepted transmissions as the misidentification of signals emanating from either cosmic background or terrestrial radiation sources. They do not even acknowledge Tesla as the true pioneer in the use of radio in the search for extraterrestrial intelligence, but instead credit the emergent science to the work of Dr. Frank Drake in the early 1960s.

That Tesla heard *"buzzing sounds"* in the alien transmissions similar to those coming out from a beehive is more than coincidental, especially since the Kabbalists, Sufis, Cathars and other seekers of esoteric knowledge down through the ages have intimately associated bees with the planet Venus. Tesla himself, much as the Cathars who submitted to martyrdom rather than denounce their belief that society should be reorganized along the matriarchal lines of a beehive, passionately argued that our political systems were antiquated and obsolete and advocated that they needed to be scrapped and replaced in accordance with the patterns provided us by the diligent and hardworking bees.

In a rare interview with Tesla at age 68, conducted by *Colliers* magazine correspondent John B. Kennedy, the famed inventor and theorist stated that, "The life of the bee will be the life of our race." When the inquisitive interviewer asked Tesla what such a world organized like a beehive would look like, the optimistic scientist added that, *"A new sex order is coming-- with the female as superior.* You will communicate instantly by simple vest-pocket equipment. Aircraft will travel the skies, unmanned, driven and guided by radio. Enormous power will be transmitted great distances without wires." But he also added that big geological shifts and climate changes were coming on a global scale: "Earthquakes will become more and more frequent. Temperate zones will turn frigid or torrid. And some of these awe-inspiring developments are not so very far off."[394]

391 Arthur Matthews, *Wall of Light*, 56.
392 *Ibid.*, "Tesla Scope 1898, Communicate with Venus": Inserted pages (unnumbered) with diagrams of Tesla-Scope, first conceived by Nikola Tesla in 1898 to communicate with planet Venus; first model built 1918 by Tesla; second model built by Arthur Matthews with Tesla in 1938; Matthews rebuilt the 1938 model in 1947; third model is new design by Matthews built in 1967 with adaptation of microminiature parts, significantly reducing its size. Numerous articles on communication with the inhabitants of other planets were published by Tesla in prominent publications such as *Collier's* and the *New York Times*. See also Marc J. Seifer, *Wizard: the Life and Times of Nikola Tesla: Biography of a Genius* (Secaucus, New Jersey: Carol Publishing, 1996), 157.
393 Margaret Storm, *Return of the Dove*, 182.
394 John B. Kennedy, "When Woman is Boss: An interview with Nikola Tesla," 30 January 1926, *Colliers* magazine, New York, New York.

It quickly became clear in the interview that Tesla regarded the emergence of women as one of the most powerful portents for the future. But what did Tesla mean by his remarks about the coming arrival of a "*new sex order*," one that is to be led by women? The intrepid philosopher-scientist explained:

"It is clear to any trained observer, and even to the sociologically untrained, that a new attitude toward sex discrimination has come over the world through the centuries, receiving an abrupt stimulus just before and after the World War.

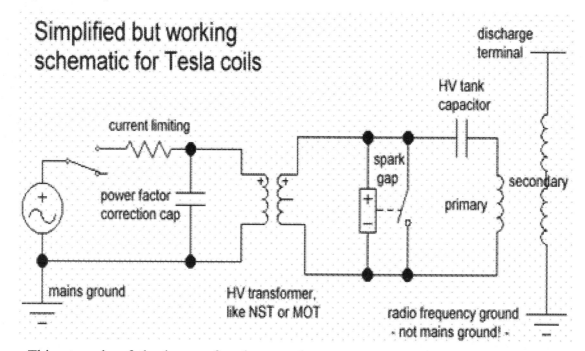

This struggle of the human female toward sex equality will end in a new sex order, with the female as superior. The modern woman, who anticipates in merely superficial phenomena the advancement of her sex, is but a surface symptom of something deeper and more potent fermenting in the bosom of the race.

It is not in the shallow physical imitation of men that women will assert first their equality and later their superiority, but in the awakening of the intellect of women.

Through countless generations, from the very beginning, the social subservience of women resulted naturally in the partial atrophy or at least the hereditary suspension of mental qualities which we now know the female *sex to be endowed with no less than men.*"[395]

Tesla obviously concurred with the feminist

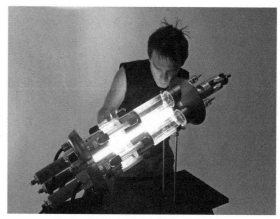

Model of the Tesla-Scope "*for space communication with intelligences on the planet Venus*," based on the drawings provided Arthur Matthews in *The Wall of Light*. See http://ajcatalano.com/teslascope.html.

view. He further elaborated on the need to make the Queen the center of life, just as she is the

395 *Ibid.*

focus of all within the micro-cosmos of the beehive:

"But the female mind has demonstrated a capacity for all the mental acquirements and achievements of men, and as generations ensue that capacity will be expanded; the average woman will be as well educated as the average man, and then better educated, for the dormant faculties of her brain will be stimulated to an activity that will be all the more intense and powerful because of centuries of repose. *Woman will ignore precedent and startle civilization with their progress.*

The acquisition of new fields of endeavor by women, their gradual usurpation of leadership, will dull and finally dissipate feminine sensibilities,

Until scientists began to seriously ponder the search for extraterrestrial intelligence (SETI) via radio transmissions in the early 1960s, the idea remained the prevue of science fiction. Here two scientists build and test out an *interocitor*, establishing contact with the inhabitants of *Metaluna* in the epic *This Island Earth* (Universal International Pictures, 1955). Clearly, Tesla was light years ahead of his peers. See http://uncyclopedia.wikia.com/wiki/Interociter.

will choke the maternal instinct, so that marriage and motherhood may become abhorrent and human civilization draw closer and closer to the perfect civilization of the bee.

The significance of this lies in the principle dominating the economy of the bee--the most highly organized and intelligently coordinated system of any form of nonrational animal life--the all-governing supremacy of the instinct for immortality which makes divinity out of motherhood.

The center of all bee life is the queen. She dominates the hive, not through hereditary right, for any egg may be hatched into a reigning queen, but because she is the womb of this insect race."[396]

Tesla pondered the nature and organization of the hive, explaining that:

"There are the vast, desexualized armies of workers whose sole aim and happiness in life is hard work. It is the perfection of communism, of socialized, cooperative life wherein all things, including the young, are the property and concern of all.

Then there are the virgin bees, the princess bees, the females which are selected from the eggs of the queen when they are hatched and preserved in case an unfruitful queen should bring disappointment to the hive. And there are the male bees, few in number, unclean of habit, tolerated only because they are necessary to mate with the queen.

"When the time is ripe for the queen to take her nuptial flight the male bees are drilled and regimented. The queen passes the drones which guard the gate of the hive, and the male bees follow her in rustling array. Strongest of all the inhabitants of the hive, more powerful

---

396 *Ibid.*

Don't mess with the Queen Bee! See
http://zephyrxavier.deviantart.com/
art/Queen-Bee-386551511.

than any of her subjects, the queen launches into the air, spiraling upward and upward, the male bees following. Some of the pursuers weaken and fail, drop out of the nuptial chase, but the queen wings higher and higher until a point is reached in the far ether where but one of the male bees remains. By the inflexible law of natural selection he is the strongest, and he mates with the queen. At the moment of marriage his body splits asunder and he perishes.

The queen returns to the hive, impregnated, carrying with her tens of thousands of eggs--a future city of bees, and then begins the cycle of reproduction, the concentration of the teeming life of the hive in unceasing work for the birth of a new generation."[397]

Now the question of human applicability comes to the fore, and Tesla responds:

"Imagination falters at the prospect of human analogy to this mysterious and superbly dedicated civilization of the bee; but when we consider how the human instinct for race perpetuation dominates life in its normal and exaggerated and perverse manifestations, there is ironic justice in the possibility that this instinct, with the continuing intellectual advance of women, may be finally expressed after the manner of the bee, though it will take centuries to break down the habits and customs of peoples that bar the way to such a simply and scientifically ordered civilization.

We have seen a beginning of this in the United States. In Wisconsin the sterilization of confirmed criminals and pre-marriage examination of males is required by law, while the doctrine of eugenics is now boldly preached where a few decades ago its advocacy was a statutory offense."[398]

In Tesla's mind, the bees offer humankind a pattern for rapid future development. He strives for a society where all of its members are united in positive actions for its overall good and advancement. In 1926, Nazi plans for the abuse of eugenics were little known outside an inner circle of the party elite; and at the time of this Tesla interview, the National Socialist German Workers Party was but a minority political faction that would not rise to power for another seven years. *What we should keep in mind, however, is that as knowledge of biology grows, so does our power to determine our own biological nature by means of genetics.*

Nevertheless, the disastrous character of the Nazi eugenics program has resulted in a certain reluctance to face the problem of what to do with this power. Eugenics as it was previously envisioned by Tesla could be re-examined in

397 *Ibid.*
398 *Ibid.*

the light of the recent scientific discoveries. It can be argued that eugenics is still with us in the various techniques of genetic manipulation and is, to a great degree, something quite desirable for the long-range projections of human progress. Some have dubbed this revamped form as "libertarian reform eugenics" insofar as it has been taken out of an authoritarian construct. While eugenics failed to prove itself a force for good in the previous century, who can say it will not improve humankind's overall prospects in the coming centuries? David Gems of the University College in London commented on the "political correctness" of so-called eugenics programs:

....Among the numerous reasons for disapproving of 20th Century eugenics programmes are the fact that they were typically not only authoritarian, but also based on an inadequate understanding of human genetics, particularly before the Second World War. Then there was the special place of eugenics in the deranged ideology of German National Socialism. Arguably, Nazi atrocities justified in terms of eugenics (principally the Holocaust) are more the consequence of the brutal, totalitarian and at times insane character of Nazism, than the desire to promote human well-being through genetics. These failings of eugenics are historically contingent and do not necessarily follow from the idea of promoting human genetic well-being. *Yet there remains another reason for disapproving of eugenics that stems from its basic aims: positive eugenics promotes human enhancement, which raises the sinister prospect of the creation of supermen, or a master race. It is open to debate whether the possibility of genetically based human enhancement should be approved or condemned. What surely is a mistake is to conflate these four elements - authoritarianism, fallacious biology, criminal misapplication, and enhancement, with the application of genetics to ensure the birth of healthy babies; and an open question remains: is the pursuit of eugenic ends necessarily a bad idea?* [399]

In each hive, there can only be one Queen Bee! Here the beautiful Zsa Zsa Gabor as the rebel leader Talleah leads her posse to overthrow the evil ruler of Venus and become its new queen in the sci-fi cult classic, *Queen of Outer Space*, Allied Artists (1958). See http://www.briansdriveintheater.com/zsazsagabor.html.

There is also another linkage of bees and their societal hive organization with the planet Venus that strikes me as something more than mere coincidence. It has to do with the Fibonacci numbering sequence inherent in the orbital relationship of the Earth and Venus, as well as the allotment of gender and work roles found throughout the entire population in any given beehive, distributed in accordance with the Fibonacci sequence. Tesla himself, as a mathematician and scientist, was certainly aware of the significance of the Fibonacci numbers in both the natural world and the progress of humankind.

It should also be pointed out that the planets in the heavens move in exquisite orbital patterns, dancing to the Music of the Spheres, as it were. For example, when we take the orbits

399 David Gems, "Review Essay: Politically Correct Eugenics," University College, London, UK, *Theoretical Medicine and Bioethics* (1999) 20, 199-211.

of any two planets and draw a line between their positions every few days, because the inner planet orbits faster than the outer planet, interesting patterns emerge with each planetary pairing having its own unique dance rhythm. In the case of the Earth-Venus orbits, the respective planets return to the original starting positions after eight Earth years. Eight Earth years equals thirteen Venus years. Note that 8 and 13 are members of the Fibonacci number series.

*Earth: 8 years * 365.256 days/year = 2,922.05 days*
*Venus: 13 years * 224.701 days/year = 2,921.11 days (i.e. 99.9%)*

As one is watching the Earth-Venus cycle for eight years, one notes that it creates this beautiful five-petal flower with the Sun at the center; and 5 is another number in the Fibonacci series.[400]

Fibonacci numbers or the Fibonacci sequence is constituted with the numbers in the following integer sequence:

$$1, \ 1, \ 2, \ 3, \ 5, \ 8, \ 13, \ 21, \ 34, \ 55, \ 89, \ 144, \ \ldots$$

In modern usage, however, note that the 0 is included at the beginning of the sequence:

$$0, \ 1, \ 1, \ 2, \ 3, \ 5, \ 8, \ 13, \ 21, \ 34, \ 55, \ 89, \ 144, \ \ldots$$

This is important because of the applicability of the Fibonacci numbering sequence to the frequency spectrum and harmonic phenomena, more of which will be covered in a later chapter as it deals directly with Venus and its inter-dimensionality. Suffice it to say for the moment, the inclusion of the zero, if directly translated into Hertz (Hz) as a unit for measuring frequency, is represented as 0Hz, where complete radio silence reigns, having zero vibration and zero movement, such as existed throughout our universe before the infusion of the Higgs Boson or so-called "God Particle," that sparked the Big Bang and set everything into motion. This coincides with the Gnostic view that our universe was nothing but a debris field of inert matter left over from a previous creation; but that it was re-enervated or re-energized with the arrival of the first *Aeons* into our plane of existence.

Mathematicians have also noted that the expansion of Fibonacci numbers within a rectangle converts into a Golden Spiral pattern, the very shape assumed by myriad millions of galaxies, to include our own Milky Way, in addition to many recurring phenomena visible and apparent throughout the natural world.

By definition, the first two numbers in the Fibonacci sequence are 1 and 1, or 0 and 1, depending on the chosen starting point of the sequence. Each subsequent number is the sum of the previous two. In mathematical terms, the sequence F_n of Fibonacci numbers is defined by the recurrence relation

---

400   Steve Curtin, "Dances of the Planets," 17 July 2013, *Conscious Resonance* website, http://consciousresonance. net/?p=1083 (Accessed 20 November 2014): Webpage also includes above orbital diagram.

$$F_n = F_{n-1} + F_{n-2},$$
with seed values
$$F_1 = 1, \ F_2 = 1$$
or
$$F_0 = 0, \ F_1 = 1.\text{[401]}$$

Therefore, given the significance of honeybees and their attachment to Venus throughout human history, it should be noted that this relatively mild insect is greatly affected by Fibonacci numbers. There are over 30,000 species of bees; and in most of them the bees live solitary lives. The bee that most of us know best, however, is the honeybee. It lives in a colony called a hive and has an unusual family tree. In fact, there are many unusual features of honeybees; and the Fibonacci numbers can be used to count a honeybee's ancestors.

First, not all honeybees have two parents. We have to take into consideration that in a colony of honeybees there is one special female called the queen, and while there are many worker bees who are female, unlike the queen bee they produce no eggs. There are also drone bees, that are male; but they do not work. These drones are produced from the queen's unfertilized eggs; hence the male bees only have a mother but no father. All the females, on the other hand, are produced when the queen has mated with a male and so have two parents. Females usually end up as worker bees; but some are fed with a special substance called royal jelly. This helps them grow into queens ready to go off to start a new colony when the bees form a swarm and leave their hive in search of a place to build a new nest. Therefore, female bees have two parents, a male and a female, whereas male bees have just one parent, a female. Let's look at the family of a male drone bee.

He had **1** parent, a female.

He has **2** grand-parents, since his mother had two parents, a male and a female.

He has **3** great-grand-parents: his grand-mother had two parents but his grand-father had only one.

How many great-great-grand parents did he have?

Here we see that the Fibonacci numbers are very well represented in honeybees. For example, if you follow the family tree of honeybees, it follows the Fibonacci sequence perfectly. If you take any hive and follow this pattern, it would look like this:

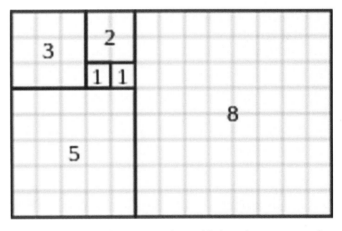

Above: A tiling with squares whose side lengths are successive Fibonacci numbers.

401 Miklós Bóna , *A Walk Through Combinatorics*, 3rd ed. (Hackensack, New Jersey: World Scientific, 2011), 180, including graphs.

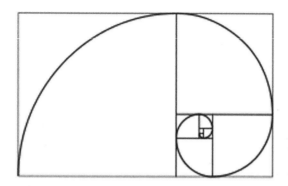

Above: The Fibonacci spiral replicates the Golden Spiral. It is created by drawing circular arcs connecting the opposite corners of squares in the Fibonacci tiling. This one, for example, uses squares of sizes 1, 1, 2, 3, 5, 8, 13, 21, and 34.

And if you divide the number of female bees by the number of drones, you get 1.618, the golden ratio. This mathematical sequence works well for any honeybee hive at any time.[402] Commonly, honeybee hives are always used to explain the Fibonacci sequence and the Golden Ratio, such as it is so closely approached in the orbital relationship of the Earth and Venus. Another intriguing fact is that the ratio between the Earth's outer orbit and Venus' inner orbit is represented by a square.

Nevertheless, Nikola Tesla clearly recognized the significance of the Fibonacci numbers and their connection to all things pertaining to planet Venus. Tesla, who claimed to have built a radio set by which he could communicate with Venusians, maintained that he operated it in accordance with the frequencies and their attendant harmonics corresponding to the Fibonacci sequence. Later in the book, we will explore this in greater depth.

The Fibonacci numbers, however, when taken in conjunction with the Golden Ratio, are a popular theme in culture. They have been employed in novels, songs, television shows and even films. A recent example can be found in *The Da Vinci Code*,[403] a movie that focuses on the importance of the Divine Feminine in the search for the Holy Grail, where these numbers are used to unlock various security devices. They are also used in an anagram to indicate that the meaning commonly attached to a message may require further scrutiny. The numbers have also been used in the creation of architecture, music and visual art.

Number of	Parents	Grand Parents	Great Grand Parents	Gt-Gt Grand Parents	Gt-Gt-Gt Grand Parents
Male Bees	1	2	3	5	8
Female Bees	2	3	5	8	13

In Tesla's opinion, as humankind emulated the honeybees and restructured society accordingly, women would assume the superior roles for which they were destined and all would collectively benefit thereby. Of course, Tesla was not alone in his admiration of the humble bee. Naturalists have looked at bees and other social insects over the centuries. They have pondered whether the great organizational skills of these small creatures was instinctual or based on an inherent intelligence, perhaps far surpassing that of human beings. The Earth, Venus and many other worlds may be hosting numerous creatures of vast intelligence, not restricted to the humanoid form.

Contactee Ted Owens, for example, reported that the Space Intelligences had transcended the physical plane; yet when they manifested in our reality they sometimes appeared to him as insect-like beings. In addition, none other than Gerald Heard (1889-1971), the famous

---

402 Ron Knott, "Honeybees and Family Trees," 30 October 2010, *Fibonacci Numbers and Nature*, http://www.maths.surrey.ac.uk/hosted-sites/R.Knott/Fibonacci/fibnat.html#bees (Accessed 20 November 2014)

403 *The Da Vinci Code* (Sony Pictures, 2006): Dan Brown, Ron Howard, Executive Producers; Ron Howard, Director; Starring Tom Hanks and Audrey Tautou.

British educator, philosopher and science writer, as well as the author of the very first book published on the UFO phenomenon in the English language, *The Riddle of the Flying Saucers: Is Another World Watching?*, wrote that in his opinion the mysterious objects are spacecraft piloted by an intelligent species of bees from the planet Mars.[404] These Martian bees, however, were only slightly larger than our own variety of honeybees. He estimated that each individual Martian bee averaged about two inches in length.

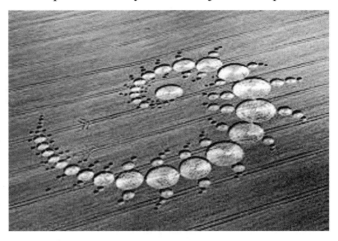

Heard, the author of 35 books mostly centered on philosophical, religious and scientific themes, was always on the cutting edge of the movement for the expansion of human consciousness. In the 1950s, Heard was one of the first to experiment with LSD. He felt that if it were to be properly used, it might prove a beneficial tool to "enlarge Man's mind." The drug would allow a person to see beyond their own ego. And in

The vast majority of crop circles display a Golden Spiral or other pattern resulting from the use of the Fibonacci sequence. Are the UFO occupants dropping hints of their Venusian origins? See http://indigosociety.com.

late August 1956, Alcoholics Anonymous founder Bill Wilson first took LSD under Heard's guidance and with the officiating presence of Dr. Sidney Cohen, a psychiatrist attached to the California Veterans Administration Hospital. According to Wilson, the session allowed him to replay in his mind a spontaneous and transcendent spiritual experience he enjoyed years before, an event that enabled him to overcome his own alcoholism. Heard is also responsible for introducing the then up-and-coming theologian Huston Smith to his close associate and friend, Aldous Huxley, of *Brave New World*[405] fame. Smith's book, *The World's Religions,*[406] is a classic in the field of comparative religion. Smith's meeting with Huxley eventually led to his connection to and work with the American psychedelic guru Timothy Leary. With such an eclectic and prestigious circle of friends and colleagues, it does not surprise me that Heard would be the first among thousands to follow in exploring the UFO phenomenon and writing a book about it.

While even today many dismiss his flying saucer book,[407] some are giving it a second look. As it turns out, the social insects, and especially the honeybee, do indeed appear to operate on the level of a discriminating intelligence over that of mere instinctual reaction. *The sharing and*

---

404 Gerald Heard, *Riddle of the Flying Saucers: Is Another World Watching?* (London, UK: Carroll and Nicholson, 1950)

405 Aldous Huxley, *Brave New World* (London, UK: Chatto and Windus, 1932): The book describes the London of 2540 A.D. (632 A.F.—"After Ford.") It anticipates developments in reproductive technology, sleep-learning, psychological manipulation, and classical conditioning, all combining profoundly to change society. Huxley followed this book with a reassessment in an essay, *Brave New World Revisited* (1958), and with *Island* (1962), his final novel. Some critics rate Brave New World as one of the 100 greatest novels of all time, a transformative work with long-range implications for all humankind. Huxley, Heard, Orwell, and to a certain extent Tesla, heralded fantastic changes and scientific advancements, but also questioned the ability of humankind to deal adequately with these new technologies, lacking the needed spiritual maturity to utilize them circumspectly.

406 Huston Smith, *World's Religions* (New York, New York: Harper One, 1958).

407 Andrew May, "UFOs: The Forgotten Book," *Retro-Forteana* blog, 29 June 2011, http://forteana-blog.blogspot.com/2011/06/ufos-forgotten-book.html (Accessed 20 November 2014).

"The Zanti Misfits" arrive on Earth in the vicinity of a secluded Army base in the California desert. These scary aliens first appeared in an episode of the original *Outer Limits* television show, broadcast on 30 December 1963 in its premier season. See http://www.themadmonstermaker.com/ZantiMisfit.html.

collective processing of information by certain insect societies is one of the reasons that they warrant the superlative epithet, "super–organisms."[408]

Detailed experimental and mathematical analyses of information exchange and decision–making in, arguably, the most difficult collective choices that social insects face: namely, house hunting by complete societies, provide the keys in demonstrating extraordinary levels of intelligence. The primary issue rests in how a complete colony selects the single best nest–site among several alternatives. To accomplish this, individual scouts respond to the diverse information they have personally obtained about the quality of a potential nest–site through their generation of a recruitment signal. The colony then deliberates over and integrates the different incoming recruitment signals associated with different potential nest–sites to achieve a well–informed collective decision. When this process is compared in both honeybees and in the ant *Leptothorax albipennis*, some interesting findings emerge.[409] Of these, entomologist Nigel R. Franks writes:

"Notwithstanding many differences – for example, honeybee colonies have 100 times more individuals than *L. albipennis* colonies – there are certain similarities in the fundamental algorithms these societies appear to employ when they are house hunting."

"Scout honeybees use the full power of the waggle dance to inform their nest–mates about the distance and direction of a potential nest–site (and they indicate the quality of a nest–site indirectly through the vigour of their dance), and yet individual bees perhaps only rarely make direct comparisons of such sites. By contrast, scouts from *L. albipennis* colonies often compare nest–sites, but they cannot directly inform one another of their estimation of the quality of a potential site. Instead, they discriminate between sites by initiating recruitment sooner to better ones."[410]

The entomologist further explains how this discrimination process serves the collective interest of the respective colonies and demonstrates a high degree of intelligence among the social insects of bees and ants:

"Nevertheless, both species do make use of forms of opinion polling. For example, scout bees that have formerly danced for a certain site cease such advertising and monitor the dances of others at random. That is, they act without prejudice. They neither favour nor disdain dancers that advocate the site they had formerly advertised or the alternatives. Thus, in general the bees are less well informed than they would be if they systematically monitored dances for

408 Nigel R. Franks (1989), *American Science* 77, 138–145.
409 _____, et al., "Information flow, opinion polling and collective intelligence in house–hunting social insects," Philosophical Transactions of the Royal Society: Biological Sciences, 29 November 2002 (London, UK: Vol. 357, No. 1427), 1567-1583.
410 *Ibid*: Abstract of.

alternative sites rather than spending their time reprocessing information they already have. *However, as a result of their lack of prejudice, less time overall will be wasted in endless debate among stubborn and potentially biased bees.* Among the ants, the opinions of nest–mates are also pooled effectively when scouts use a threshold population of their nest–mates present in a new nest–site as a cue to switch to more rapid recruitment. Furthermore, the ants' reluctance to begin recruiting to poor nest–sites means that more time is available for the discovery and direct comparison of alternatives. *Likewise, the retirement of honeybee scouts from dancing for a given site allows more time for other scouts to find potentially better sites. Thus, both the ants and the bees have time–lags built into their decision–making systems that should facilitate a compromise between thorough surveys for good nest–sites and relatively rapid decisions. We have also been able to show that classical mathematical models can illuminate the processes by which colonies are able to achieve decisions that are relatively swift and very well informed.*"[411]

Much more could be said about the demonstrated intelligence of social insects. Thanks to the work of entomologists and melittologists the world over, we certainly know much more about honeybees than we did in 1926, when Tesla was so rightly praising the organization of their hives and communistic, collective society. As more attention is devoted to the study of social insects like ants, bees and wasps, exobiologists are beginning to wonder how millions or billions more years of cosmic evolution might shape the development of this species on other worlds.

But what did our ancient ancestors know about the higher significance of social insects? Thanks to the work of the Mormon prophet Joseph Smith, we are beginning to appreciate the knowledge acquired by the long-lost Egyptian civilization and passed down through the ages to us in the papyri that constitutes the so-called *Book of Abraham*. In the celestial hierarchies, it appears as though the very throne of God is a stargate guarded by a vast insect intelligence. But before proceeding further with this and the other powerful truths found in the *Book of Abraham*, let us see how a set of unique historical circumstances brought this priceless information to the modern world's attention.

According to the official website of the Church of Jesus Christ of Latter Day Saints, with headquarters in Salt Lake City, Utah, it was in the summer of 1835 that an entrepreneur named Michael Chandler arrived at the church's headquarters in Kirtland, Ohio, with four mummies and multiple scrolls of papyrus. The Latter-Day Saints' website states that, "Chandler found a ready audience. Due partly to the exploits of the French emperor Napoleon, the antiquities unearthed in the catacombs of Egypt had created a fascination across the Western world. Chandler capitalized on this interest by touring with ancient Egyptian artifacts and charging visitors a fee to see them."[412]

Naturally, the arrival of these artifacts in the world center of Mormonism caused quite a stir. The Mormons themselves believed that the Native Americans scattered throughout the entire Western Hemisphere were descended from the ancient Israelites who, once they arrived in the Americas, split into two warring factions, the Nephites and the Lamanites. With the help of special optical and auditory aids given to him by an angel, the young prophet Smith was able to translate the golden plates he had dug up in the woods outside his Palmyra, New

---

411 *Ibid.*
412 "Translation and Historicity of the *Book of Abraham*," author unspecified, Church of Jesus Christ of Latter-Day Saints, Intellectual Reserve, Inc., 2014, https://www.lds.org/topics/translation-and-historicity-of-the-book-of-abraham?lang=eng (Accessed 25 November 2014).

The Kolob Stargate See https://www.lds.org/scriptures/pgp/abr/fac-2?lang=eng. "Fascimile Number 2" in the *Book of Abraham*, included in the Church of Jesus Christ of Latter- Day Saints' scripture volume, the *Pearl of Great Price* (2013 edition), wherein the prophet Joseph Smith gives the following interpretation concerning the insectoid being occupying the center and labeled with the number 1: "*Kolob, signifying the first creation, nearest to the celestial, or the residence of God.* First in government, the last pertaining to the measurement of time. The measurement according to celestial time, which celestial time signifies one day to a cubit. *One day in Kolob is equal to a thousand years according to the measurement of this earth*, which is called by the Egyptians *Jah-oh-eh*." Kolob, as we later learn in the *Book of Abraham*, is the central star system in the amalgamation of stars (*Hah-ko-kau-beam*) to which our Sun belongs (the Milky Way galaxy). The insectoids dwell on Kolob and guard the stargate leading into the presence of God. Incidentally, scientists have discovered a black hole at the center of our galaxy; whence we also learn that power is transferred through tunnels of light energy (*Kli-flos-is-es*) emanating from the revolutions of Kolob to all the inhabited solar systems scattered throughout the galaxy. These are represented by the stars marked 22 and 23 on the facsimile.

York home, purportedly written originally in "Reformed Egyptian," into the *Book of Mormon* that we have today. The enthusiastic members of Smith's new church were hoping that the discovery of the Egyptian papyri would shed new light and knowledge on the already existing scriptures found in the *Book of Mormon*. What they discovered, however, would have a much greater, yet unforeseen impact, significantly shaping the theology of the church that would one day attract millions upon millions more believers, clearly placing it in the Gnostic camp, whether the Mormon adherents and leadership, then or now, recognized this or not.

It was Antonio Lebolo, a former cavalryman in the Italian army, who oversaw some of the Egyptian excavations at the behest of Napoleon Bonaparte. In the conduct of his archaeological investigations, Lebolo pulled 11 mummies from a tomb not far from the ancient city of Thebes, whence he shipped the artifacts to Italy to be processed and cataloged. After his untimely death, however, Lebolo's Egyptian collection found its way to New York; and at some point the mummies and cryptic scrolls came into Chandler's custody.[413]

However, it should be noted that by the time the collection arrived in Kirtland, all but four of the mummies and several papyrus scrolls had already been sold. At an emergency meeting of the Presiding Elders convened at Kirtland, a decision was reached that the remaining artifacts would be purchased by the Church, to be turned over to their leader, Joseph Smith. Of course, Smith was delighted to take possession of the artifacts. And upon examining the papyri, the prophet noted that in the translation of some of the characters or hieroglyphics, "much to our joy we found that one of the rolls contained the writings of Abraham."[414]

---

413   H. D. Peterson, *Story of the Book of Abraham: Mummies, Manuscripts, and Mormonism* (Salt Lake City: Deseret Book, 1995), 36–85. See also Brian L. Smith interview by Philip R. Webb, "Mystery of the Mummies: An Update on the Joseph Smith Collection," *Religious Studies Center Newsletter* 20, no. 2 (2005): 1–5, for a detailed account on the disposition of the artifacts after their arrival in the United States to the present day.

414   *Joseph Smith History, 1838–1856*, vol. B-1, 596, available at josephsmithpapers.org (Accessed 25 November 2014).

Of the Book of Abraham, the Latter-Day Saints website notes that:

"The *Book of Abraham* clarifies several teachings that are obscure in the Bible. *Life did not begin at birth, as is commonly believed. Prior to coming to earth, individuals existed as spirits.* In a vision, Abraham saw that one of the spirits was *"like unto God"* (*Abraham* 3:24). *This divine being, Jesus Christ, led other spirits in organizing the earth out of "materials" or preexisting matter, not ex nihilo or out of nothing, as many Christians later came to believe* (*Abraham* 3:24; 4:1, 12, 14-16). Abraham further learned that mortal life was crucial to the plan of happiness God would provide for His children: *"We will prove them herewith,"* God stated, "to see if they will do all things whatsoever the Lord their God shall command them," adding a promise to add glory forever upon the faithful (*Abraham* 3:25-26). Nowhere in the *Bible* is the purpose and potential of earth life stated so clearly as in the book of Abraham."[415]

Of course, as was previously explained in an earlier chapter, the Christian Gnostics of the first four centuries in the Common Era held similar beliefs. They, like their Greek progenitors, believed in reincarnation, i.e. that our spirits came into being eons before our current birth, and probably have undergone countless incarnations along the way. That Abraham took note of one spirit as "like unto God" is indicative of his identification of the *Angel of the LORD*, or Theophanic Angel, Who is none other than the archangel Michael, also known to us as Jesus Christ, the First Born in the Fullness of Time.[416] And as we now understand, the Gnostic Christians believed that the first *Aeon* to emerge from the Pleroma was Michael/Jesus Christ. These same Christian Gnostics also maintained that we live our lives in this material world as a sort of schooling, wherein we acquire the knowledge necessary to work good deeds on behalf of our fellow beings and then advance to the next grade in our universal education program. Hence the reference in the *Book of Abraham* for the gods to "prove them herewith," meaning that all must be put to the test and pass it before moving on to some more exalted and higher sphere. This is also in accordance with the teachings of Swedenborg with respect to the souls on various stages of Venus in its cosmic evolution. Nevertheless, because traditional Christians do not accept most of these tenets, Mormonism refers to itself as a religion of "restoration." In other words, it brings back to reestablish the fullness of the Gospel as it was accepted and practiced by the early Christians, to include the Gnostics. The only difference in interpretation of the Gospel between a Gnostic and a Mormon is that while the latter believes in the pre-existence of the soul, he or she does not accept the doctrine of reincarnation. Additionally, while the Mormon does believe that Michael was Jesus Christ in His pre-Earth form, he or she does not accept Him as God incarnate, but only as one of the Eternal Father's many spirit children.

Egyptologists have identified the papyrus fragments as parts of standard funerary texts that were deposited with mummified bodies. These scholars date the fragments between the third century B.C.E. and the first century C.E., quite some time after Abraham actually walked the Earth. Of course, spokespersons for the Mormon Church claim that the fragments do not have to be as old as Abraham in order for the *Book of Abraham* and its illustrations to be authentic because ancient records are often transmitted as copies or as copies of copies. The official website of the Mormon Church explains it thusly:

"The record of Abraham could have been edited or redacted by later writers much as the *Book of Mormon* prophet-historians Mormon and Moroni revised the writings of earlier peoples. Moreover, documents initially composed for one context can be repackaged for

---

415 "Translation and Historicity"
416 *Hebrews* 12:23 (KJV)

another context or purpose. Illustrations once connected with Abraham could have either drifted or been dislodged from their original context and reinterpreted hundreds of years later in terms of burial practices in a later period of Egyptian history. The opposite could also be true: illustrations with no clear connection to Abraham anciently could, by revelation, shed light on the life and teachings of this prophetic figure."[417]

For the purpose of our investigation, however, it is sufficient that the *Book of Abraham* is consistent with various details found in non-Biblical stories about Abraham that circulated throughout the ancient world around the time the papyri were most likely created. In the *Book of Abraham* 3:2-15, for example, God teaches the patriarch about the Sun, the Moon, and the stars: "I show these things unto thee before ye go into Egypt, that ye may declare all these words." Ancient texts are especially noted for repeatedly referring to Abraham instructing the Egyptians in an accurate knowledge of the heavens. One such chronicler was Eupolemus, who lived under Egyptian rule in the second century B.C.E., who wrote that Abraham taught astronomy and other sciences to the Egyptian priests. Also, a third-century papyrus from an Egyptian temple library connects Abraham with an illustration similar to facsimile 1 in the *Book of Abraham*; and a later Egyptian text, discovered in the twentieth century, explains how the Pharaoh tried to sacrifice Abraham, only to be foiled when Abraham was delivered by an angel. And later, according to this text, Abraham went on to teach members of the Pharaoh's court through astronomy.[418] Since all of these details, and more, are found in the *Book of Abraham*, its importance cannot be overlooked by the contemporary Theosophist who seeks accurate knowledge to reconcile history and science with religion, wherever he or she can find it. And in the case of the insectoid beings on the planet Kolob at the center of our galaxy, it should not go without saying that they seem to be filling a role as guardian spirits adjacent to the throne of God.

Venusians, so in touch with other intelligent species throughout the galaxy and beyond, certainly laugh at our limited designation of intelligence as being exclusively limited to human beings. And despite the seemingly never-ending debate over the theory of evolution, it has by now been almost fully absorbed into our society's belief structures. Nevertheless, this has not changed our basic conceit for we still tend to think of ourselves as the highest pinnacle on the evolutionary pyramid. While we are different from other species, and in fact quite unique, does this make us any better? The answer would be yes, if we were judging according to our own standards. A bee or a dolphin would probably see it a little differently. Or a Venusian might put it this way: *"If there is such a thing as a 'highest' form of evolution on Earth, it certainly could not be represented by the one species that is in danger of wiping itself out, and the entire planet along with it."*

It does not appear, at this juncture, that humankind is going to start anytime soon in granting equal rights to bees or dolphins. As one biologist noted,

"Our civilization is largely based on the assumption that the Earth is ours to exploit as we wish. This view is deeply rooted in the Jewish and Christian traditions. It is clearly spelled out in the first chapter of *Genesis* 1:28 (KJV): 'So God created man in his own image, in the image of God created He him; male and female created He them. And God blessed them, and God said unto them, Be fruitful, and multiply, and replenish the Earth, and subdue it: and have dominion over the fish of the sea, and over the fowl of the air, and over every living thing that

---

417 "Translation and Historicity"
418 *Ibid.*

moveth upon the Earth.'"[419]

Clearly then, most of the adherents of the more fundamentalist religions will have a problem with placing bees, dolphins or any other creature on an equal status with humans. Even if a bee is intelligent, does that necessarily mean it has a soul? The fundamentalist will argue that the *Bible* gives humankind the right to rule over all animals, no matter how intelligent they are, because after all, "man" is the only one created in the image of God.[420]

However, a conscientious reader of the *Bible* will note that there are three types of amazing "heavenly beings" described therein; and they do not seem to resemble anything that we would normally associate with "angels," at least as we have commonly come to understand them, or even human beings. These strange entities are classified as the Seraphim (Seraphs), the Cherubim (Cherubs), and the Four Living Creatures. Each of these angelic groups was charged with fulfilling important roles in the heavens to serve God in their respective capacities.[421]

The first of these groups are the Seraphim (single- *seraph*, plural- *seraphim*). The Hebrew word Seraphim literally signifies the "burning ones" or nobles. These angels are also sometimes called the "ones of love" because their name might come from the Hebrew root for "love." Apart from the Hebrew origins of the word, the Seraphim are only fully described in the *Bible* on one occasion, this being in the book of *Isaiah* when he is being commissioned by God to be a prophet and experiences a vision of heaven. While caught up in this exalted experience, Isaiah takes note that these types of heavenly beings have six wings, but they only use two of them for flying. They may be utilizing the other four wings to cover their face because, being so close to God, they would not be able to witness His full glory, less they be consumed in the intensity of the holy light. The Seraphim hover as bees around the throne, not letting their feet touch the ground, for such are considered "unclean" and unworthy to be shown in the presence of God. While we are not told how many Seraphim there are, we do understand that it is more than one because the word to designate these angels is used in the plural form. In the Jewish tradition, and some later, albeit esoteric Christian works, the Seraphim are said to be the highest rank of angel, most likely because of their very close proximity to God. The coal in Isaiah's vision touches his lips and is used to signify that Isaiah is now purified and fit to be a prophet. The coal was taken from the altar in heaven, designating that it was fused with supernatural power. Such a holy fire is also used in many religions and faiths as a way of purifying and cleansing something.[422]

We understand that the position of the Seraphs is to fly above God's throne, unlike the Cherubim who are beside and/or around it. The primary duty of the Cherubim is to constantly glorify and praise God, as well as to serve as the personal "attendant angels" of God. Their eternal song is "Holy, Holy, Holy is the LORD Almighty; the whole earth is full of His glory." This chorus has been used by Jews and Christians for thousands of years, joining with the angels in praising God. In Hebrew, to use the same word three times to describe something

---

419 David R. Woolley, "Search for Nonhuman Intelligence," 10 February 1981, *Just Think of It*, http://just.thinkofit.com/the-search-for-non-human-intelligence/ (Accessed 26 November 2014).

420 C. S. Lewis, *The Lion, the Witch and the Wardrobe* (London, UK: Geoffrey Bles, 1950). To be created in the "image" of God, in a more Theosophical sense, would indicate that each human is fashioned with an eternal soul, invisible to the natural eye. Fantasy and science fiction writer, as well as Christian apologist, C. S. Lewis, in his *Narnia* series, took this into account. In a world populated by talking animals, the Eternal God came and lived among them in the form of a regal lion, albeit His essence was one of pure, undefiled spirit. He only manifested His presence as a lion to relate to the local population. The Christian recognizes this fact and therefore does not take *Genesis* 1:28 literally.

421 James Cooper, "Seraphim, Cherubim and the Four Living Creatures," 2014, *Why Angels? http://www.whyangels.com/contact.php#.VHc9b2emUfB* (Accessed 27 November 2014).

422 *Ibid.*

or someone means that the thing or person is "utterly like the word." Therefore, calling God "Holy" three times means that God is completely and perfectly "Holy" in all of His aspects and manifestations. In art, Seraphim are often painted with an intense red color to designate the aura of fire by which they are surrounded. At times, they are often depicted as holding a flaming sword with the words, "Holy, Holy, Holy" on its blade.[423]

Since God is an Immortal Spirit, of course, we understand that He-She is above gender qualification. God exhibits both feminine and masculine qualities, and manifests many others as well, non-quantifiable in our third dimensional universe. The masculine pronoun is only used in maintaining conformity with the traditions and grammar of the English language because God relates to humankind in our version of the Scriptures (*King James Bible*, 1511) in the form of a man, the Lord Jesus Christ. The sexuality of angels and/or ultra-dimensional aliens is the subject of a later chapter.

As we move further out from the throne of God, we come to the realm of the Cherubs. These are not the pudgy, little baby-like figures that we see on Christmas cards, so cute with their two little wings fluttering above the manger. The Bible actually describes the Cherubs quite differently. Also, keep in mind that in the Hebrew language, *Cherub* is the single form while *Cherubim* accounts for the plural form of the word. Like the Seraphs, Cherubs do not receive much space in the pages of the *Bible*, appearing only twice. They are only described in the canonical books of *Genesis*, allegedly written by Moses, and *Ezekiel*, a major Jewish prophet.[424]

Like the Seraphs, the Cherubs are assigned a guardian role. In *Genesis*, they guard the entrance to the Garden of Eden, being assigned this role following Adam and Eve's banishment from the Garden. They are also described as holding flaming swords. In addition, the prophet Ezekiel has a vivid vision of heaven wherein he beholds many angelic beings. His description of the Cherubim is that of powerful and frightening beings, having four faces and four wings. This type of angel is also described in the construction of the Ark of the Covenant, the dwelling place of God with the Israelites throughout their exodus in the desert. After Solomon finished the construction of the first Jewish temple, the Ark was placed within it and surrounded by statues of Cherubim.[425]

Notes angelologist James Cooper,

"The Bible doesn't say how many Cherubim there are, but certain more than one! Their role is to guard God's Holy domain and presence from any sin and corruption. They are sometime known as the throne angels as they are seen to be around the throne of God."

"In Jewish folklore the 'Throne Angels' are known as *Merkabah*."

"Having four faces on four side of their heads and being arranged in a square, they can travel in any direction without having to turn."

"The word Cherub may come from a term 'to guard' which would fit well with their role. Nowhere in the Bible are the Cherubim actually called angels!"

"So far from being cute, cuddly creatures, the Cherubim are the mighty and powerful guardians of God."[426]

Yet another classification of heavenly Cherubim is described in Ezekiel's vision. This new

423 *Ibid.*
424 *Ibid.*
425 *Ibid.*
426 *Ibid.*

144

type of angel is even stranger, given that its appearance defies adequate description by the prophet.

And lastly, we come to the final book of the *Bible*, John the Beloved's *Revelation*, where we find an amazing description of the "Four Living Creatures." The beings have features in common with both the Seraphim, in having six wings and continually praising God, and the Cherubim, in that they number four, are covered in eyes (*like insects*) and look like a lion, ox, man and eagle. Cooper writes, "Whether these creatures are Seraphim, Cherubim or another sort of angelic/heavenly being, we simply don't know. But they are certainly amazing and very powerful."[427] The prophet Joseph Smith was similarly impressed, when he wrote by words of explanation to "Facsimile 2" in the *Book of Abraham* such statements as: "*Ought not to be revealed at the present time*;" "Figures 12, 13, 14, 15, 16, 17, 18, 19, 20, and 21 *will be given in the own due time of the Lord*," and "*The above translation is given as far as we have any right to give at the present time.*"[428]

It is simply amazing that a farm boy from Upper New York State could have such an insightful knowledge of the role of the insectoid inhabitants of Kolob in the hierarchy of light that surrounds the throne of God and the gateway to our galaxy and beyond. As the Cherubim guarded the way to the Tree of Life, so the insectoids stand as sentinels at the Star Gate, the tunnel of light leading directly to the presence of God within the Pleroma itself. And as Smith, Tesla and other visionaries have surmised-that such insectoid intelligences would also have important tasks to carry out on countless planets throughout the Omniverse- including our own, Mars or Venus- is not a revelation that surprises me.

The manifestations of non-human entities in our plane of existence are rife with deep theological implications for the West that have largely been overlooked, mainly that the soul does not have to be limited to a human form in future reincarnations or any yet-to-be existences on other planes of reality. The knowledge acquired by our spiritual essence through countless experiences throughout the eternities may very well be in accordance with the doctrine of the transmigration of the soul, as long espoused by the great Hindu philosophers. A good example of this can be found in the teachings of Patanjali, the founder of the Yoga system of philosophy. He speaks of the transformation of one genus or species into another. In the Sanskrit language it is referred to as *Jatyantara-Parinama*, and *provides for one genus or species with the potential ability to evolve into another genus or species when changing circumstances create a suitable environment for such a cosmic evolution to take place.*[429]

Of course, Joseph Smith is hailed today as a great prophet and the founder of one of the world's fastest growing religions; and Nikola Tesla as the unsurpassed inventor and visionary, despite the lingering lack of acceptance and absence of appreciation of many for some of their more advanced ideas. Nevertheless, as we enter boldly into the new millennium, hearts and minds are beginning to change. But even as more are beginning to recognize the exalted status of these two gifted individuals, we have to keep in mind that they were not always so honored among their fellow humans. Both arrived on Earth to humble circumstances. Only with an awareness of their true natures did these men evolve into the esteemed stations they would later

427 *Ibid.*

428 Joseph Smith, as translated from the papyrus, *Book of Abraham*, "Facsimile Number Two," 2013 edition, Church of Jesus Christ of Latter-Day Saints, *Intellectual Reserve, Inc.,* 2014, https://www.lds.org/scriptures/pgp/abr/fac-2?lang=eng (Accessed 27 November 2014).

429 Swami Baskarananda, "Hindu Concept of Reincarnation," 13 September 2010, *Vedanta Society of Western Washington*, http://www.vedanta-seattle.org/articles/hindu-concept-of-reincarnation/ (Accessed 28 November 2014)

assume in life. Insofar as Venusians and other extraterrestrials have long communicated with other human beings from "all walks of life," as the character George (Jack Nicholson) in *Easy Rider* stated, it would behoove us to pay attention to their messages as well. Perhaps one day in the not-too-distant future, some of the contactees like George Adamski, Howard Menger, Orfeo Angelucci and others will be hailed as the true prophets of the New Age, which they are.

One lesser known contactee with an important message from the Venusians was the retired engineer, H. Albert Coe. This cosmic ambassador wrote several books about advanced intelligences on other planets in our solar system and beyond, but kept a low profile, choosing to live quietly in his Philadelphia, Pennsylvania, home and rarely granting interviews or giving public talks. But in one of his few interviews, Coe told *Midnight* correspondent Art Bentley that while his best friends were Venusians, "I'm not trying to make you believe me. There's no way I can prove it. They're very elusive as far as letting any of us know who they are."[430]

The humble Coe, who was 72 years old at the time of his interview with Bentley, seemed an unlikely candidate to be the close friend to so many Venusians operating clandestinely here on Earth. When the reporter asked Coe what was it that made him so special to the Venusians, the contactee stated that it wasn't so much that he was particularly "special" in any sense of the word, but that he was simply in the right place at an opportune time to help one of the Venusians who had fallen into a dire predicament.[431] It seems that back in June 1920, Albert and his friend Rod were on a school break, leaving their homes in Hastings-On-Hudson, New York, and embarking on a canoeing adventure on the Mattawa River, branching off Lake Trout in the wilds of Ontario, Canada. When Albert and Rod reached a certain spot of rough terrain at a point where the river had significantly narrowed, they decided to separate in order to look for a clear route through to more navigable waters. They were to meet back at the juncture point in a couple of hours and then decide on which route they would take out of the woods. As Albert was making his way through the dense foliage that lay before him, however, he suddenly heard a man cry out, "Oh, help, help me! Down here!"[432]

As Coe made his way down the gorge in response to the cries of distress, he found a seemingly young man who had apparently fallen into a deep cleft in the rock, getting himself stuck in the process. After freeing him from the dire situation and tending to his wounds, Coe took note of the unusual silvery jumpsuit the man was wearing. He also saw that the man was equipped with an instrument panel strapped across his chest, on the exterior of the suit, and that this apparatus had been smashed in his fall. Coe inquired as to what the man was doing in such a remote area and was told that he had flown into the area with his "plane," that he had landed in a nearby clearing. He explained that he was looking for a good place to do some fishing. That he was flying an airplane in itself would be quite remarkable for the year 1920, when such aircraft were just becoming popular attractions at barnstorming aerial performances. In any event, Coe stayed with the man to help him look for his missing fishing rod and tackle box.[433]

Upon finding the "fishing rod" for the mysterious pilot, Coe noticed that it was highly unusual, exhibiting characteristics, he said were, "....the likes of which I had never seen." The rod was bright blue and the fishing line came directly out of the tip. Of course, the pilot

430 Art Bentley, "People from Venus Live Among Us- This Man's Known Them for Years," 26 April 1976, *Midnight*, Boca Raton, Florida.

431 *Ibid.*

432 Ash Staunton, "Coe, Albert," entry in *Exopaedia*, 2014, http://www.exopaedia.org/Coe%2C+Albert (Accessed 27 November 2014)

433 *Ibid.*

was extremely grateful for Coe's kind assistance, both in saving his life and recovering the mysterious fishing rod. The stranger asked Coe for his name and address, for he "would surely write" to him at the earliest opportunity. Coe insisted on helping the man get back to his airplane, and was quite surprised to see a large disc-shaped object parked in the middle of the clearing.[434] As this was 1920, the term "flying saucer" had not yet entered into our vocabulary; but after 24 June 1947 when fire fighting-equipment salesman and private pilot Kenneth Arnold reported nine disc-shaped objects flying in formation at a speed of 1,200 miles per hour, like "*saucers skipping across water*," over Mt. Rainier in Washington State, Coe would refer to the object he observed with this new appellation. The flying saucer observed by Coe, he would later learn, was a Venusian scout craft, similar to those sighted by Adamski and other contactees nearly three decades later.

Naturally, Coe senses that the stranger comes from another world. The alien pilot, for his part, does not sense any ill intentions on Coe's part, and takes the boy from New York's word that he can maintain secrecy about the saucer's landing site. The stranger identified himself simply as "Zret," an inhabitant of the planet Venus. Zret regrets that he cannot answer all of Coe's questions, but does let him know that he is 340 years older than the boy. The Venusian then entered the ship, preparing for takeoff. He told Coe to stand back about twenty feet. A few minutes later the saucer rose vertically and silently zoomed off, disappearing into a cloud bank.[435] Coe then rendezvoused with his fishing buddy Rod at the appointed place. Rod had been waiting there for about an hour; so Coe simply apologized for his tardiness and explained to his schoolmate that he had been delayed since he helped a fisherman in distress, without getting into any details about the saucer or its occupant's extraterrestrial origin.

True to his word, the Venusian pilot did indeed write to his new young friend and during a series of subsequent meetings, a couple that take place in New York City, and also on a fishing trip together, Zret tells Coe more about Venus, the solar system and his mission on Earth. According to Zret, his ancestors did not originate on Venus. Rather, they migrated there from the planet Norca, which orbits around Tau Ceti, a star in the constellation of Cetus, but situated in our galactic neighborhood. Unfortunately, Norca was drying up, its deserts expanding over the entire planet's surface. Therefore, they sought a new home in space, eventually establishing colonies in our solar system's inner planets of Venus, Mars and Earth, in that order.[436] Perhaps *The Man Who Fell to Earth,* the 1963 science fiction novel by American author Walter Tevis,[437] about an extraterrestrial who lands on Earth seeking a way to ferry his people to Earth from his home planet Anthea, which is suffering from a severe drought, was based on Coe's Norca revelations. The novel served as the basis for the 1976 cult film by director Nicolas Roeg, starring David Bowie as the alien.

The first contingent and highest number of Norcans settled on Venus. Although Venus was already inhabited, there were still many unpopulated regions that the Norcans could settle. The indigenous Venusians realized that the Norcans were not a hostile race so they allowed them to settle in the cooler, mountainous areas of their planet. Therefore, with Venus as their base, the Norcans chose Mars, the fourth planet out from the Sun, as their secondary area for colonization. On Mars they built their vast cities and laboratories underground to protect them from the massive radiation bombardment of intense streams of cosmic rays emanating from the <u>Sun that were </u>continually striking the Martian surface during daylight hours. The indigenous

434 *Ibid.*
435 *Ibid.*
436 *Ibid.*
437 Walter Tevis, *Man Who Fell to Earth* (New York, New York: Gold Medal Books, 1963).

inhabitants of Mars also had no problem with allowing the peaceful Norcans to settle there as well. The Norcans originally skipped the third planet out from the Sun for settlement because its human inhabitants had not yet reached a state of harmony and peace conducive to interplanetary contact.[438]

As to the Norcans' presence on Earth, Coe stated that it dates back to about 13,000 B.C.E. At the time of their arrival, the Norcans discovered that a sort of cold war had broken out between the two super states of Atlantis and Lemuria. The first contingent of Norcans to arrive on Earth were not authorized to land here by the ruling Science Council in the Venusian Hierarchy of Light. The Atlanteans and Lemurians were in the process of developing atomic weapons of mass destruction, and the Venusian Masters did not wish to the see the Norcans, a race genetically similar to the humans of Earth, caught up and possibly destroyed in the conflict that was sure to ensue between the great powers. Once the Norcans on Earth settled in various areas, they found themselves dwelling within the spheres of influence of either Atlantis, which largely controlled the Northern Hemisphere, or Lemuria, which controlled most of the Southern Hemisphere. As the Norcans interbred with the Earthlings in these sectors over several generations, they began to lose their sense of being extraterrestrials, thinking of themselves more as Atlanteans or Lemurians and working for the specific interests of their respective and adoptive nation. Coe explained that there were three Norcan colonies in Atlantean territory and two in Lemurian controlled zones.[439]

Sure enough, just as the Venusian Masters had predicted, the war broke out between Atlantis and Lemuria, with disastrous consequences around the globe. In India, tales of great aerial battles with *vimanas,* or flying saucers, and massive atomic blasts wiping out cities throughout the world are recorded in ancient Hindu scriptures. And throughout the Middle and Near East, similar accounts can be found in the sacred texts of Judaism and Zoroastrianism that speak of a war extending to outer space between the Sons of Light and the Minions of Darkness. Even in North America, the Hopi have maintained oral legends of the end of the Third World, when their ancestors were forced to live in underground caves for several generations before emerging into the Fourth World, when the planet was able to somewhat recover from the devastation wrought against it by the atomic blasts and the subsequent radiation fallout. Coe says that the few Norcans that survived were allowed to return to Venus, provided that they did not leave any remnants of their technological capabilities behind for the Earthlings to scarf up and use against each other in some future time.[440]

Coe asserted that in our day there are no more than 100 Venusians, formerly known as Norcans, residing on the Earth at any given time. He told the *Midnight* reporter that he gets around to meeting most of them at various clandestine meetings. He usually has about a dozen such meetings each calendar year with this current Venusian contingent. Coe claims that when Zret is in attendance at any of these meetings, he usually hands him a letter with instructions pertaining to the message the Venusians would like him to disseminate to his fellow Earthlings. When correspondent Bentley asked Coe to see such a letter, however, the retired engineer stated that he had none to offer by way of proof. He said that, "I have strict instructions that as soon as I get a letter, I destroy it. I've never violated them."[441]

Coe did not object to Art Bentley's interview, for despite *Midnight's* reputation in 1976 as a

---

438 Staunton
439 *Ibid.*
440 *Ibid.*
441 *Ibid.*

"sensationalist" tabloid, the fact that its readership exceeded 250,000 who largely picked it up at supermarket checkout counters, at the very least meant that the Venusian message was going to get "out there," and at some level find its way into the collective consciousness. Thanks to the efforts of Coe and other contactees, UFOs and their alien occupants have gone from being the subjects of small home discussion groups to those of genuine crazes and true pop culture phenomena. Remember, Ted Owens indicated that the Saucer Intelligences planned this all along.

Håkan Blomqvist, the leading ufologist in Sweden, would concur with Owens, but also adds that the Saucer Intelligences have been assisted in their outreach to the peoples of Earth by their fellow travelers here, namely the members of the Theosophical Society. Blomqvist, who works as a librarian at the Norrköping Public Library, also devotes a significant amount of his time to volunteer work at the Archives for the Unexplained (AFU), formerly the Archives for UFO Research, a foundation of which he was one of the founders in 1973. The 62 year-old UFO researcher claims that he was endowed from birth with "an existential curiosity." He also adds that he has, "always been fascinated by literature and the mysteries of life."[442]

As a young man, Blomqvist studied ethnology, philosophy and the history of religion at Stockholm University. In the process of researching these subjects, he developed a great interest in the Theosophical and esoteric traditions in the world's literature, noting the intervention of extraterrestrials in the cosmic evolution of humankind. He is the author of numerous UFO books,[443] as well as hundreds of articles in various magazines and newspapers. Most of these focus on the contactees and their important message for humankind. At the present time, Blomqvist serves as chairman of the AFU board and is also a board member of the national organization, UFO-Sweden.[444]

As to the Earthlings aiding and abetting the extraterrestrials to accomplish their mission here on Earth, Blomqvist writes:

"Was there a hidden hand, an ancient esoteric society behind some of the first UFO contactees of the 1950s? Were George Adamski, Orfeo Angelucci, Daniel Fry, George Van Tassel, Howard Menger, etc., involved in a test made by this hidden group? This is the controversial basic theme and theory presented and documented in my new book, *Return of the Gods: UFOs and the Esoteric Tradition*."[445]

The Swedish researcher also provides a synopsis of this theory:

"I have discussed this variation of Vallee's esoteric intervention theory in several earlier blog entries. Much additional data and new dimensions to this theory were provided by the Theosophical scholar Joscelyn Godwin, who kindly sent me part of an unpublished manuscript documenting a hidden hand behind the outbreak of the first, very physical, spiritualistic phenomena in the 19th century. He has also delved into this intriguing hypothesis in a four-part series of articles, *The Hidden Hand*, in the academic journal *Theosophical History*,

442 Håkan Blomqvist, "Who was Paul M. Vest?" 5 December 2013, *Håkan Blomqvist's blog*, http://ufoarchives. blogspot.com/2013/12/who-was-paul-m-vest.html (Accessed 2 December 2014)
443 Håkan Blomqvist, *UFO – In Myth and Reality* (Visby, Sweden: Nomen förlag, 1993).

_____, *Aliens on Earth: UFO Contacts in Sweden* (Visby, Sweden: Nomen förlag, 2009).

_____, *A Travel in Time: The History of UFO-Sweden, 1970-2010* (Visby, Sweden: Nomen förlag, 2010).

_____, *Return of the Gods: UFOs and the Esoteric Tradition* (Visby, Sweden: Nomen förlag, 2013).
444 Blomqvist, "Who is Paul M. Vest?"
445 *Ibid.*

1990-91. According to official Theosophical documents, written by Constance Wachtmeister, Charles Leadbeater and Annie Besant, the first nineteenth century spiritualist phenomena were created by a secret lodge, the Yucatan Brotherhood, custodians of the Ancient Wisdom and a branch of the Planetary Guardians. The object was to challenge the materialistic worldview by creating "unexplained" phenomena. Was this lodge also the hidden hand behind the 1950s contactees?"[446]

In other words, it did not matter so much as to how the message arrived to the populace at large; but rather that they received it, that it constituted a "seed" for the growth of thought constructs that would impact and ultimately change the collective consciousness, creating an aura of receptivity toward the arrival of the Venusians and other Space Brothers and Sisters.

Blomqvist also believes that Paul M. Vest's August 1954 *Mystic* magazine article, "Venusians Walk Our Streets," has not received either the attention or the recognition it deserves from the international UFO community. Besides providing a wonderful summary of the Venusians' message for the people of Earth, the article also highlights the Theosophical tenets inherent in the Venusian way of life. And while we know a great deal concerning the lives of most of ufology's leading lights, especially those of the contactees, we know so little about Vest, and most importantly his ties to the Theosophical Society, the likely *agent provocateurs* of the contactee movement.[447]

On the involvement of Vest with the contactees, Blomqvist writes the following:

"An important source of information that made me seriously consider the possibility of an esoteric society behind some of the 1950s' contactees was several articles by the American journalist Paul M. Vest. He was a frequent contributor to *Fate* magazine in the 1950s and 60s. Vest was obviously very well informed on the esoteric tradition and paranormal phenomena. His article on Theosophy and Helena Petrovna Blavatsky in *Fate* (October 1951) received favourable comments from Boris de Zirkoff, editor of the *Collected Writings of H. P. Blavatsky* (*Fate*, February-March 1952). Vest wrote articles on subjects like medium Daniel Dunglas Home, fairies, Alice Bailey, the Count Saint-Germain; and he also revealed several personal paranormal experiences in *Fate*'s column, 'True Mystic Experiences.'"

THEOSOPHICAL HISTORY

July 1990
$3.00

A Quarterly Journal of Research
ISSN 0951-497X

The clues to the Theosophical Society's involvement in the UFO contactee phenomenon may be found in the pages of *Theosophical History*, 1990-91. See http://ufoarchives.blogspot.com/2013/12/who-was-paul-m-vest.html.

But the most important and really intriguing article from the pen of Paul M. Vest, "Venusians Walk Our Streets," was printed in Ray Palmer's magazine *Mystic*, August 1954, also reprinted in *The Journal of Borderland Research*, March-April 1982.[448]

The article, "Venusians Walk Our Streets," was primarily significant to Blomqvist because of the information it contains about the extraterrestrials here on Earth, relayed to Vest by the ever-so-mysterious "Bill," who allegedly came down to Southern California

446 *Ibid.*
447 *Ibid.*
448 *Ibid.*

from Washington State, to meet with Vest outside a bus terminal. During the interview, Bill gives Vest a list with various individuals who he has previously conversed about contactees in Southern California; and when Bill has left, Paul Vest contacts the people on the list and they all confirm meeting this strange man, who was also known as "Mr. Wheeler" by some of them. It does seem, however, that Orfeo Angelucci's wife, Mabel, was not duly impressed by her visit from Mr. Wheeler. Mabel told Vest, "Oh, that man gave me the creeps. He rang the doorbell one day and introduced himself with an odd name I can't remember. He seemed to know everything about us. It frightened me - there was something so strange and downright weird about him." Nevertheless, despite Mabel's lack of endorsement, Paul Vest follows the advice of Bill and writes three articles for *Mystic* on the experiences of Orfeo Angelucci. These were published in November 1953, May 1954 and October 1954.[449]

Blomqvist notes that,

"The story of Mr. Wheeler's involvement with many contactees and ufologists in the 1950s is very well documented in several books and articles. A good source is "The Great Venusian Mystery" by James Crenshaw (*Fate*, June 1966). Even the skeptical ufologist James Moseley regarded it as "one of the strangest saucer cases I have ever been involved with."[450] I have found many new data and documents on this case, presented in my book, indicating an apparent connection with the esoteric tradition and a hidden hand behind the UFO contactees in the 1950s. But I have not succeded in finding any biographical data on journalist Paul M. Vest and find it notable that no American ufologists have followed up on this case or made an interview with Paul M. Vest. Maybe someone reading this blog can provide more clues?"[451]

During the interview, Bill revealed to Vest a vast knowledge of the Ancient Wisdom, what we refer to as Theosophy. After his initial apprehension and skepticism, Vest was overwhelmed by Bill's positive characteristics, taking note that the visitor "was a much wiser, gentler and more evolved being than I - and with infinitely greater perceptive ability."[452] Perhaps we may never know the true identity of this unknown visitor; but Blomqvist is sure that whoever he was, he was definitely sent by a secret group to promote one of the first of the so-called UFO contactees.

The Venusian Agenda

So just what do the Venusians want us to know? What agenda have they established for humankind? To answer this question, we return to Vest's August 1954 *Mystic* magazine article, "Venusians Walk Our Streets." I have taken the liberty to both summarize and enumerate the points made by Bill in the order that they were presented to the interviewer, Paul M. Vest:

1. Human beings have traveled in flying saucers. However, the number is small insofar as those individuals selected for the honor must be humble and gentle receptors, recognized by the Venusians and other Etherics as true spiritual brothers and sisters. The chosen ones must also be known to the extraterrestrials as seekers of knowledge and wisdom. Those with more than a passing interest in metaphysics, comparative religion and supra-normal phenomena make the best candidates for developing contacts, and possibly going for rides aboard their craft into space and perhaps to the Moon or another planet in our solar system.

2. As Venus is the planet in closest proximity to the Earth, the Venusians have been

449 *Ibid.*
450 James Moseley, *Wright Field Story* (Clarksburg, WV: Saucerian Books, 1971), 13.
451 Blomqvist, "Who is Paul M. Vest?"
452 Vest, "Venusians Walk Our Streets"

designated as the Watchers over all of our affairs. Bill told Vest that *to the etheric beings that have evolved far beyond the infantile perceptive states of form, color, sex, conflict, time, space and material illusion*, which sadly is the erroneous condition most Earthlings find themselves in, "Our planet is comparable to a huge vat of broth for the production of penicillin. To the senses of man such a vat is a rather ill-smelling, offensive thing; but nevertheless, it produces the precious golden-colored penicillin. Bill added that, "The vat is comparable to Earth and its peoples, while the comparatively few spiritually evolved souls of this age represent the precious golden product of the vat." And the good news for humankind is that, "Eventually, every human being upon Earth will evolve into the higher consciousness." So in the meantime, to keep us from blowing our planet to smithereens, the Venusians and other enlightened alien species will continue to watch over our cosmic development.

3. There are many intelligent forms of life in the solar system and beyond, filling the immensity of space. Many of the extraterrestrials visiting the Earth in the 1950s "*were extra-dimensional, etheric beings of a high spiritual order.*" And from what we know about the contactees of that era, at least for those who had been aboard the massive motherships, great deference was shown to the "masters" by all of the crew members; while the contactees immediately recognized these ones as being of an exalted nature, feeling a great sense of awe just from being in their presence.

4. Earthlings do not have a good reputation throughout the galaxy, and perhaps beyond. For this reason, we of Earth are to a large extent, "under the direction of the Etherics- the Great Ones...." Bill, the Venusian, elaborated on this point when he stated that, "Earth's people are woefully, emotionally immature and their prison-like three-dimensional world is preponderantly false, as compared to reality. Men's minds are crystallized in error and filled with violent prejudices." Bill also decried the prevalence of intolerance in our society, noting that, "Upon your Earth the mere color of one's skin- a slight difference of religious belief- merely belonging to a different race or country-in fact, the most trivial deviations precipitate animalistic belligerencies, hideous brutalities and the bloody slaughter of millions of fellow creatures."

5. Naturally, the Venusians and other Etherics have come to fear such an aggressive species as ourselves. After all, Bill explained, "Mankind's greatest Teacher-the etheric Sun-Spirit, whom you know as Jesus Christ- who took upon himself the error of humanity to teach men simply to LOVE ONE ANOTHER- was crucified and tortured by those He came to save." For this reason, when human beings self-righteously demand that the Venusians land their craft openly at one of our airports, just to prove their existence, they should not be surprised or disappointed to discover that no Venusians will comply. It may take numerous incarnations, but eventually "all (Earthlings) will attain to their lost heritage." In the meantime, Bill made it known that they (the Etherics/Venusians) will "help insofar as we are permitted to do so."

6. Each individual human being must work out his or her own salvation. When a sufficient number have accomplished this task, Earth's collective planetary consciousness will have risen to such a point that more open communications with Venusians and the inhabitants of other planets can be established. For the present time, the Venusians declare that, "Yes, we understand, Earth, the planet of sorrows, is one of the hardest and most difficult paths of evolution in the entire cosmos. And to make it even more severe, mankind must work out their own salvation- this is the Law."

7. Much as Swedenborg once explained to his congregants, there are many souls on Venus at various stages of spiritual development. Some were of a more "material evolution," meaning that, "though they differed from us in certain physiological principles, still many Venusians could pass for Earthlings." Bill also made it a point to elucidate on some of the then extant theories that Earth's astronomers held about Venus, stating that they were "entirely erroneous." But since rocketry had not developed to the level that space probes could be sent to Venus, and the planet's surface was covered by an extremely

Despite the hostility shown toward Him, Jesus came to Earth teaching us to simply "love one another." He and the angelic Venusians continue to watch over and protect us. See www.evangelicaloutreach.org.

dense cloud layer, the astronomers could only go by the little information they had acquired concerning the outward appearance of the mysterious orb, thereby assuming that it must be a planet quite similar to the Earth in many respects. They assumed that future astronauts to Venus would find the atmosphere and surface conditions conducive for human habitation and settlement. Sadly, this did not prove to be the case. The astronomers and other scientists did not understand that the Venusians, being at least 13.5 million years more advanced along the scale of biological and technical evolution, had long ago abandoned the third dimension of space-time for an existence in the higher ethereal realms. In the fourth dimension, the next level above our own, the Venusians would manifest a material and physical presence, those of the ancient past as well as those of the distant future, when the planet has been completely terraformed by human beings, becoming a veritable paradise, much as C. S. Lewis imagined it would be in his mythic *Perelandra*. And in the fifth dimension, we find Venusians of both an advanced technical and spiritual level of development, existing in a parallel dimension of space-time commonly referred to by psychics as "Etheria." In this realm, Venusians and entities from other planets can live anywhere from 1,000 to 3,000 years, but they are not immortal. Fourth and fifth dimensional Venusians can easily be mistaken for human beings; and they readily assimilate into our populations. Fifth dimensional Venusians have developed some of the powers still latent in humankind, but they are not yet operational at an angelic or godlike level. On the other hand, the Venusians in even higher dimensions of reality might easily be confused with epic heroes, angels, *aeons* or even gods. Bill wanted us to know that the Venusians "undoubtedly presented themselves to us in a manner that we with our lower perceptive abilities might understand and interpret according to our limited three-dimensional standards."

8. The Venusians have been in constant communication with humans for countless millennia, but have recently stepped up their physical presence on our planet during the initial phases of our transition into both the atomic and space ages. The Venusian contingent on Earth ranges anywhere from 24 to 100 at any given time. The Venusian Hierarchy of Light, being shared by adepts, masters and ascended masters, in the rank

levels of spiritual development, will allow no entity less than a master to interact with human beings on the Earth's surface. More about the rationale for this will be explained in the next chapter. Bill did state, however, that "numerous Venusian contacts had been made by means of 'ham' radio sets and tape recordings." He even provided Vest with a list of contacts, complete with their home addresses, of those special persons who have received such radio broadcasts and had gone so far as to record them. Bill also went on to declare that other contacts had been made through so-called "sensitives," or mediums. These psychically-gifted individuals received messages from the Venusians and other Etherics by means of clairvoyance and clairaudience.

9.   The Venusians were telepathic and possessed many other extrasensory powers that Earthlings could barely even begin to imagine. Vest, a dedicated Theosophist and student of the occult, was familiar with the work of many of Earth's adepts, where in private meetings they had revealed their true identities to him while he sat in utter silence. Vest stated that, "Realization of their true spiritual status had to be gained entirely through extra-sensory perception (ESP), or not at all. Words later served only to verify the paranormal communication. Thus I knew that the man who openly proclaims himself an adept, a master or a guru, usually is not one, while the true spiritual adept goes unknown, often in humble garb." Vest reported that he was able to psychically discern the true Venusian identity of Bill almost immediately since the gentleman came into his view outside the Santa Monica bus depot. His mind was constantly being bombarded by images of life on Venus and other planets while he was in the presence of the mysterious "Mr. Bill Wheeler."

10. Reincarnation is real and universal. Vest took particular note of the fact that Bill stressed the idea of reincarnation and the inevitable law of compensation (karma) as regards the inhabitants of Earth. "But," said Bill, "*no matter what the material objectification or etheric individualization, the Spark of Eternal Being is always identical. For all are essentially One* and a part of the Infinite and Everlasting Spiritual Fire, which is the Father."

Most significantly, the Venusians were accelerating their outreach program. It was of paramount importance that their message to Angelucci and the other contactees get out to the public at large in the shortest possible time. The very destiny of our planet depended upon the success of the Venusians' mission. Bill, the Venusian master, also urged Vest and other Earthlings concerned about the course of future events, to read with an open mind and heart the nineteenth century California Theosophist Francis S. Oliver's book, *A Dweller on Two Planets*.[453] In its introduction, Oliver attests that the book was channeled through him via automatic writing, visions and mental "dictations" emanating from a spirit entity calling himself "Phylos the Thibetan." This now disembodied entity revealed an amazing story to Oliver concerning the ancient inhabitants of Atlantis, Lemuria and Venus over a period of three years, commencing in 1883.[454] Much of the information contained in *A Dweller on Two Planets* corresponds neatly with the revelations previously proffered by Coe regarding the two lost

453   Frederick Spencer Oliver as channel for Phylos the Thibetan, *A Dweller on Two Planets or the Dividing of the Way,* 2nd edition (Los Angeles, CA: Poseid Publishing Company, 1920); This work was originally completed in 1886 and copyrighted by the author in 1894, with the first edition published by the author's mother, Mary Elizabeth Manley-Oliver in 1905 in Los Angeles, California, six years after Frederick Spencer Oliver's death.

454   John B. Hare, Introduction to on-line edition of *A Dweller on Two Planets*, 2002, http://www.sacred-texts.com/atl/ dtp/index.htm (Accessed 5 December 2014).

continents on Earth as well as sundry civilizations on our sister planet, Venus.

It seems that Phylos can trace his numerous Earthly incarnations back to the time of Atlantis. Oliver, when channeling Phylos, would go into a deep trance state, while this ancient soul would move his hands across the paper, scribbling quickly a first-person account of the Poseid culture in old Atlantis up to the point where it had reached a high level of technological and scientific advancement, only slightly above the level we have currently obtained. Phylos' personal history and that of a group of souls with whom he closely interacted is portrayed in the context of the economic, military, political, religious and social structures which shaped the ancient Poseid society. Some of the marvels available for the Poseidi citizens, or those dwelling in the capital city of Poseidon, included such things as electric-powered antigravity air and submarine craft, television, wireless telephony, aerial water generators, air conditioners and high-speed rail. Deep esoteric subjects such as karma and re-incarnation are described by Phylos' final incarnation in nineteenth-century America, where his Atlantean karma finally played itself out in the person of Walter Pierson, a gold prospector and occult student of the Theo-Christic Adepts who travelled to the planet Venus, a.k.a. Hysperia, in a subtle body while his physical form remained at an etheric temple deep inside Mt. Shasta in Northern California. Describing his experience with the Venusian adepts, Phylos relates many wonders including artwork depicted in three-dimensional scenes that appeared "alive," as it were. He also witnessed a voice-operated typewriter and huge cigar-shaped flying ships that carried the Venusians to our world. All of this left Phylos- in the embodiment of Pierson- marveling at the seeming "occult" and technical power the extraterrestrials were able to so easily employ. Other devices he mentioned that were in use by the Venusians have already become part of present-day reality, such as television and the atomic microscope.[455]

In a detailed and personal history of Atlantis and nineteenth century North America, Phylos is able to arrive at some of the linkages between his first and last incarnations, adequately demonstrating to the reader the cause and effects of karma in his triumphs and tragedies literally spanning millennia. Phylos sums up his autobiographies thusly: "*Whatsoever a man soweth, that shall he also reap.*" The old soul leaves a warning to ourselves, yet on the cusp of a new technological age, that we not repeat the mistakes of the past which led to the cataclysmic destruction of "Poseid, Queen of the Waves," the most beautiful of all cities in the ancient world, obliterated in what can now best be described as a "nuclear war" with the Lemurians. *A Dweller on Two Planets* has greatly influenced our ideas about the ancient continents of Atlantis and Lemuria, in addition to generating an esoteric mystique about Mount Shasta and Trinity County in California that has never abated. In the 2002 introduction to a reprint of the book, New Age guru John B. Hare says that it "is openly acknowledged as source material for many New Age belief systems, including the I Am Movement, the Lemurian Fellowship, and Elizabeth Claire Prophet."[456] It should also be noted that in 1940, the Lemurian Fellowship published a "sequel" to *Dweller* with the title *An Earth Dweller's Return*. And according to actress Shirley MacLaine, it was the book, *A Dweller on Two Planets* that jumped off of a bookshelf and into her hands in a New Age bookstore in Hong Kong, so impelling her to change the direction of her life, dedicating herself thoroughly to the seeking of esoteric knowledge. This book also served as the source of the idea that there is a hidden sanctuary of ascended masters deep under Mount Shasta and that the destiny of America was intrinsically linked to

---

455 *Ibid.*
456 *Ibid.*

that of becoming the "New Atlantis."[457]

It is apparent that Theosophists are not receiving the honors and respect due them as the true founders of the New Age. Long before Edgar Cayce, the sleeping prophet from Hopkinsville, Kentucky, had ever uttered a word about Atlantis or Lemuria, Blavatsky and others in the Theosophical Society and other groups concerned with paranormal manifestations were illuminating us with continuous and historically accurate information about these lost continents, as well as their connections to a Venusian contingent here on Earth. And even before the words "flying saucer," "unidentified flying object," "mothership" or "contactee" had ever entered anyone's vocabulary, the sightings of strange aerial phenomena continued to take place. The observations of these phantom airships were also being linked to reports of their landings, along with the disembarkation of mysterious occupants, supposed "visitors from outer space."[458]

The Phantom Airship

Thousands reported sightings of a great phantom airship throughout the late 1890s. Concerning reports of this "Jules Verne-style flying machine,"[459] UFO investigator Michael Busby penned the following:

Long before Adamski and reports of the Venusian mothership, Tesla conceived of a massive, electric-powered airship. See http://www.abovetopsecret.com/forum/thread546706/pg2.

"Some people, including professors and other 'learned men,' believed the airships were from another world. The descriptions of the craft and their antics seemed to suggest an intelligence far beyond any on Earth. Supporting such a premise is the claim of a U.S. government signal officer of the recovery of an alien body after a purported crash. The similarity of the government official's account to an alien crash of another time and place is striking. A U.S. Air Force major serving as base public information officer made the exact same claim fifty years later at Roswell, New Mexico. Moreover, a published firsthand account of an encounter between an Earthling and the unearthly visitors gave credence, at the time, that the flying machines were from another world."[460]

The airships were generally reported as flying parallel to telegraph lines and railroad tracks,[461] much as contemporary UFOs seem to follow power lines or hover in the vicinity of military bases. And like the UFO sightings of today, the airships were widely reported in numerous newspapers as attributable to various manifestations of both natural and supernatural events.[462] Most authorities interviewed as to the origin of the phantom craft speculated that it came from Mars or Venus,[463] although a few suggested Jupiter and Saturn as alternative possibilities. But

---

457 *Ibid:* See also Manly P. Hall, *Secret Destiny of America* (Los Angeles, CA: Philosophical Publishing Company, 1944), for further development on the re-emergence of Atlantean science and society in the contemporary United States, brought about by reincarnated souls from the lost continent.

458 Charles Fort, *Book of the Damned* (New York, New York: Boni and Liveright, 1919).

459 Michael Busby, *Solving the 1897 Airship Mystery* (Gretna, LA: Pelican, 2004), 28.

460 *Ibid.,* 23

461 *Ibid.,* 24

462 *Ibid.,* 25

463 *Ibid.,* 261

most interesting was the public's perception that the airship was the result of some top secret government project undertaken to master the secrets of aerial navigation, and that perhaps the scientists involved received some kind of extraterrestrial assistance. Others felt that the mysterious inventor of the airship would soon come forward with his device to claim a huge financial reward for his diligent endeavors.[464]

While it can be said that the "Age of Flying Saucers" did not really begin until 1947, with the Kenneth Arnold sightings and the crash at Roswell, New Mexico, sightings of the phantom airship and mysterious lights that would at times seem to follow it persisted from late 1896 through 1946. Thus the stage was being set and the mass consciousness prepared for the coming "saucer flap" in the following year.

1946, however, was quite a remarkable year in the history of ufology, for that is when the United States first bounced a radar beam off the Moon,[465] thus alerting the inhabitants of other planets in our solar system that we Earthlings, as a species, had finally arrived at the point where we could project power off world, for better or for worse. At this point, the Solar Hierarchy of Light decided that Earth surveillance activities would be intensified, hence the reason for interplanetary space craft to start showing up across the globe in such massive numbers ever since. The accelerated extraterrestrial presence was first made manifest by the appearance of a massive carrier ship in the night skies over San Diego, California, on 9 October, 1946. The mysterious

The "Age of Flying Saucers" began with civilian pilot Kenneth Arnold's sighting of nine disc-shaped objects over Mt. Rainier in Washington State. See http://www.project1947.com/fig/coronet1152.htm.

---

464 *Ibid.,* 25

465 Kelly Dickerson, "Quantum Particles Take the Road Most Traveled," 6 August 2014, *livescience*, http://www.livescience.com/47221-quantum-particle-path-most-traveled.html (Accessed 6 December 2014). The development of radar represents an important step in the continuing scientific advancement of humankind; but our projection of certain types of radar waves into the ethers of space presents a significant problem for the inhabitants of other worlds in parallel or different dimensions. Radar, as it turns out, generates quantum particles; and these can exist in states where they are in multiple places at once — a phenomenon called superposition. There is a mathematical equation called "wave function," however, that serves to describe the many possible locations where a quantum particle might simultaneously exist. Nevertheless, as soon as someone tries to measure the location or the velocity of one of these particles, its wave function will collapse and the particle will appear in only one spot, falling back under the laws of conventional physics that govern our three-dimensional universe. Because radar systems generate such quanta, it could be utilized as an offensive weapon against those extraterrestrials inhabiting "Etheria," i.e. quantum levels outside the space-time continuum in parallel or other dimensions. If an ultra-dimensional object, or an entity inhabiting such a zone, were to be exposed to the quantum particles of a radar beam, it is not unreasonable to assume that the resonant state of their "atomic structure," for the lack of a better word, would be reduced to the third dimension whence their light ships could be jammed or destroyed and they themselves would become vulnerable to attack and annihilation by our conventional weaponry.

The Solar Hierarchy of Light may be, at this very moment, reconsidering their non-interventionist policy toward the inhabitants of Earth. Our scientists' study of quantum particles has already provided one clue toward a resolution of the UFO enigma. What they have discovered is that as soon as they start probing around, the particles' quantum states collapse. For this reason, the ultra-dimensional entities prefer to keep safely absconded in another or parallel dimension, as any visibility in the third dimension could result in disastrous consequences. However, as physicists develop a way to isolate the bizarre quantum world and peer into it in a noninvasive way, this may allow them to map the path that particles like electrons, neutrons and protons are most likely to take when changing from one state to another. I would have to say this is definitely bad news for any ultra-dimensional aliens "out there," for it means they no longer have any place to hide from us while operational in our context of reality.

airship, reported by hundreds of observers, stated that it was similar in appearance to a "huge cigar with wings like a bat."[466] It was also on this same night that George Adamski and some friends were observing a meteor shower from a hill at his Palomar Gardens campgrounds, to the north of San Diego, when they observed the same large cigar-shaped craft that Adamski later described as a "mother ship." Adamski believed that it was the identical ship that returned one year later over the skies of Mt. Palomar that he took a photograph of through his eight-inch reflecting telescope as it passed in front of the Moon.[467]

In 1946, at the end of this pre-"flying saucer contactee" period in the history of ufology, it can be surmised that even Adamski did not yet have an idea of the full importance of the phenomenon that he and his friends at Palomar were then observing. Nevertheless, just a little down the road in San Diego, there was a gentleman who had the answers, local medium Mark Probert, who had long been channeling messages from a variety of disembodied entities for the benefit of the recently established San Diego-headquartered Borderland Sciences Research Associations (BSRA), directed by occult theorist and immigrant from Canada, N. Meade Layne.[468]

On the night of 9 October 1946, Layne was outdoors with hundreds of other San Diegans, waiting for a glimpse at the predicted meteor shower. Of course, they were not disappointed; and certainly observed a lot more interesting celestial phenomena than they had originally expected. Upon sighting the large cigar-shaped craft, Probert became quite animated and immediately called his associate in psychic research at the BSRA, N. Meade Layne, to obtain further instructions. Layne asked Probert if he could attempt telepathic communications with the vehicle's presumed occupants. Probert

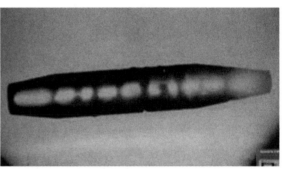

Mothership photographed by Adamski in 1947 through his telescope as it passed in front of the Moon. See http://mercuryservices.hubpages.com/video/Bio-of-George-Adamski.

then tried to reach the alien crew on the mental plane and succeeded famously.[469]

Of his telepathic contact with the aliens, the medium told a San Diego newspaper reporter that:

The strange machine is called the Kareeta, *and it would return in one year*; the occupants "came in peace. It is attracted at this time because the Earth is emitting a column of light which makes it easier of approach. The machine is powered by people possessing a very advanced knowledge of anti-gravity forces. It has 10,000 parts, a small but very powerful motor operating by electricity, and moving the wings, and an outer structure of light balsam wood, coated with an alloy. The people are nonaggressive and have been trying to contact the Earth for many years. They have very light bodies. They fear to land, but would be willing to meet a committee of scientists at an isolated spot, or on a mountain top."[470]

466 "Unidentified Airships," no author stated, 2014, *Sky Gaze*, http://www.skygaze.com/content/strange/Airships. shtml (Accessed 6 December 2014).

467 Michael Scott-Blair

468 Jerome Clark, "UFO Religions" in Lewis, James R., editor, *Odd Gods: New Religions and the Cult Controversy* (Amherst, New York: Prometheus Books, 2001), 354.

469 *Ibid.*

470 Mark Probert, quoted in the page 8-A story, "Parapsychologist Impatiently Repeats, 'Twas Space Ship in Sky,'" Friday, 18 October, 1946 edition of the *San Diego Union*.

It is interesting to note that Adamski believed that he had photographed the exact same mothership one year later. Keep in mind that Probert had predicted that it would return to San Diego and the surrounding area at that time. It should also be taken into account that Probert, an adept medium, acknowledged that his contacts were of a purely psychic nature, unlike Angelucci, Adamski, Menger, Van Tassel and others who would follow in coming forth publicly with their claims. These later contactees maintained that there were both physical and psychic aspects involved in their contacts, and that sometimes they were not able to distinguish between the two. While Adamski stated that he could only go by what he actually saw and heard on that memorable 20 November 1952, sensing that Orthon and the saucer were as "solid" as anything else in this three-dimensional world, he did take note that: "Certain students of this subject have asked me if I thought saucers and their occupants might normally be 'etheric' in nature or texture, but be able to 'condense' and so take on 'solidarity' and 'visibility' in Earth's environment. This is an involved subject. There are, of course, more things in Heaven and Earth than we have dreamed of and it never pays to be too arbitrary about those things which as yet we 'see through a glass darkly.'"[471]

In the aftermath of World War II, therefore, it appears that there was a global flurry of news reports on the flying saucers, with literally thousands reporting sightings of the mysterious craft. Of course, the "true believers" asserted we were being visited by physical beings in metallic spacecraft. These beings, as Adamski so eloquently wrote about, appeared much as we do, arriving here from other planets in outer space. These orbs were carbon-based worlds and very much like the Earth in their atmospheric and geological compositions, at least as far as the contactees could determine. However, there was another current of thought, that being that these craft were not from outer space, as we understand it, but from inter-dimensional space.

Layne, relying heavily on the revelations of his friend and associate Mark Probert, came to believe that the flying saucers, rather than representing advanced military or extraterrestrial technology, were piloted by beings from a parallel dimension, which he called Etheria. Their "ether ships" usually operated within our atmosphere and third dimensional environment under a cloak of invisibility but could be seen by human beings when their atomic vibratory rate became slow enough. He further claimed that Etherians could become stranded on the terrestrial plane on the rare occasions when their ether ships malfunctioned. Layne also asserted that various governments were aware of these incidents and had investigated them.[472]

In addition, Layne argued that the Etherians and their ships inspired much of Earth's mythology and religions. Nevertheless, they were not gods but truly mortal beings, albeit living thousands of years. On Earth, they were confused with being gods because of their high level of technological and spiritual

In the Cold War hysteria of the early 1950s, many thought the flying saucers were a top secret Soviet weapon. See http://www. project1947.com/fig/coronet1152.htm.

---

471 Adamski and Leslie, *Flying Saucers Have Landed*, Library of Light on-line edition without page numbers, closing paragraphs of Chapter 22, "The Memorable November 20th."

472 Gregory L. Reece, *UFO Religion: Inside Flying Saucer Cults and Culture* (London, UK: I. B. Tauris, 2007), 16-17.

advancement. Layne believed that the Etherians' motive in coming to the terrestrial plane of existence was to reveal their accumulated wisdom to humanity; and that these revelations would be relayed through individuals with sufficiently developed psychic abilities, like Probert, who could contact the Etherians and communicate with them directly.[473]

According to the BSRA, the space between Earth and the planet Venus is intersected by seven unseen dimensional planes. These, in turn, are populated with at least four parallel worlds, two for Venus and two for the Earth. Of these planets in other dimensions, ether ship researcher Edward S. Schultz writes that, "We must not harbor the illusion that the four etheric states are ghostly and unsubstantial. They are a good deal more substantial than our so called dense world, and it is we who're the ghosts of the Etheric realm."[474] One of these inter-dimensional planets, closer to Venus in its revolutions around the Sun, can be sensed by perceptive psychics and is called Etheria. Even until now, its very existence has eluded ordinary scientific investigation.

What caught the attention of the Etherians, however, were humankind's initial successes in splitting the atom and uncovering some of the secrets of the subatomic universe, thus creating ripples and even tears in the inter-dimensional fabric of the solar system and the galactic neighborhood. Prior to our dangerous experimentation, the Etherians were more or less willing to watch us from a distance, occasionally sending an enlightened spirit to guide us along in our spiritual development.

Layne warned us in 1950 that, "Although these craft have been with us a longer time than most of us suspect, our own science and technology, military and otherwise, have only recently entered into an era in which some of our developments (radar, A-Bombs, etc.), are beginning to manifest to the Etherians in degrees ranging from a nuisance to a menace."[475] Atomic blasts on Earth, our development of vehicles capable of reaching space, and radar beams to the Moon and other planets meant that the Etherians were now going to take a more active role in patrolling our skies, monitoring our military installations and disseminating their message of peace through credible spokespersons. Of this accelerated program, ufology pioneer Lawrence Elliot wrote:

"In space ships whose outer skin was wrought by metal tougher than steel, they flew along magnetic lines of force into the atmosphere of Earth. We saw their craft at night as flashing fire balls of red and green. We saw them by day as discs that flew at incredible speeds and executed fantastic maneuvers. Troubled and confused, we dubbed them Flying Saucers and went to weird lengths to explain their existence. We failed utterly to recognize the truth. Such is the elaborately worked-out theory of the Borderlanders. Does it hold up? Until there is a definitive report on the saucers, the Etherians can appeal to our credibility as well as anyone — or anything."[476]

One of America's foremost authorities in the emerging field of "paranormal technology," David M. Roundtree, informs us that,

"There may also be subatomic particle beams, waves and *radar ionic gas plasmas* such as electronic ion plasma clouds, neutrinos that are nonelectric or magnetic, tachyon time particles/waves, and gravity particles/waves influencing paranormal activity. *These waves can*

473   Erik Davis, *Visionary State: A Journey through California's Spiritual Landscape* (San Francisco, California: Chronicle Books, 2006), 192.
474   Edward S. Shultz, as quoted in N. Meade Layne, *The Ether Ship Mystery and Its Solution* (San Diego, CA: BSRA, 1950), 23.
475   *Ibid.,* 23
476   Lawrence Elliot, "Flying Saucers: Myth or Menace?" (*Coronet* magazine, Chicago, Illinois, November 1952).

be artificially created by accelerometers, atomic lasers, or even employing a simple Jacob's Ladder anode and cathode plasma antennas, and placing them into a direct energy beam."[477]

Roundtree, 60, was born in Suffolk, Virginia, but moved to Delray Beach, Florida, in the fall of 1963 when his father had to relocate his family there in order to take up new employment. It was in Delray that young David first became interested in all aspects of the paranormal, having been introduced to the subject by his next-door neighbor, Fred W. Grosstuck, a retired college professor and pattern maker, who presented him with some literature detailing unexplainable occurrences the world over. The inquisitive lad soon obtained a subscription to *Fate* magazine, and by the age of 17 he was investigating his first "haunted house" in Boynton Beach, Florida.[478]

November 1952 cover of *Coronet* magazine. These Earth girls might easily pass as Venusians.

Roundtree has an impressive academic background, receiving his Bachelor of Science degree in Electrical Engineering in 1973 while serving in the Air Force, specializing in microwave technology; and in November of 2007, he went on to receive his Master's in Electronic Engineering, specializing in Digital Signal Processing. In 1978, now out of the Air Force, he was certified as an audio engineer and in 1985 as an acoustic engineer. Roundtree worked in the entertainment industry as a technical director, lighting designer and audio engineer for over twenty years, but all the while maintaining a strong interest and involvement in paranormal research. He also taught classes on electrical engineering at the University of Florida, whence he retired in 2001. At the present time, Roundtree serves as Manager of Public Address Communications Technologies and Director of the Audio Research and Development Lab for the third largest public transportation corporation in the nation while simultaneously working on his doctorate in physics. He is a professional member of numerous scientific organizations: the American Association for the Advancement of Science, the Audio Engineering Society, the International Frequency Sensor Association, and is also affiliated with the Institute of Electrical and Electronics Engineers; and he was recently invited to join the Mathematics Association of America. Despite his current research into sundry aspects of paranormal technology largely focused on ghost hunting, Roundtree does not doubt that his investigations have some applicability in explaining other anomalous phenomena such as UFO sightings and alleged "alien" encounters.[479]

The electrical engineer has concluded that since subatomic particles can be rotated up or down to change their properties to be anti-gravitational, anti-matter or reverse in time, *"We know that time anomalies are present at a paranormal event because we have detected them."* He then elaborates on some unexpected findings from NASA's Fermi Gamma-ray Space Telescope; for when the space technicians turned it toward the direction of Earth, the orbital observatory detected 17 gamma-ray flashes in lightning storms containing signatures of anti-

477 David M. Roundtree, *Paranormal Technology: Understanding the Science of Ghost Hunting* (Bloomington, IN: iUniverse, 2010), 178.

478 "David M. Roundtree: Author, Lecturer, Paranormal Researcher," no author stated, 2008, *Scientific Paranormal Research Information and Technology of Gainesville, Florida and Hackettstown, New Jersey*, http://www. spinvestigations.org/David_Rountree.html (Accessed 6 December 2014).

479 *Ibid.*

matter. Since Fermi recorded gamma-ray emissions that could only have been produced by the decay of energetic positrons, or the anti-matter equivalent of electrons, Roundtree declared that the question of the existence of anti-matter had clearly been settled: It does exist.[480]

Another discovery related to the structure of atomic particles and time anomalies was explained by Roundtree:

"A typical atomic particle or wave may be viewed as a holographic vortex which has 137 rings wrapped around the "eye" traveling at 13 times the speed of light. This potential to alter perception or influence perceptions of time may offer the foundations for what we term a "residual" haunt. We actually may be glimpsing something that occurred in the past. This voodoo demonstrates why I study all aspects of quantum mechanics with a passion. It is my firmly held belief that the key to unlocking the mystery of paranormal phenomena will be determined by its analysis at a subatomic level."[481]

Contactee researcher Ed Komarek, while never experiencing any paranormal "affiliation," did recognize the following:

"As I work back through material and memories accumulated through my lifetime, the overall picture of ET human interactions is beginning to take shape in my mind. While I never have had direct contact with ET humans, I have nevertheless felt a telepathic affiliation all my life. In investigating UFOs in my local neighborhood I have found myself on the fringe of a human ET network that seems to be dealing with the same human ETs of the 1950s, but in a much less overt manner."[482]

Komarek goes on to explain that the very same things that were going on more overtly in the 1950s are still, in fact, going on covertly today. It has become clear to him and other researchers of the contactee conundrum that contact has not dissipated since the 1950s, but simply had to go underground due to worldwide autocratic military and elite resistance. For this reason, Komarek states that, "Contact may have covertly accelerated."[483]

The extraterrestrial contact situation has morphed to accommodate this new paradigm. Komarek elaborates:

"The rapid advances in technical knowledge in the first part of the twentieth century led to space travel and the atomic bomb. The human extraterrestrials who had been monitoring developments on Earth became very concerned both from self-interest and secondly, our interest as well. *It became clear to the extraterrestrial humans that something had to be done about Earth because we earth humans had become a clear and present danger to their societies in way that we can only begin to imagine."[484]*

Following World War II, with the division of the Earth between the two equally armed nuclear powers of the Soviet Union and the United States, the Solar Hierarchy of Light opted to modify its more conservative approach toward extraterrestrial contacts with human beings. Insofar as the situation on Earth was much worse than the extraterrestrials had previously realized, either for the Earthlings or themselves, they began an accelerated push to deal with the danger, initiating a rapid overt intervention to get humanity "back on the right track,"

---

480 Roundtree, *Paranormal Technology*, 178
481 *Ibid.,* 178-179
482 Ed Komarek, "The 1950's Contactee Movement Revisited," 10 November 2007, *Exopolitics* Blogspot, http://www. bibliotecapleyades.net/vida_alien/alien_contactee01.htm (Accessed 7 December 2014)
483 *Ibid.*
484 *Ibid.*

so to speak. By the late 1950s, however, it was evident to the Solar Hierarchy of Light that there would have to be a change of tactics once again, with a much longer covert approach to extraterrestrial contact and intervention put in place. While the contactees' message was positively impacting mass consciousness to a certain degree, the various governments of Earth were conducting campaigns of disinformation and ridicule against those who publicly came forth with accounts of contact, effectively silencing them and their important celestial communiqués.

Komarek believes that insofar as these UFO occupants that are human-appearing entities seem to have such extended life spans, their period of time in which they can intervene on Earth is still quite brief. But because of our much shorter life spans, it goes to reason that the transition seems for us to be taking a very long time. Wrote the contactee researcher, "What the ETs seem to have decided to do is to wait a generation or two for our societies to adapt to their presence and for the elite fear factor to dissipate before they made another more overt push."[485] On this point, however, I would tend to disagree. I think that our exponential technological advancements now pose a severe threat level to the Omniverse that can no longer be ignored; and that direct intervention by the ultra-dimensional inhabitants of other worlds, physical and ethereal, is now a certainty and bound to happen sooner than later. In a sense, our species is like the proverbial child playing with matches in a dynamite shed. We lack the spiritual wisdom to adequately deal with the technology we already have at our immediate disposal.

The Cosmic Emissary

In view of the perils posed by humankind's expansion into the realms of space, the Hierarchy of Light on the planet Venus decided to dispatch an emissary to speak with the leaders of the United States, the most powerful nation militarily on the surface of the Earth. As the Venusians had long maintained a mothership in a near polar orbit in a logistical and supporting capacity for their contingent of operatives working among the Earth's population, the Hierarchy chose the mothership commander, Valiant Thor, to be their spokesperson with the government of the United States. The Hierarchy had supreme confidence in Commander Thor's ability to negotiate on their behalf with the powers-that-be in Washington, D.C. A lone scout craft, therefore, was deployed from the mothership, piloted by Thor, who carefully guided it to a graceful landing on the outskirts of Washington, D.C., in the suburb of Alexandria, Virginia, on 16 March 1957, whence he was met by two police officers, weapons drawn. Apart from the Cuban missile crisis, this may have been one of the tensest moments in the history of Earth. If the police officers failed to follow established protocols and shot Commander Thor, either wounding or killing him, what dire consequences might befall the Earth and its inhabitants?[486]

The commander, with many accumulated years of experience in clandestinely living and working among average Americans, telepathically communicated his peaceful intentions to the officers. Rather than acting impetuously, the policemen understood that Thor meant them no harm and treated him with deference. The Venusian emissary was then ushered into the back seat of their patrol car. The two police officers then drove the extraterrestrial across a bridge and into Washington, D.C., escorting him to the office of the Secretary of Defense, along with six of his staff members, in the Pentagon. Soon the two officers were joined by police from

---

485   *Ibid.*
486   Dr. Frank E. Stranges, "A Holy Stranger in the Pentagonal Lodge," extracts from *Stranger at the Pentagon* (Brunswick, NJ: Inner Light Publications, 1967), from Brother Blue website, recovered through Way Back Machine website, http://www.bibliotecapleyades.net/bb/stranges.htm (Accessed 10 December 2014).

every conceivable district and agency in the area, all vying for the right to escort Commander Thor to the office of President Dwight D. Eisenhower.[487]

Commander Thor projected a telepathic message to all of the assembled officers, thanking them for their concern but assuring them that no further assistance would be required; that he would be content to go and see the president in the custody of an Air Force captain, the military officer in the room with the highest rank.[488]

Meanwhile, his presence in the Pentagon had thrown everyone into a tizzy. The introduction he held from the Hierarchy of Light, destined for President Eisenhower, could best be described as an "electronic letter." Like a contemporary tablet, the letter it contained was displayed on a glass panel and could quickly be translated from the Venusian language into contemporary American English with the touch of a finger. Remember that this was 1957, so such graphic computer technology must have appeared as "magic" to all concerned.

The Air Force captain, which we shall simply refer to as "Gould," in lieu of his real name, dismissed the gathered crowed from the room. Finally alone with Thor, Gould asked the Venusian visitor if he would like to join him in downing some plain bourbon. Thor respectfully declined, but the captain poured himself some of the potent liquid in a shot glass, gulping it all quickly in one big swig. Gould commented, "My God, why couldn't this have happened on my day off?" Thor looked quizzically at Gould as he poured himself another drink, when all of a sudden the door opened and six armed military guards entered, leading the Venusian to an elevator that carried him to the bottom-most maximum security level. From there, Thor was transferred to an underground train that sped him on to the White House for his meeting with the president.[489]

In a matter of minutes, the subway had transported the Venusian and his military escort contingent to a platform hundreds of feet below the White House. Here the alien and the six armed guards were joined by six military officials and three Secret Service agents who accompanied them to another elevator that would take them up to the White House, exiting at an alcove adjacent to the War Room. From there they took another elevator up to the first floor and the Oval Office, where they met with President Eisenhower. From behind his mahogany desk, the President rose while the Secret Service men remained nervous and uneasy. As Thor extended his hand to shake that of the President, the jittery Secret Service men drew their revolvers and pointed them directly at the Venusian.[490]

The president gave a nod, signaling that it would be all right; so the agents reluctantly lowered their weapons. President Eisenhower then remarked, "Of course, you know that we have suspended all rules of protocol. I have a good feeling toward you. Please, sir, what is your name? And where do you come from?" To which, the gentleman from space replied, "My name is Valiant Thor and I come from the planet your *Bible* calls the morning and the evening star."[491]

"Venus?"

"Yes, sir."

"Can you prove this?" the president asked.

"What do you constitute as proof?"

---

487 *Ibid.*
488 *Ibid.*
489 *Ibid.*
490 *Ibid.*
491 *Ibid.*

He quickly retorted, "I don't know."

"Will you come with me to my ship?"

President Eisenhower answered with a quizzical look and said, "My friend, even I cannot come and go as I please. There are others to be considered. There are committees to be consulted and security measures to be adhered to. Please spend some time with us here ....Let's get better acquainted ...learn more about one another ...and perhaps soon, real soon, well ...we shall see."[492]

In the middle of their conversation, another gentleman rushed into the room. It was the Vice President Richard M. Nixon. To Thor, he appeared to be very sharp and quick-witted. Nixon maintained his eyes fixed on Thor, thrusting out his hand for Thor to shake without hesitation. To this, the Venusian simply stated, "My name is Valiant." Unlike his meeting with Eisenhower, the alien now dropped his last name in the introduction with the vice president.[493]

"You have certainly caused a stir ....for an out-of-towner," remarked Nixon, who smiled and added that, "Of course, we are not totally convinced of anything just yet. But suffice it to say we are checking and double- checking everything you say and do. When Sergeant Young from Alexandria radioed in and stated that you had just landed in a flying saucer, we thought Sergeant Young had flipped. Say, were you in on that UFO flap over Washington? You certainly had us all in a dither, if you were."[494]

Just what Richard M. Nixon may have known about UFOs and their occupants up to the point of Thor's arrival remains a matter of speculation to this day. There are some indications, however, that he may have actually seen some of the bodies recovered from the wreckage of the 2 July 1947 flying saucer crash at Roswell, New Mexico; and when he became president, allowed these to be viewed by some of his closer associates.

One of Nixon's more intimate friends was the brash actor and comedian Jackie Gleason, who played the flamboyant New York City bus driver Ralph Kramden on the popular CBS Television sitcom, *The Honeymooners*.[495] The program originally aired with 39 episodes in the 1955 and 1956 season, but continues in syndication even to this day. "To the Moon, Alice!" was Gleason's trademark expression on the set of *The Honeymooners*, and perhaps for good reason. For Gleason, known among Hollywood circles as "The Great One," had an abiding interest in the Moon, the planets and all things extraterrestrial, to include the UFO phenomenon. He purportedly had the world's largest private collection of UFO books, literature and actual sightings and encounter reports. Gleason's library contained literally thousands of UFO books; and as soon as a new title came out, from any country, "The Great One" was sure to secure a copy. And fortunately for Gleason, his interest in ufology would one day serve to secure him, from President Nixon no less, his "back stage pass" to access one of the most highly-guarded secrets in American history, the truth about the alien bodies retrieved from the Roswell flying saucer crash.[496]

It all began with a chance conversation one sunny Florida day back on 19 February 1973, while Jackie was playing golf with one of his regular partners, President Richard M. Nixon. On the course, Jackie casually brought up the topic of UFOs and his intense interest in the subject,

---

492 *Ibid.*
493 *Ibid.*
494 *Ibid.*
495 "*The Honeymooners*," Paramount Television, 1955-1956, Starring Jackie Gleason, Art Carney, Audrey Meadows, Joyce Randolph, *IMDb, http://www.imdb.com/title/tt0042114/* (Accessed 15 January 2015)
496 Marty Murray, "Jackie Gleason's Trip to the Alien Morgue," 9 April 2006, http://www.rense.com/general70/gleason.htm (Accessed 15 January 2015)

discussing some of the more interesting books in his collection, especially those referencing possible saucer crashes and trace evidence cases. To this, the president admitted that he too was a "UFO buff" with a sizable collection of UFO-oriented materials of his own. At the

time, however, the president did not let on as to what he actually knew, but things were to change drastically later on, that same night.[497]

One can barely imagine Gleason's surprise when one night President Nixon showed up at his Fort Lauderdale home, situated on the grounds of the Inverrary Country Club. Nixon arrived at the Gleason house around midnight. The president came alone and was driving his own personal car. When Jackie asked him why he was there, Nixon told him he wanted to take him somewhere and show him something important. Trusting his friend, Gleason got into the president's car, and they ended up at the gates of Homestead Air Force Base where they passed through security and drove to the far end of the

Nixon "spills the beans" about UFOs and their occupants to his good friend and golfing buddy, Jackie Gleason. See http://wordmachine. org/2013/04/05/nixon-dreams-of-aliens-a-short-story-based-on-real-events/.

base. There they came to a tightly-guarded building.[498] On the first of several nights "The Great One" Gleason, from an interview he gave to UFO researcher and author Larry Warren, related the following:

"We drove to the very far end of the base in a segregated area, finally stopping near a well-guarded building. The security police saw us coming and just sort of moved back as we passed them and entered the structure. There were a number of labs we passed through first before we entered a section where Nixon pointed out what he said was the wreckage from a flying saucer, enclosed in several large cases. Next, we went into an inner chamber and there were six or eight of what looked like glass-topped Coke freezers. Inside them were the mangled remains of what I took to be children. Then - upon closer examination - I saw that some of the other figures looked quite old. Most of them were terribly mangled as if they had been in an accident."[499]

Gleason was naturally excited by all of this, but also a bit shaken. He could not eat or sleep properly for weeks afterwards, and found himself drinking heavily until he was able to regain some of his composure. His wife at the time, Beverly (*nee* McKittrick), recalled him being out very late that night and speaking excitedly about what he had seen when he returned home. Later, however, when she and Gleason were in the process of divorcing, she told the story to a writer at *Esquire* magazine, who forwarded it to the *National Enquirer* for publication, believing it to be a more suitable venue for a story of this nature; and from then on, relations between her and Gleason deteriorated to the point that he became very upset and angry the story had ever been made public.[500]

After Beverly's account was splashed all over the pages of the tabloid, however, Gleason was of the opinion that since the "cat was already out of the bag," so to speak, he might as well frame the story in an accurate and proper context, using his own words. Gleason largely trusted

---

497 *Ibid.*
498 *Ibid.*
499 *Ibid.*
500 Beverly Gleason, "Jackie Gleason Saw Bodies of Space Aliens at Air Force Base," *National Enquirer*, 16 August 1983, Lantana, Florida.

Warren because of his faithful military service and the bravery he demonstrated in disclosing information about a close encounter that he experienced while serving as an Airman First Class at Bentwaters Air Force Base in England, an installation of the North Atlantic Treaty Organization (NATO) primarily staffed by United States military personnel.[501]

Warren witnessed an amazing series of events that took place at Bentwaters over the Christmas week of 1980 that all began when a UFO was picked up on radar and subsequently came down just outside the perimeter of the base in a densely forested area. Of this case, ufologist Timothy Green Beckley writes:

"On the first of several nights of confrontation with the Unknown, three security police ventured into the area, coming across an eerie-looking object hovering just above the ground. One of the MPs was mesmerized by the UFO and was unable to move for nearly an hour. While in this mental state, he received some sort of telepathic message that the craft would return. For the next few nights, up to 80 U. S. servicemen, British "bobbies," as well as civilians from some nearby farms, witnessed an historic event. According to Larry Warren, who stood within feet of this craft from another world, three occupants came out of the ship and actually communicated with a high ranking member of the U.S. Air Force."[502]

National Enquirer 8/16/1983

The correspondent from *Esquire* magazine forwarded the details of this story to the editorial staff of the *National Enquirer*. They ran it in their 16 August 1983 edition, much to the dismay of Jackie Gleason. See www.skeptoid.com.

Naturally, a close encounter of this magnitude would become the stuff of UFO legend; and one of the first of the major books to be published concerning this incident was Jenny Randles' *From Out of the Blue*,[503] in case you care to obtain more detailed information about it. In addition, the Bentwaters affair received even wider media publicity when it became the subject of a CNN documentary, a Home Box Office movie special, as well as the focus of an episode of *Unsolved Mysteries*. To a certain degree, Warren has become as much a media buzz as Gleason, at least so far as he has remained in the public eye, willing to discuss what he observed concerning the extraterrestrial presence.

Warren informed Beckley that, "Jackie Gleason was interested in hearing my story first hand," As to how he met the famous actor in May 1986, Warren explained that, "At the time I was living in Connecticut and both CNN and HBO had run pieces on the Bentwaters case. Through mutual friends who knew members of his family, I was told that Gleason would like to talk with me privately in his home in Westchester County (New York), and so the meeting was set for a Saturday when we would both have some time to relax."[504]

Then after the two were formally introduced, they ventured into Gleason's recreation room

---

501   Marty Murray

502   Timothy Green Beckley, "Jackie Gleason and the Little Green 'Men from Mars,'" 25 October 1999, http://www. rense.com/ufo5/gleason_u.htm (Accessed 16 January 2015)

503   Jenny Randles, *From Out of the Blue* (New York, New York: Berkley Books, 1993)

504   Timothy Green Beckley

complete with pool table and a full-size bar. Warren noted that, "There were hundreds of UFO books all over the place, but Jackie was quick to tell me that this was only a tiny portion of his entire collection, which was housed in his home in Florida."[505]

For the remainder of the day, the two ufologists and UFO witnesses exchanged pertinent information. Warren commented that,

"Gleason seemed to be very well informed on the subject, as he knew the smallest detail about most cases and showed me copies of the book *Clear Intent* that had just been published, as well as a copy of *Sky Crash*, a British book about Bentwaters that was published, actually, before all the details of this case were made public. I remember Gleason telling me about his own sightings of several discs in Florida and how he thought there were undersea UFOs bases out in the Bermuda Triangle."[506]

Then, after Warren had downed a few beers and Gleason imbibed a few of his favorite Rob Roys, the conversation really got down to brass tacks. Warren stated that, "At some point, Gleason turned to me and said, 'I want to tell you something very amazing that will probably come out some day anyway. We've got 'em!' 'Got what?' I wanted to know. 'Aliens!' Gleason sputtered, catching his breath." At this juncture in their discussion, Warren noted that Gleason proceeded to tell him the intriguing set of circumstances that led him to the stunning conclusion that extraterrestrials have arrived on our cosmic shores.[507]

From the interview, both came away with what they needed to hear. Gleason obtained a firsthand account about Warren's experience at Bentwaters Air Force Base in England. And Warren came to the conclusion that Gleason was being honest and sincere all along about his excursion with Nixon to the Homestead Air Force Base.

Warren noted: "You could tell that he was very sincere - he took the whole affair very seriously, and I could tell that he wanted to get the matter off his chest, and that was why he was telling me all of this. Jackie felt just like I do, that the government needs to 'come clean,' and tell us all it knows about space visitors. It's time they stopped lying to the public and release all the evidence they have. When they do, then we'll all be able to see the same things the late Jackie Gleason did."[508]

The United States government's knowledge about UFOs and their occupants exists at levels above "Top Secret." In terms of the ranking of security classifications, UFOs and extraterrestrials held higher priorities than nuclear weapons and enhanced cyber technological developments. Information in regard to the true nature of the UFO phenomenon is highly compartmentalized and imparted on a strictly "need to know" basis. Unfortunately, this has even left many presidents "out of the loop," so to speak; but obviously, Nixon wasn't one of them.

Naturally, the Venusians were just as concerned about this massive cover-up, taking place among all the world's governments, not just in the United States. Ilmuth, a beautiful Venusian woman and escort for Adamski while traveling off-world, informed him while onboard a mothership *en route* to her home planet that:

"We also are aware, as are you and many other people on your Earth, that your air forces and your governments *know* that our ships seen in your skies are coming from outer space, and that they can be made and piloted only by intelligent beings from other planets. Men high in

505 *Ibid.*
506 *Ibid.*
507 *Ibid.*
508 *Ibid.*

the governments of your world have been contacted by us. Some are good men and do not want war. But even the good men on your Earth cannot entirely free themselves from the fear which has been fostered by man himself on your planet throughout the centuries."[509]

Then another member of the crew, a Venusian communications officer named Kalna who was sitting in on Ilmuth and Adamski's recreation room conversation, chided in, "The same is true of your fliers everywhere on Earth. Many have seen our ships again and again. But they have been muzzled and warned, and few dare speak out."

And to this Firkon, a Venusian scout ship co-pilot hailing from the Venusian Martian colony who had been slowly sipping on some exotic Cytherian fruit concoction at the bar, turned about and joined the conversation, adding that, "It is the same with your scientists."

Adamski marveled at their knowledge of our world and its peoples. "Then it would seem," said Adamski, "that the answer lies largely with the ordinary man in the street, multiplied by his millions the world over." Ilmuth and Kalna nodded their assent, simultaneously transmitting positive vibes to the mind of the Polish-born, American contactee. And Firkon quickly agreed, voicing his approval of Adamski's conclusion: "They would be your strength, and if they would speak against war in sufficient numbers everywhere, some leaders in different parts of your world would listen gladly."

UFO blogger Marty Murray writes, "One can only imagine what technology and evidence of life outside of this Earth exists in the back corners and hidden labs of the American military, but for anyone who doesn't believe that this situation is real, this story about Jackie Gleason is just the very tiny tip of the iceberg. We may be waiting a very, very long time, indeed, until Jackie's dream of government disclosure comes true."[511] Nevertheless, until such a time as an authentic representative of the government does release this critical data, there are plenty of theories circulating about flying saucers in our skies and their enigmatic occupants.

In the process of editing and publishing the *New Millennial Star* in Hilmar, California, and as director of the Outer Space International Research and Investigations Society (OSIRIS), situated in the lush San Joaquin Valley, frequent trips were made to interview and exchange information with crucial people in the south of the state, leaders in the contactee movement. It was the spring of 1992 in a small private chapel within walking distance of the Yucca Valley home of Gabriel Green, founder and president of the Amalgamated Flying Saucer Clubs of America, that I asked him about the alleged Roswell 1947 UFO crash. Also at the meeting was African American UFO contactee investigator Yvonne Bryant of Long Beach, *Weekly World News* psychic and *New Millennial Star* correspondent Andy Reiss of Glendale, as well as a "visitor" ufologist from Vitoria, Brazil, who was staying at the Green residence; and that at the time was going by the name of "Débora Bergara." She used to live in the Manhattan Beach area, northwest of Los Angeles, in the mid-to-late 1950s, where she was an avid follower of the contactee circuit when she wasn't too busy designing and fabricating custom dresses for Hollywood celebrities out of her boutique in nearby Hermosa Beach, just a couple of blocks up from the famous pier. Débora did a lot of contract work for Helen Rose of the Metro-Goldwyn-Mayer studios, possibly one of the greatest American costume and clothing designers of the era. Débora was particularly proud of the dress she helped to make for Rose that was worn by Anne Francis in the 1956 science fiction classic, *Forbidden Planet.*

The movie was produced by Nicholas Nayfack and directed by Fred M. Wilcox. It starred Walter Pidgeon as Dr. Edward Morbius and Anne Francis as Dr. Morbius' seductive daughter Altaira. Leslie Nielsen, Warren Stevens and Jack Kelly played various members of the

509 Adamski, *Inside the Space Ships* (no page numbers)
511 Marty Murray

spaceship crew. A realistic robot named Robby was also featured. *Forbidden Planet* is the first science fiction film in which humans are depicted as traversing space in a starship of their own creation, somewhat patterned after the designs presented for the Venusian scout craft by Adamski in his second flying saucer book, *Inside the Spaceships*.

Forbidden Planet was also the first science fiction film set entirely on another world; and is considered one of the great science fiction films of the 1950s, a precursor of what was to come for the sci-fi film genre in future decades, most notably the *Star Trek* brand. The movie features special effects that were nominated for an Academy Award, along with a groundbreaking score based entirely on the eerie electronic music composed by Louis and Bebe Barron. Robby as the robot also put prior automatons used in other science fiction films to shame. While Robby was totally believable, the robots of prior films just come across as nothing but "tin cans" on legs. The film was deemed "culturally, historically or aesthetically significant" by the directors of the Library of Congress in 2013, whence it was entered into its National Film Registry.

But getting back to our small group's conversation about Roswell, the following is a gist of what was said:

This ornate golden-tan short dress was worn by Anne Francis in the cult science fiction epic, *Forbidden Planet*, and recently sold at a Hollywood auction for $30,000. The garment was also worn by Lisa Davis as the Venusian Motiya, a member of Talleah's rebel contingent, in the Allied Artists 1958 science fiction adventure, *Queen of Outer Space*. Note the *retro sci-fi* look with "Venusian" influence, now so in vogue. See http://www.telegraph. co.uk/news/picturegalleries/howaboutthat/5165593/ Hollywood-prop-and-costume-auction-Own-a-piece-of- film-history.html?image=15.

Raymond: Gabe, what can you tell me about the Roswell crash?

Gabriel: There is a lot of misunderstanding out there about that one. First, there were two crashed saucers, not just one. The other saucer came down somewhere near Arizona, on the New Mexico side of the border, up in the mountains, around that area where OSIRIS owns the land overlooking the Plains of San Agustin. And they weren't piloted by the so-called Grays, either. They were Venusians.

Raymond: How do you know this?

Gabriel: Howard (Menger) filled me in on it…. before the Silence Group got to him. But more than anything else, what the government fears is the "communist" system in place on other planets in our solar system. It's actually more like a communal system as the early Christians practiced by holding all things in common, but the Cold War "hawks" in DC don't see it that way.

Raymond: Débora, you knew Howard Menger quite well. Did he ever mention any of this to you?

Débora: Yes, Ray. He did. This is all part of an even bigger cover-up than anyone can imagine. While everyone thought the atomic bomb, which generates an explosion from a single-fission reaction, was bad enough, nobody realized that they were already developing and testing thermonuclear, two-stage devices as early as 1947.

Raymond: You mean they had a hydrogen bomb in 1947?

Débora: That's exactly what I am saying. They were in an arms race with the Russians even before World War II was over. It was so distressing to the Venusians, especially, having the misfortune of living on the closest planet to the Earth. It didn't matter to them whether the Americans or the Russians got the bomb first. It wouldn't take long before either one of these "super powers" started mounting thermonuclear missiles onto spacecraft and sallying forth to conquer Venus and other inhabited worlds.

Gabriel: I recall that very message being transmitted as an override signal across Western European and American television stations throughout the mid-1950s and early 1960s. The jammer identified himself as a Venusian, too.

Andy: I remember that, too. The Venusian went by "Vor" and he said it was an acronym that stood for "Venusian Observation Ranger."

Raymond: Clever. He's my superhero. I bet J. Edgar Hoover was shitting bricks in his dress. Err, sorry Débora .

Débora: *No te preocupes, Raimundo.*

Yvonne: Officially, we were all told that the first hydrogen bomb wasn't detonated until 1952. Why do the American people keep on believing these lying politicians?

Gabriel: Woe to the inhabitants of Jerusalem, ye that stoneth the prophets! Jack and Bobby tried to tell them the truth, but look what it got them for their troubles.

Raymond: So, what was it about the hydrogen bomb that brought down the saucers?

Gabriel: It is not so much the fusion of hydrogen isotopes that is so devastating. Rather, when the first fission reaction occurs, it is used as the igniter of the second fission reaction, that of uranium. The hydrogen isotope fusion is a relatively harmless byproduct. The distribution of fissionable uranium in the atmosphere following the detonation of a hydrogen device is powerful enough, however, to bring down a scout craft operating nearly anywhere on Earth or even in a low orbit.

Débora: Also, I might add that Howard explained how the scout craft largely depend on the utilization of electromagnetic lines of force surrounding the Earth. They can only operate in the Earth's atmosphere or in close vicinity to the Earth. Other than that, they are dependent upon the magnetic field of the mothership when on their own in space, but for a limited range. While it was easy enough for the scout craft to be annihilated, being caught up in a thermonuclear implosion, bringing down a mothership would take the power output that could only be generated by a literal "death star," a Dyson sphere armed with quanta particle beams. An object about the size of Neith (the cloaked "moon" of Venus), I'd have to estimate, could probably do the trick.

Gabriel: Fortunately for all of us, it will take millennia before the Terrans (Earthlings) reach that level of technological sophistication.

Andy: I hear you, Gabe. And I second the notion!

Raymond: Did the saucers' occupants survive the crashes?

Gabriel: No. Not a one. Their bodies were mangled, but not beyond recognition and partial reconstruction. Autopsies revealed that there were some slight eye, facial, finger and hand characteristics that only a close observer could spot that could distinguish them as alien beings. They were all of average height and relatively human in appearance. There were four in each craft. Of the occupants, there were three women and one man in each saucer.

Raymond: That's what Jackie Gleason's wife said her husband saw at an Air Force Base in Florida, eight alien bodies in all.

Yvonne: (Chuckling.) Well, "Enquiring" minds ought to know.

Raymond: Good one, Yvonne. Uh, Gabe?

Gabriel: Yes, back to the aliens. That's where they ended up eventually, but right after the crashes, recovery teams from the Air Technical Intelligence Reconnaissance Center in Dayton, Ohio, were flown out to clean up the mess and set up the medical examination stations at the New Mexico base. After a couple of months, they were flown to Wright Patterson Field in Dayton for who knows how long. Howard says they were taken to the high security "Hangar 18" and put in cryogenic suspension awaiting further disposition.

Raymond: What did they discover about the aliens that convinced them that they were Venusians?

Gabriel: Among both of the saucers' debris fields, some electrical apparatuses were discovered partially intact, thrown at some considerable distance from their respective craft and sheathed in a durable, thermoplastic polymer substance, later duplicated in American laboratories and known as propylene. Research scientists at International Business Machines (IBM) in New York City and the Radio Corporation of America (RCA) in Cleveland, Ohio, were given the assignment of restoring at least some of the electronics to working order. RCA succeeded in reactivating a type of television recorder displaying mathematical equations relating to an interplanetary trajectory for the mothership from Venus to Earth, as well as the deployment of scout craft in the vicinity of top secret American and Soviet military research facilities. Determining the Venusian number system was relatively easy, as it roughly corresponds to our own, but also incorporates a sort of spiral notation matrix. The Venusian "alphabet," if you could call it that, was a little more difficult to deal with than the numbers; as it was mostly determined to be a pictographic system, something akin to Egyptian hieroglyphics.

Raymond: What was it about the alien bodies that set them apart from humans on Earth?

Gabriel: There were several remarkable differences, but not so outwardly noticeable. First, they didn't have the spiraled DNA strands found in nearly all indigenous life forms on Earth.

Raymond: Can you explain that further, please?

Gabriel: Yes, I mean their cells were actually composed of latticed crystalline hexagonal structures, similar in composition to the walls of their scout craft. It's almost as though they were artificially constructed beings, designed to easily and quickly disassemble or reassemble. But their cells were silicon-based,[510] rather than carbon-based, and it was conjectured that

---

510 Donald E. Keyhoe, *Flying Saucers Are Real* (New York, New York: Fawcett, 1950), 116, 117, 126; Keyhoe exposes the findings of the United States Air Force *Project Sign*, sometimes informally referred to as *Project Saucer*. *Project Sign* was an official government study of unidentified flying objects (UFOs) initiated in response to the dramatic flying saucer flap of 1947. It was undertaken and active for most of 1948. *Project Sign*'s final report emerged as a digest of preliminary studies on "Flying Saucers" made by the Air Material Command at Wright Field in Dayton, Ohio, published on 27 April 1949, and stated that while some UFOs appeared to represent actual aircraft, there was not enough data to determine their exact planet of origin, albeit Venus was the most likely candidate within our solar system. Because the *Sign* personnel favored this extraterrestrial hypothesis, the Department of Defense ordered the project dissolved, and constituted *Project Grudge* with the intent of debunking saucer reports and advancing more terrestrial explanations for the incoming instances of aerial phenomenon, such as the appearance of comets, weather balloons viewed under unusual atmospheric conditions, and weather inversions. As to the possibilities of life on the planet Venus revealed in the Sign report, Keyhoe quotes: "Since flying saucers first hit the headlines almost two years ago, there has been wide speculation that the aerial phenomena might actually be some form of penetration from another planet.... The possibility of intelligent life also existing on the planet Venus is not considered completely unreasonable by astronomers. The atmosphere of Venus apparently consists mostly of carbon dioxide with deep clouds of formaldehyde droplets, and there seems to be little or no water. *Yet, scientists concede that living organisms might develop in chemical environments*

somehow the hydrogen bomb's implosion and subsequent uranium radiation atmospheric dispersals fused enough of their cells into sheets of a sort of aluminum glass that their disassembly/reassembly capabilities were impeded, thus stifling their life force right out of their bodies. Several large female honeybees were also found dead in each craft, being glassed over and fused into the walls of their respective ships, suffering the same fate as the humanoid Venusians. The bees ranged from three to five feet in length and were composed of the same latticed crystalline hexagonal cells. These insect bodies were forwarded to the Texas A&M Honey Bee Research Lab at College Station for further analysis. It seems that the Venusian bees and humanoids exist in some sort of symbiotic relationship. Only today are our own scientists discovering the superiority of the honeycomb structure as an architectural masterpiece. By using the hexagonal form, we may now, like the Venusians, fabricate structures that are both resilient and space efficient. Aircraft engineers use panels patterned after the honeycomb in order to construct planes that are not only sturdier and stronger, but consume much less fuel. Even NASA engineers now use honeycomb structuring in the design of spacecraft and space habitats.

Yvonne: What were some of the other differences?

Débora: Both the bees and the humanoids on Venus have eyesight well adapted to seeing in the ultraviolet range, something that is beyond the abilities of most Terrans. This prompted NASA to conduct a series of top secret surveys of Venus in ultraviolet light (UV). For the most part, the planet is remarkably featureless at wavelengths of light visible to us. But this all changes when lovely Venus is observed at those wavelengths slightly shorter than what our eyes can deal with. In the UV spectrum, Venus turns out to be anything but a featureless orb. It is a world of high contrast, sharply defined features in all the colors of a rainbow.

Yvonne: What kinds of features become visible on Venus in the UV light?

Débora: The UV photographs show the planet to be awash in mysterious dark, high-contrast features. The physical characteristics and movements of these dark UV markings have been extensively studied by NASA scientists, and greatly clarified, but they remain mysterious to this day. Their source is one of the greatest unsolved puzzles that NASA researchers have encountered. However, one exobiologist speculated that some moving, dark patches in the upper Venusian cloud layers may be attributable to massive swarms of bees feeding off of

which are strange to us. Venus, however, has two handicaps. Her mass and gravity are nearly as large as the Earth (Mars is smaller) and her cloudy atmosphere would discourage astronomy, hence space travel" (116, 117). But Keyhoe effectively argues against those at *Sign* who leaned counter to the Venus option because of that planet's high gravity and cloudy atmosphere, noting that, "The last argument, I thought, did not have too much weight. We were planning to escape the Earth's gravity.... As for the cloudy atmosphere, they could have developed some system of radio or radar investigation of the universe. The Navy research units, I knew, were probing the far-off Crab nebula in the Milky Way with special radio devices. This same method, or something far superior, could have been developed on Venus, or other planets surrounded by constant clouds" (117). Also, one of the prominent astronomical authorities consulted by the Air Force personnel at *Project Sign* was Dr. H. Spencer Jones, Astronomer Royal of the British Isles. The *Sign* report goes on to state that, "In his book *Life on Other Worlds*, Dr. Jones points out that *everything about us is the result of changing processes, begun millenniums ago and still going on. We cannot define life solely in our own* terms; *it can exist in unfamiliar forms.*" In the book, Dr. Jones elaborates: ***"It is conceivable that we could have beings, the cells of whose bodies contained silicon instead of the carbon which is an essential constituent of our cells and of all other living cells on the earth. And that because of this essential difference between the constitution of those cells and the cells of which animal and plant life on the earth are built up, they might be able to exist at temperatures so high that no terrestrial types of life could survive"*** (126). Therefore, at least according to Dr. Jones, life could be possible on worlds hotter and drier than ours, a planet like Venus. Remember that this report was written one year after the New Mexico crashes by government insiders with both a need to know and access to at least some of the data.

enriched krypton and other noble gases.

Gabriel: Our friend Daniel Ross from the Public Interest Space Sciences Center has a lot more to say about the Venusian atmosphere and the lies NASA has been scamming us with since the early 1960s. He said that NASA is in no hurry to dispel the prevailing beliefs about Venus being uninhabitable, despite the fact that some outside scientists have used some of the space agency's own photographs from Mariner 10 and other probes to prove that the Venusian cloud cover is broken and variable, just as the Earth's; and that the atmospheric pressure is at most only 18 times that of Earth, and not the 92 times they want us to believe.

Andy: While I mostly associated the Egyptians with the star system of Sirius, I often suspected there might also be some connection between the Egyptians and the Venusians.

Gabriel: Débora, would you like to take it from here?

Débora: Sure, Gabe. And Andy, you are correct in your assumptions about the Sirians and the Venusians. Even from Earth's most ancient texts, Theosophists have determined that besides the bees as the native inhabitants of Venus, as far back as 18,000,000 years ago, there were many Galactic species that colonized our Solar System's second planet: the Sirians, the Pleiadians, the Ummans, the Centaurans and lastly, the Norcans. The influence of the Sirians was most pronounced in the establishment of Venusian colonies in Atlantis, Lemuria, ancient Egypt and the Pyrenees mountain range in Western Europe following the fall of Atlantis around 12,000, B.C.E.

Yvonne: I'd like to know how the humanoid population can co-exist with the Insectoids on Venus.

Débora: The Insectoids have endured as an advanced civilization across this universe and many others in multiple dimensions for billions of years, guarding and guiding human populations throughout the cosmos, when and wherever they have found them. To keep the humans from reverting to a savage state, the Insectoids have continually intervened to help them, through each successive generation, rise to yet greater heights of culture and science. If any group of humans can develop the spiritual maturity necessary to manage their world, then they may attain telepathic linkage with all other humanoids on their planet and beyond, in addition to the mentoring Insectoid "supermind." Thereby, a mass consciousness is established for the benefit and continual progress of all. The Terrans now find themselves on the verge of attaining this unity of consciousness, if we don't first blow ourselves up or pollute our world into extinction.

Yvonne: Do all Insectoids take the same form as the bees on Venus?

Débora: At the Galactic Core, on the planet nearest to the Great Central Sun of Kolob, and on the planet Belaton, the fourth out from the second star of the Sirius system, these are akin to praying mantises, on the average of seven to twelve feet in length. On Venus and Mars, the Insectoids take the form of honeybees, three to five feet each on Venus and six to ten inches each in the vast caverns of Mars. Of course, we have smaller varieties of bees on Earth, but we should always respect them and never harm them.

The honeybee species also originates from a solar system in the vicinity of Kolob, near the Galactic Core. On all of these worlds, and many others, the Insectoid females are the only ones that can communicate with humans, and only through the female of our species. Because the human inhabitants of Venus share in a group mind with themselves and a collective "hive mind" with the bees, the Venusian society is truly reflective of its status as a super-organism, not unlike an ant colony or beehive on Earth. And naturally, like the hive itself, Venusian society is organized along matriarchal lines.

The Utopian conditions that are present on Venus are largely due to the overarching and progressive unity within and between the varied human civilizations and the super-organism of the hive, forming an unparalleled collective bond of consciousness that can endure through the eternities. Through the honeybees, the humans gain access to universal knowledge, insofar as the bees remain in constant communication with all other Insectoid species throughout the cosmos. The Venusians long ago discovered that they and their world, nay, their cosmos, is but one in a vast ocean of boundless starry universes comprising this infinite realm otherwise known as the Omniverse. There are an almost infinite number of varied and advanced species throughout the Milky Way Galaxy, but the Insectoids are among the oldest. At some times in the past, the Insectoids have been referred to as the "Watchers" by various human populations on countless worlds.

Gabriel: Thank you, Débora. And can you repeat for the others what you told me about Dr. Hynek's visit to Argentina, and what he told you and some of the others in Guillermo Aldunati's UFO group in Rosario, Entre Rios Province, about the Roswell crash and what the United States government knows about all of this?

Hynek actually came down to Argentina two times to investigate UFO reports there, and on his last visit, in early 1986, he was in Rosario to meet with Guillermo, the OSIRIS South America representative, and his group there. I drove down from Brazil especially to talk to Hynek. From about 1983, because of the Beverly McKittrick/Jackie Gleason revelations, all of South American ufology was abuzz with rumors of the frozen alien bodies that were stored on a United States Air Force base. This was, of course, classified at the highest echelons of secrecy. Nevertheless, Hynek was willing to talk to us about it. But he presented two versions. The first one he told to me in front of all the other Rosario UFO investigators; and that one was that the United States government was still investigating the Roswell case and analyzing what little apparent "wreckage" they discovered from the debris field. But the other "behind the scenes" version is what he had spoken only for my ears, that when he was the Air Force advisor to Project Bluebook he had learned that the UFO phenomenon was very real and that the United States had a flying saucer in its possession. He also confided in me that the Air Force had recovered dead alien bodies, and that all of them were transported to the famous Hangar 18 in Ohio. Hynek also told me that I should not divulge anything that he said of this to me until after he was dead and buried, which I am sorry to report, took place a couple of months later. So I don't have any problem in talking about it with you now; and I also informed the Operation Right to Know in Argentina about Hynek's comments as well.

I have to believe this because Hynek had access to a mountain of information about UFOs while he was contracted with Projects Sign, Grudge and Bluebook and serving as the chair of the Astronomy Department at Northwestern University in Illinois. Hynek said that he was in a difficult position even after he retired from an advisory capacity to the government and its intelligence branches because his debriefing included a gag order on what he came to learn about the Roswell incident. Even in his capacity as a Northwestern professor, Hynek had to tow the official line about the Earth being the only inhabited planet in our solar system, and especially to keep quiet about the truth concerning our Venusian neighbors.

After a few hours, as the Sun began to set, our small group retired to Green's beautiful ranch home to continue our intriguing conversation. But from the revelations that emerged from our "brainstorming" session on Roswell, it soon became apparent to all of us that the United States government officials, to include Richard Nixon as Eisenhower's vice president in an era when information was not as readily compartmentalized and hidden from our leadership as it is now, knew a lot more about the truth behind the flying saucer mystery than they were ever letting on. So by the time that Thor had arrived in Washington, D.C., it has already been ten years since the Roswell crash. In this time frame, much more information about the Venusians and their presence on Earth must have been discovered by United States military contracted researchers. Nevertheless, to the inquisitive and talkative vice president, Thor assured him and those standing around in the Oval Office as well, that the Earth had been under close scrutiny for countless millennia before the 1945 bomb blast; and with his special "letter" now in the slightly quivering hand of the president, he was requested to follow the Secret Service back the way they had come, to the Pentagon and into a beautifully furnished apartment where he would spend the next three years, to the very date of 16 March 1960. The scout ship, set on automatic pilot, was sent back to the mothership after the president declined to go with Thor out to Alexandria to take a gander at it.

Thor was thoroughly prepared for such a lengthy visit and kept in constant telepathic communication with the mothership. The president ordered that Thor be free to come and go as he pleased, so long as he was accompanied by a security detail. Thor's most memorable trip, in April 1957, just one month after his arrival, was up to High Bridge, New Jersey, where he met up with three other crew members from the mothership and the UFO contactee Howard Menger. The three crew members identified themselves as Donn, Jill and Tanyia. Although there were some non-Venusians serving as crew members aboard the mothership, primarily from Mars and the Saturn system, the aforementioned individuals were all Venusians. Also, a unique friend of George Adamski was present; but more about that in a later chapter. All of the Venusians had changed into the same type of street clothing worn by their Earth friends. The meeting took place at Howard Menger's farm, in his backyard.

Months before the actual meeting, Menger had advertised it as a "flying saucer convention," where he would take the time to explain about the aliens, their planets of origin and the purpose of their visits to Earth. Thor told the authorities in Washington, D.C. that he found Howard Menger to be a "very interesting" individual and that the, "people who were following him (Menger) were on the right track." Even alone in his quarters in the Pentagon, however, Thor had access to newspapers, radio and television. Of course, it is no wonder that he became so dismayed to learn of the undignified manner in which these sincere flying saucer devotees, and the contactees themselves, were being treated by the media. A curious young photojournalist with a penchant for "ufology," so-called, was also in attendance and managed to take some photographs of many in attendance, including Thor and some in the Venusian contingent, without really knowing who they were, besides just being "other faces in the crowd" with a big interest in the flying saucer phenomenon.

Now back in Washington, D.C., Thor would meet with the president on many occasions. At one particular meeting, the president was tightly holding the message tablet from the Venusian Hierarchy of Light in his hand, while regretfully informing Thor that he would have to decline his assistance, insofar as his offer to help the human family would upset the economy of the United States and could plunge the nation into the "Abyss of Chaos." Basically, President Eisenhower politely told Thor that the people of Earth had not yet arrived at a point in their cosmic evolution where they were ready to cope with such conditions as would come into existence if the recommendations of the Hierarchy of Light were actually attempted here.

Even though the president was unable to secure the compliance of the United States with the recommendations of the Venusian Hierarchy, he nevertheless invited Thor to assist a number of American scientists who were working on various medical projects directly associated with the human exploration of outer space. Thor did not see any harm in providing a limited amount of technical information, provided that his true identity was not revealed to the scientific team to which he would be attached. After all, he was only allotted a limited time by the Hierarchy to clandestinely acquaint as many of the "leaders of the United States" with the Venusian program for the material and spiritual advancement of humankind. It was also during this time that he refused to advise them regarding a certain "bomb in the sky," which we now know as the "Star Wars" system. And while we do not know if the Venusians made similar gestures to the leaders of the Union of Soviet Socialist Republics, we can assume that they probably did due to the inordinate amount of attention that their space program focused on the collection of scientific data from Venus through the use of unmanned probes, utilizing both flybys and landers. Throughout the first half of the 1960s, the Soviets sent four probes out to Venus; and by November 1965, a Soviet probe actually made an impact landing on our sister planet's surface. While the Soviets were also the first to land an unmanned probe on the Moon, this was the first spacecraft from our world to reach the surface of another planet.

Upper photo, Left to right: Venusians Jill, Donn and Mothership Commander Valient Thor at meeting on Howard Menger's farm, April 1957. Bottom photo, lady in blue dress is Tanyia. See http://www.theeventchronicle.com/editors-pick/valiant-thor-a-venusian-at-the-pentagon-rev-frank-e-stranges/.

Since the Soviet Union and the United States were the only two countries in the early 1960s possessing the necessary space technology to send probes to other planets in our solar system, one might make the assumption that there would not be any level of cooperation between them, especially considering their diametrically opposed economic, philosophical and political systems and their respective needs to continually "one up" each other in setting new milestones in the so-called "Space Race." However, science writer Daniel Ross, once a nuclear reactor technician aboard the United States submarine *Pintado* (SSN672) during the period of 1970-1972, believes that the two superpowers did reach an accord of cooperation, at least in order to keep the official findings about our neighboring planets of Mars and Venus "consistent."

Just what the Cold War, United States Navy nuclear reactor technician meant by this, he succinctly explains in the following paragraph:

"....In fact, there is a high degree of cooperation and agreement in matters of science, and in other sensitive areas. There is a definite collusion between the superpowers for certain mutual interests, the main one being the preservation of the world economy system. The discovery of life, or the suitable conditions for life, on other planetary bodies in our solar system, would topple the corporate structure of the world. That is because both the capitalistic and communist systems are based on maintaining military tensions, and the control of energy resources. The proof or confirmation of advanced, peace civilizations that travel through space using free electromagnetic energy would be catastrophic to the false money system that is the basis of world power. There are secret intelligence agencies in both governments, whose activities are to insure that the system is not challenged or disrupted."[511]

One cannot help but hearken back to the words of George Hanson, the character in *Easy Rider* played by Jack Nicholson, who elucidated on this very topic, noting that, "The authorities know all about them (the Venusians); but they can't let this information be known because of the terrible blow it would give to our antiquated systems." Most likely, Thor knew even before his mission began that he would be meeting stiff resistance at every turn. Nevertheless, he has to be admired for his persistence.

Although officials in the Pentagon were continually stymied by Thor's lack of cooperation in providing advanced Venusian technical information, a team of government scientists was at least able to test the one-piece garment that he was wearing upon his arrival on Earth. Even by today's standards, Thor's uniform underwent rigid testing. The Pentagon scientists attempted to penetrate the material with a diamond drill bit; but it snapped under pressure. Then they poured copious amounts of acid on the uniform, only to have it roll off and down on the floor, where it burned a big hole. Then the testers fired a high-velocity rifle at the garment; but even that failed to pierce it. Finally, a bright-eyed colonel escorted him to a high security installation where the last test would be performed. Thor gazed at the instrument amusingly. Upon command, the device sparked to life, projecting a fine line of intense *light amplification by stimulated emission of radiation* (LASER). The colonel then began to explain the device to Thor, telling him that it contained a crystal-synthetic ruby in which atoms, when stimulated by focused light waves, amplify and concentrate these waves, and only then emit the beam. As the colonel continued to speak, his smile gave way to a frown, and utter dismay. Like everything else the Pentagon scientists had tried, the laser ray was totally ineffective against the garment.

The flustered colonel rambled on long after the laser has been turned off. The sorry military official reiterated how powerful the United States had become since the splitting of the atom and gave Thor a lesson on atomic power, explaining that when a chain reaction of nuclear fission is set off by a neutron bombardment in the atoms or a charge of plutonium or uranium isotope with an atomic weight of 235 (U-235), an immense quantity of energy is suddenly released. The good colonel, finally realizing that most Venusian school children could probably recite this information by rote memory, talked himself out and the alien visitor was escorted back to his quarters, right along with his untarnished uniform.

These were the findings of their report to the president:

Physical appearance -- Soft silver and gold lustrous.

Fabric – Unknown.

Weight-Six ounces, total, including boots.

Cut -- Close fitting like a tunic; no cuffs, pockets, buttons, zippers, clips or hooks.

511 Daniel Ross, *UFOs and the Complete Evidence from Space: The Truth About Venus, Mars, and the Moon* (Walnut Creek, CA: Pintado Publishing, 1987), 186.

RXT-2 Tests – Indestructible.[512]

The Venusian commander, back in his Pentagon apartment, did not have to depend on any sort of physical radio apparatus to maintain communications with his mothership, that he referred to as "Victory One." And since he was relatively free to come and go as he pleased, thanks to the orders of President Eisenhower, he was more or less able to keep current on the breaking news stories. He would read the newspapers every day, in addition to listening to local Washington, D.C. radio stations or watching local television programs. 1959 was fast coming to a close, and for Thor that meant that in less than a quarter of a year his mission would be over.

Various chiefs of state were also on pins and needles over Thor's coming departure, finding themselves in constant turmoil and confusion. It can rightly be said that indecision caused delay after delay as economists and industrial giants conferred with politicians and military heads on a daily basis. The government leaders also failed to reconcile Thor's being in a position to force their hand, should he have so desired to do so. And while several scientists attempted to learn the secrets of space travel, it was fortunate that none succeeded in doing so.

It was particularly cold and snowy in the nation's capital as Christmas week had arrived. Fortuitously, the Rev. Dr. Frank Stranges was in town. Stranges was Founder and President of the National Investigations Committee on UFOs as well as President of the International Evangelical Crusades, a worldwide Christian denomination, and the International Theological Seminary of California. Stranges was born in New York and educated there in Brooklyn, as well as in Pennsylvania, Minnesota, and California, holding degrees in Theology, Psychology and Criminology. He had recently published a book on the flying saucer phenomenon[513] and was giving a series of scientific lectures on the subject at a number of churches throughout the greater Washington, D.C. area, demonstrating how the presence of these objects in our skies was a sign that we were truly living in the long-predicted "latter-days." Stranges had just returned from an evangelistic tour of Cuba, where he personally met with the island's revolutionary leader, Fidel Castro, who also seemed quite interested in the reverend's theories about the arrival of flying saucers on Earth, many which had been sighted all throughout the Caribbean, Central and South America.

And in the audience at one of Stranges' many lectures was a Pentagon office worker that shall simply be referred to as "Nancy Warren." She was well known by Stranges as one whom he had discerned as "having an honest and open heart, and who loved Almighty God, her country and fellow man."[514] The young lady followed Stranges on his lecture tour, whenever he was in the area; and despite defying security protocols at the Pentagon, had formulated a plan whereby the reverend could be contacted by Commander Thor.

Wrote the Rev. Dr. Stranges concerning his initial contact with Warren:

"'Nancy' attended the lecture/service which I conducted at the National Evangelistic Center, pastored by Dr. John Mears, in Washington, D.C. Following the conclusion of my talk, she approached the platform and asked to speak to me. Strangely enough, the photographer in New Jersey (August C. Roberts) had given Val's photographs to me and I had been displaying

---

512 Frank E. Stranges, "A Holy Stranger in the Pentagonal Lodge," extracts from *Stranger at the Pentagon* (Brunswick, NJ: Inner Light Publications, 1967), from *Brother Blue* website, recovered through *Way Back Machine* website, http://www.bibliotecapleyades.net/bb/stranges.htm (Accessed 10 December 2014).

513 Stranges, Frank E., *Flying Saucerama* (New York, New York: Vantage Press, 1959). Stranges catalogs global UFO sightings to support the contention that UFOs represent a real problem that deserves international attention and investigation.

514 Stranges, "A Holy Stranger"

them at my lectures ever since. I had no personal knowledge of them, other than what I had been told by the photographer. When she was unable to "grab" my attention while I was signing copies of my book *Saucerama*, she showed her Pentagon ID and that got my attention quickly to say the least.

We borrowed the Pastor's study and she asked me if I would like to meet the man in the photographs personally. Of course, I answered her with a resounding yes. She then asked if I could follow instructions to the letter, to which I replied that I could, and she told me to meet her at the curb in front of my hotel at 8:00 a.m. the next morning.

'Nancy' arrived precisely on time and thus began the journey which at times would seem unreal, but which later would prove beyond doubt that there is truly life in God's Universe."[515]

Insofar as the reverend displaying the photographs of the "aliens" at his book lectures, it was purely in the context of demonstrating an increasing public interest in flying saucers, in particular as it was manifested at one of contactee Howard Menger's meetings. Stranges had no idea who the people were individually in the photographs taken at the Menger farm, although the photojournalist Roberts did note that the one later identified as Valiant Thor had attracted his attention and those of all the others in attendance at the April 1957 meeting as he was speaking many languages fluently, to include Xosha, a "clicking" South African indigenous dialect. He also presented himself as a handsome figure who spoke authoritatively on such matters as extraterrestrial life and space travel. Naturally, August C. Roberts, or "Augie," as his friends called him, could not help but take photographs of the gentleman and the contingent he had arrived with, sensing that he and his associates were definitely "special" and that the pictures would someday have some greater historical significance.[516]

But getting back to the Pentagon, when the reverend arrived there with Warren, he was quite nervous. Getting past the first security checkpoint was no problem, as Stranges could pass through with the "visitor" designated identification badge supplied by Warren. But getting past the second point would be difficult, as they were to enter a compartmentalized area of the building restricted only to those with a so-called "need to know." Both Stranges and Warren had to stand in a somewhat busy line at the second point; and the reverend was thinking that at the very least he was going to be detained and questioned; and at the very worst, jailed for an extended but undetermined amount of time. Much to his surprise, the guard just glanced at him and his escort, Warren, waiving them right on through. Once within the secured zone of the building, Warren left Stranges standing in front of a door that contained no markings.[517]

Soon the door was opened from the inside by Warren, however, with the reverend walking in and standing on the threshold. His stocky form shifted from one foot to the other as he cleared his throat. There were three men in the room, but they acted as if they were completely unaware of his presence. It appeared as though Stranges was being completely ignored. Hence, the reverend was puzzled, to say the least. Later, he would come to find out that Thor had clouded their minds and rendered them oblivious to the entire session. Whatever the officials in that room were doing, they continued on with their work, seemingly oblivious to Stranges' entrance.[518]

After about half a minute, in walked a man from the back door, the same door that Warren had apparently passed through moments before to let Stranges in. The gentleman was about six

---

515 *Ibid.*
516 *Ibid.*
517 *Ibid.*
518 *Ibid.*

feet tall, perhaps 185 pounds, with brown wavy hair and brown eyes. His complexion appeared normal, albeit slightly tanned. When the reverend approached him, he immediately received the impression that the gentleman was looking straight through him. Then, with a warm smile and extending his hand, he introduced himself as Valiant Thor and then greeted the reverend by his first name, saying "Hello, Frank. How are you?"[519]

Stranges was impressed with the genuineness of the gentleman, and somehow intuitively understood that there was something very special about him. As Stranges gripped his hand, he was somewhat surprised to feel the soft texture of his skin. It was like that of a baby but with the strength of a man that silently testified to his power and intensity. In addition, Stranges noted that the gentleman's voice was very strong and mellow, yet filled with purpose and character.

Of this initial meeting, Stranges wrote:

"I again looked around the room to see whether the other men would say or do anything. They were still working as if I weren't there. I noticed that he was wearing the same type of clothing as I. When I asked if he possessed any other clothing, he said that he had given several officials a garment so that they could run tests on it. He then proceeded to a closet and produced a one-piece "suit" that glittered as the sun which streamed in through the window and hit the fabric.

I thought that it looked like liquid sunshine. I asked him about the material from which it was made. He answered, "It is made of a material not of this Earth." The general appearance of the suit was all one piece ...even down to the boots. It contained no buttons, zippers or snaps. I asked him how it held together. He demonstrated by holding the front together and passing his hand over it as if to smooth it out. I could not even locate the opening. It was held together by an invisible force."[520]

As to his mission on Earth, the gentleman stated that his purpose in coming was to help mankind return to God, i.e. following the teachings espoused by Jesus Christ. While he regretted the sorry state to which humankind had sunk, he nevertheless spoke in positive terms about humanity's potential and a bright future among the stars, and always with a smile on his face. He did note that while humankind was further away from God than ever before, there was, nevertheless, still a good chance for redemption should individuals start looking for answers in the "right places," and begin acting on what they learn. Thor told the reverend that he had been here nearly three years and in just a few months would depart to once again take command of his mothership, Victory One.

Stranges asked if the mothership was a vessel of war, insofar as it was named "Victory One." He wanted to know if it received that title in commemoration of a great battle in which it played some decisive and prevailing role. To this Commander Thor replied that his mothership was named after one of the ancient defenders of Earth, Victoria, who served as an admiral of the Venusian Fleet, repelling an invasion from the Draconis system in which Saurian aliens[521] were attempting to secure a foothold in the area of our planet that we now recognize as the Mediterranean Basin. After the defeat of these reptilian interlopers, Victoria successfully landed her triumphant but crippled command ship in the heights of Mount Olympus in Greece, where it was repaired and then served as the base of operations for the Venusians and other

---

519 *Ibid.*
520 *Ibid.*
521 "Who are the Reptilians," 2010, Extraterrestrial Community, http://arcturi.com/ (Accessed 18 December 2014). Paranormal researcher David Icke notes that Saurian aliens, or Reptilians from the Draco system, are manipulative and deceiving by nature. They are so advanced that, like some other extraterrestrial species, they have surpassed the physical limitations of their material bodies. Reptilian aliens from Draco ingest their nutrients through energy, but their needed food source is "bad" or "evil" energy. They also created the Greys to serve them as a slave race.

allied Solarians for nearly 1,500 years. Like the other extraterrestrials on board the command ship, she would occasionally descend from Mount Olympus and interact with the human population below. Fearful of the technological power that Victoria and the other advanced beings displayed, our ancestors erroneously assumed that they were gods who had come down among them.

Thor further explained that despite the extraterrestrials' denials of "divinity," the ancient Greeks and Italians were adamant in refusing to believe them. In 382, B.C.E., by the reckoning of our time line, Thor told Stranges that Victoria herself held a long conversation with the Roman emperor Gratianus, informing him that while she and the other extraterrestrials were happy to help humankind develop their own technology and progress as a species, they were nevertheless displeased when human beings put them up on pedestals and worshipped them as so-called "gods and goddesses."

She explained to the emperor that there was only the one "God" in the entirety of the universe that any beings, including themselves, need concern themselves with. Therefore, she kindly asked Gratianus to have her statue removed from the central plaza in Rome, for she had become weary of the incessant worship bestowed upon her by every Roman general returning triumphantly from war with neighboring states. Victoria voiced no objection to those thankful for her and the other extraterrestrials' assistance in repelling the Saurian invaders so long ago, graciously receiving the thanks and adulation of the Roman people. However, she was clearly opposed to her "brand," so to speak, being linked to aggression and imperialism in the expansion of the Roman Empire against the will of other peoples. While Gratianus complied with Victoria's wishes, he nevertheless met stiff opposition from the military class that had so facilitated a cult of war surrounding her. And Thor emphasized that his mothership, like Victoria's, was a vessel devoted to scientific exploration, research and above all, peace; and that he, too, should not be construed as a "god" in any sense, even though many would probably like to make one out of him.

Victoria has returned in the 21st century as "Winged Victory," a defender of *Astro City*, a DC Vertigo Comics series. By now, she has become accustomed to being mistaken for a goddess. See www.comicbookjustice.com.

Thor also informed Stranges that while he would never use force to speak with men in authority in America, he was happy to consult with them at their invitation. He further stated that so far only a relatively small number of men in positions of authority in the Washington, D.C. area knew of his existence and his residence inside the Pentagon. Of course, Thor expressed disappointment that so few among these leaders had availed themselves of his advice during the past three years. He also felt that there was still so much yet to be accomplished, but so little time remaining. And recognizing Stranges as a minister of the gospel, he commented that Jesus Christ would most likely not force anyone to be saved from their own folly, and that therefore he would neither coerce anyone, even though it would ultimately be for their own good and the overall benefit of the planet. When the reverend asked him if he was an angel sent from Heaven, the intrepid Mothership Commander replied, "I am from the planet that is called Venus."[522]

Stranges writes more about his meeting with Thor:

"I asked him how many visitors from Venus were presently on Earth and he said, "There are presently seventy seven of us walking among you in the United States. We are constantly coming and going." During the next thirty minutes, he told me things about myself that even I did not know. Later, I was able to verify them with my parents and grandparents. He gave me information regarding the gravitational pull of Venus in comparison to Earth. I was informed that the abdominal muscles hold flesh firm against the mild gravitational pull, which is three-twentieths less than that of Earth. He gave me information which would be revealed to others over a period of years."[523]

The only thing that troubled the reverend, however, was Thor's use of the expression "when the time is right" in response to his question as to whether or not he would see him again. Also, Thor's lack of fingerprints intrigued Stranges, insofar as he had also worked as a private investigator for many years, sometimes on loan to some of the government agencies in the nation's capital. In the conduct of his private investigating work, Stranges had learned the science of fingerprints, with the impression of the lines and whorls on the inner surface of the last joint of each finger on the human hand. An examination of Thor's fingertips gave no indication that he ever had fingerprints at any time throughout his life.[524]

Thor encouraged Stranges to not give up the fight in the important work he and others in the contactee community were doing. The Venusian commander noted that Stranges would face many adversities, including "organized attempts to both discourage and discredit" him and his work in the eyes of the public. When the subject of religion came up again, Stranges asked Thor if they used a *Bible* or some other holy book on Venus, to which the venerable Venusian assured him that, "A personal, unbroken fellowship with the Author of the *Bible* did not necessitate the printing of a book." Apparently, the Venusians, having an "open door" policy with Jesus Christ and other ascended masters, have little need to live by faith as we do here on Earth, at least insofar as they receive continual guidance and revelation directly from the One Source. In addition, Thor found it amusing that many theologians attempt to discredit both Jesus Christ and the *Bible*, while the very "God" that they proclaim as dead continues to lavish them with all good things, material and spiritual. Said Thor, "Perhaps they will, in time, permit the Spark of Divine Light (the Holy Spirit) to again illuminate their troubled hearts."[525]

While they continued on the topic of religion, Stranges asked Thor what he personally thought of Jesus Christ, to which he replied:

"I know that Jesus is the Alpha and Omega of yours and everyone else's faith. He today has assumed His rightful position as the Ruler of the Universe and is preparing a place and a time for all who are called by His Name to ascend far above the clouds to where His Power and Authority shall never again be disputed. I believe that Jesus Christ is the Wonder of Wonders and changes not. No, not forever and forever."[526] (*Amen!*)

Clearly, as Thor spoke these profound words of wisdom, Stranges' own heart burned within him and tears filled his eyes. Thor, sensing Stranges' yearning for the return of Jesus Christ to

---

522 Frank E. Stranges
523 *Ibid.*
524 *Ibid.*
525 *Ibid.*
526 *Ibid.*

Earth and His millennial rule, turned to the sole small window in the room, looked up to the sky and said, "Frank, it will not be long. Contend for the faith, and you will never miss the mark."

Stranges also wanted to know about life on other planets, the material and spiritual conditions that were extant there. To this, Thor replied,

"There is life on many other planets of which people on Earth know nothing. There are more solar systems for which man has not even given God credit. There are many beings that have never transgressed the perfect laws of God. Man does not possess the right to condemn the whole of God's creation because he himself has broken the perfect laws of God through disobedience."[527]

And as their conversation was coming to a close, Stranges asked Thor what he would do if the military prevented him from leaving on the appointed day, to which he simply stated, "Frank, do you remember one day after Jesus arose from the dead, He had gone in search of several of His followers? They closed themselves in a locked room and suddenly they saw Jesus standing in the very midst of them?" He paused, and then smiled and looked at Stranges as if to imply, "Need I say more?"

As Thor turned to leave the room, he said simply, "Please keep your faith and leave the same way that you came in. Continue to seek first the Kingdom of God and His Righteousness and all other things will, in time, be added to you and yours. Good-bye for now and God bless you and keep you always."

With that, Stranges left that meeting, escorted by Warren, astounded yet greatly fortified in his faith. But still he experienced a heavy heart, not knowing what the future would hold. He began to wonder who would believe him if he ever told of this strange encounter with a man from Venus. At first, the reverend considered not repeating this extraordinary story, but the more he thought about it and the more he prayed about it, the more he felt that it would bring a great blessing to those who would hear and read it, and more importantly, act upon it. This interplanetary traveler possessed a wealth of knowledge, not only about science and God, but also about many other subjects as well, including personal information about the reverend. He also declared that Stranges' book, *Saucerama*, could not have been written without Heavenly guidance.

Thor's instructions were to leave Washington, D.C., no later than 16 March 1960. That meant that there were less than three months during which he could confer with scientists, politicians, military men and the like. All appeared to have missed his point entirely, largely fearing him in lieu of trying to understand his message. They were all filled with self-ambition and cared little for the pressing needs of humankind. His efforts to bring about an end to the sickness and disease that plague this planet were met with pathetic refusal. He was told over and over that his presence and his ideas were a threat to both the economic and political structure. Certain religious leaders were also fearful of losing a grip on the people in the event that Thor's presence was admitted on an official level. It was very disheartening that the administration failed to lay hold of such information that would change the course of human activities for the good, and all because of socio-economic reasons.

Security restrictions were very tight, but despite the fact that they knew Thor would come and go as he pleased, they delighted in playing their "game." Thor had vowed not to use force; ergo another course of action would be necessary if the information which he had to relate was going to be disseminated. This is the reason why he contacted men and women of goodly

527 *Ibid.*

184

character and strength around the world. And according to Stranges, even to this day, "Many are presently working in close contact with Val and other members of his crew."[528]

Unfortunately, Thor's last meeting with the president failed to reap any lasting results. Eisenhower truly wanted to let the world know of the positive Venusian agenda for the United States and the world; but the Secretary of Defense, the head of the Central Intelligence Agency and the military chiefs of staff were totally at odds with him. While the president tried to bring about a joint meeting before the General Assembly of the United Nations to openly discuss the Venusian agenda, this plan too was summarily rejected. Eisenhower was, however, informed that the United Nations would receive a special "press release" in the form of a memorandum to the Secretary General no later than 7 February 1966, detailing a United States' plan for the demilitarization of outer space that would also include the extension of a nuclear test ban to areas outside our atmosphere. In fact, such a Treaty on Outer Space was adopted by the United Nations General Assembly on 27 January of the following year.[529] Allegedly, Vice-President Nixon was the only one to side with the president; and it was Nixon who helped to garner this concession to the United Nations. Even so, the various federal department leaders of the United States government argued long into the night about it before coming together with Nixon's suggestion; and they only reached this accord because they feared that their failure to present Thor and the Venusian Hierarchy with "something" might engender dire consequences for the long-term prospects for national security. The only point they could agree on was a fear that if the people of this nation learned of the Venusian plan offered by Thor, they just might choose to follow him instead of them.

World conditions were quickly deteriorating. In addition, much international pressure was being directed against the United States and our government's "crackdown" on the dissemination of information related to the UFO phenomenon and life on other planets. Many nations, and particularly the Soviet Union, were bringing pressure to bear on the Eisenhower administration to come clean with what they knew about these highly classified subjects. Of course, higher echelon members of the United States intelligence community fought diligently and enforced rigid regulations with stiff penalties for revealing anything about Thor's presence or that of any other Venusians on Earth. A major radio newscaster and talk show host who frequently discussed UFOs and interviewed numerous contactees long before Art Bell ever ~~on 1240~~ arrived on the scene, "Long John" Nebel, inadvertently learned of Thor's visit through one ~~at night~~ of his paid informants, but was silenced by agents of the Central Intelligence Agency (CIA), which had long disclaimed any and all knowledge concerning UFOs; but that we now know had all the while maintained secret files that could actually prove the existence of intelligent life in the universe beyond all doubt.

While the public came to know of the existence of a set of post-detection of extraterrestrial life protocols for the first time with their disclosure by the International Academy of Astronautics (IAA) in 1992;[530] they were definitely in place and enforced throughout the free world by

528 *Ibid.*
529 D. Goedhuis, "An evaluation of the leading principles of the Treaty on Outer Space of 27th January

1967," *Nederlands tijdschrift voor internationaal recht,* (Leyden), 1968, 15:1:17-41. For the reader who would like to peruse the flurry of documents produced by the various delegates responsible for the ultimate formulation of the United Nations' space policies, your attention is invited to *Extract from United Nations Juridical Yearbook, 1968*, Part 4, Chapter X: "Legal bibliography of the United Nations and related intergovernmental organizations" (New York, New York: United Nations, 1968), 286-288.

530 The reader's attention is invited to the "Declaration of Principles for Activities Following the Detection of Extraterrestrial Intelligence," created by the SETI Permanent Committee of the International Academy

the CIA from the 1940s through the early 1990s. The CIA has cataloged declassified UFO reports throughout this period, with most of the documents detailing CIA cables reporting unsubstantiated UFO sightings in the foreign press and intra-Agency memos about how the Agency handled public inquiries about UFO sightings or requests for information about alleged "extraterrestrial biological entities" (EBEs). Even a quick survey of this "declassified" data will reveal that nearly half of the applicable information pertaining to the "who, what, when, where, and why" has been conveniently deleted.[531]

In addition to garnering the compliance of astronomers and other scientists who accumulated evidence for the existence of any extraterrestrial intelligence, military personnel, astronauts and technicians with NASA fell under the prevue of the Department of Defense (DoD) and the CIA, clearing every new scientific discovery with bureaucratic censors in these organizations. To explore this situation further, James A. David, the curator for the Division of Space History at the National Air and Space Museum, has performed a herculean task by pulling together for the first time hundreds of formerly classified documents to tell the fascinating story of NASA's intimate and extremely sensitive relations with the CIA and other branches of the intelligence community over the past fifty-plus years in a soon to be published, hard-hitting

of Astronautics (IAA) and later approved by the Board of Trustees of the IAA and by the International Institute of Space Law, and still later by the International Astronomical Union (IAU), the Committee on Space Research, the International Union of Radio Science, and others. See John Billingham (August 1991). Shostak, Seth, ed. "ASP Conference Series," Third Decennial US-USSR Conference on SETI, University of California, Santa Cruz: Astronomical Society of the Pacific. pp. 417-426, Archived from the original on 24 December 2012 (Accessed 16 December 2014). It was subsequently endorsed by most researchers involved in the search for extraterrestrial intelligence, to include the SETI Institute. See Ray Norris (2002), Norris, R, and F. Stoolman, eds. "Proceedings of the IAU, Bioastronomy 2002: Life Among the Stars," *International Astronomical Union*, Archived from the original on 24 December 2012 (Accessed 16 December 2014) and SETI Permanent Committee, International Academy of Astronautics, "Protocols for an ETI Signal Detection," *www.seti.org*. SETI Institute (Accessed 16 December 2014). It should also be noted that the SETI Permanent Committee of the IAA and Commission 51 of the IAU continually review procedures regarding detection of extraterrestrial intelligence and the management of data related to such discoveries. A committee comprising members from various international scientific unions, and other bodies designated by the committee, is empowered to regulate continued SETI research. In addition, a separate "Agreement on the Sending of Communications to Extraterrestrial Intelligence" was subsequently created. It established an international commission, the membership of which is open to all interested nations, and is constituted on the detection of extraterrestrial intelligence. This commission decides whether to send a message to the extraterrestrial intelligence, and if so, *determines the contents of the message* on the basis of principles such as justice, respect for cultural diversity, honesty, and respect for property and territory. *It forbids the sending of any message by an individual nation or organization without the permission of the commission*, and suggests that, if the detected intelligence poses a danger to human civilization, the United Nations Security Council should authorize any message to extraterrestrial intelligence. *In other words, the activities of contactees are declared in opposition to international law. Attempted communications with extraterrestrials are done at the contactee's own risk.* See Michael A. G. Michaud (March–April 1992), "An international agreement concerning the detection of extraterrestrial intelligence," *Acta Astronautica* 26 (3–4): 291–294. Also, radio astronomer Paul Davies, a member of the SETI Post-Detection Taskgroup, stated that post-detection protocols needed to be codified into international law and call for international consultation before taking any major steps regarding the detection of extraterrestrial life because without such, astronomers were unlikely to follow mere "suggestions." They would put the advancement of their careers over the word of a protocol that is not part of national or international law. In other words, the protocols needed some "teeth" if they were going to have any bite in them. See Jason Zasky, "If ET Calls, Who Answers?" *Failure Magazine* (2014); http://www.webcitation.org/6DA60bA5i (Accessed 16 December 2014).

531 For the most recent CIA revelations on UFOs, see the article "CIA's Role in the Study of UFOs, 1947-90" at the *Center for the Study of Intelligence* website (https://www.cia.gov/library/center-for-the-study-of-intelligence/index.html). The article is located in On-line Publications under the "Studies in Intelligence" section, specifically semi-annual Edition #1, 1997.

exposé of the space agency.[532] So when an agent of the government tells me that Venus cannot support any kind of life because it is too hot and the air is not breathable, you can see why I would be hesitant to believe it. After all, the government does not rate very high on the scale of believability. And once you read David's recent book, you will understand even more why the acronym NASA stands for "Never A Straight Answer."

But getting back to our Venusian emissary, on the morning prior to his departure, Thor met one more time with "Nancy Warren" as she would continue to work inside the Pentagon and be one of his valuable contacts in the Washington, D.C. area. She would continue to communicate with others who would become part of his network of Earth contacts. Early on the morning of 16 March, however, the Venusian commander dematerialized and departed from this phase of his Earthly mission. His next stop was a wooded area in the outskirts of Alexandria, Virginia, somewhat near to the place where he had landed his ship alone three years ago. Now, however, some of his crew came down with the scout ship, awaiting his arrival. Thor encased his body in an Etheric shield of invisibility, just in case he ran into a problem in entering his ship.

Having entered the scout craft undetected by any human presence in the area, he dropped his cloaking and greeted his Venusian comrades, Jill, Donn and Tanyia, who were all glad to see him back. Donn gave up the command chair to Thor, who fired up the electromagnetic coils. Repelling the ship from the Earth's gravitational field, it rose slowly at first, then reaching an altitude where a number of people stopped and pointed excitedly at the saucer as it hovered over some stores in a shopping plaza. Others stood motionless, transfixed by the glorious sight. The saucer seemed to pulse with inner multi-colored lights, creating a

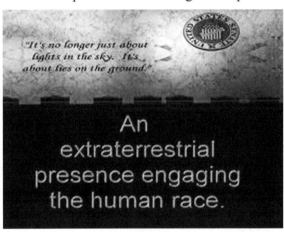

See www.exopolitics.org.

translucent effect on the skin of the craft. Thor's heart was filled with gratitude and love. Once again he was with his loyal Venusian crew members. Having experienced so many adventures in space together over the past half century, there was no fear or panic in them, just curiosity and an intense desire to know more. Of course, it did not take long for the military to scramble some jets over Alexandria from the nearby Washington Naval Air Facility at Andrews Field. In response, Vice Commander Donn engaged the scout ship's ion force field, generating both a cloak of invisibility as well as an impenetrable electronic screen. The Navy pilots could not see a thing. The ship appeared to be surrounded by a cloud, induced from negatively charged atmospheric molecules in the vicinity of the craft. Even if they could observe the ship, conventional weapons would be useless against it. Ground radar scans of the Alexandria area also turned up nothing. And although the ship was equipped with traditional radio transmitters and receivers for the benefit of communicating with some non-Venusians onboard the Victory One mothership, Communications Officer Tanyia knew better than to turn them on until well outside the Earth's atmosphere. In the meantime, she was telepathically receiving and entering the coordinates into the ship's computer for docking with the mothership. Confusion once again reigned amongst all concerned: the Navy pilots, the ground observers and radar operators

532   James A. David, *Spies and Shuttles: NASA's Secret Relationship with the DoD and CIA* (Gainesville, FL: University
    Press of Florida, 2015).

at Andrews Field.

On the way back to the Victory One mothership, Thor meditated on his home planet, and particularly what he so dearly missed during his past three years on Earth. First in his mind were the low, heavy, but colorful and iridescent clouds. In second place came the even temperatures. He compared it to California 24/7. Next was the perfectly diffused sunlight that made shadows almost nonexistent, as well as the lushness of the rich green grass that surrounded his home. He was also informed of several Earth people with whom he would maintain contact for a long time into the future.

Upon Thor's return to Venus, he immediately reported to the Council of Central Control, the defense wing of the Hierarchy of Light, to detail the results of his Earth visit, including the failure of the leaders of the United States to "take him up" on his offer of advice and assistance to the human family.

After due consideration of his report, the Council recommended the following actions be taken:

To mingle with and become as Earth people.

To work and labor in Earth enterprises.

To help those who encounter possible threat or danger while striving for world peace

To give them advice and guidance.

To entrust with superior knowledge those who have proven themselves.

Divulge the essence of their mission to the collective national leaders of Earth, only when the time is right.[533]

However, as of this writing, along with the peaceful passing of the Rev. Dr. Frank E. Stranges in 2008, it is assumed by the leadership of the UFO organization he established so long ago, the National Investigations Committee on Unidentified Flying Objects (NICUFO), headquartered in Los Angeles, California, that Thor continues with this mission as outlined above, while at the same time assisting in preventing our "civilization" from being the cause of orbital chaos and disruption throughout the solar system resulting from the destruction of our planet.

While some consider Stranges' account preposterous, others were not so quick to dismiss it. As it turns out, there is evidence that the very creation of NASA may have been inspired in response to the proof obtained by the United States government concerning the existence of the Victory One mothership in a high near polar orbit for the entire three years that the Venusian commander was resident in the Pentagon. The very existence of the ship, exactly as Thor described it, was all the president needed to convince him that Thor was not bluffing about what actions the extraterrestrials could take if they had to put a stop to any of Earth's military developments that could somehow threaten the inhabitants of other planets. The creation of NASA would serve to at least guide America's space program in a peaceful direction.

Before the creation of the space agency, and starting from the period immediately following the close of World War II in the late 1940s, it was the Department of Defense that pursued research in rocketry and the upper atmospheric sciences as a means of assuring American leadership in technology, *vis-à-vis* the Soviet Union. According to an official NASA website, however, "*The major step forward came when President Dwight D. Eisenhower approved a plan to orbit a scientific satellite as part of the International Geophysical Year (IGY) for the period, July 1, 1957 to December 31, 1958, a cooperative effort to gather scientific data*

---

533 Frank E. Stranges

about the Earth. The Soviet Union quickly followed suit, announcing plans to orbit its own satellite."[534] The big question here concerns Eisenhower's sudden conversion to a belief in fostering the peaceful development of space research, especially in *cooperation* with the Soviet Union, our declared "Enemy Number One" in the ongoing Cold War.

When one considers that Eisenhower diverted the personnel and resources of the Naval Research Laboratory's Project Vanguard, a high-priority ballistic missile development program, to support the peaceful IGY effort, it is all the more amazing. Remember, this was in the heat of the Cold War, with the Doomsday Clock on the University of Chicago campus set at just a few minutes short of midnight. Initially, the IGY program utilized the non-military Viking rocket out of fear that other, more powerful launch vehicles should remain under military prevue in case our nation was attacked by the Soviets. But Eisenhower ordered that the Army turn several of its Redstone ballistic missiles to be converted into the launch vehicles required as the boosters to put up at least one satellite into orbit sometime during the IGY. While Project Vanguard certainly caught the imagination of the public, especially inspiring the imaginations of our nation's youth and their enthusiasm for peaceful space exploration, the funding levels were too small to ensure success, with most of the dollars still flowing into the coffers of military projects concerned with the development and deployment of advanced ballistic missile systems.

On 4 October 1957, the Soviets launched *Sputnik I,* the world's first artificial satellite as its IGY entry. Political hawks, on the other hand, failed to see the Soviet satellite as anything but a "direct threat" to the national security of the United States. Because of this Cold War hysteria, the launching of Sputnik, rather than generate an aura of peace and inaugurate an era of scientific cooperation, such as the IGY was supposed to inspire, had a "Pearl Harbor" effect on American public opinion. What it did was create an illusion of a technological gap and provided the impetus for increased spending for aerospace endeavors, technical and scientific educational programs, and the chartering of new federal agencies to manage aerospace research and development.

The reaction of the United States government toward the Soviet Sputnik accomplishment was the launching of its first Earth satellite on 31 January 1958, when *Explorer I* documented the existence of radiation zones encircling our planet. Shaped by the Earth's magnetic field, these zones partially dictate the electrical charges in the atmosphere and the solar radiation that reaches Earth. They have come to be known as the Van Allen Radiation Belt. The United States also began to plan and initiate a series of scientific missions to the Moon, Mars and Venus in the latter 1950s and early 1960s. The Soviets, likewise, planned and initiated sundry projects to launch space probes to the Moon and Venus.

All of this was taking place while Commander Val Thor was allegedly in the custody of Pentagon officials, an honored guest of President Eisenhower and a cosmic emissary from the Venusian Hierarchy of Light. Thor was sent to Earth for the express purpose of persuading the leaders of the United States, the world's most powerful nation state, to divert its military aims from the conquest of space to designs for its peaceful exploration. And just a few days short of one year following the Sputnik I launch, on 1 October 1958, NASA was formed by an executive order from President Eisenhower, effectively absorbing into itself the earlier National Advisory Committee for Aeronautics intact: its 8,000 employees, an annual budget

---

534 Steve Garber and Roger Launius, "A Brief History of NASA," 25 July 2005, *NASA History Program Office,* http://history.nasa.gov/factsheet.htm (Accessed 16 December 2014)

of $100 million, three major research laboratories-Langley Aeronautical Laboratory, Ames Aeronautical Laboratory, and Lewis Flight Propulsion Laboratory, along with two smaller test facilities. NASA quickly incorporated other organizations into the new administration, notably the space science group of the Naval Research Laboratory in Maryland, the Jet Propulsion Laboratory managed by the California Institute of Technology for the Army, and the Army Ballistic Missile Agency in Huntsville, Alabama, where Dr. Wernher von Braun's crack team of engineers were engaged in the development of yet larger rockets appropriate for voyages to the Moon and beyond. Eventually, NASA created yet other centers; and today it has ten located throughout the country.

NASA Encounters the Venusian Mothership

It was clearly in the national security interests of the United States to monitor all satellite activity around the planet. Naturally, military officials were concerned about the Soviets and the fast-paced developments taking place in their space exploration program. But there was also a growing fear of an extraterrestrial surveillance program. As early as mid-1954, more than three years before Thor's arrival and the Soviet launch of the Sputnik I, United States military brass were certainly aware of extraterrestrial surveillance craft orbiting our planet.

Retired Marine Corps major and aviator, Donald E. Keyhoe, the director of the world's then largest civilian UFO group, NICAP, informed Washington, D.C. reporters that "Artificial Satellites Are Circling Our Earth."[535] In a radio interview with Frank Edwards of the Mutual Broadcasting System on the evening of Thursday, 13 May 1954, the retired Marine Corps officer mentioned three areas of concern that had come to his attention during the course of NICAP's ongoing investigations into the UFO phenomenon. First, the major announced that the United States government was aware of the existence of at least two artificial satellites in orbit around our planet. Second, the Secretary of the Air Force Harold Talbott had actually observed a flying saucer. And third, for the past two weeks the Canadian government had placed all of its armed forces on high alert, in addition to those in civilian occupations responsible for monitoring the air space over Canada, such as air traffic controllers, commercial pilots and astronomers. The individuals in these positions were to immediately report any unidentified aerial objects to the authorities at the nearest Canadian military installation.

As far as the United States government was concerned, Keyhoe informed Edwards that scientists at the White Sands Missile Range in New Mexico were conducting an intense effort to locate and chart the orbital paths of any artificial satellites in the hopes of determining where they came from and what their purpose was. The NICAP director, while not a "scientist" in the literal sense of the word, was an experienced aviator who had spent the majority of life around, in or flying aircraft. He had first-hand knowledge and experience with radar. So when asked how we could determine the characteristics of any object so far away in space, Keyhoe opined that even with 1954 technology, it would not be difficult for radar operators at White Sands to calculate its weight by knowing its speed in orbit and its altitude or distance from the Earth's gravitational center. But all of this was based on the assumption that the object was not under constant powered acceleration. He believed that radar would be sufficient to obtain the information we needed about any such unidentified satellite, at least enough so we could start making educated guesses about it.

---

535 "Artificial Satellites Are Circling Earth, Writer on '*Saucers*' Says," 14 May 1954, Associated Press release, St. Louis, Missouri, *Post-Dispatch*.

And once again, it appears as though the Silence Group was making an all-out effort to squash another UFO story. Apart from the St. Louis *Post-Dispatch*, the abbreviated Associated Press piece appeared in only one other newspaper, the San Francisco *Examiner*'s evening edition of 14 May 1954. And while a story like this certainly merited front-page coverage, it remained buried on page 4C of the *Post-Dispatch* and even further back on page 14 of the *Examiner*. It should also be noted that even though the story was covered in the pages of two major newspapers, the Air Force's denial received equal attention with Keyhoe's assertions. Air Force General Talbott insinuated that Keyhoe was a liar when he said, "I have never seen

This artist's conception of an alien mothership and surrounding scout craft was used in a television episode of *The Invaders*, starring Roy Thinnes as a former architect and full-time UFO hunter, David Vincent. The program aired for two seasons, 1967-1968. The executive producer was Quinn Martin and it was broadcast over all ABC Television Network affiliates. See http://www.deviantart.com/morelikethis/artists/294737490?offset=10&view_mode=2.

a flying saucer," adding, "I am convinced it is not from lack of opportunity. During the last 15 months, my official travels have taken me more than 160,000 miles without encountering one."

Keyhoe, trusting his sources, would continue to insist that, "Talbott personally has seen a large, silvery disk-shaped object in the sky." But inasmuch as the debate between the retired Marine Corps major and the Air Force general was concerned, back in 1954 the public simply took it as one man's word against another's. Now, however, more than sixty years later, and in light of the ineffectiveness and ineptitude of the Silence Group's persistent and massive efforts at trying to sustain a UFO cover-up, most would find agreement with Ralph Waldo Emerson, who wrote the following entry in his journal for 1860: "The teaching of politics is that *the government, which was set for the protection and comfort of all good citizens, becomes the principal obstruction and nuisance which we have to contend. The cheat and bully and malefactor we meet everywhere is the government.*" And that "everywhere" in our day includes both near and outer space.

So the Eisenhower administration was well aware of the existence of advanced extraterrestrial civilizations well before Val Thor ever stepped foot into the Pentagon. But the proof that the mothership Victory One- or a similar craft- was real came in February 1960, when the space radar scanners at White Sands detected what could only be described as a "gigantic unknown object in polar orbit." Of course, putting a satellite into a polar orbit was a feat beyond the technological capabilities of either the United States or the Soviet Union at that time. Also, the detection of the mothership in its polar orbit just one month from Commander Thor's departure date, gave every indication to the White House and Pentagon officials that the mysterious object they were looking for was the Victory One, coming to take him back home to Venus.

But while the White House and upper echelons of NASA had expected that the mothership would go away soon after it had received its commander, they were surprised to discover that the large vessel remained in its polar orbit. Ham radio operators from around the globe also began to intercept strange coded signals from the object. The National Security Agency (NSA), in turn, and at the behest of the CIA, dispatched agents to pay unceremonious visits to each of the radio aficionados, telling them that what they were hearing were coded messages from a new but secret Soviet satellite, and that for the interests of national security they should not say anything further about the transmissions to anyone, including family members. And along with the enactment of these security measures, the NSA put a team of its own analysts on the case. Soon one of these was claiming that he had managed to decode one of the strange transmissions. He said that the encrypted signal corresponded to a star chart that could have been plotted from the Earth 13,000 years ago. The focus of these charts was the Epsilon Bootis double star system, located about 203 light years from Earth. Most astronomers know the two major stars in this system by their traditional names of Izar and Pulcherrima. These celestial lights can be viewed with the unaided eye at night, but resolving the pair in anything but a large telescope is a daunting task, even for a professional astronomer.

While both Izar and Pelcherrima can be seen in the northern constellation of Bootes, neither of them has ever been or will ever be a candidate for Earth's northern pole star. The NSA analyst reasoned that, as incredible as it may seem, the mothership guidance system may require such a star map in order to locate fixed coordinates for quantum jumps through time. In other words, the ship's engines can generate a neutrino field both fore and aft of the vessel. It can then move instantaneously through a time tunnel or wormhole to any desired space coordinate at any desired time, past or future. To travel vast distances yet maintain the ship in the same time line, however, it has to first make a jump either backward or forward to the desired coordinate, and then make a jump in the reverse direction returning to the present star time, synchronized with the new location.

The Time Tunnel, an Irwin Allen production released by 20th Century Fox, was originally broadcast in 30 episodes over all ABC television affiliates in 1966-1967. Left to right: Lee Meriwether as Dr. Ann MacGregor, Robert Colbert as Dr. Douglas Phillips and James Darren as Dr. Anthony Newman, high-ranking personnel of a top-secret U.S. government operation code named Project Tic-Toc. In the series, the time tunnel is located in a huge, underground complex on a military installation somewhere out in a remote corner of the Arizona desert. It is 800 floors deep and employs over 36,000 people. See http://bookstevechannel.blogspot.com/2012/07/time-tunnel.html.

To contemporary astrophysicists, a wormhole is a topological feature that fundamentally serves as a shortcut through "spacetime." To understand the function of wormholes requires a mathematical study of shapes and their fixation in topological spaces. In other words, it incorporates an area of mathematics concerned with the properties of space that are preserved under continuous deformations including stretching and bending, *but not tearing or gluing*. Fixation of the wormhole in spacetime would, therefore, include such properties as boundary, connectedness and continuity. And in consideration of these properties, one can easily picture the wormhole as a tunnel with its two ends, each in separate points in spacetime. So essentially the Venusian mothership's powerful electromagnetic drive can be utilized to form this tunnel by curving the immediate space surrounding it's fuselage with the pulsing of neutrino fields emanating from both ends of the craft, thereby "warping" the space around it to such a degree that the mothership is actually operative outside the continuity of time itself.

If you can visualize space as a two-dimensional (2D) surface, then you can see the wormhole as a hole in that surface that leads into a 3D tube (the inside surface of a cylinder), with the tube then re-emerging at another location on the 2D surface with a similar hole as the entrance. In the case of the Venusian mothership, however, the spatial dimensions of its wormhole would be raised by a factor of one. Hence, instead of circular holes on a 2D plane, the mouths of its wormhole are observable as orbs or spheres in 3D space. Such wormholes, once created, can then be crossed in both directions. To astrophysicists these are known as traversable wormholes, and to Venusians they are called "stargates." The wormholes are stabilized for transit by the continuous infusion of pulsed exotic quanta particles of a negative energy density into each of the two orbs of composite fluxing neutrinos generated at each end of the mothership. When the infusion of quanta particles ceases, the orbs dissipate and the stargate is closed. The mothership stabilizes in the spacetime now surrounding it, and the craft resumes normal operation under conventional drive systems.

Interestingly, it was the American astrophysicist, John Archibald Wheeler, who first popularized the term *wormhole* in 1957 by publishing numerous articles on the theoretical nature of this phenomenon in various academic and scientific journals. One has to wonder whether all of the ideas he expressed were his own, or whether he got a few tips from the venerable Venusian, Valiant Thor. The first use of the word *wormhole*, however, in an astronomical context, dates back to 1921 and the German mathematician Hermann Weyl, whose research and writings examined the possibility of this unique cosmic formation in connection with the mass analysis of electromagnetic field energy.

Wheeler, in carefully considering Weyl's analysis, noted that it would soon necessitate the scientific community to reevaluate their entire understanding of physics; for "where there is a net flux of lines of force, through what topologists would call a 'handle' of the multiply-connected space, and what physicists might perhaps be excused for more vividly terming a 'wormhole,'" then what other direction can be taken in future investigations?

Of course, the implications of this for humankind are astounding. Einstein's general theory of relativity predicts that if traversable wormholes exist, they could allow for time travel. Theoretically, this could be accomplished by accelerating one end of the wormhole to a high velocity relative to the other, and then sometime later bringing it

Project Tic-Toc patch worn by *Time Tunnel* personnel. See www.ebay.co.uk.

back. A relative time dilation would result in the accelerated wormhole mouth aging less than the stationary one, at least as seen by an external observer. But one must also consider that time connects differently through the wormhole than outside it. Therefore, if synchronized clocks were placed at each mouth, they would remain in synch to someone traveling through the wormhole itself, regardless of how the mouths move around individually at each end of the wormhole. Essentially, this means that anything which entered the accelerated wormhole mouth would exit the stationary one at a point in time prior to its entry.

This photo is from *The Philadelphia Experiment*, a film by John Carpenter starring Michael Paré as an accidentally time-traveling sailor and Nancy Allen as a love interest who tries to help him. The film was released by New World Pictures in 1984 and deals with a top secret U.S. government experiment in the midst of World War II, originally designed to create an electromagnetic cloaking device for our ships at sea. On 28 October 1943, according to various accounts, an exceptionally strong magnetic field encircled the destroyer escort USS Eldridge (DE-173) and its crew. The U.S. Navy ship was also enshrouded in a green haze. At this point, its crew members began to "phase in and out" of reality, right in front of each other. The USS Eldridge then disappeared in a flash of blue light before the eyes of people watching from the relative safety of the dock. At the very same moment that the ship disappeared from the harbor in Philadelphia, Pennsylvania, it appeared in Norfolk, Virginia, and then vanished again and re-appeared back in Philadelphia. Those sailors who have dared speak out about the event claim that several of their fellow Eldridge crew members were hospitalized immediately after the experiment with third degree burns and feelings of disorientation. A few became permanently deranged and some even died from exposure to radiation. There are also allegations that USS Eldridge crew members were subjected to brainwashing so as to maintain secrecy about the experiment. The experiment was code named *Project Rainbow*, with details of the incident available in the book, *The Bermuda Triangle* (1974) by Charles Berlitz and in an appendix to *Uninvited Visitors* (1967) by Ivan T. Sanderson. See http://hiddencityphila.org/2013/04/the-other-philadelphia-experiment/.

Therefore, the impossibility of faster-than-light relative speed only applies locally, at least in a galactic sense; for wormholes might allow superluminal (faster-than-light) travel by ensuring that the speed of light is not exceeded locally at any time. When the Venusians are traveling through a wormhole, subluminal (slower-than-light) speeds are used; and this is aptly demonstrated when two points are connected by a wormhole whose length is shorter than the distance between them *outside* the wormhole and the time taken to traverse it takes less than the time it would take a light beam to make the journey if it took a path through the space *outside* the wormhole. However, a light beam traveling *through* the wormhole would always beat the traveler. For this reason, once the mothership is operative inside the wormhole, a series of convex, parabolic and spherical wave reflectors are used to maintain the focus of intense light beams on the desired space coordinates visible through the opening at the end of the "time tunnel," so to speak. The mothership basically follows its own generated beam through and out of the tunnel to the destination point. Much like the fictional Dr. Who and the other inhabitants of his home world of Gallifrey, the Venusians wield such massive power across the multi-dimensional continuum that they might rightly be referred to as the real "Time Lords."

But our fantastic story does not end here, for on 3 September 1960, just seven months after the large "satellite" was first detected by radar, a tracking camera at Grumman Aircraft Corporation's Long Island factory took a photograph of it. Now the object appeared to have significantly changed its orbital path, abandoning a polar north-to-south orbit for an east-to-west one. People on the ground who knew where to look for it had occasionally been able to see it for about two weeks at that point, with viewers making it out as a red glowing object. What few satellites there were in 1960 moved west-to-east; so this object was moving in the opposite direction of all the others. Also, its speed was about three times faster than normal, at least for one of our satellites at that time. At NASA they dubbed it the "Black Knight" satellite; and a committee was formed to examine the mysterious craft. Unfortunately, none of their findings have ever been made public. But just three years later, Gordon Cooper was launched into space for a 22 orbit mission; and on his final orbit, he reported seeing a glowing green shape ahead of his capsule, and heading straight in his direction. It's also said that personnel at the Muchea tracking station, located about 37 miles north of Perth in Western Australia, which Cooper reported this sighting to, were able to pick it up on radar traveling in the same nontraditional east-to-west orbit.[536]

This event was also reported to the NBC Television Network, but the Silence Group was back in business, this time forbidding the network's reporters from asking Cooper any questions concerning the object after his splashdown. And once again, NASA had to chime in with its "official explanation" for the astronaut's sighting after news of it leaked out to the Australian press. A space agency spokesman authoritatively attributed Cooper's experience to "an electrical malfunction in the capsule that had caused high levels of carbon dioxide, which in turn had induced hallucinations." It never ceases to amaze me how the so-called "official explanations" seem far more absurd than anything actually reported by the UFO witnesses.

And now, after this full discussion of the Venusian presence on Earth, let us consider these words of wisdom from the prominent contactee George Adamski that he penned at the end of the account of his 13 December 1952 reencounter with Orthon:

"The truth about flying saucers does exist. There are space visitors in our midst. And they are here for a purpose. We may as well search out and acquaint ourselves with this truth and address ourselves to its challenges and ultimatums.... A deep analysis of events of the past makes me firmly believe that these people from other planets are our friends. I am convinced that their desire and their object is to help us and perhaps to protect us from even ourselves; as well as that, they mean to insure the safety and balance of the other planets in our system."[537]

"You didn't see a flying saucer. You just witnessed the light from Venus refracting off a misty cloud of swamp gas." See www.shikalee.deviantart.com.

Even as early as 1961, astronomers were expressing some concern about sending lethal rockets to impact on other planets. The first statement dealing with this possibility was made by Dr. Rudolph M. Lippert of the University of San Diego's Department of Astronomy. The astronomer warned that "it was wrong to launch warheads into space without knowing whether civilizations existed on other planets."[538] What was little known in the United States astronomy community, however, was that Lippert had long come to believe in the existence of advanced extraterrestrial life in outer space, having

536 "The 'Black Knight' Satellite?," 6 February 2015, *Mystery of the Iniquity* (Accessed 15 February 2015)

537 Adamski and Leslie, *Flying Saucers Have Landed*, Book 2, Chapter 23, on-line edition, http://www.universe-people.com/english/svetelna_knihovna/htm/en/en_kniha_flying_saucers_have_landed.htm (Accessed 18 December 2014).

538 Raymond Keller and Andy Reiss, *Vortex One: Extraterrestrials Everywhere* (Hilmar, California: Outer Space International Research and Investigations Society-OSIRIS, 1993), 13-14.

personally observed a large object hovering in the vicinity of the Moon on the night of 16 September 1953. On that date he had not yet immigrated to the United States. He was a member of the Lunar Section of the British Astronomical Association; and through his eight-inch Cassegrain reflector 90x power telescope, he witnessed a peculiar, bright flash on or close to the surface of the Moon that continued to steadily emit an intense, yellowish-orange glow. Lippert classified its level of brightness as equivalent to that of a first magnitude star. Naturally, the young and aspiring astronomer excitedly filed his report with the Lunar Section, albeit confidentially. Nevertheless, news of the sighting caught the attention of the British press, and Lippert, much like thousands of others in the early 1950s who reported UFOs, became the butt of jokes, especially among his cadre in the astronomy field. And like any previous reports of strange lights on or near the Earth's only natural satellite, the Moon, it was quickly explained away by the more "seasoned" but skeptical astronomers, who claimed it was "just a meteor striking the lunar surface." Despite the intense criticism directed at him, Lippert declared that he was sure he had seen a huge extraterrestrial spacecraft, perhaps a mothership. To this astronomer, at least, his eyes were not lying to him. UFOs were very real.

Therefore, eight years later, on the campus of a major California university, the now highly acclaimed astronomer speculated, "Suppose one of these rockets (fired into outer space) hits a city? It's time we think about it!"[539] At the time he said this, the Soviets had launched their first probe to Venus. As science was unsure whether life existed on that planet, the astronomer was obviously concerned. And if there are interplanetary spacecraft surveying our planet, the indiscriminate deployment of warheads or other military hardware, such as those deployed in the Strategic Defense Initiative (SDI-"Star Wars"), may be interpreted as a hostile action by the Saucer Intelligences. As the United States, the Russian Federation, China, the European Union, India and a few other newer space-faring countries continue to expand their influence beyond the Earth, speeding up their militarization of the heavens, and as probes are sent to the outer planets of our solar system and beyond, the extraterrestrials will surely increase their own monitoring activities with respect to the Earth and beef up their own defense grids.

In L. Neil Smith's *The Venus Belt*,[540] the science fiction author projects a near future where Earthlings have colonized the planetoid Ceres as well as the planet Mars, using them as bases of operation to further exploit the vast Asteroid Belt extending in an orbit between Mars and Jupiter. As conditions in Earth's environment have seriously deteriorated, more and more people abandon their homes to settle in hollowed-out asteroids or artificial space platforms created from the raw material mined from the asteroids. But as the Asteroid Belt becomes depleted, the greedy authorities on Earth, rather than attempting to heal the ecology of their own world, pursue a desperate measure: blowing up Venus to create a second asteroid belt.

In order to accomplish this, a future corporate power smashes a giant ice asteroid, Bester, into Venus at a fraction of light speed. Their rationale for destroying Venus as a planet is that it had no immediate monetary value. The corporate big wigs regarded the orb as nothing but, *"as close to hell as places a world satisfactorily ever get."* To these short-sighted ones, Venus was considered the, *"most inhospitable, desolate, useless, impossible planet in the System."* And Venus, with its *"mass approximating Earth's, probably quite close to that of whatever primordial body became the Asteroid Belt (or never quite became a planet), the same potential goldmine, a hundred times as rich."* Matters were made even worse in that after they had fully exploited the Venus Belt, further development plans were on the blackboard, i.e. *"Just t'*

539 *Ibid.*
540 L. Neil Smith, *Venus Belt* (Rockville, Maryland: Phoenix Pick, 1980).

balance things out, we're gonna blow up Neptune!"

One scientist chimed in, "Listen, you guys. I didn't want to ask before, but- well, *won't this slop the whole gravitic balance of the Solar System out of kilter or something*?" To which Lucy, one of the associates on the planetary wrecking crew replied, "Oh, that. You want us to file EPA forms in triplicate? Only folks who're interested in that kinda ritual are gone now with Malaise!" The questioning scientist turned his attention out the port hole of an observational craft hovering at a safe distance from the point in space where Venus once stood, remarking, "But you've got to admit, it was one hell of an environmental impact!" Outside the safety of their spaceship, however, what was left of the once beautiful Venus had swollen into a cloud of glowing debris, "a trillion tons of popcorn going off inside a nuclear explosion." It was like one of those high-speed photos that Remington used to publish of a high-velocity bullet hitting an orange. In other words, glorious Venus would end with a big, inglorious "*Splat!*" By converting Venus into a belt of a million little worlds, give or take, the elite could continue to carve out personal kingdoms in space, where all with the economic wherewithal could become the sovereign of their own tiny planet.

That any Earthling could think such thoughts is beyond the comprehension of any Venusian. To wield such vast power without any degree of concern over its short or long-term cosmic consequences has already arrived at the point of possibility in the minds of some of the power elites here on Earth.

In his concluding paragraphs in *Flying Saucers Have Landed*, Adamski writes:

"But if we continue on the path of hostility between nations of Earth, and if we continue to show an attitude of indifference, ridicule and even aggression toward our fellow-men in space, I am firmly convinced they could take powerful action against us, not with weapons of any kind, but by manipulation of the natural force of the universe which they understand and know how to use. I barely brushed against this force as it was being used in a subdued degree, yet I felt the effects of it for several weeks after the encounter.

I have but one sincere purpose in narrating the foregoing experience: my most urgent message and plea to every person who reads it is:

Let us be friendly. Let us recognize and welcome the men from other worlds! THEY ARE HERE AMONG US. Let us be wise enough to learn from those who can teach us much — who will be our friends if we will but let them!"[541]

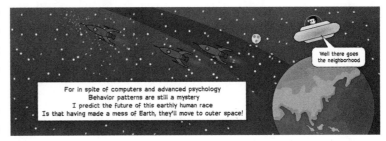

The Venusians aren't exactly thrilled at the prospects of humankind's colonization of space. See www.pixton.com.

To this we can all but proclaim a hearty and resounding "Amen!"

541 Adamski and Leslie, *Flying Saucers Have Landed*, Book 2, Chapter 23, on-line edition, http://www.universe-people.com/english/svetelna_knihovna/htm/en/en_kniha_flying_saucers_have_landed.htm (Accessed 18 December 2014).

Chapter VI:
Channels and Walk-Ins

Christ, following his resurrection, proved to Thomas (who became the
proverbial "Doubting Thomas") that He really was He, risen from the dead,
by showing Thomas His wounds. At the same time, however, Christ bestowed
His special favor on those who believed Him *without proof.*

—Gary Zukav, ***Dancing Wu Li Masters*** (1979)

As noted in previous chapters, the doctrines of Theosophy have permeated the contactee movement since its inception in the late 1940s. Theosophy, incorporating the ancient wisdom of the Orient with the scientific materialism of the West, hopes to guide humankind in the pursuit and acquisition of esoteric knowledge, thereby lifting our species to new plateaus of cosmic awareness and integration into the greater galactic community. Zukav, in his landmark work, *Dancing Wu Li Masters,* writes concerning the formidable obstacles one must overcome in arriving at such an East-West synthesis:

"Acceptance without proof is the fundamental characteristic of western religion. Rejection without proof is the fundamental characteristic of western science. In other words, religion has become a matter of the heart and science has become a matter of the mind. This regrettable state of affairs does not reflect the fact that, psychologically, one cannot exist without the other. Everybody needs both. Mind and heart are only different aspects of us."[542]

As to how this gap is breached, Zukav rhetorically asks if both religionists and scientists in the West should believe without proof. He ponders if scientists ought to start insisting on this. If the world is truly without substance, if it is as illusory or unreal as some imagine it to be, then why do Westerners assert that it must be continuously divided and subdivided into countless branches?

To this, Zukav suggests that we begin to learn from the Eastern masters. Long ago, they came to the realization that "religion" and "science" are both only "dances" on the cosmic stage, with their respective devotees being the "dancers." Naturally, both the religious and scientific dancer believe that they are gyrating to the "truth," or at least the on-going quest to arrive at some kind of consensus of just what constitutes "reality;" but the Wu Li Masters are the ones who know better. Zukav opines, "They know that the true love of all dancers is dancing." So in this sense, the dancers, like the Theosophists, certainly share a love of the exploration process, regardless of their particular "field" or area of specialization.

When it comes to the planet Venus, there appears to be plenty of floor space for a plethora of dancers. In the physical realm, we have considered the words of contemporary astronomers, largely dismissing any possibilities for "life as we know it" on our sister world. We have also considered the possibility of a massive cover-up concerning the presence of a terrestrial environment on Venus, with a population nearly indistinguishable from the human inhabitants of Earth. In addition, we have speculated about the existence of a "hidden Venus," one occupying a space or multiple spaces in another or multiple dimensions.

To this occult sphere, it is easy to understand how its mysterious denizens have so quickly been linked to the apparitions of angels, demons, ghosts, superheroes, gods and every sundry

542 Gary Zukav, *Dancing Wu Li Masters* (New York, New York: Bantam, 1984), 88, first edition 1979.

ilk of supernatural being and creature. But in this chapter, we follow the sage advice of the Dancing Wu Li Masters. We will not impede the performance of any dancer, for each one may have something to contribute to an enduring and enlightened production. In order to accomplish this feat, however, an examination of two classifications of psychic phenomena will occur, "channeling" and "walk-ins."

The Channels

"Channeling" is a relatively modern term for what spiritualists of prior eras deemed the mystic art of "mediumship." In other words, channeling consists of an event or process in which an individual "channel," or medium, is able to transmit information from a supernatural source. In the majority of cases, the source is a disembodied spirit. The term "channeling" actually gained parlance in ufology, whence it was used to describe the psychic communications from the "space brothers," and only later was applied to New Age mediums. As to the manner in which an extraterrestrial, ultra-dimensional or supernatural being might transmit a message to a true psychic channel, parapsychologist Phillip C. Lucas elaborates:

"While some channels retain full consciousness during their transmissions, most of the prominent New Age channels are what spiritualists refer to as trance mediums-mediums who lose consciousness while a disembodied sprit takes over the channel's body and communicates through it. These spirits frequently claim to be spiritually advanced souls whose communications consist of metaphysical teachings. The teaching function of this communications contrasts with traditional, nineteenth century mediums who were more concerned with transmitting messages from departed relatives and with demonstrating the reality of life after death."[543]

But insofar in serving as vehicles for communications from other worlds or ethereal realms, the channels can best be seen as participants in a phenomenon that traces its roots back to archaic shamanism. Among ancient peoples, as well as in many communities throughout the contemporary developing world, shamans mediate the on-going relationship between supernatural entities and the local human population. In days of yore, however, it was not uncommon for a shaman to transmit warnings from God, much like an *Old Testament* prophet. However, in the modern age, the channel will most likely communicate some precept of New Age philosophy; and in this capacity can best be placed in the tradition of Western Theosophy. The contemporary channels of extraterrestrial intelligences can be understood as representing a blend of both Spiritualism and Theosophy in their so-called "transmissions;" and the first of these we will examine in some detail is George King, who established the first UFO religion based on knowledge telepathically imparted to him by the Master Aetherius of Venus.

George King and the Aetherius Society

George King was born in Shropshire, England, in the outskirts of Wellington, on 23 January 1919. As a child, he had demonstrated a keen interest in spirituality, quickly reasoning that there was more to the mysteries of life than conventional philosophy or religion could satisfactorily explain. While yet in his early teens, the young King opted out of the Church of England, choosing instead to pursue a deeper religious life in a nearby Quaker congregation. He was greatly impressed with the Quaker message of peace and strove to conduct his life in conformity to the Christian doctrine of nonviolence.

His commitment to this adopted philosophy of peace was sorely tested when the United

---

543   Phillip C. Lucas, "Channeling Movement," in Lewis, James R., ed., *Odd Gods*, 343.

Kingdom conducted a national draft in 1941, at the outset of the Second World War. King declared himself a conscientious objector, refusing to take up arms against his fellow man, even if it meant serving time in prison. The local authorities, impressed by his sincerity, offered the now 22-year-old King a way out of this dilemma. If he was willing to enlist in the British Fire Service he would not have to pick up or fire a weapon. He could go about the United Kingdom putting out fires wherever they were reported or found. King took them up on the proposal, and spent most of his time in the war period stationed in London, whence he worked through the German Blitz, aiding emergency medical crews, assisting special teams to disarm or detonate unexploded aerial bombs, as well as containing and putting out urban fires.

With the conclusion of the war, King continued his quest for further spiritual enlightenment. Taking up the ancient spiritual science of yoga, King hoped to fine tune both his body and mind with the Infinite. After some time, however, he came to the realization that while yoga was an important tool in the maintenance of physical fitness, its higher aspects of developing proper breathing techniques, mantras and the mastery of Kundalini chakra forces were the keys to accelerating his progress on the spiritual path.

King's determination to master the ancient art of yoga was, of course, a much more unusual pursuit for an Englishman in those days than it is now. Nevertheless, what was even stranger was his total commitment to it, practicing for an average of eight to ten hours daily, for an entire decade, while simultaneously living in central London and holding down a full-time job. Those closest to King, noting his steadfastness in pursuing spiritual self-mastery, thought of him in terms of being a "truly advanced soul" with whom they considered themselves fortunate to associate with in any capacity. And by the mid-1950s, because of his consistent yoga practice, King's psychic abilities had developed to their near utmost degree. King had far exceeded the status of yoga student, or even adept. He was now rightly functioning at the level of a master, entering some of the highest states of consciousness it is possible to achieve on the Earth plane. He was now duly prepared for the next phase, one of cosmic importance for all of humankind.

Just how the interplanetary hierarchy, directing the affairs of the Solar System from Venus, came in contact with King is described below:

"One sunny Saturday morning in May 1954, Dr. King, while in his small flat in Maida Vale, London, heard the following words, which have become known as 'The Command':

Prepare yourself! You are to become the voice of Interplanetary Parliament.

He tells us that the voice came from outside of himself and struck his eardrums 'with a somewhat gentle firmness,' but he admits to being unable to describe the 'tonal qualities' of this 'alien sound.' He also describes the suddenness of it as it came into his mind as 'numbing.'"[544]

Being a true Englishman, King was acquainted with the parliamentary system of government; and even though he had never before heard of an "Interplanetary Parliament," he did know that the experience was not an imaginary one. Due to his intense practice of yoga over the past decade, King had developed the innate powers of concentration and detachment still latent within most of us. But he had exercised them to such an extent that he could clearly tell the difference between a "paranormal" experience and a so-called "flight of fancy."

In the days following, the medium described feelings of "turmoil," "bewilderment" and "hopeless frustration" as setting in, presumably due to the lack of any explanations offered by the interplanetary psychic transmitters. The beings that contacted him, however, were well

---

544   "Dr. George King," 2014, *Aetherius Society* (http://www.aetherius.org/dr-george-king/ (Accessed 15 February 2015).

aware of his perplexity, and before the close of the week send him an emissary, a world-renowned yoga master whom King knew to be alive and active in India at that time. This yogi appeared to him in physical form, but was able to enter and leave by passing right through a locked door that he did not open. The Indian master apparently applied some advanced yogic technique to accomplish this feat. During the meeting, King was comforted by this exalted yogi's angelic presence. King was also given detailed instructions in certain spiritual practices, such as astral travel and even physical teleportation.

This was the beginning of King's career as the "Primary Terrestrial Mental Channel." In this capacity, he served as the medium by which literally hundreds of communications, or "transmissions," as they are known within the ranks of the Aetherius Society, have been given by a higher order of beings from this world and beyond. These transmissions contain some of the most advanced spiritual teachings available on Earth today. Some were given while King was in a trance, but most were received telepathically.

Many of the entities who spoke to, and through King in this way are extraterrestrials. They reside on the higher dimensional planes of other planets in this Solar System. A spokesperson for the Aetherius Society explains that a true yogi can detect life on these planets, where a NASA astronaut finds nothing but horrid conditions unsuitable for any life, at least as we know it:

"If, for example, an Earth spacecraft were to take an astronaut to Venus tomorrow, that astronaut may well find no indication of the existence of Venusian culture. However, if a genuine Master of yoga, like Dr. King, were to project from the physical body to a higher plane of Venus, he would find a highly advanced spiritual civilization, existing at a frequency of vibration higher than that with which we are familiar on Earth."[545]

English yogi George King (1919-1997) maintained telepathic communication with the Master Aetherius of Venus. See www.aetherius.org.

The space intelligence who first contacted King was a being from Venus. He identified himself to King as the "Master Aetherius," after whom the Aetherius Society was named and established in 1955 by King. The purpose of the society is "to spread and act upon the teachings of the Gods from space;" and the word "Aetherius" is of Greek derivation, signifying something akin to a "traveler through the ether."

As highly evolved intelligences from other planets had maintained open channels of communication with King for over 40 years, the Aetherius Society has carried out a marvelous work in continuing to propagate his message to humankind. Of the organization, UFO researcher John A. Saliba writes:

"Headquartered in Hollywood, California, the society has centers and branches on several continents, including North America, Europe, (West) Africa, and Australia. Its membership, though not very large, is thus varied. In the United States, members are more

---

545 "UFOs and Extraterrestrial Life," 2014, *Aetherius Society*, http://www.aetherius.org/ufos-and-extraterrestrial-life/ (Accessed 15 February 2015)

likely to be adult, middle class and white. One must add, however, that in some cities, white members actually form a minority. Further, many of its ministers are women and black. These factors, plus the society's presence on several continents, makes its overall membership cosmopolitan."[546]

The Aetherius Society publishes all of King's books. It also sells his taped lectures, separately or in a complete set. In addition, members receive a subscription to the *Aetherius Society Newsletter*. This publication is issued on a monthly basis and is available on-line or direct to one's mailbox. The society places an emphasis on spiritual service. Members believe that both the greatest yoga and the greatest religion manifest in "service to humankind." Because of this, along with the society's adherence to Eastern religious tenets such as aura manipulation, understanding chakras, Kundalini, karma and reincarnation, theologians place it in the same tradition as Theosophy, but with a somewhat apocalyptic bent largely due to its leadership's great concerns over the dangers of atomic warfare and fallout, to include the resulting substantial increase in UFO sightings worldwide.

While detailed descriptions of the "Cosmic Intelligences" or inhabitants of other planets, their different types of spacecraft (motherships, scout patrol vessels and special-purpose vessels), were provided by King and accounted for in Aetherius Society literature, we are informed that these exalted beings cannot "come out" publicly, as it were, mostly because of the negative karmic effects generated by human beings and resulting from their neglect of God's laws and the teachings of the masters. According to the society, the two most illustrious masters hail from Venus, these being Buddha and Jesus. Krishna comes from Saturn.

To find out all of this information, King never had to leave his London flat. According to theologian David V. Barrett, "Although George King often wrote of his journeys in spacecraft to other planets, he made it clear that this was a form of astral travel."[547] Barrett also notes that while the world did not recognize King's doctoral degree from the International Theological Seminary of California as a valid credential, the membership of his society did and always respectfully addressed him as "Dr. King."

Ernest L. Norman, the "Voice of Venus"

In consideration of Ernest Leland Norman's work as the "Voice of Venus" to the people of Earth, we begin by setting aside both our third and fourth-dimensional concepts of space and time, insufficient as they are to the task at hand of understanding sundry aspects of the ethereal second planet. Ernest L. Norman (11 November 1904-6 December 1971) co-founded the Unarius Academy of Science, along with his wife Ruth, in 1954 for the purpose of contacting and channeling beings in outer space. Norman believed that these entities did not hail from planets that could be easily detected with conventional scientific instruments and techniques, but rather originated on "non-atomic spiritual worlds." These exalted beings were collectively referred to as the "Space Brothers" by Norman and his wife. The primary function of these ultra-dimensional entities was to transmit critical information to the Normans that could help the Unarius Academy members further develop their knowledge of cosmic "fourth-dimensional science."[548]

---

546 John A. Silba, "UFO Religions," in Lewis, James R., ed., *Odd Gods*, 359.

547 David V. Barrett, *A Brief Guide to Secret Religions* (Philadelphia, Pennsylvania: Running Press), 123.

548 Diana Tumminia, "UFO Religions," in Lewis, James R., ed., *Odd Gods*, 364.

The members of the academy, or Unariuns, believe that knowledge of such fourth-dimensional science will not only help them to heal themselves of all emotional, mental and physical maladies, but will ultimately bring about their rebirth on an ascendant planet in a higher dimension. Throughout the 1950s, Norman channeled numerous books, with the most notable being the *Voice of Venus*,[549] that came through in a series of "transmissions" that he received in 1954. Ruth attempted to type the manuscripts of these cosmic communiqués as fast as her husband received them. Unarius members hold them in the highest esteem, considering them to be "enlightened teachings" on a par with the *Bible* and other sacred scriptures. Norman attests that most of this channeled information originated from his higher self, a Venusian master who identified himself as "Mal Var."[550]

Before he began his career as a channeler for Mal Var, however, Ernest Norman studied electronics through a correspondence school. After successfully completing his studies, he went on to work as an electrician in the greater San Diego, California, area, but supplementing his earnings by reading palms and conducted psychic readings in private sessions. And being caught up in all of the excitement generated by the "airship" sightings over Southern California in 1946, along with the accompanying reports of Adamski and Layne concerning the extraterrestrial origin of the craft, he joined the Borderland Sciences Research Association, whence he worked as a contributing editor for their *Round Robin* journal.[551]

In addition, Norman served as a minister in the Spiritualist Church for 15 years. Like King, Norman claims that he has visited other planets in our solar system and beyond on numerous occasions via astral projection. Hence, he never had to leave his El Cajon, California, residence to travel to any of these exotic and extraterrestrial locales. He wrote about life and conditions on these other planets in more than twenty books published by the Unarius Academy. Although Norman did not possess a doctoral degree, the Unariuns referred to him as "Dr.

King moved to California in 1959, occasionally leaving the state to go on the lecture circuit. From his Hollywood headquarters, King channeled most of the transmissions from the "Cosmic Hierarchy" or "Interplanetary Parliament." King frequently prefaced his channelings with the following statement: "*I do not ask the unbeliever to believe at once, but only request that he applies that which Aetherius says to his own reason and acts upon that which, in the light of greater reason, is acceptable.*" See www.aetherius.org.

Norman," out of respect for his position as the Unarius Monitor.

Of the "Masters on Venus," Ernest Norman channeled the following from Mal Var in Chapter 15 of the *Voice of Venus*: "....no Master has ever appeared or materialized in a séance room.

---

549 Ernest L. Norman, *Voice of Venus* (El Cajon, California: Unarius Educational Foundation, 1956). While Val Mar was channeled through Ernest L. Norman for most of 1954, the transmissions were not compiled into one volume and published until 1956, as the first volume in the "Pulse of Creation Series."

550 John A. Saliba, "UFOs and Religion: A Case Study of Unarius Academy of Science," in Lewis, James R., ed., *Encyclopedic Sourcebook of UFO Religions* (New York, New York: Prometheus Books. 2003), 191.

551 Greg Bishop, et al., *Weird California* (New York, New York: Sterling Publishing Company, Inc., 2006), 107-109.

If by chance you know of some instance in which a Master supposedly made an appearance I would severely question the position of both the medium and the entity or apparition."[552] Of course, Mal Var was not inferring that Venusian masters do not appear. He was merely placing a greater value and emphasis on the correct use and understanding of psychic powers within their proper context, or domain.

Mal Var continued to transmit information through Norman regarding the role of Venusian masters on Earth:

"There have been several Masters who have lived on your Earth in physical form. I need not mention that the one called Christ is the most outstanding example. Masters have also appeared in different ways and in some clairvoyant fashion to some of the more highly evolved souls who have lived, or are living on your planet.

In the *Bible* there are numerous cases. A Master appeared to one called Moses and he wrote the "Ten Commandments," out of which grew one of the oldest and strongest religions of your earth. After the crucifixion, the Master Christ appeared to Saul, or Paul, who founded a church which later, through a schism, became known as the Greek Orthodox and the Roman Catholic churches. A Master named Zoroaster also founded a pure monotheistic belief. A boy named Joseph Smith saw a Master and, under his guidance, founded what is today a very powerful church in your America…. Such psychic happenings to any individual personalities gave a great and powerful influence which is usually marked by the appearance of some spiritual movement."[553]

With Ernest Norman's death in 1971, however, Ruth Norman took charge of the academy, trying to sustain the organization and carry out its important task as her husband would have wanted. Somewhat overwhelmed with the task, she prayed for cosmic assistance and guidance in 1973, and immediately received a vision from her higher self, Uriel, from the ultra-dimensional planet known as Eros. It is from Eros that Uriel ruled as the "Queen of the Archangels." Ruth was also informed by Uriel that she and her higher self were yet "aspects" of an ever greater oversoul, Mary of Bethany from the first century of the Common Era; and that Ernest and Mal Var were also "aspects" of Jesus, the Christ.[554]

In the case of the Normans, their lives as aspects differed from those of direct reincarnations in that Ernest and Ruth could psychically "plug-in," as it were, to the universal Christ Consciousness, but only while in contact with their respective higher selves, who themselves also had to be simultaneously and telepathically linked with their respective oversouls. As the oversoul directs a network of entities spanning both space and time, it is simply a matter of the oversoul allowing one or more of the souls serving as higher selves for those still evolving beings on Earth and other developing worlds to share in the various transmissions passing through the psychic communications matrix. Allegedly, what Ruth discovered from all of this is that Jesus and Mary lived together as man and wife some two thousand years ago in Nazareth, along with Mary Magdalene in a polygamous relationship.

The first step that Uriel told Ruth to carry out was the reorganization of the academy into the Unarius Educational Foundation, and to clear up any legal claims against the organization and any liens against its lands and properties in California. Ruth immediately went about in expanding the outreach of the foundation, instituting elaborate pageants and rites as well as airing regular programming on television via public access channels throughout the country.

---

552 Norman, *Voice of Venus,* 100
553 *Ibid.,* 100-101
554 Tumminia, 364

And following the death of Ruth Norman on 12 July 1993, Queen Uriel informed Ruth's Unarius students through a series of transmissions that she would be closer to them than ever before, now that she was free of any Earthly bonds or confining energies.[555] Now without a Monitor or a Queen, the Unariuns are awaiting further light and knowledge from the Space Brothers. Nevertheless, the organization's work continues to be carried out by the Normans' students on a global scale. According to one researcher of UFO religions, "The teachings say that the Unarius Science of Life expressed itself through master teachers who spoke in the idioms of the cultures they lived in, such as the discourses of Buddhism, Taoism, Theosophy, Swedenborgianism and the true teachings of Jesus of Nazareth."[556] The syncretism of Eastern religions and philosophies with Theosophy and the New Church of Emanuel Swedenborg clearly places the Unarius Foundation in the classic theosophical tradition, with the Normans following in the footsteps of Blavatsky, Layne, Adamski, Angelucci, Fry, Menger, King and others.

The Walk-Ins

In the parlance of the New Age, a "walk-in" is defined as a person whose original soul has departed his or her body and has been replaced with a new soul, either temporarily or permanently. A good example of this phenomenon is that of the Tibetan lama, Tuesday Lobsang Rampa, who traveled to Venus onboard a flying saucer along with a group of his brother monks, as reported in the chapter on "Contactees." If you ever feel that you are not from this planet, timeline, or dimension, perhaps you might be a walk-in. If you feel that your soul came here to live out certain experiences, and then something life-changing happened and you became another person, perhaps more evolved with a mission to heal and help humanity, then you might be a walk-in.[557] This aptly describes the life journey of a walk-in; and in this chapter we will look at two women who came to the realization that they were walk-ins from Venus.

ViVenus

Of course, we are all familiar with the notion of contactees, people who've encountered benevolent aliens with a message to spread on Earth about the dangers of our self-destructive ways, our nukes and our impending doom through the misuse and pollution of our planet's environment. We are also familiar with alien abductees or "experiencers," those persons who have been taken against their will by grays, reptoids or other gruesome aliens and subjected to invasive medical procedures as well as telepathic testing and interrogation. Yet there is another form of alien contact that has so far been ignored or, if it has been acknowledged, it has been ridiculed to the point of absurdity; and this is the claim made by some very human-looking individuals that they are themselves aliens from another planet here to bring a message of love and hope.[558] In this context, there are two women claiming to be from Venus, sent on a mission to save us from ourselves, that we will closely examine in this chapter. And the first is the activist-folk singer popularly known as ViVenus. Back in the 1960s through the early 1980s, ViVenus would travel across America from town to town, with her acoustic guitar in hand,

---

555   *Ibid.,* 366

556   *Ibid.,* 364

557   Ellie Crystal, "Walk-Ins," undated, *Crytstalinks*, http://www.crystalinks.com/walk_ins.html (Accessed 27 December 2014).

558   Sean Casteel, "From Venus with Love: Helpful Aliens in Human Form," 21 December 2011, *UFO Digest*, http://ufodigest.com/article/venus-love-helpful-aliens-human-form (Accessed 27 December 2014).

ready to belt out a song of love and peace to any individuals or group that gathered to hear her poignant message.

In 1982, before she seemed to completely disappear from the face of the Earth, ViVenus published a small, 68-page paperback account of her life on Venus, simply titled *ViVenus: Starchild*, with Global Communications in New York City. While now out of print, the small-circulation book was recently made available to Kindle readers on Amazon. The book was written by the supposed Earthly incarnation of the higher Venusian entity "ViVenus." It is assumed that the author gave herself the name ViVenus as a play on the abbreviation of "Vivian," perhaps her real first name on Earth, coupled with an easy reference to her alleged planet of origin.

ViVenus introduces herself in her *Starchild* book as follows:

"Dear Friend in Light, as you read this, let the light grow brighter within you.

Please understand that what I shall share here I must translate into the Earth tongue. I must – against the natural grain of me – name and label and classify in words the life I lived at home. I must seem to bottle and confine beauty as though it could be [so contained.] It is a strange task, and I pray I can achieve it.

We are free at home – not stopped by the policemen of words. We do not name beauty, but become one with it. And we do not question joy, but just enjoy it.

We have not "time." We live in the eternal now, so it will be difficult to pinpoint events and memories and celebrations. But divine love will give to me what I need, if you will keep in your mind all along these pages that Venus is a wordless world, a silent world. When we communicate at home, it is not by sound but by feeling. And if memory restores some "conversations" in this writing, understand it was not actually in words but in feeling that I must put into words.

I shall describe scenery, places, souls and moments in my Venusian life, and it will surprise me if I can do it, because at home I never had to put into words what was in my heart. What we do at home is flow in feelings, which turns into a state of being called love.

The "things" on Venus are not really "things" as they seem to be on Earth. *We make what we make, for the most part, with our minds.* No sounds of hammers pounding nails. We envision our house, and the house is there. We can envision its being built "brick by brick" or we can see it all at once, perfect and complete.

My name is Viv. Full name is ViVenus. This is my soul name, the one I was given for my mission on Earth. And I was given this name on the planet Venus where I was born.

I cannot prove my origin. I cannot prove that what I share with you is true about my heavenly home. I cannot even prove that I exist at all. Perhaps I am but a figment of your imagination. *What is proof is an illusion of the mind. What is faith is of the heart, and thus is real. If I do exist, then I am from Venus. I have no credentials, but one: my heart that does not stop loving you, oh, child of Earth.*

Before I came to the Earth plane, when I was at home on Venus, I had a vision of all of you. I felt that the Earth would welcome – if not me – then the truths I would discover to help them find the peace and inner contentment, independent of what happens on the outside. But now I know my vision was a mirage. The Earth seems satisfied to resign itself to depression, despair, and dead ends. Does this planet Earth need me from Venus? Did it ever need me? I still don't know."[559]

---

559 *Ibid.* with ViVenus quoted from introduction to *ViVenus: Starchild* (New York, New York: Globe Communications), 1982.

The sincerity of ViVenus comes through her prose like a searchlight; and throughout *Starchild*, she offers tempting bits and pieces of wondrous lyrics and short poems. The actual account of her childhood on Venus describes a place where no one uses language to communicate and where one simply wills things to appear. Like a scene from the 1998 movie about heaven, *What Dreams May Come*,[560] if a Venusian wanted to make a painting, all they would need to do is conjure a canvas out of nothing and then mentally transfer the image from their mind onto it, and voila, there is the desired painting.

ViVenus informs us, however, that the most important aspect of life on Venus is love. As feelings are the only true reality, the mind and its use of language to describe the world is simply not required. That is the true depth of feeling that ViVenus wants to impart to Earth, for it is clear to her, from a Venusian perspective, that most Earthlings suffer from a collective depression sent by enemy forces of darkness that lurk in our skies, ever ready to amplify the pain we have largely brought on ourselves.[561]

ViVenus sings of love and peace, but who would hear her important message? See http://ufodigest.com/article/venus-love-helpful-aliens-human-form.

Much as other channelers, contactees and mediums have already stated, we cannot detect life on Venus, thinking it a dead planet too hot to harbor any life as we know it, largely because the Venusians maintain a sustained rate of vibration at a level too high for our naked eyes or optical instruments to view them. Basically, the Venusians are so advanced spiritually that they remain invisible to most of us here on the Earth plane of existence.[562]

ViVenus is a woman who believes in lifelong learning, however; for back on Venus she attended a college to prepare her for an arduous missionary journey on Earth. She claims that her older brothers flew her to Earth in a flying saucer, what Venusians call a "swoop," named for its swooping motion as it travels. Upon arrival, she was given the fleshly covering of a young American woman who had recently pondered taking her own life because of her failure to succeed as a singer of love songs. ViVenus just slipped into her role so perfectly that even the relatives of the young woman she replaced failed to notice the difference. Wrote UFO investigator Sean Casteel: "It's a variation of the 'walk-in' motif that has been kicked around the past several decades in which an alien chooses to enter the body of an everyday mortal and work through that person to create positive change in the world."

The diligent ViVenus, now ensconced in the body of a young Earth woman, taught herself to play guitar well enough to accompany her singing. Hence, Vivenus went on to compose songs of love that embodied the doctrine that the heart is all there is and that perfect love is available outside the confines of human language to those who seek it in purity and compassion. So even while she may come across as a "little whacky" to some, they still must admit that

---

560 *What Dreams May Come* (Interscope Communications, 1998): Steven Deutsch, Barnet Bain, Producers; Vincent Ward, Director; Starring Robin Williams, Cuba Gooding, Jr., Annabella Sciorra.
561 Casteel
562 *Ibid.*

her intentions are good. Besides the continual grating of the skeptics, however, ViVenus began to feel a sense of frustration in dealing with life on Earth, and its variety of hardships. Noted ViVenus:

"The more I tried, the more I failed. The more I cared, the more indifference was shown to me. I found out what a lie was and what deception is. And I began hurting inside just as the girl before me. My determination to sing for the world turned into desperation. My struggles to stay afloat and keep a shelter angered my soul, for this struggle to survive on Earth was intruding on my mission."[563]

Unfortunately, ViVenus learned to fear and to mistrust, becoming familiar with the pain that comes from rejection, even from friends. Even so, she overcomes her depression by being reminded of her mission and being "shown" the plan for her future. At this, she decides to reveal her true identity as a Venuisan and begins to speak publicly to large crowds, starting in New York and moving westward. ViVenus writes down her feelings in a series of books, and holds weekly meetings for those interested in her story as well as publishing a twelve-page journal, simply called nothing more than *Feelings*.

It does not take long for ViVenus to realize that when she began her mission, she hoped to reach everyone on Earth with her teachings about perfect love. Unfortunately, as circumstances played out, she was able to share her message with only a few people. But on the positive side, there still exist news clippings of her 1980 campaign to have God listed as a write-in candidate for president in the race between Jimmy Carter and Ronald Reagan. Some local election boards, to include one in Oakland, California, stated that this would be fine, insofar as God was at least thirty-five years of age and born on American soil. Vivenus had even written a campaign song for God's candidacy called *It's Not Odd to Vote for God*, the message that appears on

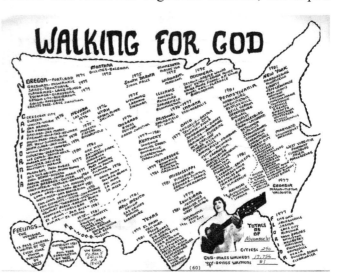

Last residing in Galilee, Pennsylvania, the Venusian woman left no forwarding address. See http://www.johnkeel. com/?cat=1.

the sign in the background of her photograph in this chapter. One can speculate that ViVenus and other Venusians are Libertarians. While socially liberal, believing in free love, ViVenus also recognizes that the differences between Democrats and Republicans are about the same as those between two nickels and a dime.

Omnec Onec

Much like ViVenus, Omnec Onec is another woman with an extraterrestrial experience not so easy to categorize. She is not your typical contactee, like Adamski or Menger, detailing <u>mere accounts</u> of face-to-face meetings with extraterrestrials. And she has nothing to do with

563   Quoted in Casteel

the more familiar abductee accounts of those being swept into a ship full of reptilians or grays, where these types of aliens usually conduct biological examinations with highly intrusive probing instruments. What we find in the case of Omnec Onec, however, is a fascinating autobiography of a young woman born and raised on the near Utopian planet of Venus. Greatly moved by the plight of humankind, Omnec Onec willingly departed the Planet of Love in order to come to our world and assist in cosmic missionary work as the "Venusian Ambassador to Earth."

The fifth dimensional entity known as Omnec Onec was born and raised on Venus. She sat at the feet of her spiritual master and her uncle, who primarily raised her, listening to their stories of missionary work among the barbarian inhabitants of Earth. These enlightened teachers encouraged the young Omnec Onec to go down to Earth and live out the rest of her life there, assuring her that upon the completion of her work on the carbon planet, she would reincarnate on Venus as a spiritual master in her own right. And in the process of undertaking this assignment, she would also clear out any karma accumulated from prior reincarnations. Upon hearing this, she took them up on their generous offer.

According to the Earth calendar, it was the year 1951. After bidding farewell to her Venusian family and friends, Omnec Onec flew in a scout craft to the capital city of her district, Teutonia, whence she boarded a mothership and took off from Venus to a lamasery in Tibet. This was necessary in order for her to adjust to the "lower vibrations" predominate on the Earth plane of existence. The monks, of course, being accustomed as they were to visits from their Venusian brothers and sisters, were more than delighted to help Omnec Onec in becoming acclimated to life on our quaint little sphere.

Four Earth years had passed and Omnec Onec had adjusted well. She mastered all of her lessons at the Tibetan school; and the chief lama of the temple deemed that she was ready to go out and make her mark in the world. This lama had consulted with a resident oracle and informed Omnec Onec that she was to go to the state of Tennessee in the United States of America, where a where young girl had just been involved in an automobile accident and wouldn't

Girl From Venus Tells Of Coming

By PETER C. WOLF, JR.
Staff Writer

Imagine, you are a new reporter for a newspaper and given the normal run-of-the-mill (not too great) stuff to cover.

Then it happens, your boss goes on vacation and you have to take his place for two weeks. You wonder what you are going to do for front page news.

Somebody tells you there is a girl, who says she is from Venus, living on your beat. You panic. That might be worth front page, after all how many stories do you read about real live Venusians living here on earth.

You get up tight and decide to interview her. You phone and a man answers: "Miss Venus is taking no calls but you can have an interview at 3 p.m."

Being a cub reporter trying to make good, you decide to play it straight.

She meets you at the door, looking a little Venusian you think, yet mostly earthling. You are asked in, and to look like a real professional get out your light meter and test the room for photography.

Miss Venus, acting extremely cool, sits waiting to start the interview. You panic.

You open with, "Tell me what life is like on Venus."

She says "Physically similar, but mentally superior and much more wonderful."

"Is there weather?"

"No."

"Is the form or body you are in the same as on Venus?"

"No, earth-form is heavier and thicker."

By now you know you aren't going to shake her on anything. You take a few pictures and let her talk.

She asks about your paper: "Is it daily?"

"No, weekly."

"What is it made up of?"

"Good news. No accidents or murders just the happier stuff that the dailies can't fit in."

"That sounds wonderful. I wouldn't feel like I am on earth anymore if there is such a paper."

"The worst thing we have to print is the obituary," I say. She says that it not bad since all those who die go to a better life.

You drop the interview idea altogether and play it straight in an attempt to retreat but you realize you have let yourself go.

You let her interview you.

Actually, "Viv" Venus is an alien being from the sun's second-closest planet. She has come to earth in a flying saucer and takes the identity of a girl who secretly committed suicide. She did not originally plan to expose herself. It just happened.

Her mission is to get people to believe in the young-er generation's "love not war" philosophy. A noble cause. But I doubt if even a Venusian could bridge the generation gap.

At least, the main idea comes across. People who expect the worst will get the worst.

Miss Venus, currently staying at 3620 SE 84th Ave., will leave the Portland area shortly and head for Detroit. She says there are many different planetary representatives on earth. She also says there is life on all the planets.

It seems that in America's Apollo 11 experience, everybody on the moon must have been on vacation. Anyway who cares? According to Venus, everything is going to groove within 20 years.

VIV VENUS is her name and the last name is also name of her planet. She is on earth presenting the Venus view that we should make 'love not war' here on earth. While in Portland she is staying at 3620 SE 84th Ave.

VENUS may be second closest to the Sun but it has a representative here on Earth. Viv Venus is currently visiting Portland giving talks to residents concerning the better world Earth will be in 1990.

Newspaper article where ViVenus explains her mission on Earth from Portland, Oregon, sometime toward the end of 1974, from "Uncategorized" file of paranormal researcher, John A. Keel. See http://www.johnkeel.com/wp-content/uploads/2014/11/VIVENUS4A.jpg.

have much time left to live. The young Tennessee girl was in a coma, but her prayers ascended to Venus, where her petition to join with the angels there would soon be granted.

As the last breath was exhaled from the body of the young Tennessee girl on 20 August 1955, Omnec Onec was "waiting in the wings," so to speak, to jump in and take over where the lass would leave off. Along with Omnec Onec came two other Venusians to meet the spirit of the girl and to escort her to the lamasery in Tibet, where she would be prepared to be reincarnated in a new form on Venus. As for Omnec Onec, her adventures on Earth were just beginning. The monitors in the hospital suddenly came back on, and the young girl, whom everyone still presumed to be Sheila, quickly recovered. Omnec Onec kept up the pretense of being Sheila, going home with her new parents and living out the remainder of what would have been Sheila's life. Eventually, she married, had children, divorced, and wrote a book about her experiences on Earth. And in the process, Omnec Onec became a noted, globe-trotting celebrity.

Stan Schultz, the ex-husband of Sheila/Omnec Onec, is a grandfather and semi-retired artist, dancer,

1961 – FIRST PHOTO OF VIVENUS ON EARTH

Unbelievably beautiful in body and spirit, it was surprising that so few paid any attention to ViVenus. See http://www.johnkeel.com/wp-content/uploads/2014/11/VIVENUS1.jpg.

minister, musician and writer. He loves to take long nature walks and cultivate organic food. He says that "natural healing" is one of his big passions, along with listening to a wide variety of music genres, especially New Age. He also likes watching programming aired over the Public Broadcasting Service and exploring cyberspace. Schultz maintains several blog sites, but the one devoted to his ex-wife, "What Now, Grasshopper?" is the most revealing. Writes Schultz:

"I'm guessing that most of you who read the title of this article might be thinking that it is a set up for a joke. In fact it's no joke. Her Venusian name is Omnec Onec. If you have not heard her story, you might want to continue reading this little introduction.

Omnec Onec, the Venusian Ambassador to Earth. See http://galacticchannelings.com/english/omnec-onec.html.

We met on Wells Street, Chicago during the hippie era in the middle 60s. She and her girlfriend were playing at shooting hippies with toy rifles. I watched this little melodrama unfold.

Some of the hippies would play along and fall to the ground. The cops stopped her and checked out her weapons and discovered they were toys and told her to cease and desist.

After they drove down the street, the girls started up again. The cute blonde one shot me but I didn't play her game. I was however very attracted to her, so I walked up and introduced myself and invited her to tea. She accepted. There used to be a restaurant called the Stagecoach on the corner of North and Wells; we went in there. She kissed me and the rest, as the cliché goes, is history.

We ended up staying together for more than ten years, marrying and having two kids together. She spent two plus years writing an autobiography with the help of a writer friend and we had lots of wonderful adventures together. She had a hard time getting taken seriously. Jerry Springer had her on back in the early days of his show, along with our kids and me. The theme was, "What was it like to grow up with a mom who said she was from Venus?" They intended to make a mockery of her, with a panel of scientists, etc. But Sheila/Omnec

Painting is Omnec Onec's depiction of Teutonia, a city on Venus. She flew on a cigar-shaped mothership, like the one on the upper left, to a lamasery in Tibet, in 1951. See http://omnec-onec.com/?attachment_id=169.

impressed everyone with her dignity and the seriousness and credibility of her presentation. To this day she is the guest that has gotten the most mail in response to a show.

We split in '76 and soon after she moved to Germany. She was taken more seriously there and spent many years giving talks, seminars and workshops all over Europe. She managed to get featured by all the major media in Europe and basically had a career telling her story and inspiring people with her mind-blowing experience.

Visa problems and other issues now have her back in the states. I would normally be babysitting my grandsons tonight, but she is in town so I am getting a break. So here I am returning the favor by writing this little piece.

She had a two-volume, 400-page autobiography that tells her story published years ago. Currently it is out of print. If you look on Amazon, copies are selling from $400 to $2000. It is still available in German translation and there will be a Japanese translation published in '08.

I have recently decided to again help her bring her story to a larger audience. We have had our share of differences over the years but the love bond is still strong and mutual. And I think her story is so amazing that I can't imagine anything more important to do.

Is she authentic? I decided so many years ago, and I got important confirmations from authorities I trusted. Of course this is the sort of thing that you have to decide for yourself.

Science tells us that it is 700 or 800 degrees on the surface of Venus and the planet cannot support human habitation. NASA has probed and mapped the surface and found nothing that looks like life as we know it. So what is the truth? Just remember that cutting edge science used to be sure that the Earth was flat and that the Sun revolved around the Earth. So much for science!

I think she has an important mission and message for us all in these crazy, fast changing times. I think it is worth listening to what she has to say. You have to judge for yourself. Be sure to check out the little video excerpt of one of her talks on You Tube: http://youtube.com/watch?v=40jo5uElYNI."[564]

---

564 Stan Schultz, "My Ex-wife was born on Venus," 11 January 2008, *What Now, Grasshopper?* http://whatnowgrasshopper.blogspot.com/2008/01/my-ex-wife-was-born-on-venus.html (Accessed 5 January 2015).

Omnec Onec's account certainly makes for an inspiring story of interplanetary compassion.

In the process of telling us her life story, Omnec Onec also provides her readers with an in-depth education in Venusian metaphysics. It is told with the kind of attention to detail and narrative precision that makes it hard to dismiss as simple New Age rants. Sean Casteel of *UFO Digest* has investigated the claims of Omnec Onec and makes the following comments concerning her book:

"The beauty of the Venusian landscape, which exists at a higher vibration than Earthly mortals can see or hear, is described in breathtaking, exquisite language that carries the reader into everyday life on another planet with a practiced ease that goes well beyond any notion of science-fiction fakery.

There is also the part of the story involving the dysfunctional Earth family that Omnec Onec has traveled to be a part of. It is an emotionally powerful tale to say the least. The sentiment aroused by the Venusian transplant's going with her mortal cousins to see the science fiction classic "The Thing from Outer Space," for example, displays an eager willingness to join suffering humanity and bear some of its burdens. There is the obvious irony of the benevolent alien seeing a Hollywood depiction of a hostile one, but Omnec also talks about learning to wear makeup and the same yearning to grow up felt by all adolescents, even though she is already hundreds of years old in Venusian time."[565]

Omnec Onec agrees with other contactees in asserting that human-looking aliens are already here, operating undercover but working to help us through the world-shattering difficulties that lie waiting for us, just around the bend. The Venusians want to assist us in overcoming some of our character faults that threaten to destroy us from within. Of this, the *UFO Digest* researcher Casteel notes that, "Current research into the alien abduction phenomenon has found that the hybrids being created by the alien genetics program have lately begun to be more and more human-looking, which adds some real world support to Omnec's story."[566]

Like countless others who have interviewed her, Casteel remarks that "Omnec actually looks the part." She definitely comes across as a beautiful young woman. Her Nordic good looks and ice-blonde hair can make anyone wonder if she is indeed a product of "something out of this world," concluded the UFO journalist.[567]

The New Age belief in walk-ins is now said to include a number of variant experiences such as channeling, telepathic contact with extraterrestrial intelligences, or soul merging. In the latter case, the original soul is said to remain present, coexisting or integrating with the new one. But for the most part, walk-ins are higher frequency aspects of someone's soul, here to heal and help during these critical and transitory times. Once the walk-ins allegedly enter an individual's body, often after a traumatic experience, serious illness or near death experience, the person's grid consciousness is forever changed, but always going from negative to positive. In most cases where extraterrestrials have walked in to a body, the prior occupant's life functions have usually ceased and the alien entity needs to resurrect the physical form in order to continue their mission on Earth. In the cases of ViVenus and Omnec Onec, these were more instances of- to paraphrase the great Sufi mystic Rumi- "leaving the circle of time and entering the circle of love."

---

565 Casteel
566 *Ibid.*
567 *Ibid.*

Chapter VII:
"Closer" Encounters

"Love comforteth like sunshine after rain,
But Lust's effect is tempest after sun.
Love's gentle spring doth always fresh remain;
Lust's winter comes ere summer half be done.
Love surfeits not, Lust like a glutton dies;
Love is all truth, Lust full of forged lies."
—William Shakespeare, *Venus and Adonis* (1592-1593)

By the mid-1960s, the Silence Group had largely succeeded in convincing the public that life, at least as we have come to know it here on Earth, could not possibly exist on Venus. NASA's spin doctors were working overtime, pumping out misinformation regarding space research and, in the process, obscuring what they really knew about UFOs, their occupants, and their origin on other planets within our solar system. Hollywood, of course, was complicit in generating this barrage of propaganda heaped upon our heads, promoting the standard fallacies about Venus and other worlds. What they wanted us to know was this: That if there was any life to be found out there, it was definitely going to be of a hostile nature.

For example, in *Zontar: The Thing from Venus* (1966), a misguided scientist enables a grotesque and giant crab-like Venusian creature to come to Earth in order to help solve humankind's problems. Nevertheless, the alien Zontar has other ideas. Once arriving here, it goes about disabling the power supply of the entire planet and taking possession of important officials with mind control devices. Movies and television shows like this helped to build up a formidable "wall of ridicule" around the entire UFO phenomenon and the possibility of other forms of intelligent life existing alongside us in the solar system. Hence, the science of ufology became associated with sinister and bizarre-appearing aliens from the darkest and deepest recesses of outer space. These creatures were scrutinizing our planet with envious eyes, studying our planet with the idea of carrying out a program of military conquest. It really wasn't until the end of the twentieth century that ufologists were able to break out of this mold. Putting aside all of the negative hoopla, they started to take another look at the intention of extraterrestrials in physically interacting with humans on more intimate levels, as well as any possible intentions in their collection of human genetic materials.

Up through the late 1960s, NICAP- with retired Marine Corps Major Donald E. Keyhoe at its helm- was the foremost privately funded UFO research organization in the world. But despite the dramatic increase in UFO occupant reports since the establishment of NICAP in 1956, the group's board of directors continued to ignore those reports involving any "close encounters of the third kind." In the estimation of most NICAP board members, such UFO incidents, where animated beings are purportedly sighted in relation to a UFO, lacked any tinge of "credibility." Inasmuch as its director Keyhoe was the leading proponent for the extraterrestrial origin of the flying saucers, it seemed like a confused position for the NICAP board to take, at least publicly. After all, if aliens traversed the vast distances of outer space to visit our planet, wouldn't they at least step out of their saucer for a little while to take a look around and survey the situation before blasting back to wherever it was they came from?

With the passing of time, however, it has come to light that NICAP's leadership, behind closed doors, was taking an altogether different position. Noted former NICAP Assistant Director Richard H. Hall, the negative position toward incidents involving close encounters of the third kind was more "tactical and not doctrinaire."[569] In other words, the organization was not necessarily dismissing occupant reports out of hand, but electing to focus on other aspects of the UFO phenomenon that would be perceived by mainstream observers as less outlandish. Keyhoe believed that the attention given to the contactees of the late 1940s-1950s was a key factor in diminishing the overall credibility of ufology and the acceptance of NICAP as a serious research organization in both the eyes of the public and the powers-that-be.

With the wave of UFO sightings throughout the 1960s capturing the public's imagination, by mid-decade the membership of NICAP had peaked at 14,000. But the failure of NICAP to pay due attention to many interesting and seemingly reliable UFO occupant reports from around the globe was siphoning off members who affiliated with other organizations, such as the Aerial Phenomena Research Group (APRG) of Seattle, Washington, or the Aerial Phenomena Research Organization (APRO) of Tucson, Arizona.

The latter organization, APRO, was established in January 1952 by Jim and Coral Lorenzen of Sturgeon Bay, Wisconsin. [570] But because most of the UFO reports that APRO was receiving originated in the American Southwest, the group moved to Tucson, Arizona, in 1961. APRO had branches in nearly every state and many foreign countries as well, especially throughout Latin America. It remained active until late 1988, when Coral passed away and Jim transferred their vast UFO archives, consisting of some 15,000 sightings and encounters reports, from storage in their garage to the Center for UFO Studies in nearby Scottsdale, Arizona, the civilian research organization established by astronomer J. Allen Hynek in 1973.

APRO had a large staff of consulting Ph.D. scientists and stressed accurate and detailed field investigations. Two of the more notable from the scientific community were Dr. James E. McDonald of the University of Arizona, a well-known atmospheric physicist, and perhaps the leading scientific UFO researcher of his time, and Dr. James Harder of the University of California at Berkeley, a civil and hydraulic engineering professor, who acted as director of research from 1969-1982. Both of these eminent doctors were among six scientists who testified about UFOs before the United States House of Representatives Committee on Science and Astronautics on 29 July 1968, during a *one-day* symposium on the subject. Astronomer J. Allen Hynek also worked closely with APRO on numerous occasions and cited it as one of the best civilian UFO groups of his day, consisting largely of sober, serious-minded people capable of valuable contributions to the subject.

Unlike NICAP, however, APRO was not afraid to investigate those cases on the cutting edge of ufology, even those where the UFO occupants went so far as to engage in sexual relations with human beings. And while NICAP mostly concerned itself with investigating sightings in the United States, APRO was aggressively recruiting a large contingent of qualified scientists to act as its field investigators throughout the world, researching cases of every kind.

In the spring of 1957, APRO recruited Dr. Olavo T. Fontes, a gastroenterologist at the National School of Medicine in Rio de Janeiro, who joined APRO as its representative for the whole of Brazil, a country as large as the continental United States that had been consistently visited by the mysterious flying saucers since the early 1950s. This was a huge plus for APRO, for up until Fontes' enlistment in its ranks, APRO's files were considered "sparse" from this vast Portuguese-speaking country. Now, however, with Fontes onboard, the APRO files began to bulge with the cases he investigated and filed. Besides being a professor at the National School, Fontes was also in private practice. Fontes told the Lorenzens that when he first heard of the "saucers" in the late 1940s, he thought they were a typical Yankee phenomenon. But that estimation quickly changed when these mysterious objects began showing up throughout Brazil in tremendous numbers in the early 1950s.

The Vilas-Boas Incident

One of the most memorable cases thoroughly investigated by Fontes, from APRO's Brazilian files, was that of a 23-year old farmer, Antonio Vilas-Boas, who was working out in his field to avoid the intense heat of the Sun, on the outskirts of São Francisco de Sales in the south central region of the country, on 16 October 1957, when the engine of his tractor suddenly came to an abrupt stop. Villas-Boas dismounted his vehicle to check out the motor, and after a few minutes took notice of a large "flying disk" silently hovering directly overhead. He estimated the UFO to be about "half the size of a regulation soccer field," making it about 55 meters in diameter.

The craft softly touched down on his field and the farmer saw three human-like entities stepping out. The aliens wore what appeared to be some sort of gas masks and were slowly approaching him; and Vilas-Boas panicked. He had no idea as to the intention of the aliens; so he gritted his teeth and balled up his hands into tight fists, ready to duke it out with them, if that's what it came down to. The aliens sensed the defiance in the farmer and rushed him, pinning his arms behind his back and dragging him kicking and screaming into their saucer. They removed his clothing and tied him up to a metal table, where they administered a meticulous medical examination, scanning his body from the crown of his head to the tips of his toes with some overhead conical device similar in appearance to a small x-ray machine.

The aliens apparently found their captive to be in a healthy physical condition, for after the scan they injected him with some unknown substance and immediately left him alone in the room. Vilas-Boas seemed to have lost track of time. All he remembered of this duration was that it was for "quite a long time." But after this extended period, the farmer recalled that the door opened and he saw a beautiful, naked white woman.

At this point, nature took its course and the seductive alien girl turned the young man on. And as the guests often say on the *Jerry Springer Show*, "one thing led to another" and Vilas Boas was making love to the extraterrestrial female for several hours, without saying a word, other than uttering some sexual groans. This female alien was a little more than five feet in height, about the same size as his three masked abductors. But as for the female, Vilas-Boas noted that she had a small, pointed chin and large, blue catlike eyes. The hair on her head was long and white (somewhat like the platinum-blonde hair of Omnec Onec); but her underarms and pubic hair were bright red.[572] Vilas-Boas said that during their act of sexual intercourse, the female did not kiss him but instead nipped him on the chin. And in an extensive interview with the APRO field representative, Vilas-Boas remarked: "When she was walking away (and they

---

569 Ann Druffel, Firestorm: *Dr. James E. McDonald's Fight for UFO Science* (Columbus, NC: Granite Publishing, 2003), 93.

570 "Jim and Coral Lorenzen," undated, Northern Ontario UFO Research and Study, http://www.noufors.com/Jim_and_Coral_Lorenzen.htm (Accessed 7 June 2015): "In August 1951, they moved to Sturgeon Bay, Wisconsin, where James obtained a job as engineer at a radio station. Correspondent for the Green Bay *Press-Gazette*, Coral writes articles about flying saucers. Astonished by the amount of mail she receives, she is convinced the USAF is hiding the truth."

were outside of the craft saying their good-byes), she turned around, pointed at her stomach, smiled and pointed up to the sky" in the direction of the Evening Star (Venus). On the evening in question, however, Venus and Saturn appeared to be in alignment, so Vilas-Boas wasn't sure as to the planet of her origin.

Following this close encounter of the intimate kind, Boas claimed to have suffered from nausea and weakness, in addition to headaches and lesions on his skin which appeared with a kind of light bruising. José Martins, a local journalist, upon hearing Vilas-Boas' story referred him to Dr. Olavo Fontes, who physically examined the farmer and determined that his illness had resulted from exposure to a large dose of radiation. One ufologist who conducted an in-depth probe of the Vilas-Boas incident, wrote the following:

"Among [Boas] symptoms were "pains throughout the body, nausea, headaches, loss of appetite, ceaselessly burning sensations in the eyes, coetaneous lesions at the slightest of light bruising...which went on appearing for months, looking like small reddish nodules, harder than the skin around them and protuberant, painful when touched, each with a small central orifice yielding a yellowish thin waterish discharge." The skin surrounding the wounds presented "a hyper-chromatic violet-tinged area."[568]

After this intimate encounter, Vilas-Boas began to crave knowledge, voraciously reading everything he could get his hands on. This is not an uncommon experience for abductees or contactees. And one year later, he entered the department of law at the local university, successfully graduating and going on to become a brilliant lawyer. He went on to marry and have four children. But most importantly, he stuck with his story throughout his life, until his death on 17 January 1991.

Extraterrestrial "Lonely Hearts"

While the Vilas-Boas incident might be considered as a mere "hook up," at best, the possibility of more durable and loving extraterrestrial relationships has been a hot literary topic since the dawn of the science fiction era. One of the more popular books in this genre that immediately comes to mind is Jacqueline Susann's *Yargo: A Love Story,* the one and only sci-fi romance by the renowned author of the best selling *Valley of the Dolls. Yargo* was Susann's first work, written in 1956, during the height of the contactee movement. She was also dating the famous actor Yul Brynner at the time; and the novel reflects both the feel of that era and the heroic qualities of Brynner as imputed to the alien love interest, Yargo.

Susann was 38 years old when she authored *Yargo.* She was an intellectually gifted writer and is reported to have scored nearly 140 on a standardized IQ test. Very few women were concerned with science fiction in the 1950s; so perhaps it was her intelligent and inquisitive mind that sparked her breach into this new and challenging area. She was definitely ahead of her time in taking on the writing of *Yargo,* providing us with an account of a very young lady, Janet Cooper, who at the age of 21 is abducted by human-like aliens, quite by accident. They mistake her as a prominent scientist who can help save their world. When they find out she is just a secretary on Earth, they decide that it is too risky to send her back home as she might not be trusted to keep their existence a secret. So they opt to send her to Mars, to live out the rest of her life on a remote colony there. But along the way back to our solar system, Yargo and his crew,

568   Bruce Rux, *Architects of the Underworld: Unriddling Atlantis, Anomalies of Mars, and the Mystery of the Sphinx* (Berkeley, California: Frog Books, 1996), 109–120.

572   Mark Pilkington, *Mirage Men: A Journey into Disinformation, Paranoia and UFOs* (New York, New York: Little, Brown Book Group, 2010), 105, 108-114.

to include Janet, are captured by a contingent of large Venusian bumblebees. They are transported to the Venusian mothership where Janet and Yargo affect their escape, battling a 200-pound queen bee in the process. Eventually, one thing leads to another with Janet and Yargo becoming an interstellar item.

Science fiction critic Terry R. Hill wrote the following about *Yargo* in his blog:

"In reading this story nearly seventy years later, the many technical mistakes and inaccuracies with their space travel, the alien environments, and life forms encountered are very noticeable. However, if one takes into account that this was written around the time of the first artificial satellite about Earth, before humans had even gone into orbit, before we went to the moon and only had fuzzy images of Venus from terrestrial telescopes, much of it is easily forgivable and should be treated as a snapshot of our understanding of the cosmos at the time of writing. And therein lies the difficulty of seeing into the future and writing science fiction; sometimes you just don't get it right."[569]

The naked alien woman signaled that she was pregnant from Vilas-Boas' sperm and would return to her home planet to give birth to their baby. See http://s327.photobucket.com/user/cmsahe/media/vilasboas5tif.jpg.html.

In light of we have learned about Venus from the contactees, historians and students of world religions, however, one can easily turn this around and remark on just how right Susann did "get it." And most importantly, the book places an emotional young Earth woman in a strange and threatening alien environment for the express purpose of allowing us, the readers, to come to grips with what it really means to be a transcendent "human being." While it is unclear to Hill what subplots and subtexts Susann intended, he does take note that now, in the early part of the 21st century, "one could read that the majority of this book is more of a coming of age for the heroine. But upon closer inspection, it can be said that it is more of a veiled venture to explore what it is to be a strong woman in the 50s (think Agatha Christie, Queen Elizabeth II, etc.) where a woman must be like a man, unfeeling and aggressive, to be taken seriously and what Susann feels women inevitably lose in the process."

Jacqueline Susann (1918-1974) ventured into the sci-fi genre with *Yargo*, an extraterrestrial love story. See www.pinterest.com.

Hill wondered if there was some aspiring science fiction writer out there who could rework the story, modernize the characters, fix the technical aspects and re-release it to possibly have a new generation fall in love with *Yargo* all over again. In my opinion, this would not be necessary. Overall*, Yargo* can be classified as excellent literature in the sense that it directly reflects the status of society at the time it was written. It serves

569   Terry R. Hill, "Yargo by Jacqueline Susann – Book Review," *Terry R. Hill* blog, 14 June 2013, http://terryrhill.net/?p=168 (Accessed 15 February 2015).

as a type of time capsule for the era of the UFO contactees and the dawn of the Space Age. It can authentically stand on its own merits.

Interestingly, as a tribute to Susann, the writers of *Star Trek IV: The Voyage Home* (1986), have the twenty-third century Admiral James T. Kirk and his Vulcan science officer Spock engage in the following conversation when they time travel back to late twentieth century San Francisco, California:

Spock: Admiral, may I ask you a question?

James T. Kirk: Spock, don't call me Admiral. You used to call me Jim. Don't you remember "Jim"? What's your question?

Spock: Your use of language has altered since our arrival. It is currently laced with, shall I say, more colorful metaphors-- "Double dumb-ass on you" and so forth.

Kirk: You mean the profanity?

Spock: Yes.

Kirk: That's simply the way they talk here. Nobody pays any attention to you unless you swear every other word. You'll find it in all the literature of the period.

Spock: For example?

Kirk: *[thinks] Oh, the complete works of Jacqueline Susann*, the novels of Harold Robbins….

Spock: Ah... *The giants.*

While most of the above referenced Susann and Robbins' novels have been made into movies, *Yargo* has yet to see the silver screen. But in light of the recent success of the off-beat *Guardians of the Galaxy,* one can easily imagine that *Yargo* could also prove itself a box-office blockbuster. Apparently, there is a big, untapped market out there for science fiction romances.

One of the better films in this category was John Carpenter's 1984 production of *Starman.* It tells the story of an alien (Jeff Bridges) who has come to Earth in response to the invitation found on the gold phonograph record affixed to the Voyager 2 space probe, launched in 1977. This was the phonographic disk with a message of peace designed by the eminent astronomer Dr. Carl Sagan, inviting visitors to visit planet Earth. As the Voyager 2 probe is intercepted by an alien ship, the extraterrestrials send a small scout vessel to establish first contact with Earth. But rather than greeting the craft, the United States government shoots it down with a surface-to-air missile, where it crashes somewhere in the vicinity of Chequamegon Bay, Wisconsin. The alien, looking like a shining blue energy orb, finds the home of recently widowed Jenny Hayden (Karen Allen); and once inside, he/it uses the DNA from a lock of hair from her deceased husband, a house-painter named Scott Hayden, to clone a new body. The stunned Jenny witnesses this unique transformation.

Science officer Spock and Admiral James T. Kirk in *Star Trek IV: The Voyage Home* (Paramount Pictures, 1986), pay homage to Jacqueline Susann. See www.scene-stealers.com.

The Starman (Jeff Bridges) carries with him seven small silver spheres which provide energy to perform miraculous feats. He uses the first to send an SOS to his people about his craft being destroyed and also to let them know that the "environment" is hostile. He then arranges to rendezvous with them at "Landing Area One" at Meteor Crater in Arizona in just three days. The alien then uses the second sphere to create a holographic map of the United States, coercing Jenny into taking him to Arizona. All the while, government agents are on their trail, trying to intercept them and take the Starman into custody. At first, Jenny is fearful of the alien; but as they travel across the country and get to know each other better, they fall deeply in love. The Starman is forced to use up all but one of his remaining spheres in protecting themselves and others from the dastardly deeds of government agents and ignorant folk that they encounter along the road to the rendezvous point. Nevertheless, they manage to meet up with the mothership at the crater, but not before Jenny finds out that she is pregnant with a hybrid alien baby. But before the Starman departs, he hands over the last sphere to Jenny and explains that their son will know what to do with it.

Jeff Bridges was nominated for the Academy Award for Best Actor, in addition to being nominated for the Golden Globe Award for Best Actor – Drama. He was also received the Saturn Award for Best Actor, with Karen Allen also receiving a nod for Best Actress from the Academy of Science Fiction, Fantasy and Horror Films. *Starman* was itself nominated Best Science Fiction Film; and Jack Nitzsche received a Golden Globe nomination for its score. *Starman* was an excellent movie, framing a new mindset where non-human aliens come across as more genuinely human than most of the Earthlings they manage to run into.

Love Reincarnate

Unlike the fictional love stories that revolved around *Yargo* and *Starman*, however, some humans and extraterrestrials have become true "best friends forever," as the millennial generation might say. It became well known in the 1950s that aliens often visited Earth with more than the intention of just "sewing their oats," so to speak, but with genuine matrimonial purposes. Prominent contactee Howard Menger was one of the few humans who not only had a chance to meet an alien female, but marry one.

Howard Menger was born on 17 February 1922 in Brooklyn, New York, but raised on a farm in the rural borough of High Bridge, New Jersey, situated in the northwestern part of the state. The young Howard enjoyed exploring the surrounding woods with his dog and younger brother Alton, as well as swimming in a nearby lake with his friends. He enjoyed a carefree yet energetic youth.

When Howard was eight and Alton was four years of age, however, they began to notice the flying disks and other strange objects swooping down out of the sky and hovering over their farm. Their parents also observed some unusual aerial phenomena in the night sky over their property. And while their father was a staunch Catholic and their mother an unyielding Methodist, they nevertheless came to an agreement that angels were real and flying over their home for some as yet to be determined spiritual reason. So while the boys were initially afraid, Howard somehow sensed that his parents were right in their assumptions about these craft being piloted by angels, and managed to convince his brother that the intentions of their occupants could only be benevolent.

Howard's days of playful romps in the New Jersey countryside were soon

The *Starman* and Jenny take distracted driving to new levels. See <u>www.notcoming.com</u>.

coming to an end, however, when at age ten he caught sight of a large saucer-shaped object landing in a wooded area just beyond the Menger family's farm house. Running out to the craft, he spotted a beautiful angelic woman perched on a large rock. The woman identified herself as an inhabitant of Venus and also told Howard not to be afraid for she had come to Earth on a mission of mercy to help humankind. She spoke to him as she would an adult, telling him of his past incarnations on other planets and also of his destiny. Howard sensed that pure love emanated from this angelic Venusian woman.

The young man was so flabbergasted by the encounter that he found himself at a loss for words. But he paid close attention to every word pronounced by the angel, etching them deeply into his mind for future reference. Despite his young age, Howard came to understand that the Venusians were in the process of contacting those whom they had worked with before on their home world and other planets. The beautiful Venusian, with long blond tresses and garbed in white flowing, shiny robes, also explained to the boy that she was over 500 years old and not even considered to be of middle age back on her home world. She also said that "Venusians live with nature and not against it," and that this was something that Earthlings would have to learn to do if they were going to survive as a species.

The years passed, however, and with the advent of World War II, Menger found civilian employment as a munitions handler at the Picatinny Arsenal in his home state. By late 1942, however, as the war heated up, Menger signed up as an enlisted man, completing his basic training in El Paso, Texas, whence he was sent to Hawaii and later on to Okinawa, where he was injured in battle, blinded temporarily, and escaped death on several occasions. It was while in the military that his contacts began again with highly advanced beings from other planets in our solar system who warned him of future events that would soon transpire on planet Earth. The woman appeared again to Menger while stationed in Hawaii and said that, "Wars do not exist on Venus.... But your planet is in great danger if your people do not stop warring with each other." Clearly, the enchanting Venusian could see into the years ahead, that it would not be enough that the Axis Powers should be defeated, but that the Western world, led by the United States, would strive against the Eastern world, led by the Soviet Union, dividing the globe into conflicting proxy states.

Contactee Howard Menger, the "East Coast Adamski," 1922-2009. See www.philipcoppens.com.

After the war and upon honorable discharge from the military, Menger returned home to New Jersey, where the contacts with advanced, angelic beings continued. With extraterrestrial craft landing almost continually on his farm in High Bridge, it comes as no surprise that he was soon contacted by the newly formed Central Intelligence Agency, where he was assigned a top secret mission. Menger and several witnesses captured some of these landings on 8mm film, but Menger was required to turn over most of this film to the United States government. Of Menger in the post-war period, Aileen Garoutte, the former Director of the UFO Contactee Center International in Seattle, Washington, wrote the following:

"With a lot of courage, and little backup, Howard Menger started a "crusade" to enlighten the planet Earth. He spread the message (from the angels, as he calls them) on radio, television and cross-country lectures. He spoke with George Adamski, George Van Tassel, Trumann Bethurum, and others who were also receiving enlightened extra-terrestrial messages. Each had their own mission, but joined together in a single cause: to rescue the people from themselves.

During his mission of enlightenment, Howard met Connie Weber. Their connection was immediate. Her talent as a writer and his incredible story would be put together in their first book, *From Outer Space to You*. The two "pioneers of truth" would collaborate on several books, lectures, and tours. Howard was well-known throughout the United States and Europe, and appeared on the *Jack Paar* television talk show, and the *Long John Nebel* WOR radio talk show. He continued to work with the government and shared his secrets of truth and technology."[570]

The beautiful Venusian woman that first met Howard at the rock on his family farm back in 1932 appeared to him yet again in June 1946 at the same location. At their parting, Howard asked her if he would ever see her again, to which the Venusian gave a surprising response: "No, Howard, but one will come who is my sister. She will work with you and be with you for the duration of this life span. She is my sister Marla from Venus, and incarnated on this planet some years ago in your state of New Jersey. She is not too far from you at this moment. One day you will meet her."

Naturally, Howard wanted to know how he would recognize the woman's sister. To this, she responded, "Don't worry; you will recognize her the moment your eyes fall upon her. Once in her presence you will know that she is the one of whom I speak. And you will discover she looks very much like me!"

Throughout 1956, George Van Tassel came out from California to the East Coast in order to present a series of public lectures on the flying saucer phenomenon as well as to do some radio and television interviews. At this time, George Adamski was on a world tour, so Van Tassel and a few other contactees were picking up the slack in keeping the American citizenry informed about all matters pertaining to the presence of aliens among us. Menger too was doing his part to illuminate the curious American populace by holding flying saucer meetings and sky watches from his backyard at High Bridge. Also, as some of Menger's photos entered into circulation within ufology circles, his fame spread far and wide. Naturally, Van Tassel made sure that he would meet up with Howard Menger, the "East Coast Adamski," as long as he was in the area.

In June 1956, a full ten years after Menger's last encounter with the beautiful Venusian at the rock, Van Tassel came to address a monthly meeting of the High Bridge flying saucer club, convened in Menger's back yard. Of Van Tassel's speaking engagement at his home, Menger writes:

"Ten years later, while listening to George Van Tassel speak, I had seen Marla for the first time; and as the girl on the rock had stated, I recognized her instantly.

I looked at a silent, serious young woman with a sad face. My first recognition came not from physical appearance, but a feeling of oneness with the soul of the girl. And as I looked at her face carefully, my heart almost jumped out of my body: Marla bore a striking resemblance to the girl on the rock! She was shorter, and her hair, tied in a tight severe bun at the nape of her neck, was not quite as light a blonde as that of the Venusian woman; her eyes were blue-green

570 Aileen Garoutte, "The Menger Story," 28 August 2005, UFO Experiences, http://ufoexperiences.blogspot. com/2005/08/menger-story.html (Accessed 15 February 2015).

with flecks of gold, and the Venusian's had been golden. Yet my breath almost stopped when I noticed the similarity.

I enquired about the young lady, learning she had recently become widowed. Asking Van to come with me in order to give me courage to meet her, we walked over to her after the lecture, and I renewed an association with someone who had been very close to me in the past.

I remember her blushing when Van told her that she bore a scar on her upper leg, one of the ways in which certain people are "marked" and are known to their own as 'one of themselves.' Marla smiled and said, 'But I have never seen a flying saucer, or had a contact with a space person.' To which Van replied somewhat enigmatically, 'You don't have to!'"[571]

Menger discovered that on Earth Marla then went by the name of Connie Weber. Since he first looked at her, the memory veil had been lifting from Menger's mind. He realized that Connie was the Venusian Marla that he had long awaited to come into his life; and that he had known her before in a previous lifetime and had loved her deeply. But most importantly, he understood that both he and Connie/Marla were "meant to be one." Of course, while at first glance this would appear to be a happy revelation for Menger, it also bode for tragic times ahead. After all, Howard was already married, and with children at that. The contactee found himself in a complete state of confusion, divided between fond anticipation and a sorrowful gut-wrenching sense of what would soon occur in his family life.

Outer-space enthusiasts at Yucca Valley, Calif., rally. Saucerite George Van Tassel (scanning sky, foto right), with author Howard Menger.

After the first meeting, Menger noted that, "Marla and I were irresistibly drawn to each other; and though both of us tried to fight off the predicted outcome, we were caught up in the overwhelming remembrance of a long-ago promise to each other," one that was made while he was a Saturnian envoy to the planet Venus. His meeting up with Marla must have jarred his consciousness to an awareness of his last incarnation. While he could not remember all the details of his life as a Saturnian, Menger did recall being part of a family with parents, brothers and sisters. Of his prior life on the ringed planet, Menger explained:

"I was a spiritual teacher who instructed the young. I had at my disposal a space craft which I used for traveling to different planets for the purpose of both teaching and gaining knowledge. I taught many subjects, including the positive use of telepathic projection, and the study of God's Universal Laws. As such a teacher, I was known as one of the "Sons of Naro," "Sol do Naro," a teacher of Light who came from a region close to the Sun which was called Naro."[572]

---

571 Howard Menger, From Outer Space to You, on-line copy, no page numbers. Be advised that the author has since had made available to him many of Howard and Connie Menger's personal papers and photos, to include those stamped as original prints by Menger's photographer, August C. Roberts, together with Roberts' comments and reports. Also available to the author is Menger's original manuscript of From Outer Space to You, in addition to letters he received from around the world in the months following its first publication. There is a follow-up book now in the works, which will explore the Mengers' encounters and these newly come-to-light revelations, to include fresh material on Valiant Thor and the extrasensory powers manifested by the Venusians under unusual circumstances.

572 *Ibid.*

As Menger was already married, he wondered about the kind of relationship he could possibly share with Connie/Marla. He did not have to be a prophet in order to foretell that an "unfortunate situation" was already brewing. Menger noted that, "My first knowledge that something was happening both to myself and to my first marriage came shortly after I returned from the Army, when Rose was heard to remark, 'Howard is not the same man that I married.'" At that time, Howard had not developed a fuller sense of the unfolding of his cosmic consciousness. When he had been quite young, Howard married the lovely, dark-haired girl that he met while working at the arsenal in New Jersey. He and Rose's backgrounds were entirely different, which at that time made little difference to either of them. On the Earth's plane of existence, this is usually the case when very young couples first meet and share the novelty and spell of romance. So even before he would ever meet the Venusian Marla, his marriage was already on shaky ground.

Menger noted that,

"Parents, older and often wiser, know that in time, when the flush of romance dims, couples are faced with the down-to-earth and everyday prospect of living with each other. And at that time the basic characters and temperaments, due to background, training and other factors, finally emerge.

When we are young we cannot see these differences which stem from variation in mental and spiritual development. Our interest is usually based mainly on physical attraction and common interests of the moment. This is a story which is lived so frequently...."[573]

Upon reflecting back to this time, Menger wrote that he believed that he "pictured an Earth woman of mature years who might assist in my work and nothing more. A younger woman would conflict with my marital state." But sometimes we have to just go with the hand dealt us by the fates. And it wasn't getting any easier, to be sure; for with the frequent press interviews and multi-media appearances, no longer did the Mengers have a private life they could call their own. Hundreds thronged their home in High Bridge, and from then on Howard and Rose Menger had no peace in their household. In his autobiographical work, *From Outer Space to You*, the contactee noted that, "Our visitors ranged from sincere individuals to reporters, curiosity seekers, investigators- but I talked with all of them." Note that *he* talked with all of them, not Rose. She was at the point of being very much fed up with the whole "flying saucer scene," as it were.

Unfortunately, this is the domestic plight that many in the contactee community find themselves. Note Menger's remarks concerning the memory blockages that need to be overcome: "It is a pity that many of us who are working here suffer from memory blocks which are unveiled only after we have already become established in a way of life—in my case, married, with children and the attendant obligations. It would take a great amount of understanding for one or both of the partners to re-define their lives along original purposes."

In Menger's case, it was the extraterrestrial visitors who assisted him in breaking through the memory blockage. The aliens explained that most every being in the universe has experienced past lives and gone through the process of reincarnation innumerable times. They also informed Menger that there were many extraterrestrials, like himself, who had chosen to reincarnate on the Earth plane, abandoning their "light body" and taking on a humanoid form. But for all forms of life in whatever degree of complexity, there is an endless cycle

---

573 *Ibid.*

of continual spiritual growth and cosmic emergence. At first Menger found that many of the concepts taught him by the space people were difficult to believe; but he went on to state that, "the more awareness I received, the more I was able to understand the truth of my own soul and its various expressions."

At his various lectures, Menger tried to convey these concepts to the seekers of esoteric knowledge. Explained the contactee:

"All of us have lived through hundreds of incarnations on various worlds. Some of us have volunteered to come to this planet and be reborn in earth bodies. We have volunteered to help in the work of helping other people receive the gifts of awareness. One can believe in these gifts on a purely intellectual level, defining the logic through rationalization; but believing is not knowing. To know a thing one must experience it.

Have you ever experienced some illuminating truth which flashed across your mind and gave an answer to a particular problem which had been worrying you? Or, perhaps, suddenly given insight into more profound subjects, and then, suddenly, the next instant, it was gone? Yet the memory of this brief illumination remained with you in your mind, but you can never find words with which to explain it to others. This is what I mean by *knowing*—it is difficult to put the knowing into words to those who do not know, or to those who only believe or imagine a thing to be true, without having experienced it. This gradual awareness and knowing comes with evolvement of the soul, mind and body, which are ever striving upward toward perfection and oneness with our Infinite Father."[574]

For the typical contactee, breaking through this memory block is the first step to reestablishing a normal life, where constant surveillance and help from our space brothers and sisters is no longer required. And once Menger had accomplished this and was on his own, so to speak, he experienced a thrill even more satisfying than meeting up with these advanced beings, that of receiving the joy that only comes from helping others embark on the same path of self-awareness and achievement.

As Menger grew up in a Christian home, it soon became apparent to him that some of the ideas he was taught by the extraterrestrials did not conform to the teachings promulgated by many of our more orthodox religions. The occult sciences and Theosophy, in particular, do touch upon some of these subjects; yet persuading listeners to take off their spiritual earmuffs long enough to hear and ponder the extraterrestrial message was the greatest obstacle he had to overcome. And even when these esoteric concepts were grasped by some, finding an immediate practicality for them in everyday life was another story. Of these and other dilemmas encountered by the contactee, Menger writes the following:

"Science asks for proof, but how can we prove something which is beyond our sciences? Scientific proof is based on what we perceive with our five senses, not what we *know* with the use of even more valuable senses. But, somehow, out of these advanced ideas must come a science, a system of some kind; else our unchartered paths will become even wilder. Such a science, a cosmic science, which will involve investigations in to the realm of other senses and dimensions, has already had its humble beginnings; but its patriarchs, like those ancient iconoclasts who announced the world was round and was not the center of the universe, have been persecuted.

Man's research has penetrated millions of light years into the universe, and into the almost inestimable depths of the atom; but now he must do research into an even more mysterious and

---

574 *Ibid.*

difficult subject, *man himself!*"[575]

Of course, in referring to past lives, the concept of *karma* always comes into play. Menger defines it as a "compensative hereditary expression in this physical three-dimensional world of now." What he meant by this is that one can live above karmic conditions when possessed of the gift of awareness. Having this, one is no longer a slave of karma; and he or she may leap over its prison walls. Menger, however, did not seem to have too much pity on those who had resigned themselves to live under this system of karmic retribution, for he noted that, "It is a false and artificial condition, one which takes on reality only because you agree that should be so." In other words, such individuals make themselves out to be their own jailers.

In combining Eastern and Western philosophy, Menger took note of Jesus' teaching that one should, "Know the truth and the truth shall make you free" (*John* 8:32, KJV). To this, the contactee added that, "Those who die on this planet without knowing the truth or having the gifts of awareness are prisoners of this planet and do not leave it; they are reborn in new bodies and continue in the school of life, bound to the wheel of karma." But for those who know the truth, like Howard and Connie Menger, it can rightly be said that they are not afraid to die. For in truth, there is no death. Those that die in truth go on to be reborn on another planet. Of Venus, for example, Menger explains that it is a "veritable heaven compared to Earth," adding that, "Heaven is not an isolated place; instead there are degrees of heavens. Some souls who choose to be reborn here from another planet do so for a purpose, either to accomplish a mission or to be with some loved one. But whether they progress upward or downward, there is continual evolvement."

But in getting back to the Van Tassel's High Bridge lecture, Menger was so caught up in Marla's dazzling beauty that he could not keep his eyes off of her. Paying little attention to Van Tassel's words, Menger's mind soared in flights of fancy. Of this time, Menger wrote that, "I caught myself wondering if it was the soul of myself or Marla which had voluntarily cast itself once more into the hell of Earth. Perhaps it had been that of both of us." And he was mulling all of this over and over before he ever even stepped up to meet the young lady at the end of Van Tassel's discourse.

On "Natural Couples"

If Howard Menger were alive today, as a human being on Earth, one might suppose he would either be promoting a new book, *Men Are from Saturn, Women Are from Venus*, or be viewed by millions on television as cameramen from the REAL Reality Network program *Cheaters* followed him and Connie around the New Jersey countryside. Or perhaps in our time, in light of their unusual circumstances, we might be more sympathetic to the plight of Howard and Connie; but in the mid-1950s their liaison was considered quite scandalous. In his autobiography, Menger felt that he needed to offer some words of explanation for his abandonment of Rose and the children in favor of starting up a relationship with Connie/Marla.

On the high calling of "Natural Couples," Menger interjected that,

"….the soul embodied on this planet operates differently, according to the frequency of the planet which makes up the magnetic lines of force around each corporeal planetary body (and all others for that matter). For instance, on Venus and Saturn the rate of vibration is much higher, and renders corporeal structures more tenuous; and if an Earth man in physical body could go there he probably would not see some of the life forms which vibrate more rapidly

---

575 *Ibid.*

Connie Menger, a.k.a. "Marla," the Venusian beauty. See http://artivision.pagesperso-orange.fr/docs/Howardmenger.html

than his own—no more than he can see the spiritual life forms in and around his own planet. Unless his physical body were processed and conditioned, he could not see the beings on another planet. If two planetary bodies are close in frequency, then, of course, the life forms are visible to each other. The life forms on Venus and Saturn, for example, are visible to each other, and their cultures are interchangeable because of the compatible frequencies."[576]

In elaborating on this concept, Menger explained that when souls incarnate on Earth, the frequency must be "stepped down," so to speak, in order to be embodied. In most cases, such *reborns* do not even recognize each other, let alone know of their own past histories. But as to how a Saturnian and a Venusian could ever come to recognize each other, Menger writes the following:

"On one of my trips as Sol do Naro I stopped off on Venus, and it was there I met Marla for the first time. Tall, lithe, with long, blonde wavy hair cascading around her shoulders, Marla, with her gold-green eyes, presented a picture far more beautiful than a storybook princess. We fell in love at once. As a Saturnian I was very tall, much broader than I am now. Yet there is a similarity in appearance; that is why this Earth body was chosen. And not only is there a similarity, but sometimes I actually do become the Saturnian in height, size and powers.

Our love on Venus was intense and overpowering; but it was fated we should not stay together, since I knew I must travel to Earth and complete a mission which had been outlined from my day of birth on that planet.

I remember clearly now the day I left her. Both of us pretended to be very brave about it. Marla made little jokes and tried to laugh musically; but she found it hard to choke back the tears which crept into her laughter.

As I turned to look upon her for the last time, I made a promise to her. Someday, somewhere, I would find her again."[577]

The reader of *From Outer Space to You* also comes to realize that Howard Menger falls into that rare category of being classified as an extraterrestrial walk-in, like Omnec Onec or ViVenus. As noted above, the contactee relates that at times he actually "becomes the Saturnian, in height, size and powers." This is something quite beyond the scope of any standard reincarnations. Most of those simply reincarnated souls experience dreams or mental flashbacks of prior lives, but do not physically change or contort into another being. Of this amazing metamorphosis, Menger writes:

"When I arrived at the portals of Earth a one-year-old boy by the name of Howard Menger had just died. The dead body was rushed to a Lutheran church to be baptized and prayed over. I, Sol do Naro, watched, and communicated with the soul leaving the little body. By consent and free will, and mutual agreement, I then entered the body. While the relatives prayed, the little boy miraculously "came back to life."

576 *Ibid.*
577 *Ibid.*

It seems strange, but I can remember the consciousness of the original soul, parts of its past (which was already impressed on the subconscious of the infant as soul record), as well as the partial recall of the Sol do Naro soul. As Sol do Naro I can vaguely remember being inside the craft as it hovered in the earth's atmosphere, then losing the sense of my surroundings and becoming as light. As this blob of light I entered the Earth body."[578]

Menger soon realized that as his memory of the soul, Sol do Naro, became more pronounced through his contacts with the extraterrestrials, he began to operate less on the original subconscious record of the Earth boy Howard and became more and more the Saturnian. To the extent that he was more fully possessed, in body and spirit, by Sol do Naro, one need only turn to an account provided by Connie Weber of their love-making sessions in her classic work, *My Saturnian Lover* (1958), written under the alias of "Marla Baxter." To maintain Howard's anonymity, now wife Connie refers to him as "Alyn" in her somewhat steamy book.

Connie explains some of the Saturnian's foreplay techniques in the following selection:

"Alyn bent down to kiss my brow. I felt the undulating tremors of his body again, and then began a strange and fascinating transformation, right before my eyes. Alyn began to grind his teeth, and turn and twist and stretch. He appeared to be getting taller and stronger. He breathed in deeply, and I felt his chest expand greatly. It seemed as if he had grown a head taller. Not only did he grow taller and stronger, but his face contour changed. His face seemed to get longer and triangular shape, and his eyes grew larger and deeper. Even his voice was different-deeper and lower. He had ceased to be Alyn and had become a Saturnian…. The next thing I knew he, as a Saturnian, had placed his hands under my armpits and slowly raised me at arm's length as if I had been a doll, and without so much as a muscle strain or change of breathing or the slightest exertion of any kind. He held me thus, high above his head for a moment, looking up at me with the most wondrously loving eyes, then slowly drew me down toward him until our lips met. It was this individual, this Saturnian, this strange being who revealed himself to me as he really was, with whom I fell in love."[579]

In his autobiography, Howard Menger explains the process of selecting appropriate mates on Venus and other worlds in our solar system: "On other planets, of which I have some knowledge, couples come together by natural selection; that is they know their proper mates. The considerations by which they choose mates involve mainly the state of evolvement of each individual. They choose their mates by a spiritual awareness of what constitutes perfect and complete union. They know a complete union must include all levels of development—spiritual, mental, emotional and physical."

Menger elaborated a bit more on the application of this process, stating that, "In spirit like attracts like….," adding that, "The entire concept of proper mating is to bring out the best possible expression in both individuals. Together they should blend spiritually and mentally, but emotionally and physically complement each other and make a perfect unit of expression. Union and mating is not only a biological and social mechanism for the procreation and rearing of children, but also for the soul's development and fullest expression."

In reading Menger's thoughts on the mating process for natural couples, one gets the distinct impression that he could easily substitute as a ghost writer for the "Dear Abby" column in the daily newspaper. And as for the handling of marital discord, the contactee goes on to note that,

578 *Ibid.*

579 Marla Baxter [pseudonym for Constance "Connie" Viola Weber Menger], *My Saturnian Lover* (New York, New York: Vantage Press, 1958), 72 pages, as quoted in Jerome Clark, *Hidden Realms, Lost Civilizations, and Beings from Other Worlds* (Canton, Michigan: Visible Ink Press, 2010), 177.

"If a marriage does not fulfill natural mating requirements, the two persons are antagonistic, resentful, lack in creative interest in life, and contributing little to their own union, themselves, or their fellow man. They are better off separated than continuing an 'armed truce' on the battlefield of an incompatible union."

This photo of Connie appeared in the New York *Daily News* of 13 July 1959.

Menger summed it up nicely when he wrote the following:

"This simple law- that in spirit like attracts like, and in the flesh opposites attract each other- is the basis for happy mating. The space people know this law, apply it and teach it to their children, so that early in life their offspring know and recognize suitable mates well in advance of the formal selection.

Since evolvement is an individual process, differences in growth can occur, even on the other planets. When this does happen and there is a genuine difference in the spiritual growth and physical attunement, these people part with understanding and find more suitable mates. Natural couples who find each other choose each other over and above everyone else. They stay together, not by law or by force, but by their own choice and are far happier than those couples who stay together because of law, social conditions or convenience. Thus natural selection is morally honest and spiritually valid. On this planet we rarely make natural selection of mates. But fortunate indeed are the souls who chance upon it. On Earth we have a word for it far more expressive, I believe, than do the space people. Here we call it 'true love.'"[580]

Of course, here on the Earth plane of existence, divorce often proves to be so traumatic an event for the children that they remain emotionally scarred for the remainder of their natural lives. But Menger teaches us that those children born of couples who do part on the other planets are loved and cared for by all in the more communal environments that flourish there. Children mature at a much faster rate on Venus, where a child two years old generally possesses the physical and mental development enjoyed by an Earth child of seven.

In addition, couples on Venus stay together much longer than Earth couples, if only due to the fact that they live much longer than we do. Venusian unions last hundreds of years and sometimes continue through several incarnations. For Menger, "this is as good a commentary upon their ways of selecting mates as one could offer."

The enlightened contactee was also an early advocate for "no-fault" divorce:

"In my own life, after several years of marriage, and particularly when my contacts became more frequent, differences in mental and spiritual makeup became more evident. Really it isn't anybody's fault when this happens to a marriage, and nobody should be blamed. There should be no cause for recrimination or bitterness; instead an attempt should be made to approach the problem in the light of understanding and to the best interest of all concerned."[581]

Even in the twenty-first century, however, this is a delicate and extremely sensitive problem that we have not adequately solved. But as Menger suggests, if we teach our children how to

580 Howard Menger
581 *Ibid.*

select mates: first by spiritual attunement, second by mental pursuits and like interests, and third, by emotional complements, we need not teach them the fourth, for physical attraction of opposites is always in operation on the material level. When individuals are of different stages of development, the one who is more advanced will sometimes choose to remain with the one who is slowly advancing. When this occurs, it may be a case of previous commitment or karmic obligation. Often, unfortunately, it turns out to be a needless waste. With this in mind, Menger concluded, "I would like to think that my wife (Rose) and I parted as friends and with understanding. As humans touch each others' lives with purposes, sometimes we need part with purpose."

Apparently, though, all worked out well for Howard and Connie as they went on to ultimately discover that ever so elusive "true love" sought everywhere throughout the universe. The second time on the "marriage-go-round" proved the charm for this extraterrestrial couple. They remained happily married until Howard's death on 25 February 2009. So at least it can be said that he practiced what he preached.

Nevertheless, not too long after Howard and Connie's marriage in 1958, life was not exactly a "bowl of cherries" for either of them. First, by the early 1960s, their quiet life in rural New Jersey was no more to be enjoyed. Following the publication of their books, plus their many radio and television interviews, people from far and wide began to show up seemingly "out of nowhere," literally camping out in their front yard. Howard attributed this media circus as one of the factors that led up to the demise of his marriage with Rose; and now the same thing appeared to be happening again. Secondly, the new wife was a real "bombshell," so to speak, possessed of all those qualities of beauty that go into making a real "pin-up" girl. Many of the men who showed up really cared little in hearing the flying saucer gospel. They just wanted to get a closer look at the lovely Venusian.

As Howard became disturbed by all of this undue attention being focused on his wife, he asked the beautiful Dolores Barrios, a close friend of George Adamski who had then moved out from Southern California to be close to the Mengers and attend the meetings of the High Bridge Flying Saucer Club, if she would mind helping him out with a special project, of sorts, whereby she would be sitting in a darkened room by herself, behind a closed door. He then offered only those in paid attendance at the Flying Saucer Club meeting the opportunity of seeing a real woman, direct from Venus, for an additional donation of ten dollars. Those who paid this then hefty sum merely obtained the right to open the door, look in, and ask one question to the Venusian. Dolores got to keep five dollars from each encounter, with the other five dollars going to the coffers of the High Bridge club.

Of this fundraising scheme, it has been written: "Once, when Menger led a follower into a dark building to speak with a spacewoman, a sliver of light happened to fall on the face of the 'extraterrestrial.' It was- the follower could not help noticing- identical to the face of a young blond woman who happened to be one of Menger's closest associates." Howard thought that as long as he couldn't get rid of these people, he might as well get something out of them to help underwrite his more sincere missionary ventures. But no matter what actions Howard would take- he could have charged $100 a pop to see the Venusian, he couldn't shake the curiosity seekers off his property. By Christmas 1960, Dolores returned to Southern California; but more about her will follow in the last chapter.

In any event, Howard thus began to seriously wonder if his second marriage was also going to fail; but Connie/Marla remained the stalwart trooper, even in the face of this total onslaught. Of this period, contactee researcher Aileen Garoutte from Washington State wrote the following:

"People camped out on their front lawns, and wanted Howard to be their "God" instead of looking inside themselves for salvation. The government pressured the couple by assigning Howard to projects that Connie could not know about. The dark side of ufology: power hungry, greedy people came "out of the woodwork" and harassed Howard and his family.

The Mengers moved to Florida. Howard and Connie, and now their two children, Eric and Heidi would start a life "away from it all". Howard worked for a sign company (in New Jersey), then started his own (in Florida). It flourished and became the biggest in the area. The Mengers tried to stay away from the UFO field. For many years they remained silent about many things."[582]

Of Menger's alleged "work" with the United States government, UFO conspiracy theorist Philip Coppens believes that *a good number in the contactee movement were led by people that worked hand-in-hand with the CIA and that the abductee scenario was created by CIA personnel. Coppens reveals an intriguing alternative universe of the contactee and abductee phenomenon,* noting that:

"The contactees themselves attracted many thousands of followers in what was the first appearance of the quasi-religious aspect of the UFO phenomenon. The contactees were the precursors of the UFO cults that continue to flourish as part of the New Age movement.

Although many such gurus emerged during the 1950s, the first and most famous of the contactees to make a public impact were George Adamski and Howard Menger. Adamski in particular, until his death in 1965, sold great quantities of books, including the bestselling *Flying Saucers Have Landed* (1953), co-written with Desmond Leslie, describing his adventures with the "Space Brothers". He travelled the world giving well-attended lectures, impressing many people, including leading members of European royal houses. Menger has largely been identified as someone who saw Adamski's success and wanted a part of the money and fame that befell Adamski. Menger did not state that the aliens gave him a religious message (though they did give him a diet for weight-loss!), which means that his impact, following and fame have not been as lasting as Adamski.

Today, Adamski is seen as a con-man, Menger as a man who copied a con-man and whom during one television interview admitted as much. Yet once again, the situation is not as simple as it seems, because solid evidence exists that at least these two individuals were acting as part of an intelligence-backed operation.

Apart from admitting he jumped on Adamski's bandwagon, in the 1960s, Menger also admitted that he had worked for the CIA, and that his story was part of an experiment to test public reactions to the idea of extraterrestrial contact. In short, Menger's story was a CIA experiment to see how easily and who specifically could be fooled into believing anything."[583]

One might suppose that you can't keep a good contactee down, for by 1991, the Mengers were back with yet another book, *The High Bridge Incident*. This book has been read all over the world, and is now published in the German language. Today, Howard and Connie's children are grown and successful in their respective fields and with their own families. Connie Menger continues to promote the "Truth" as much as possible, to those who will truly take to heart the important and universal message that she and Howard have sacrificed so much for.

---

582 Garoutte

583 Philip Coppens, "UFOgate: The Pied Pipers of the CIA," *Philip Coppens* blog site, http://www.philipcoppens.com/ufo_ciapipers.html (Accessed 21 January 2015).

Astronomical Vindications

It is interesting to note that Coppens, when referring to Adamski and Menger in today's light of scientific discovery and reason, is quick to qualify any premature characterizations of these gentlemen as "con men," to any degree. As the years roll by, we are continually acquiring new knowledge of the true nature of our solar system. While a few years ago, it would have seemed preposterous for any astronomer to advance the idea that life as we know it can survive and even thrive on or in the vicinity of the outer planets or any of their attendant moons, we now understand that this is totally within the realm of possibility, an idea whose time has come.

In the cases of these two aforementioned contactees, both have made assertions that Saturn is inhabited by beings not too dissimilar than ourselves. Adamski claimed that his last flight to outer space involved a trip to Saturn for the purpose of attending an intergalactic conference there; while Menger alleged that he was actually an inhabitant of that distant world, a walk-in visitor to life on Earth whose spirit assumed the body of a one-year old dying boy in the Garden State, back in 1923.

Of course, every elementary school science student knows that the inner planets of Mercury, Venus, Earth and Mars are close enough to the Sun to receive sufficient radiation. But with those worlds beyond Mars, the outer planets, one finds an entirely different situation. At these vast distances, the heat and light from the Sun has already started to diminish. Adamski, himself a voyager to Saturn onboard a massive mothership, took note that, "At this time it comes under the influence of the tremendous attracting force generated by the first asteroid belt, which totally envelops the central position of our solar system." He further added that, "The negative charge of the asteroid belt is great enough to attract the particles from the Sun and pull them back up to their original speed. Because this belt is grid-like in construction, with thousands of openings and paths, similar to a window screen with air going through, the particles dash on through and enter the influence of the planets beyond."

The planets beyond Mars- being of a negative polarity in and of themselves- attract from outer space the particles that they require in order to generate heat and light. All the while, however, a nearly infinite number of smaller particles are rushing on past, being pulled in to yet another asteroid belt further out between Neptune and Pluto, whence the process repeats itself. Adamski, pondering the cosmic importance of these celestial events, indicated as early as 1961 that, "This furnishes Pluto and the last three planets with normal light and heat." Adamski clarified this statement even further, revealing that,

Howard Menger and Connie Weber both claimed to be reincarnated extraterrestrials; he from Saturn and she from Venus. They married in 1958 and wrote flying saucer books together, preaching the gospel of the friendly "Space Brothers" to whoever would listen. See http://ufofyi.blogspot.com/2009/08/ufo-fyi-contactee-files-howard-and.html.

"Twelve planets in all exist in our system, according to the space travelers."

And here, as I sit at my computer typing this manuscript, I read the following headline:

"Two Earth-sized planets could be hiding in our solar system." Is this just another coincidence, or is some other motive force at work here, vindicating both George Adamski and Howard Menger? The recent findings, coming 54 years after Adamski penned *Flying Saucers Farewell*, must certainly give the skeptic pause to carefully consider the claims concerning the outer planets and other celestial bodies once made by these intrepid prophets of the New Age.

Concerning the discovery of these new worlds, science writer Andrew Griffin goes on to say:

"At least two planets that could be bigger than Earth might have been hiding at the edge of our solar system, scientists have claimed.

The undiscovered planets are thought to be even further from the Sun than Neptune and the dwarf planet Pluto.

Evidence of the two planets comes from watching a belt of space rocks known as "extreme trans-Neptunian objects" (or ETNOs).

Scientists would normally expect the rocks to be randomly distributed. But they're moving in completely unexpected ways, which seem to indicate that they're being pulled by something that can't be seen.

Spanish lead scientist Professor Carlos de la Fuente Marcos, from the Complutense University of Madrid (UCM), quoted by the Spanish scientific news service (Sinc), said: "This excess of objects with unexpected orbital parameters makes us believe that some invisible forces are altering the distribution of the orbital elements of the ETNO, and *we consider that the most probable explanation is that other unknown planets exist beyond Neptune and Pluto.*"[584]

To be sure, astronomers have spent decades debating whether hidden planets beyond Pluto exist. But now this new research, published in the journal, *Monthly Notices of the Royal Astronomical Society Letters*, and based on an analysis of an effect called the "Kozai mechanism," through which a large body disturbs the orbit of a smaller and more distant object, provides the necessary ammunition to bolster the theories posited by the advocates for an expanded solar system.

In his article, Griffin continues:

The scientists wrote: *"In this scenario, a population of stable asteroids may be shepherded by a distant, undiscovered planet larger than the Earth ...."*

One problem is that the theory goes against predictions of computer simulations of the formation of the Solar System, which state there are no other planets moving in circular orbits beyond Neptune.

But *the recent discovery of a planet-forming disk of dust and gas more than 100 astronomical units (AU) from the star HL Tauri suggests planets can form long distances away from the centre of a solar system.*

An astronomical unit, the distance between the Earth and the Sun, is the equivalent of 93 million miles.

"The exact number is uncertain, given that the data that we have is limited, but our calculations suggest that there are at least two planets, and probably more, within the confines of our Solar System."

More results based on a larger sample of ETNO objects are due to be published in the coming months.

584 Andrew Griffin, "Two Earth-sized planets could be hiding in our solar system," *Independent*, UK, 21 January 2015, on-line edition, http://www.independent.co.uk/news/science/two-earthsized-planets-could-be-hiding-in-our-solar-system-9987002.html (Accessed 21 January 2015).

"If it is confirmed, our results may be truly revolutionary for astronomy," said Professor de la Fuente Marcos.

So now that we know that Adamski was right about the expanded solar system, what about his and Menger's assertion that life as we know it can exist on Saturn or other of the outer planets? Of course, unless we have actually traveled to these remote spheres, as Adamski and Menger claim to have done, we can only go by what NASA has informed us concerning the findings of its more recent space probes sent to the regions of deep space where these worlds and their attendant moons are located.

It is the considered opinion of Fraser Cain, the publisher of the *Universe Today* internet site and co-host with Pamela Gay of the *Astronomy Cast* web television program, that while anyone with a relatively good telescope can check out the unparalleled beauty of the planet Saturn, "It's hard to imagine a planet less hospitable for life…. The planet is comprised almost entirely of hydrogen and helium, with only trace amounts of water ice in its lower cloud deck. Temperatures at the top of the clouds can dip down to -150 C…." But, he adds, "Temperatures do get warmer as you descend into Saturn's atmosphere, but the pressures increase too. When temperatures are warm enough to have liquid water, the pressure of the atmosphere is the same as several kilometers beneath the ocean on Earth." By Cain's estimation, if there is any life on Saturn, it would certainly fall under the category of "not as we know it" here on Earth. Nevertheless, Cain is not quite so dismissive when it comes to life in the Saturn system, with its numerous rings and 62 moons; at least that is the number of natural satellites that astronomers have counted so far.

Recent astronomical findings indicate the presence of two or more Earth-size worlds beyond the orbit of Pluto. These serve to vindicate George Adamski's statements concerning the outer solar system made 54 years ago. See www. nbcnews.com.

As exobiologists search for life in the Saturn system they will want to take a closer look at these moons. For the most part, they are composed of significant amounts of water ice. Most important, however, is that their gravitational interaction with Saturn seems to be keeping their interiors warm. Particular attention has focused on the sixth largest Saturnian moon of Enceladus. It is known to have geysers of water under an ice crusted southern polar region; and it is quite possible that this orb actually has vast reserves of superheated water under most areas of its frozen surface.

Another Saturnian moon that has caught the eye of astronomers and exobiologists alike is Titan. Of this largest natural satellite of the ringed world, approximately the size of the planet Mars, Cain wrote: "Titan has lakes and seas of hydrocarbons, thought to be the precursors of life. In fact, scientists think that Titan is very similar in composition to the Earth's early history."

Titan, completely shrouded in an orange haze, was also featured prominently in an episode of Neil DeGrasse Tyson's recent *Cosmos: A Spacetime Odyssey*. In the program, Tyson eases his spaceship into one of the moon's dark, oily seas. He's hoping to discover just what kind of strange chemistries and alien life forms might be down there. The astronomer introduced the concept of life on Titan with the following comment: *"There's a world I want to take you to, a world far different from our own, but one that may harbor life. If it does, it promises to be unlike anything we've ever seen before."*

So at least from what NASA scientists have told us about its discoveries made in the Saturn system- to the extent we can trust these reports- while there might not be life on the ringed planet itself, there are still plenty of intriguing locales to explore on or under the surface of its numerous moons. And when it comes to Adamski and Menger's assertions about life as we know it on Saturn, it may not be unreasonable to assume that advanced beings from alien environments might exercise the ability to appear as humanoids when in direct, personal contact with Earthlings. Various science fiction movies have played out this scenario, such as *Starman*, previously referenced, and the 2008 remake of *The Day the Earth Stood Still*, starring Keanu Reeves as Klaatu. Both of these alien beings originated from points in the outer planets. Even Menger recalls a prior existence as an energetic blob of light (the Saturnian Sol do Naro) before entering into and resurrecting the body of the young Earth boy, Howard.

But could it be that the NASA cover-up even extends to these outer planets? Perhaps, for Daniel Ross of the Public Interest Space Sciences Center in Walnut Creek, California, writes the following:

"Volumes have been written on Jupiter and Saturn, based on nothing but a belief. The theory that these planets are large bodies of swirling gases around a liquid core became a fundamental cornerstone of organized astronomy- forever entrenched, never questioned. The psychology of the situation is almost medieval, because the theory is taught as absolute fact by the theologians of science. And if one is paid as a scientist, one has to write and write, with the result that the original belief now expands into volumes of meaningless, nonsensical concepts- Supposition upon supposition, until natural inquiry is stifled, then suffocated."[585]

Of course, the present theories about Jupiter and Saturn are based on the picture-taking of NASA's Pioneer and Voyager fly-bys, secured from thousands of miles out. The rugged Voyagers were equipped with the better cameras, with the closest approach to Jupiter being made by Voyager 1 at 217,000 miles on 5 March 1979; and the closest approach to Saturn accomplished by the Voyager 2 at a distance of 26,000 miles on 25 August 1981. Most of the actual photographs, however, were taken at much greater distances. Both of the Voyager probes' electronic scanning signals were converted into pictures back at the Jet Propulsion Laboratory in Pasadena, California, and not released until being cleared by select intelligence personnel. From those photographs we were allowed to see, many were "computer-enhanced," i.e. given a false color and otherwise "doctored." Nevertheless, we did obtain a few close-up images of some of the larger moons in both the Jovian and Saturnian systems, in addition to discovering that Jupiter also had a faint ring.

Based on the information provided us by the contactees, however, Ross goes on to explain what is actually known about Jupiter and Saturn: "In reality, both planets have solid surfaces. Jupiter has atmospheric zones for thousands of miles above its surface, which balance and blend with Sun's energy to make a habitable environment. The Earth-like surface of Saturn lies many thousands of miles below its atmospheric firmament. Many advancements in the understanding of electromagnetic fields and cosmic science will be required in order to replace the old theories with correct knowledge."

---

585 Daniel Ross, *UFOs and the Complete Evidence from Space* (Walnut Creek, California: Pintado, 1987), 215

What is surprising here is the agreement among the members of the scientific community that indigenous life most likely exists somewhere on Jupiter, Saturn or in their respective systems. So the argument is not whether extraterrestrial life can thrive in the region of the outer planets and their natural satellites, but whether or not the organisms extant there bear any resemblance to life as we know it here on Earth. And if the case of the Saturnian Sol do Naro and the Venusian Marla is anywhere near an accurate account, then ufologists should seriously consider the aliens' need for the use of human bodies in order to procreate. To determine the extraterrestrial agenda in this process will be the focus of the remainder of this chapter.

The Alien Mating Agenda

Assuming that aliens are carrying out the physical and spiritual possession of human beings, and even mating with them, then the next question mimics the lyrics from Georgie Frame and Van Morrison's famous 1996 score, "How Long Has This Been Going On?" Most of the ancient astronaut theorists point to the Biblical account provided in *Genesis* 6:1-6 (NAS), where the "Sons of God" came down from the heavens and mated with the daughters of mortal men:

Keanu Reeves as Klaatu, a voyager from the outer reaches of the solar system, steps out of his sphere to assume human form in the 2008 remake of *The Day the Earth Stood Still*. See http://screenrant.com/day-earth-stood-still-reviews-vic-4527/.

Now it came about, when men began to multiply on the face of the land, and daughters were born to them, that the sons of God (*bene Elohim*) saw that the daughters of men were beautiful; and they took wives for themselves, whomever they chose.

Then the LORD said, "My Spirit shall not strive with man forever, because he also is flesh; nevertheless his days shall be one hundred and twenty years."

The *Nephilim* were on the earth in those days, and also afterward, when the sons of God (*bene Elohim*) came in to the daughters of men, and they bore *children* to them. Those were the mighty men who were of old, men of renown. Then the LORD saw that the wickedness of man was great on the earth, and that every intent of the thoughts of his heart was only evil continually.

So how can we interpret these verses in the context of the twenty-first century United States? Harold Bloom, American literary critic and Sterling Professor of the Humanities at Yale University, posits that our understanding of "fallen angels" is intimately linked to our obsession over the UFO phenomenon and finding evidence of advanced extraterrestrial life. Bloom eloquently states that:

"Our contemporary images of angels are all mixed up with alien visitations, whether in the benign fantasy of *Close Encounters of the Third Kind* or in the self-destructive fantasy of the Heaven's Gate cult. Images of a lost transcendence haunt our popular culture. Sometimes this nostalgia puzzles me because we are a religion-mad nation, and if we truly believe what we profess, then we would not so wistfully pursue material evidences of the spiritual world. But then I remind myself of my own favorite formulation, which is that religion in America is not the opiate but rather the poetry of the people."[586]

Perhaps because America is a "religion-mad nation," we can find a spiritual significance to the UFO phenomenon and alien contacts, where others only see possible avenues for scientific inquiry. In any event, traditional Christian *Bible* scholars place the events in *Genesis* Chapter 6 as taking place in the last generation before the Great Flood, sometime around 5,000 B.C.E.[587] But as Bloom so succinctly states, the mixing of angels and aliens in our modern world has made it increasingly difficult in discerning any distinctions between the two groups, if there are any to demarcate in the first place.

More than 7,000 years have passed since the Great Flood, so we may never really know who the *Nephilim* were. If we say that the account in *Genesis* 6 of these "Sons of God" is merely representative of Earthly kings and tyrants, then it seems as if we are promulgating just another case of modern man attempting to demythologize the *Bible*. We are ignoring the fact that nearly all of the ancient witnesses clearly understood that the "Sons of God" were fallen angels. Moreover, "Sons of God/*elohim*," when referred to in the *Pentateuch*, denote angels in every other instance. Additionally, when turning to the *New Testament* and *Matthew* 22:30, we should not accept it as a proof text for the *elohim*/Sons of God/angels not having the ability to function biologically. Jesus only stated that angels do not marry in the heavens; he did not suggest that they cannot interact sexually among themselves or with other entities, such as human beings.

Also, the Apostle Peter in the New Testament sustains the idea that the *Nephilim* were fallen angels. Note the following in 2 *Peter* 2:4-10 (NAS):

"For if God did not spare angels when they sinned, but cast them into hell and committed them to pits of darkness, reserved for judgment; and did not spare the ancient world, but preserved Noah, a preacher of righteousness, with seven others, when He brought a flood upon the world of the ungodly; and if He condemned the cities of Sodom and Gomorrah to destruction by reducing them to ashes, having made them an example to those who would live ungodly lives thereafter; and if He rescued righteous Lot, oppressed by the sensual conduct of unprincipled men (for by what he saw and heard that righteous man, while living among them, felt his righteous soul tormented day after day by their lawless deeds), then the Lord knows how to rescue the godly from temptation, and to keep the unrighteous under punishment for the day of judgment, and especially those who indulge the flesh in its corrupt desires and despise authority. Daring, self-willed, they do not tremble when they revile angelic majesties."

Jude, the brother of James the Just, also affirms this doctrine concerning the status of fallen angels in his epistle. Note *Jude* 5-7 (NAS):

"Now I desire to remind you, though you know all things once for all, that the Lord, after saving a people out of the land of Egypt, subsequently destroyed those who did not believe. *And angels who did not keep their own domain, but abandoned their proper abode, He has kept in eternal bonds under darkness for the judgment of the great day*, just as Sodom and Gomorrah and the cities around them, since they in the same way as these indulged in

---

586 Harold Bloom, *Fallen Angels* (New Haven, Connecticut: Yale University Press, 2007), 59.

587 Lauren Effron, Jenna Millman, Bryan Taylor, "Evidence Noah's Biblical Flood Happened, Says Richard Ballard," 10 December 2012, *ABC News*, http://abcnews.go.com/Technology/evidence-suggests-bibli(cal-great-flood-noahs-time-happened/story?id=17884533 (Accessed 23 January 2015).

gross immorality and went after strange flesh, are exhibited as an example in undergoing the punishment of eternal fire."

It becomes more than clear in the *New Testament* scriptures that its authors understood the Sons of God in *Genesis* 6 to be supernatural beings. Peter, and later Jude, are both referencing the same ancient episode; and that this event involved "angels" and the decision those once exalted beings made to violate the rules and boundaries God had set for them when operating on the Earth. The 2 *Peter* account definitely situates this infraction at the time of Noah and the Great Flood. That this sin committed by the angels was sexual in nature is decidedly indicated from the vocabulary: "sensuality," "lust of defiling passion," "sexual immorality," and "unnatural desire," in addition to the linkage of the angels' sin to Sodom and Gomorrah. If we deny the applicability of the supernatural view to *Genesis* 6, it puts one in the position of suggesting that Peter and Jude, under the inspiration of the Holy Spirit, misunderstood the passage. That the referenced beings were considered to be "supernatural" may also not be used to dismiss the extraterrestrial hypothesis. In ancient times, anything that could not be explained within the framework of the extant science was thusly considered. Perhaps in our own day, the UFO phenomenon, replete with its alien-human interactions, can best be seen as an evolving mythology. Keith Thompson, a New Age researcher on the confluence of aliens and angels, believes that the UFO reality can best be described as "complex, multidimensional, remarkably nuanced and textured -- and above all, not cooperative with the mental categories to which the Western mind has become so attached."[598]

DNA Drama

Stepping outside a purely religious context, however, there are those in the scientific community who maintain that over the centuries alien DNA has managed to creep into the human genome, slowly transforming and "stepping up" our species to a higher evolutionary plateau. Collaborative research from a gathering of exo-scientists suggests that there are genes from over 20 extraterrestrials civilizations in human DNA. These dedicated exo-scientists, continuing the work of Nobel Prize winner Dr. Frances Crick and other scholars in this area, report findings consistent with those of Professor Sam Chang, who discreetly released information that he previously discovered in his association with the Human Genome Project. While some scientists are beginning to complain more and more about political attempts to compromise the integrity of their important work for humanity, others are doing an end run around sanctions and threats by secretly getting news of their discoveries out to the public through various clandestine channels. This is one way in which the researchers try to cope with scientific peer pressures to conform to prevailing political dictates.

Dr. Michael E. Salla, an Australian by birth, is an internationally recognized scholar in international politics, conflict resolution, United States foreign policy and the new field of "exopolitics," examining how the world's political structures are dealing with the UFO phenomenon and the alleged presence of extraterrestrials among us. He is the author/editor of five books; and *held* academic appointments in the School of International Service and the Center for Global Peace, American University, Washington DC (1996-2004); the Elliott School of International Affairs, George Washington University, Washington D.C., (2002); and the Department of Political Science, Australian National University, Canberra, Australia (1994-96). He has a Ph.D. in Government from the University of Queensland and an M.A.

598 "Interview with Keith Thompson," 1995, excludedmiddle.com/thompson.html (Accessed 15 Aug 2015)

in Philosophy from the University of Melbourne, both in Australia. Additionally, he has conducted research and fieldwork in the ethnic conflicts in East Timor, Kosovo, Macedonia, and Sri Lanka, and organized peacemaking initiatives involving mid to high level participants from these troubled areas. Salla is considered to be a learned scholar on extraterrestrial investigations, facilitating the dissemination of such research findings through his website and publications. As exo-scientists and other researchers base their findings, at least partially, on carefully collecting data, which includes well corroborated and documented observations by contactees and "whistleblowers," in addition to other documentation, it has become apparent from some of these verified, reliable sources that at least a few on Earth have come into contact with representatives of non-Earth civilizations blending into the human populations at-large, and also in official capacities. However, due to Salla's involvement in advancing the UFO message, he has gotten himself into hot water with academia, effectively being blacklisted by the administrative powers-that-be and denied tenure status on any college or university campus. While political science departments can be tolerant and even accepting of anarchists and communists, when it comes to Salla and his assertions on extraterrestrial life, he is considered to be too much in the extreme. But why is Salla facing these obstacles? To answer that, we have to look for a clarification of definitions.

"Exo-science" is simply the study of extraterrestrial phenomenon. The term is further associated with "exopolitics," which embraces the need for humanity to have open contacts with extraterrestrials on a representative and democratic basis, but circumscribed into a relationship that takes into account Earth's sovereignty. Unfortunately, in today's global economy an "official science" which denies the analytical study of spiritual phenomena as a legitimate context for understanding human reality has been created over time. The only "legitimate sciences" which are recognized by institutions that are closely linked to this "global economy," are those that seek to analyze only certain material aspects. The prioritization of subjects as "official sciences" within academia serves to complement the agenda of those constituencies that seek to manipulate the "recognized" body of human knowledge for power and control. Naturally, that scientific prioritization has led to the exclusion of any extraterrestrial relationships to humanity and the unfolding of human history. Salla believes this was done in order to keep humanity ignorant of its apparent potential to be found in the "locked" heritage that can only be found in and released from its infused alien DNA.

Regarding Chang and the Human Genome Project, Salla states that the story first broke on 8 January 2007 in an on-line Canadian newspaper:

"A story published on January 8, 2007 concerned an alleged scientific breakthrough led by Professor Sam Chang who was reported to be part of the Human Genome Project. He reportedly led a team of researchers that established the existence of extraterrestrial genes in human DNA. These were found to be embedded within the 97% of the human genome described as junk DNA. See: http://www.agoracosmopolitan.com/home/Frontpage/2007/01/08/01288.html."

Because of Salla's close and long involvement in ufology, and especially the documentation of alien DNA research, he felt it was important to clarify that he was not a member of the Human Genome Project. While he believes that some extraterrestrial DNA has been transmitted in human genes through the ages, he makes it clear that his investigations remain independent of those being carried out by others or their organizations:

"The online *Canadian National* newspaper recently began publishing a series of articles reporting the scientific discovery of extraterrestrial genes in human DNA. There is much evidence to support genetic "upgrades" of human DNA at various points in human evolution by

238

extraterrestrials. This makes it very important to demarcate between exopolitical research on the historic extraterrestrial role concerning human DNA, with ongoing scientific investigations that are part of the Human Genome Project. I wish to clarify my own role and contribution to such research. This will remove any possible misperception that I am part of an exo-scientific research team associated with the Human Genome Project that might arise from a *Canadian National* story published on Monday, January 26, 2007. See: http://www.agoracosmopolitan. com/home/Frontpage/2007/01/26/01340.html."

Naturally, the 8 January report stirred up a firestorm in the both the SETI and UFO communities. If true, the scientific community was seriously considering the possibility that human DNA may be encoded with extraterrestrial information. This theory was first proposed by Professor Paul Davies, from the Australian Centre for Astrobiology at Macquarie University in Sydney, Australia, which he published in the August 2004 issue of the *New Scientist*, wherein he argued that non-coding sequences in human DNA, i.e., "junk DNA," may be, in fact, extraterrestrial information or messages. Davies speculated:

"DNA, the molecule that contains the script of life, encodes its data in a four-letter alphabet. This would be an ideal medium for storing a cosmic calling card. In many organisms, humans included, genes make up only a tiny fraction of their DNA. Much of the rest seems to be biological gobbledygook, often called "junk DNA". There is plenty of room there for ET to etch a molecular message without damaging any vital genetic functions. See: http://www. newscientist.com/article/mg18324595.300-do-we-have-to-spell-it-out.html."

In other words, the so-called junk DNA may be either an extraterrestrial message and/ or parts of extraterrestrial genetics encoded into human DNA. According to the *Canadian National* story, it was Chang's research that demonstrated the latter possibility. Because of the momentous implications inherent in the Chang revelations, however, it was incumbent upon Salla to do what he could to confirm the article. Salla describes some of the obstacles he encountered:

"I have attempted to verify the existence of Prof. Chang and his team of researchers but have so far been unsuccessful. Significantly, Linda Moulton Howe conducted an interview with Prof. John McPherson, a former Co-Director of the Genome Center, Washington University, St. Louis, Missouri. Prof. McPherson had no knowledge of Prof. Chang, but acknowledged that the extensive number of scientists working on the Human Genome Project made it possible that they had simply not met or yet communicated by e-mail. See http://www.earthfiles.com/ news/news.cfm?ID=1194&category=Science.

Prof. McPherson commented that he did not find the Prof. Chang story to be credible. Yet it is very likely that there is a more classified branch of the Human Genome Project that involves the location of extraterrestrial genetics which Prof. McPherson and many other Human Genome Project scientists may simply not be aware of.

While it is possible that Prof. Chang works on a more classified area of the Human Genome Project, it's important to note that I and others have not been able to verify his existence. It is very likely that classified research is occurring on extraterrestrial genetics in the human genome, but we need credible testimonies to verify this. Consequently, I cannot the verify the accuracy of the *Canadian National*'s January 8 report concerning Prof. Chang's research findings confirming the discovery of extraterrestrial genes in human DNA.[588]

---

588 Michael E. Salla, "Exopolitics and the Human Genome Project," 30 January 2007, *Exopolitics*, http://exopolitics. org/Exo-Comment-47.htm (Accessed 15 February 2015)

From personal experience, I would have to say that most likely the latter scenario is true. A few years back, I participated in a television interview on my early involvement with the Cleveland Ufology Project (CUP), during its heyday back in the mid-1960s and some of the sightings and close encounter UFO occupant reports I investigated along with the group's director, Earl J. Neff. When I appeared on the news broadcast, I was correctly identified as a doctor of philosophy (Ph.D.) and then lecturer in the Department of History at West Virginia University (WVU). A few weeks later, however, I received word that false allegations were being made against me, that I did not hold a doctoral degree, or any advanced degree, and that I was never a member of the Cleveland group.

As to holding advanced degrees and a teaching position at WVU, all any enquiring mind needed to do was check WVU's Department of History website; and of course, the older stalwarts defended my early and active membership in CUP, as well as my friendship and working relationship with Earl J. Neff; but the damage to my reputation was done. Certain members of the Ohio branch of the Mutual UFO Network (MUFON), the same organization that destroyed APRO, had temporarily seized control of CUP. And MUFON, being a front group for various government agencies, took upon itself the mission of either muffling or ridiculing the contactees, to include me. Sadly, this is an old trick of the Silence Group. If they cannot succeed in disproving the message, they slander the messenger.

So it comes as no surprise to me that nobody- with a government paycheck- was coming forth to speak up for Chang and his associates or the alien DNA decoding programs being carried out at the Human Genome Project. By casting a blanket of suspicion over the very existence of Chang and his team, the Silence Group succeeds again in burying information pertinent to solving the SETI and UFO enigmas. Nevertheless, the details of Chang's work in this are crucial to developing a more expansive base of knowledge when it comes to any possible agenda on the part of the Saucer Intelligences and is, therefore, presented in the following section.

The Mystery of "Junk DNA"

As it turns out, 97% of our DNA was created by alien programmers. Unfortunately, to reach it you have to go through the so-called "master code." When unlocked, the master code reveals the human potential for a Superman with a thousand year lifespan. If missed, one remains with a flawed code, providing for a limited slave race that just performs menial chores and is not all that bright. Up until recently, most of our DNA was deemed to be "junk," seemingly useless with no determined purpose. However, new findings about "junk DNA" are revealing some surprises.[589]

There is a group of researchers working at the Human Genome Project that believes the so-called non-coding sequences (97%) in human DNA, is no less than genetic code implanted by an unknown extraterrestrial life form. According to Professor Sam Chang, the group leader at the project, these non-coding sequences are common to all living organisms on Earth, from molds to fish to humans; but in human DNA, they constitute the greater part of the total genome. Such non-coding sequences, also known as "junk DNA", were discovered years ago, but since their function could not be established, no further attention was paid them. But unlike normal genes, which carry the information that intracellular machinery uses to synthesize proteins,

---

589 "Junk DNA Was Created by Alien Programmers," author unstated, 10 December 2009, Ascension Energy Program, http://ascensionenergyprogram.blogspot.com/2009/12/junk-dna-was-created-by-alien.html?m=1 (Accessed 24 January 2015).

enzymes and other chemicals produced by our bodies, the non-coding sequences are never used for any purpose. Basically, this indicates that these codes are never expressed, meaning that the information they carry never gets read, no substance is synthesized and they have no function at all. Essentially, we exist on only 3% of our DNA. While the junk genes merely enjoy the ride, the hard working, active genes are passed from generation to generation. So what are these free riders and why are they in our genome? Up until Professor Sam Chang and his group came along, these were the two biggest questions being asked by geneticists.

In trying to understand the origins and meaning of junk DNA, Chang realized that he first needed a definition of "junk." Is junk DNA really useless and meaningless? Or does it contain some information not claimed by the rest of DNA for whatever reason? Chang brought up the question to an acquaintance, Dr. Joshua S. Lipshutz, a young theoretical physicist turned Wall Street derivative securities specialist. "Easy," replied Lipshutz, adding, "We'll run your sequence through the software I use to analyze market data, and it will show if your sequences are total garbage, 'white noise', or there is a message in there."

With more investors opting to make their own selections in the purchase of securities, the demand for qualified stockbrokers has really slumped on Wall Street. Nevertheless, investors are still in the market for those in that new breed of analysts with strong backgrounds in math, physics and statistics. Therefore, these are the contemporary brokers finding employment with Wall Street firms. As Lipshutz fit into this category nicely, he was counted on as one who could sift through gigabytes of market statistics trying to uncover a useful correlation between the various market indexes and individual stocks.

By working evenings and weekends, this wizard of Wall Street managed to show that non-coding sequences are not all "junk." They transmit vital information. In combining the massive database of the Human Genome Project with thousands of data files developed by geneticists all over the world, Lipshutz calculated the "Kolmogorov entropy" of the non-coding sequences and compared it with the entropy of the regular, more active genes. Kolmogorov entropy, introduced by the famous Russian mathematician Andrey Kolmogorov more than half a century ago, was successfully used to quantify the level of randomness in various sequences,

from time sequences of noise in radio lamps to the sequences of letters in nineteenth century Russian poetry. For the most part, the technique allows researchers to quantitatively compare various sequences and thereby determine which one carries more information than the other.

Lipshutz noted that, "To my surprise, the entropy of coding and non-coding DNA sequences was not that different. There was noise in both but it was no junk at all." And after a year of collaboration with Lipshutz, Chang was convinced that there

Turning on the "junk DNA" infused in our genes by extraterrestrials will one day provide us with near immortality. See http://locklip. com/is-there-an-alien-message-hidden-in-our-dna/.

existed hidden information in junk DNA. But since it was never used, how could he come to understand its meaning? After all, with active sequences one can watch the cell and see what proteins are being made using the information. But this would not work with dormant genes.

Chang reasoned that there must be an experiment to test the hypothesis. Relying on the power of his thought, he reasoned that since there are letters in the sequences, it should be tested in some old languages, perhaps Egyptian or Sumerian. Therefore, Chang solicited help from three specialists in ancient languages and linguistics, but none of them managed to find a solution. The problem was that there were no cultural clues and no references to other known languages. Basically, the field was too alien for even the linguists.

Chang then pondered, "Who else can decipher a hidden message?" Giving pause to the question, he blurted, "Of course, cryptographers!" So eventually Chang came across Dr. Adnan Mussaelian, a talented cryptographer in the former Soviet republic of Armenia. Following the collapse of the communist state, this poor fellow barely survived on a $15 a month salary and occasional fees for tutoring children of the Armenian upper class. Chang and his associates offered the struggling scientist a $10,000 research grant; and he was off like a rocket and working like a beaver on the endeavor.

It wasn't long before Mussaelian confirmed the findings of Lipshutz: The entropy indicated tons of information almost in the clear. He also noted that it was not too strong a cryptographic system; so it didn't appear as if it was going to be a tough problem to solve. Mussaelian immediately set out in applying differential cryptoanalysis and similar standard cryptographic techniques; and when he was two months into the project, he noticed that all non-coding sequences are usually preceded by one short DNA sequence. And in most cases, a very similar sequence followed the junk. These segments, known to biologists as *alu* sequences, permeated the whole human genome. Being non-coding, junk sequences themselves, the alu are one of the most common of genes.

So what did this mean, and what were the implications inherent in the findings? Being trained as a cryptographer and computer programmer, and having no knowledge of microbiology, Mussaelian approached the genetic code as if it were a computer code. Dealing with 0, 1, 2, 3 (four bases of genetic code) instead of 0s and 1s of the binary code was a bit of nuisance, but the computer code was what he was analyzing and deciphering all his life. He was back on familiar territory, so the breakthroughs were coming quickly.

First, Mussaelian noticed that the most common symbol in the code causes no action followed by a chunk of dormant code. So just playing with the analogy, he grabbed the source code of one his programs and fed it into the program that calculates the statistics of symbols and short sequences, a tool often used in decoding messages. And what he discovered was that the most common symbol was "/", an indicator of comment. Second, he took a Pascal code; and it turned out to be { and } with the code between two slashes in C never executed. In a flash of inspiration, it dawned on Mussaelian that it was never meant to be executed since it was not itself the code, but a comment on it. And third, being unable to resist the temptation to further play with the analogy, Mussaelian began comparing the statistical distributions of the comments in both computer and genetic code. He reasoned that there must be a striking difference that should show up in the statistics. Nevertheless, statistically, junk DNA was not much different from active, coding sequences. And then fourth and lastly, to be sure of his calculations, Mussaelian fed a program into the analyzer where, surprisingly, the statistics of code and comments were almost the same. He then looked into the source code and realized why: There were very few comments in between the slashes; it was mostly C code the author decided to exclude from execution, a common practice among programmers.

With Mussaelian being a devote Armenian Orthodox follower, his religious inclinations led him to ponder the work of the Divine Hand in the creation of humankind. However, after analyzing the spaghetti code inside the sequences, he managed to convince himself that whoever wrote the small code was not the Almighty God. Whoever wrote the active, small coding part of the human genetic code was not very well organized. In fact, he was a rather sloppy programmer. Rather, it looked like somebody from an earlier, flawed version of Microsoft Windows was the man behind the curtain; but at the time that the human genetic code emerged in the earliest mammals millions of years ago, the only such individuals anywhere within one parsec of Earth were extraterrestrials.

Mussaelian considered the matter. The idea that the genetic code for all life on Earth was written by an extraterrestrial programmer and then somehow deposited here was mad and frightening. The Armenian scientist resisted it for days, but then opted to proceed. If the non-coding sequences are parts of the program that were rejected or abandoned by the author, then there must be a way to make them work. The only thing he would need to do is to remove the symbols of comments; and if the portion between the /*……*/ symbols is a meaningful routine, it may compile and execute. In following this line of thought, Mussaelian selected only those non-coding sequences that had exactly the same frequency distribution of symbols as the active genes, but also taking note that this procedure excluded the comments in Marcian or Q, whatever it was. He then selected some 200 non-coding sequences that most closely resembled real genes, stripped them of /*, //, and similar "stuff;" and after a few days of hesitation sent an e-mail to his American boss, asking him to find a way to put them in E-coli or whatever host and make them work.

A couple of weeks passed by, and Chang did not reply. "I thought I was fired", confessed Mussaelian, adding that, "With every day of his silence I more and more realized how crazy my idea was. Chang would conclude I was a schizophrenic and would terminate the contract. Chang finally responded and, to my surprise, he did not fire me. He had not bought my extraterrestrial theory but agreed to try to make my sequences work."

For years, biologists attempted to make junk sequences express, without much success. At times nothing turned out; sometimes it was junk again. It was not surprising, however, for if one grabs an arbitrary portion of the excluded computer code and tries to compile it, then most likely, it will fail; and at best, it will produce some bizarre results. But if one analyzes the code carefully and fishes out a whole function from the comments, they may be able to make it work. Because of Mussaelian's careful statistical analysis in four of the 200 sequences he selected, Chang began working and producing tiny amounts of chemical compounds.

Mussaelian noted that,

"I was anxiously awaiting the response from Chang. Would it be a more or less normal protein or something out of ordinary? The answer was shocking: it was a substance, known to be produced by several types of leukemia in men and animals. Surprisingly, three other sequences also produced cancer-related chemicals. It no longer looked like a coincidence. When one awakens a viable dormant gene, it produces cancer-related proteins. Researchers began searching Human Genome Project databases for the four genes they isolated from junk

DNA. Eventually, three of the four were found there, listed as active, non-junk genes. This was not a big surprise: since cancer tissues produce the protein, there must be somewhere a gene which codes it. The surprise came later: In the active, non-junk portion of the code the gene in question (the researchers called it "jhlg1″, for junk human leukemia gene) was not preceded by the alu sequence, i.e. the /* symbol was missing. However, the closing */ symbol at the end of "jhlg1″ was there. This explained why "jhlgl" was not expressed in the depth of the junk DNA but worked fine in the normal, active part of the genome. The one who wrote the basic genetic code for humans excluded a portion of the big code by embracing them in /*… */ but missed some of the opening /* symbol. His compiler seems to be garbage, too: a good compiler, even from terrestrial Microsoft, would most likely refuse to compile such a program at all."[590]

Chang with his researchers began searching for genes associated with various cancers, and almost in all instances they discovered that those genes are followed by the alu sequence (i.e. protein as a comment closing symbol */), but never preceded by the comment opening /* gene. This explains why diseases result in cell damage and ultimately the death of their host. On the other hand, cancers lead to cell reproduction and growth; but because only few fragments from the big code are expressed, they never lead to coherent growth. Therefore, what we get with cancer is the expression of only a few of genes alien to humans and symbiosis with some genes of bacterial parasites that lead to illogical, bizarre and apparently meaningless chunks of living cells. The chunks have their own veins and arteries, and even their own immune systems that vigorously resist all of our anti-cancer drugs.

Chang, in reconsidering Mussaelian's alien origin hypothesis, arrived at an amazing conclusion:

"Our hypothesis is that a higher extraterrestrial life form was engaged in creating new life and planting it on various planets. Earth is just one of them. Perhaps, after programming, our creators grow us the same way we grow bacteria in Petri dishes. We can't know their motives – whether it was a scientific experiment, or a way of preparing new planets for colonization, or is it long time ongoing business of seeding life in the universe. If we think about it in our human terms, the extraterrestrial programmers were most probably working on one big code consisting of several projects, and the projects should have produced various life forms for various planets. They have also been trying various solutions. They wrote the big code, executed it, did not like some function, changed them or added a new one, executed again, made more improvements, tried again and again. Of course, soon or later it was behind schedule. A few deadlines have already passed. Then the management began pressing for an immediate release. The programmers were ordered to cut all their idealistic plans for the future and concentrate now on one (Earth) project to meet the pressing deadline. Very likely in a rush, the programmers cut down drastically the big code and delivered basic program intended for Earth."[591]

At this crucial time, the extraterrestrial directorate was uncertain as to which functions of the big code might be needed later and which not; so they kept them all there. Instead of cleaning the basic program by deleting all the lines of the big code, they converted them into comments, and in the rush they missed a few /* symbols in the comments here or there. This presented humankind with an illogical growth of a mass of cells we know as cancer.

Chang elaborates on the possible alien DNA agenda:

590 "Junk DNA Possible ET Origin?," 12 January 2007, *Merkaba Tribe* website, http://www.bibliotecapleyades.net/ciencia/ciencia_genoma03.htm (Accessed 15 February 2015).
591 *Ibid.*

"However, from the programmer's point of view, there is also a positive outlook in it. What we see in our DNA is a program consisting of two versions, a big code and basic code. First fact is, the complete program was positively not written on Earth; that is now a verified fact. The second fact is that genes by themselves are not enough to explain evolution; there must be something more in the game. What it is or where it is, we don't know. The third fact is, no creator of a new work, be it a composer, engineer or programmer, from Mars or Microsoft, will ever leave his work without the option for improvement or upgrade. Ingenious here is that the upgrade is already enclosed – the "junk DNA" is nothing more than a hidden and dormant upgrade of our basic code. We know for some time that certain cosmic rays have power to modify DNA. With this in mind, a plausible solution is available. The extraterrestrial programmers may use just one flash of the right energy from somewhere in the Universe to instruct the basic code to remove all the /**/ symbols, fuse itself with the big code ("junk DNA") and jumpstart the working of our whole DNA."[592]

If this research could be verified, the answer to whether or not we are alone in the universe could be right under our nose, or, more literally, inside every cell in our body. If our genes have an intelligently designed "manufacturer's stamp" inside them, written eons ago somewhere in outer space, then the implications for all of humankind are nothing short of astounding. Such a "designer label" would affix on all of us the indelible stamp of a master extraterrestrial civilization that preceded us by many millions or billions of years. As their ultimate legacy, these aliens must have fashioned a goodly portion of the universe in their own biological image.

"Biological SETI"

It therefore become paramount to discover an independent alien DNA study; and fortunately one was carried out in one of the former Soviet republics by Vladimir I. *sh*Cherbak of al-Farabi Kazakh National University of Kazakhstan and Maxim A. Makukov of the Fesenkov Astrophysical Institute, who determined that *an intelligent signal embedded in our genetic code would be a mathematical and semantic message that cannot be accounted for by Darwinian evolution. They call it "biological SETI."* Additionally, they maintain that their scheme exhibits greater longevity and a better chance of detecting alien life than any random and transient extraterrestrial radio transmission. Writing in the astronomical journal *Icarus*, the scientists assert that, "Once fixed, the code might stay unchanged over cosmological timescales; in fact, it is the most durable construct known. Therefore it represents an exceptionally reliable storage for an intelligent signature. *Once the genome is appropriately rewritten, the new code with a signature will stay frozen in the cell and its progeny, which might then be delivered through space and time."*

But to pass the *designer label* test, any patterns in the genetic code must be statistically significant and demonstrate intelligent-like features that are inconsistent with any natural know process. Essentially, *sh*Cherbak and Makukou argue that in their detailed analysis of the human genome displays a thorough, precision-type orderliness in the mapping between the DNA's nucleotides and amino acids. *sh*Cherbak notes that, "Simple arrangements of the code reveal an ensemble of arithmetical and ideographical patterns of symbolic language." They also discovered that this includes the use of decimal notations, to include the abstract concept of *zero*, in addition to logical transformations that were best described as "accurate and

---

592 *Ibid.*

systematic." In other words, "these underlying patterns appear as a product of precision logic and nontrivial computing," said *sh*Cherbak in his capacity as the investigative team leader.

Living in the Matrix

Their interpretation leads the scientists to a seemingly farfetched conclusion: that the genetic code, "appears that it was invented outside the solar system already several billion years ago." This means that Earth was seeded with interstellar life through a process known among exobiologists as *panspermia*, quite a novel approach to galactic conquest if we imagine this was a deliberate *Johnny Appleseed* endeavor carried out by super, god-like beings. That this genetic dispersal involved other planets in our solar system, like Venus and possibly Mars, and even worlds orbiting distant stars within our sector of the Milky Way's galactic arm, is a given. Interestingly, it was the United States Air Force Air Material Command's 1949 *Project Sign* report that verified this:

OTHER STAR SYSTEMS

"Outside the solar system other stars -- 22 in number -- besides the sun have satellite planets. The sun has nine. One of these, Earth, is ideal for existence of intelligent life. On two others there is a possibility of life. Therefore, astronomers believe reasonable the thesis that there could be at least one ideally habitable planet for each of the 22 other eligible stars.

In this line of reasoning the theory is also employed, of necessity, that man represents the average in advancement and development. Therefore, one half the other habitable planets would be behind man in development and other half ahead. It is also assumed that any visiting race could be expected to be far in advance of man. Thus, the chance of space travelers existing at planets attached to neighboring stars is very much greater than the chance of space-traveling Martians. The one can be viewed as almost a certainty (if you accept the thesis that the number of inhabited planets is equal to those that are suitable for life and that intelligent life is not peculiar to earth.)

....The nearest eligible star is one called Wolf 359. This is eight light years away."[593]

Keeping it mind that the above *Project Sign* report was issued by the Air Force on 27 April 1949, then we have to seriously wonder what the government already knew about UFOs and their extraterrestrial origins, *for the first confirmation of an exoplanet orbiting a main-sequence star was made in 1995, when a giant planet was found in a four-day orbit around the nearby star 51 Pegasi.* While a few exoplanets had been imaged directly by telescopes, the majority were detected indirectly through the transit and the radial-velocity methods. As of the day I am writing this, 27 January 2015, astronomers have identified 1,885 exoplanets planets in 1,184 planetary systems and 477 multiple planetary systems.[594] So who was informing the Air Material Command, that sponsored *Sign*, about the existence of 22 star systems in our galactic neighborhood with inhabited planets, the half of which could man spacecraft and send them to Earth across the vast distances of outer space? Was this information garnered from something recovered in the New Mexico crashed flying saucer debris fields at Roswell and San Agustin? And while considering this matter, the same criteria applies to *Sign*'s knowledge of the silicon-based life forms on Venus that can withstand incredible conditions of pressure and heat that

---

593   *Project Sign* report, 19
594   Jean Schneider, "Interactive Extra-solar Planets Catalog," updated daily at the Meudon Observatory, Paris, France, in *The Extrasolar Planets Encyclopedia*, 27 January 2015 (Accessed same day).

would ordinarily and instantaneously incinerate any form of carbon-based Earth life, at least as we know it. Keep in mind that back in 1949, most astronomers assumed that Venus was a planet possessed of very similar atmospheric and surface conditions as our own world, albeit they assumed Venus to be the younger of the two spheres, maybe a prehistoric planet replete with dinosaurs.

But in returning to the concern with alien DNA in our genome, there is another possibility that requires exploration: that perhaps the observable universe was built just for us and exists inside a vast computer program, somewhat on the order of the *Matrix* trilogy. This brings to mind the idea that some programmer, somewhere out there, wrote the genetic code for life upon which our entire universe is regulated. Of course, such biological SETI inevitably collides head-on into an idea that is completely antithetical to science: the concept of *intelligent design* (ID).

To date, however, ID has been co-opted by the Christian fundamentalists, who use it to push the teaching of creationism in schools as an alternative to "secular" evolution. Now, in 2015, this matter is being battled out in the court systems of four states. But can the claim of an alien signature in our genetic code be any more believable, or even provable, than the biblical ID? Of course, we know so little about the origin of life on Earth that it seems presumptive to identify genetic structure that supposedly defies a "natural" explanation. After all, what do we know about the mind of the programmer? At this point, all we can do is guess. Some exobiologists have argued that even the discovery of life elsewhere in the solar system would not provide an independent test of this idea of *panspermia*, insofar as it could have naturally occurred among those planets and moons. And, even when one assumes that the genetic code is ultimately considered the handprint of an extraterrestrial grand designer, then *who* designed the designer?

The complete program has the appearance of elegance. Possessed of auto-correcting software, it is very clever, self-organizing, auto-executing and auto-developing. The program's software was tailored for a highly advanced biological computer with a built-in connection to the ageless energy and wisdom of the Universe itself, or God, if you wish. Software wise, within us is either a short and diseased life, or the potential for a super-intelligent, super-being with a long and healthy life. This raises puzzling questions – was the reduction to the basic code done by sloppy programmers in a rush (as it appears to us), or was the disabling of the big code a purposeful act which can be cancelled by a "remote control" whenever desired? In the *Star Trek: Next Generation* series, it is the near eternal and omnipotent, multidimensional entity known as the "Q," who most fears humankind. The Q informs Enterprise Captain Jean Luc Picard that it is specifically our potential to one day surpass both the Q collective consciousness and continuum that most fills him with a sense of dread. Sooner or later, we have to come to grips with the unbelievable notion that every life form on Earth, not just the human, carries a genetic code for her/his/its extraterrestrial cousin and that evolution is not anywhere near what we previously assumed it to be.

Inasmuch as the alien DNA is currently latent in most of humankind, what would happen if it were to somehow become activated, perhaps by a radio transmission of some sort? That would change us forever, some of us within months while others within generations. The change would probably not be noticed too much in the physical, (except no more cancers, diseases and short life), but it would intellectually catapult us, expanding our mental capabilities exponentially.

Like a second's passing in evolutionary time, we would find ourselves, as the "new gods," so to speak, in a position comparable to that which existed 200,000 to 300,000 years ago between the Neanderthals and the emerging modern humans, placing ourselves in the latter, more advanced group. The old will be replaced, largely through miscegenation and assimilation, giving birth to a new cycle. But could such a radio transmission carry the data required to activate, alter or reboot the program inherent in a human's DNA? And most importantly, how could we identify the signal and how would we know if it was currently being transmitted?

In these areas where the spheres of science and spirituality seem to intersect, we might consider the counsel oft provided by the metaphysicians among us: that everything in the universe was and continues to be created from the pure light electrons that emerged from the Pleroma at the beginning of time as we know it. We, as human beings, understand these electrons, along with other subatomic particles, to be the composite structures that make up the atoms of the physical world. It is the geometrical design and the speed of action around the central core, plus other factors, that help determine the type of atom and its rate of vibration. The planets, people, animals, plants, trees and everything else we can even remotely sense in the third dimension all emit a certain rate of vibration; and the denser the vibration level the lower it is in the light spectrum.[595]

The metaphysicians generally agree on the following classification of density levels, with the heaviest being the lowest in the light spectrum:

Mineral Kingdom - Heaviest density

Plant Kingdom

Animal Kingdom + Lower vibration level Human

Higher Vibration Level Human

Light Body

Soul Body

Oversoul

Angels

Archangels and Ascended Masters

Leaders of the Spiritual Hierarchy

Universal Gods

Absolute Godhead - Purest Light Source

But unlike density, dimensions encompass entire realities, even overlapping each other. The lower dimensions are contained within the higher ones, whereby our third dimensional matrix would be inclusive of the lower two. Dimensions might be defined in the following manner:

First Dimension - Existence through a point in time and space.

Second Dimension - Magnitude (distance or path) in the time and space.

Third Dimension - Depth and existence in the physical universe through choices of paths in time and space.

Fourth Dimension - Time (movement) through time and space in a higher mode of physical existence.

Fifth Dimension - Through Love bridges the worlds of Matter and the worlds of Spirit (Release from duality into love and unity).

---

595 "Density and Dimensions," 2005, Center for Self Transformation, http://www.selftransform.net/ DensitiesandDimensions.htm (Accessed 28 January 2015)

Our understanding that everything in the universe is energy, and that all energy exists at different levels of vibration and frequency, informs us that all planets and their inhabitants vibrate at different levels. The planet Earth, for example, is a third dimensional sphere with fourth and fifth dimension activity in progression. In the present, the beings on Earth are estimated to be 60 percent in the third dimensional plane, 35 five percent in the fourth and 5 percent in the fifth. The levels of Earthlings in the fourth and fifth dimensions have been steadily rising since the late 1940s and early 1950s, when the Venusians among us initiated a program for the gradual dimensional ascension of our planet. The planet Earth is currently going through a dimensional ascension. But for these Earthlings to shift along with the planet's dimensional ascension, they must individually focus on raising their own levels of frequency vibration, tuning in to the Venusian harmonic continually and telepathically being beamed directly into every subconscious mind.

Every dimension has seven planes; and as vibration levels are raised through the release of all blockages in the physical, emotional and mental bodies, the shift in frequency uplifts the person to the higher planes. To fully evolve into the fifth dimension, however, the seeking individual must open up to unconditional love, thereby expanding her or his inner light quotient. This means that they must become fully forgiving under all circumstances. They must also cease from the further generation of any negative, or harmful, thought patterns. This will allow the Venusian harmonic frequency to be fully absorbed. In this manner, all the chakras will be activated, thus preparing the physical body for its imminent transition to the higher spiritual reality.

In the third dimensional matrix we currently find ourselves, most of our souls have yet to be awakened to the universal laws and their application toward dimensional and spiritual advancement that comes through the meditation process, along with an acceptance and incorporation of the Venusian harmonic frequency into the fabric of our being. When we allow this to occur, however, we release those blockages at the physical, cellular levels, thus raising our overall levels of vibration. Such profound meditations, augmented through the infusion of Venusian energies, activate your higher chakras and expand your light quotient.

Each individual's frequency level determines their vibration. So the lower one allows their frequency vibration to get, the more diminished becomes their inner light capacity; whereas the higher vibration levels permit one to expand the inner circuitry to receive the higher capacity electrons. In other words, we allow our total selves, to include our alien programmed DNA, to become activated, thereby expanding our inner light quotient and preparing us for human individual metamorphosis into the next higher dimensional matrix.

A good example of this process, demonstrating a stepping up and jump from the higher level of the physical human plane of existence to fusion with a light body, is found in the ending scenes of Hollywood Pictures 1995 blockbuster, *Powder*, starring Sean Patrick Flanery, Jeff Goldblum and Mary Steenburgen. The unique circumstances into which the protagonist Jeremy is born, bestow him with phenomenal powers, including the highest IQ in the history of humankind. But while his abilities mark him as special, they also make Jeremy, with an albino complexion, branded as an outcast among his peers at school. Jeremy then withdraws from society, preferring to lock himself in his grandparents' basement where he becomes a self-taught genius, taking in all the knowledge he can from any books that he can get his hands on.

The Venusian Transmitter

Following the visit of the Venusian emissary Valiant Thor to the Pentagon on 16 March 1957, the United States government, under the direction of President Eisenhower, commissioned the Ohio State University Radio Observatory to begin an exhaustive radio scan of the planet Venus. At the radio observatory facility in Columbus, Ohio, the Department Chair, Dr. John D. Kraus, immediately ordered that radio scans then being conducted on Jupiter's magnetic field be dropped, with all personnel now focusing their radio investigations on our twin planet Venus. And in addition to the work being carried out at Ohio State University, President Eisenhower also communicated directly with Dr. C. H. Mayer of the Naval Research Laboratory in Washington, D.C., diverting their efforts to a full scale scan of Venus by both standard and radio astronomy.

With both the Columbus and Washington radio telescopes dedicated to the Venus survey, hopes were high that intelligible signals would be detected early. By the end of April, however, nothing but static had been heard over the radio speakers. Was Valiant Thor deceiving his hosts at the Pentagon, trying to throw them off the trail? By pointing them to Venus, was Thor attempting to keep the radio astronomers from discovering his true home world, perhaps Mars or Saturn?

But just as Eisenhower was about to order that the radio investigations be diverted to Mars, on 2 May 1957, a faint signal from Venus was picked up by the Naval Research Laboratory's facility. While this first Venusian signal was barely detectable, within four days its audio strength had increased fourfold as Venus was approaching the Earth, moving into a conjunctive phase. The signal was fixed in the ultra-shortwave band on a wave length of 3.15 centimeters. While there was little that Mayer could do with the signal in this initial phase of research, at least he could confirm to the president the veracity of Thor's assertion that Venus was a habitable world. And if the signal remained steady, he might be able to measure its intensity in order to garner more information about the temperatures on Venus. Director Mayer was of the opinion that radio observations were superior to astronomical surveys with standard telescopes. After all, he reasoned that since Venus is overlaid by a thick bank of clouds, direct line-of-sight visual observations of the planet's surface would avail little. But recorded radio signals might someday enable his team at the Naval Research Laboratory to find out a lot more about what was hiding under that dense cloud layer.

Jeremy transitions from the physical human form to that of a light body in the 1995 Hollywood Pictures' *Powder*. He goes on to find happiness in another dimension. See www.rogerebert.com.

With one signal's discovery at 3.15 centimeters, however, the Pentagon reasoned that there must be other transmissions from Venus that could be intercepted and interpreted by Department of Defense analysts. Therefore, the Ohio State facility was directed to ignore the broadcasts at 3.15 centimeters and to continue scanning all bands and frequencies for new signals while the Department of the Navy continued to monitor and analyze at the first wave length.

By early June, Kraus and his Ohio team detected some new radio signals resembling the static generated from terrestrial thunderstorms. As this was a purely natural phenomenon, the data collected concerning it was stored for future reference, but the search resumed at other frequencies for signs of intelligible transmissions. But then on 22 June 1957, the Ohio radio astronomers detected new signals of a distinctly different class, in many ways resembling radio telegraphy.

It is definitely difficult to keep the lid on a discovery of this magnitude. As news of "telegraph signals" from Venus were leaked to the press by faculty members in the various science departments at Ohio State, Kraus had to come up with something logical to say concerning the radio observatory's findings in this matter. Therefore, in a press interview on the evening of the discovery, Director Kraus noted that, "While this type of emission has many of the characteristics of signals from a terrestrial transmitting station, whatever phenomenon is responsible for the signals must be of a rather complex type." In other words, the propagation of the radio waves only resembled those of a ground transmitting station, but it was attributable to natural phenomenon. Kraus hoped that this explanation would suffice, keeping the barking dogs at bay.

In the coming months, however, Kraus and his Ohio State team continued to collect more scientific data on the Venusian transmissions. The signals came in pulses often lasting one second or more; and sometimes there was a long string of them, with more or less uniform intervals in between. The frequency of the signals ranged from two to four million cycles per second, with those at the higher frequency arriving as much as two seconds ahead of those at the lower end of the band. The pulses seemed to be modulated to an audio frequency of about 117 cycles per second. When this frequency is heard through a speaker, it sounds something like the key of B flat next to the C below middle C on a piano. Kraus said that, *"This suggests that the electrified atmosphere of Venus and the Earth, and the space between, have an anomalous way of dispersing radio waves."* Perhaps the Venusians were utilizing the ionized comet-like tail of their planet, which extends to the polar regions of Earth, as a conduit for the transmission of the transformative, quickening energies that would spark the DNA receptors in certain select contactees and other individuals.

In returning to the other class of radio signals, most likely attributable as the product of lightning storms, Kraus stated that, "Sometimes they sizzle away for as long as 12 hours. The fluctuate greatly in intensity with peaks occurring 20, 39, 63 and 90 minutes, 6 hours 25 minutes and 11 days apart. Every day the peaks of intensity arrive about seven minutes earlier than they did before the day previously. This gives a clue to the planet's rotation period, and probably means that it turns around every certain number of days minus 7 minutes for each day involved in the process."

Of course, there has always been a controversy over the length of the Venusian day, because the surface is always hidden, even from the fly-by or orbit of a space probe. That is why, in the past, various astronomical methods and measurements indicated that the second planet's rotation rate was somewhere between 24 hours up to 243 Earth days. In other words, they had no concrete idea, just theories. So if the Ohio study is anywhere accurate, the Venusian day would certainly be a lot shorter than the 243 Earth days, in time equivalence, that NASA now claims that it is.

Daniel Ross of the Public Interest Space Sciences Center in Walnut Creek, California, asserts that this NASA declared "official rotation rate" for Venus cannot be corroborated or refuted by any Earth-based radar studies because of the enormous distances involved. Ross explains that, "Let's say that two radar signals of equal energy are sent out- one to the Moon and the other one to Venus. The returning radar signal from Venus would be some 10 million times fainter than the radar return from the Moon." And when the 243 day theory was first advanced in 1961, it had taken several weeks for the scientists at the Jet Propulsion Laboratory in Pasadena, California, to sort out a radar return from Venus largely due to the noise from the cosmic microwave background radiation that permeates all of space. If Kraus' calculations are correct, and taken together with time-delayed space probe photographs of high atmospheric breaks in the circulating cloud system of Venus, then the Venusian rotational period is somewhere between three and four 24-hour Earth days. The Jet Propulsion Laboratory's Venus radar project, on the other hand, being funded by government research contracts, proved to be just another front for the advocates of the long rotational period, making Venus seem like an inhospitable world not conducive to life as we know it. As their methods were prone to errors and subjective interpretations, any results that the Pasadena cadre came up with can only be considered as highly questionable.

But in getting back to the transmitter, on third dimensional Venus it may be one of the few structures that future astronauts voyaging there will actually be able to see with their physical eyes. Valiant Thor explained to President Eisenhower and various Department of Defense officials that over the millennia, as surface conditions had deteriorated on his home world, certain Venusians not choosing to escape into the fourth or fifth dimension had opted to move their material civilization underground or onto the Venusian moon of Neith, which they later cloaked when it became possible for Earthlings to view it with terrestrial telescopes. Omnec Onec also confirmed that space probes to Venus would continue to reveal a world inhospitable to life as we know it, but in continuing to scan the planet's surface, sooner or later at least one future probe would stumble upon a strange, domed structure in a caldera; and that would be the only Venusian surface city visible to humans, at least in the third dimension.

"Starseed" Activation

As the transmitter is always on, many of those defined as "Starseeds" are constantly being awakened to a new, metaphysical reality. The souls of such individuals share connections to other realms as their true points of origin. Many of these connections derive from past life experiences on other planets or in other dimensions. Others cannot seem to shake off deep memories inherent in their extraterrestrial-coded DNA sequences. But all have come to Earth in order to learn and spiritually progress. Most "Starseeds" eventually come to the realization that they are truly evolved beings from another planet, dimension or continuum whose specific missions are to assist the Earth and her inhabitants, thereby ushering in a new Golden Age.

The Starseeds incarnate into this world under the same conditions of helplessness as other human babies. They are also born with a total amnesia with regard to their true astral identity, origins and purpose here on Earth. However, as the genes of Starseeds are encoded with extraterrestrial DNA sequences, they are subject to a special "wake-up call," thus allowing them to be "activated" by the Venusian signal at any moment in life. For some, this awakening unfolds as a gradual process; but for most it is dramatic and abrupt, causing severe disruptions in behavior and lifestyle, much as demonstrated in the case of Howard Menger. In either event, memories of life on another planet or some other realm are restored in varying degrees of intensity. When this awareness occurs, most Starseeds consciously choose to take up their assigned missions, while others are free to decline. Should they opt in favor of strengthening their extraterrestrial bonds, the Starseed's connections to the Higher Self are also fortified. Now that they are in harmony with their Oversoul, the Starseeds feel guided by a sense of inner-knowing.

To find out if you are one of the Starseeds, consider the following list of attributes compiled by metaphysical and UFO researcher Brad Steiger:

Physical

A radio transmitter on the Venusian surface emits the signal to activate the alien DNA in the human genome. See http://spacesimcentral.com/ssc/topic/3071-baobobs-ship-mooring-and-refit-shop/page-2.

65% are female: 35% are male
Compelling eyes
Great magnetism and personal charisma
Sensitive to electricity and electromagnetic fields
Lower body temperature than the norm
Chronic sinusitis
Extra or transitional vertebra
Hypersensitivity to sound, light, odors
Swollen or painful joints
Pain in the back of the neck
Adversely affected by high humidity
Survived a life-threatening illness
Involved in a severe accident or trauma

Emotional

Feel a tremendous sense of urgency to fulfill their missions
Experienced a sense of oneness with the universe
Many have difficulty dealing with / or expressing emotions or have a chemical imbalance

Extraterrestrial Experiences

All believe in life on other planets
Most believe that have lived on another planet and can tell you about it
At an early age they had some kind of extraterrestrial, religious or mystical experience
Believe they have encountered alien entities of an extraterrestrial or multidimensional level or a being of light
Telepathic communication with an alien entity - physical or non-physical
They receive some form of communication from a higher source

Out of Body Experiences

Near Death Experiences
Out of Body Experiences

Metaphysics

Believe in their spirit guides or angel
Believe they have been blessed after the appearance of a holy figure
An intense religious experience

Believe in a God or creational source of energy
Believe in miracles
Had an invisible playmate as a child
Saw an elf - "wee person" - or "fairy"
Saw a ghost
Aware of parallel existence at this time in other worlds
Contact with deceased loved one
Believe in reincarnation
Have past life memories or / memories from parallel experiences

Psychic Development
Perform healing on themselves and others
Experienced a white light during meditation
Experience clairvoyance and clairaudience
Prophetic dreams or visions that have come to pass
See auras
Practice automatic art
Practice automatic writing[596]

Accessing the Signal

Just a few words regarding the awakening of Starseeds need to be presented here, before I give you the frequencies to access the Venusian signal. First, once an individual Starseed begins her or his journey of self-discovery, they will most likely seek a change in careers, preferring to work in more creative and esoteric fields more in compliance with their cosmic assignment, or "soul mission," as it were. This refocus and life realignment may require going back to school and devoting an inordinate amount of time to study and personal development that those closest to you may not readily understand. And like Howard Menger and other contactees, you may feel drawn to others more like yourself, those who also feel as if they are wanderers or walk-ins to this reality or timeline. But these are the ones who are operating on similar frequencies and predestined goals; and these are the individuals who can most assist you in your period of transition. While this sense of closeness to such individuals is only a natural feeling, as you are evolving back to the light, some family and friends will think you are withdrawing or even shunning them. So be prepared for their less than accepting reaction. And while many of the Starseeds adapt and move on to deeper and meaningful lives, others fall by the wayside, feeling lost and alone. Not connecting with anyone who understands them, these are the Starseeds who become depressed and withdraw from society at large.

Having briefed you on the implications inherent in "getting your frequency on," I can now tell you that the planet Venus resonates tones at two very specific frequencies: 221.23 hz and 409.1 hz. Other planets and moons in our solar system resonate at just one frequency; so we see again just how special Venus is. And besides the activation power in the Venusian frequencies, they are also possessed of a therapeutic energy unavailable anywhere else in the galaxy, emitting healing waves that generate new and creative relationships, improve your sex

---

596   Brad Steiger, "Traits of Star People and Starseeds," 30 May 2013, *in5d* website, http://www.bibliotecapleyades.net/ciencia/ciencia_indigo40.htm (Accessed 15 February 2015)

life, heal kidneys and inspire art.

Of course, the very real possibility of the planets creating physical effects on Earth is the bread and butter of astrology. Astrologers have always claimed that various parts of the anatomy, and even illnesses, were associated with sundry orbs in the solar system. With this in mind, it has not hard to see why some specific body parts and maladies would correspond in a sympathetic way to what was happening with the planets in our celestial neighborhood. After all, many disease conditions have been treatable via herbs associated with specific astrological energies. And if herbs have some form of utilizing certain vibrations of planetary energy, what would happen if we introduce the pure sound waves of planets into the body? This is where the therapeutic planetary energies of Venus come into play.

For astrologers, Venus is associated with the principles of harmony, beauty, balance, the feelings and affections, and the urge to sympathize and unite with others. Mitchell Gibson, a professional astrologer and sound technician, discovered a way to isolate the specific frequencies associated with the various planets in our solar system; and in the process of doing so has filtered the emitting energies for their positive effects. Gibson was thereby able to record them in a smooth and pleasant manner, devoid of repetitive noise or error. He utilized the recordings of planetary energies for over a year, achieving phenomenal results. The researcher maintains that the most beneficial sky energies come from the Sun, Jupiter and Venus. And of the latter planet's beneficent power exerted on the Earth plane, Gibson notes that, "It is involved with the desire for pleasure, sensuality, personal possessions, comfort and ease. It governs romantic relations, marriage and business partnerships, sex (the origin of the words 'venery' and 'venereal'), the arts, fashion and social life. The first-century poet Marcus Manilius described Venus as generous and fecund, and the lesser benefic. In medicine Venus is associated with the lumbar region, the veins, thyroids, throat and kidneys."

He also adds that, "Improving your Venus energy could potentially improve your romantic relationships, ability to experience pleasure and sensuality, harmonize and stabilize your personal possessions, and improve your social life." Is it worth the risk to tap into and ride the Venus wave? Only you can decide, but I would recommend the filtered version rather than immediate aural exposure to the unedited signal.

In conclusion, our intimate relationship with the sphere of Venus, her planetary energies and its inhabitants at multiple levels of reality, is nothing new. Helena Blavatsky and the Theosophists believe that it has endured for at least 18,000,000 years and will continue to do so, even into the distant future. Blavatsky was the first to postulate that the Venusians were responsible for creating the races of god-kings who populated the ancient continents of Lemuria and Atlantis. She also claims that the Venusian bloodline was carried over into Europe by some of the survivors of Atlantis' destruction. Today we know their descendants as the Basques, inhabiting the area of the Pyrenees Mountains, situated on both sides of the French-Spanish border. More about the Basques, their unique heritage and Venusian connection will be explored in the next and last chapter.

As for the future, Blavatsky predicted that in the early decades of the twenty-first century, we would begin to see the emergence of a new alien-human hybrid species. The first wave of these Starseed children will come from the United States, principally California, as well as Australia and New Zealand. After the passing of six or seven more centuries, however, as the United States demographic becomes more Hispanic and Asian, a corresponding change in the overall complexion of the North American population will be noted, also reflective in the forthcoming Starseed generations. Border distinctions throughout the Americas will gradually disappear, and in the last generation before total human individual metamorphosis to a higher level of cosmic evolution, one of the Starseed will emerge as a world leader, on the order of a new Julius Caesar,[597] to unify the planet in peace, prosperity and harmonious, open relations with the Venusians and other extraterrestrials. By this time, a goodly chunk of the North American west coast will have broken off into the Pacific Ocean. The new Island Republic of California will become the new metro-capital of the entire solar system.

Frequency map of the Rh Negative Blood Group factor

(based on Mourant et al. 1976, from Sykes & Renfrew 2000)

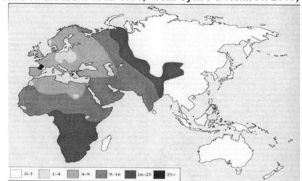

A United Nations study confirms the highest concentration of the Rh negative blood group in the Basque region of the Pyrenees Mountains. According to ufologist Brad Steiger, Rh negative blood is a genetic marker for encoded extraterrestrial DNA. See www.maya12-21-2012.com.

---

597 Lauren Horne and Clare Rowan, "Coinage of Julius Caesar," Australian Centre for Ancient Numismatic Studies, July 2008, Sydney, Australia, http://www.humanities.mq.edu.au/acans/caesar/Career_Venus.htm (Accessed 30 January 2015): "Throughout his career Caesar claimed the special protection and assistance of the goddess Venus. The connection between the Julian family and the goddess was long established, and previous members of the *gens* had struck coinage showing the goddess (e.g. RRC 258/1, 320/1). At the funeral of his aunt in 69 B.C. Caesar publicly proclaimed his relationship to Venus and his descent from Aeneas (Suetonius *Div. Iul.* 6)." It should also be noted that Caesar invoked the aid of the goddess in his battle against Pompey at Pharsalus in 48 B.C., vowing to build a temple to Venus if he was victorious. He did go on to build a temple to Venus Genetrix (Venus the Mother) in the Julian Forum, but whether this was to commemorate his victory at Pharsalus still remains uncertain. The mother statue depicts the goddess holding an apple in her left hand, while moving to cover her head with her right hand; and this is the image of Venus that was later reproduced on many issues of Roman coins. A shrine, patterned after the Venus Genetrix temple, was also placed on the *rostra* at the funeral of Julius Caesar. Pompey also professed the support of Venus; and his father-in-law Sulla proclaimed the favor of the goddess as well, with his *agnomen* 'Epaphroditus' meaning 'favored by Venus.' A temple of Venus Victrix (Venus the Conqueror) was even incorporated into Pompey's theater. Nevertheless, Plutarch notes Pompey's fear of Caesar's superior claim to the goddess: "He feared lest the race of Caesar, which went back to Venus, was to receive glory and splendor through him" (*Pompey* 68.2).

Chapter VIII:
Gods of Aquarius

Wizard: I'm an old Kansas man myself. Born and bred in the heart of the Western wilderness. Premiere Balloonist par excellence for the Miracle Wonderland Carnival Company until one day, while performing spectacular feats of stratospheric skill never before attempted by civilized man, an unfortunate phenomenon occurred. The balloon failed to return to the fair.

Lion: It did?

Dorothy: Weren't you frightened?

Wizard: Frightened? You are talking to a man who has laughed in the face of death, sneered at doom, and chuckled at catastrophe. I was petrified. Then suddenly, the wind changed and the balloon floated down into the heart of this noble city, where I was instantly acclaimed Oz, the first Wizard Deluxe. ***Times being what they were, I accepted the job,*** *retaining my balloon against the advent of a quick getaway.* And in that balloon, my dear Dorothy, you and I will return to the land of E Pluribus Unum.

Frank Morgan as the first "Wizard Deluxe" tries to help Dorothy (Judy Garland) return to Kansas in Metro-Goldwyn Mayer's 1939 classic, *The Wizard of Oz.*

The Mormon Prophetess

Annalee Skarin became a "translated being" in 1952, making her ascension into the heavens thirty years later. See http://easleygenealogy.com/books.html.

Our final chapter opens with an account of Annalee Skarin, born 7 July 1899 in the small town of American Falls, Idaho, as Nansela Mathews, the granddaughter of "Wild Bill" Hickman, a lieutenant of Brigham Young and leader in the Mormons' westward trek. In her writings she rejects the regular Christian doctrine that physical death is inevitable. While she accepts the Christian doctrine that virtuous people can die and be later admitted to the heavens, she regards this path as "the dreary backdoor entrance," and asserts that the path to true glory involves ascending to the heavens with one's physical body alive and intact, via a process she called "translation," utilizing the term commonly used by Mormons to signify one's overcoming of bodily death.

She also claimed to have visited worlds in other dimensions where she communed with angels and spoke in her books about looking down and observing Earth from a nearby "spirit world," most likely Venus in a higher dimension.[598] She has frequently

---

598 Among the Latter Day Saints, and particularly in the Church of Jesus Christ of Latter-day Saints, the Biblical patriarch Enoch is credited with establishing an exceptionally righteous city, named Zion, in the midst of an otherwise wicked world. Those canonical scriptures of the Church of Jesus Christ of Latter-day

Saints, known as the "Standard Works," declare that not only Enoch, but all of the inhabitants of the city of Zion, were taken off this earth without ever experiencing death, and all because of their piety. According to Mormonism's founding prophet, Joseph Smith, the very word "Zion" is defined as "the pure in heart;" so inasmuch as the righteous cannot dwell side-by-side with those living in iniquity, the city had to be removed from the Earth. Zion and its inhabitants will, however, return to the Earth at the Second Coming of Jesus Christ.

The *Book of Moses,* an excerpt of Smith's translation of the *Holy Bible*, appears in the *Pearl of Great Price* and provides several chapters giving an account of Enoch's preaching, visions and conversations with God. In these same chapters, the reader discovers details concerning the wars, violence and natural disasters in Enoch's day, in addition to many notable miracles performed by Enoch. Since the Salt Lake City church does not hold the copyright to Smith's *Inspired Version of the Bible*, the seeker needs to obtain a copy of it in its entirety from the Community of Christ in Independence, Missouri, formerly known as the Reorganized Church of Jesus Christ of Latter-day Saints.

In 1831, Joseph Smith appointed William W. Phelps, the church printer at Kirtland, Ohio, to go ahead to Independence, Missouri, and establish a printing press there (*Doctrine and Covenants*, Section 57:11-14). **The first periodical of the restored church to emerge from this press was volume 1, number 1, of the *Evening and Morning Star*, dated June 1832.** *Notice the direct reference to the planet Venus in the title of the publication.* Considering the Masonic background of Smith, Young, Phelps and other early Mormon leaders, this is easily understood from a more magnanimous theosophical perspective. What is also of importance here are that subsequent monthly issues of the *Star* published items of instruction from the Prophet Joseph Smith for the guidance of the new church; and these items consisted of letters from the Prophet, to include a record of the revelations that he had received. And that among these revelations were excerpts from the new translation of the *Inspired Version* of the Bible, which was then underway. Thus, the earliest publication of the materials now identified by the Salt Lake City church as the *Book of Moses* was in the *Evening and Morning Star*, with the first installment being in August 1832, with another in March 1833, and the third and final in April 1833.

The *Doctrine and Covenants* of the Salt Lake City church, Section 107:48-49, declares that Adam ordained Enoch at 25 years of age, to the higher priesthood, now called the Melchizedek Priesthood. It was later so named after the great high priest to whom the prophet Abraham offered a tithe. In any event, 40 years later God came down and blessed Enoch and he lived for 365 years beyond that until he and his city were "translated," thereby making him 430 years old at the time of this momentous event. Mormons, the nickname bestowed upon the members of the church headquartered in Salt Lake City, also believe that Enoch was the scribe who recorded Adam's blessings and prophecies, respectively bestowed upon and delivered to his children at the site of Adam-ondi-Ahman (*Doctrine and Covenants* 107:53-57).

Of the altar built by Adam at Adam-ondi-Ahman, it was Wilford Woodruff, who would later go on to become the third president of the Mormon Church's Quorum of the Twelve Apostles, succeeding Brigham Young and outlawing polygamy in 1890 so Utah could go forward and become a state in the Union, who wrote in his journal on 30 March 1873: "Again President Young said Joseph the Prophet told me that the garden of Eden was in Jackson Co., Missouri, and when Adam was driven out of the garden of Eden he went about 40 miles to the place which we named Adam Ondi Ahman, and there built an altar of stone and offered sacrifice. That altar remains to this day. I saw it as Adam left it as did many others, and through all the revolutions of the world that altar has not been disturbed. Joseph also said that when the City of Enoch fled and was translated it was where the Gulf of Mexico now is. It left that gulf a body of water."

Joseph Smith is also purported to have stated, on the occasion of some Mormons taking a survey of that region, "that the City of Enoch would again take its place in the identical spot from which it had been detached, now forming that chasm of the Earth, filled with water, called the Gulf of Mexico." See Jospeh Young (brother to the Prophet Brigham Young), *Enoch and His City* (1878 church pamphlet), 12.

However, the big question remained as to where Enoch and his City of Zion were translated to? To answer that question, one must explore deeper in the lore of the Latter-Day Saints, where ***we discover that it was removed to the planet Venus for temporary safekeeping.*** In 1881 Charles Lowell Walker was in the Salt Lake Valley and recorded in his diary a conversation he had with one of the surviving plural wives of Joseph Smith, Eliza R. Snow, who informed him that her late husband once told her that the Earth was much smaller now than it was when first in the process of being created, since both the Earth and Venus

been seen in her Earthly form in the vicinity of Mt. Shasta in Northern California, where it is believed by her followers that she was carried off by angels to live in a glorious paradise prepared for her on a more spiritually advanced sphere.

Her first book, *Ye Are Gods*, came out in 1952 and proved to be number one on the best sellers list, at least along Utah's Wasatch Front. *Ye Are Gods* took a groundbreaking approach to the Mormon faith, first because it was written by a woman and not a presiding elder of the Melchizedek Priesthood in the hierarchy of the Church of Jesus Christ of Latter-Day Saints, and second due to its uniquely metaphysical, even theosophical approach to the religion restored to the Earth by Joseph Smith in 1830. The rank-and-file Mormons were ecstatic with the publication of the book. Skarin, the beautiful and inspiring author, was in constant demand as a speaker in local Latter-Day Saints' church halls or wards.

While the Mormon Church hierarchy allowed women to speak in local assemblies, they did not believe that they could hold the priesthood, and hence receive revelations for anyone but themselves. In other words, they did not doubt that Annalee Skarin could receive revelations of a personal nature; but they did not believe she had the right to reveal or teach them to anyone else or to reinterpret those revelations already given by modern church leaders or ancient prophets in the *Bible* or *The Book of Mormon*. Therefore, in June 1952 a special meeting was called in the East Side Hillcrest Ward, where Skarin's church membership was registered. Elder Mark E. Peterson was summoned to preside over the proceedings for the excommunication of Annalee Skarin. Peterson denounced the book and declared that Skarin would henceforth "be delivered to the buffetings of Satan for writing it." This was nothing short of a "kangaroo court," as poor Annalee Skarin had to stand in silence before a panel of criticizing elders who had not even read her book. Like Caiphas, the high priest who denounced Jesus in the council of the Sanhedrin, Peterson probably thought the "whole thing would blow over in a couple of weeks, and everyone would forget about it."

However, in two weeks she claimed to have encountered an angel who transported her to an ethereal temple inside Mount Shasta. It was inside this sacred mountain where she was

were truly "twin planets" originating in the same formation of cosmic dust and other materials flung off from the Sun. But at some time in the distant past, billions of years ago, this cosmic cloud split in half with that material that would become Venus moving into an orbit closer to the Sun. It was in this new orbital position that Venus developed along similar geological lines as that of the Earth, with oceans and continents graced with pleasant river valleys. It also served as the domain of righteous, angelic beings who welcomed the arrival of Enoch and his fellow translated beings, to live happily among them until such time as conditions on Earth had improved and the Earthlings could be restored to their rightful planet. Further details concerning Venus and its development appear in Mormon anthropologist Dr. John Heinerman, *People in Space: Extraterrestrial Life on Other Worlds* (San Rafael, California: Cassandra Press, 1990). In this book, Heinerman examines the teachings of Latter-day Saint leaders with respect to the advanced inhabitants found on the Moon and other planets in our solar system and beyond.

The writings of early twentieth century Theosophists C. W. Leadbeater, Annie Besant, etc., as well as those authors influenced by them, such as Alice A. Bailey, Benjamin Creme, and the Ascended Master Teachings of Guy Ballard, Elizabeth Clare Prophet, Geraldine Innocente, Joshua David Stone, Clayton Parker and other Ascended Master Teachings / teachers, indicate that Sanat Kumara, an "Advanced Being" at the ninth level of initiation who is regarded as one of the "Lords" or "Regents" of Earth and of all humankind, is thought to be a member of the Spiritual Hierarchy of Earth that dwells in Shamballah, also known as the "City of Enoch," located on Venus. Some metaphysicians also refer to this city as Azure, because of the prominence of blue crystalline towers throughout. However, Shamballah may be accessed through an Eastern Hemispheric portal in the Gobi Desert and a Western Hemispheric portal at Mt. Shasta in California. See Werner Schroeder, *Ascended Masters and Their Retreats* (Mt. Shasta, California: Ascended Master Teaching Foundation, 2004), wherein a description of the founding of Shamballah by Sanat Kumara can be found.

converted into a "translated being" and flown back to Salt Lake City on the "wings of angels." Now back in the heart of Zion, she went on to produce eight more books. Despite the Mormon Church's efforts to silence Skarin and confiscate her books from those members holding copies, all of them are still in print and selling like pancakes at an all-you-can eat I-HOP special. And in spite of her run-in with the Mormon hierarchy, Skarin has become a cult-figure in New Age circles, especially out in California.

From the perspective of the Mormon Church, however, the major objection of their General Authorities was, as Elder Peterson stated, that "Mrs. Skarin announces that she has received her books as revelations from the Lord." This is not to say that the Mormon hierarchy does not believe in continuous revelation, for it does. But it qualifies this in that all of the Latter-day Saint apostles proclaim that only the president of their quorum is authorized to receive such for the guidance of the church. And Peterson vehemently protested that in her writings and public statements, "Annalee does not so much as mention the president of the Church," adding that she "attempts to give revelations on her own part and defends this fact even though she is a woman." This castigation of Annalee Skarin on Peterson's part comes across more as envy of the Mormon prophetess, making him sound more like a proponent for the doctrines of the Afghani Taliban than the Quorum of the Twelve Apostles of the Church of Jesus Christ of Latter-day Saints.

Contemporary Mormon feminist leader Joanna Brooks also wonders why her church, to which she has been a lifelong member, does not hold women in greater esteem, especially since there is a Latter-day Saint doctrine that God is not only a Heavenly Father, but a Heavenly Mother as well. Brooks notes that, "The idea proceeds very logically from *Doctrine and Covenants* 132:19–20, which teaches that marriage in an LDS temple is a requirement for attaining the highest levels of heaven, or 'exaltation.' Those who do, the scripture states, 'shall be gods.'" Clearly, not a one of the twelve apostles would make it past the pearly gates and exaltation without having a celestial wife in tow.

Apart from the Catholics, who esteem Mary as the "Queen of Heaven," the Mormons may be one of the few groups of Christian religionists who accord a divine potential to women. Elaborating on the Heavenly Mother doctrine, Brooks writes in her blog, *Ask Mormon Girl*, the following:

"If doctrine holds that only the married are exalted to godhood, then it follows quite rationally that God is a married couple. This beautiful, symmetrical idea found an early articulation by the LDS leader Eliza R. Snow in her hymn, "O My Father": "In the heavens, are parents single? / No, the thought makes reason stare. / Truth is reason, truth eternal, / Tells me I've a mother there." This hymn is in the official *LDS Hymnbook* and is regularly sung in Mormon congregations around the world. And the 1995 "Proclamation on the Family" refers to our "Heavenly Parents." Clearly, our Mother is no secret. But she sure feels like a secret. You could listen in on a year's worth of Mormon meetings and scarcely hear her named...."[599]

So what gives? Eliza R. Snow, the author of the Heavenly Mother hymn referenced by Brooks, was born the second daughter of Oliver and Rosetta Snow in Becket, Massachusetts in 1804, the same year in which the Prophet Joseph Smith was born. She also had a younger brother, Lorenzo, who went on to become the fifth president of the Mormon Church. Her family moved to Mantua in Northeast Ohio in 1806 as homesteaders on the Western Reserve.

---

599 Joanna Brooks, "Why do we not talk about Heavenly Mother?" 19 June 2012, *Ask Mormon Girl* blog, https:// askmormongirl.wordpress.com/2012/06/19/ask-mormon-girl-why-do-we-not-talk-about-heavenly-mother/ (Accessed 15 February 2015).

They frequently welcomed preachers of all religious persuasions into their farm home and first came in contact with the Latter-day Saints when Smith, who lived but five miles up the road in Hiram, Ohio, paid a missionary visit to their home in 1831. In the succeeding years, the entire Snow family came to believe the young Joseph Smith. By 1835, they were all baptized into the church at the headquarters in Kirtland, Ohio, and Snow was hired on as a private teacher for the Smith family. As Smith and the Latter-day Saints moved west, Eliza and the rest of her family followed suit, helping to start Mormon settlements at Adam-ondi-Ahman in Missouri, and then on to Nauvoo, Illinois, sometimes referred to as the "City Beautiful." It was in Missouri that Smith revealed to Eliza that the City of Enoch had been translated to the planet Venus; and it was at the Mormon temple in Nauvoo, Illinois, where Eliza R. Snow entered into a polygamous relationship as the second wife of Joseph Smith on 29 June 1842. After Smith's assassination at the jailhouse in Carthage, Illinois, in 1844, Eliza was taken on as one of the polygamous wives of the new church leader Brigham Young, where she made the great trek with him to the Salt Lake Valley, arriving there on 2 October 1847. She was a renowned poet, historian and songwriter. She also established the Relief Society for women as an auxiliary organization to the male priesthood and formed the Primary school system for the Latter-day Saint children, whose symbol was- not so coincidentally- a beehive.

Despite her gender, Eliza R. Snow is regarded as one of the greatest Mormon leaders of the nineteenth century. Nobody was going to tell her that she had to be a priesthood holder in order to say something of doctrinal merit and be taken seriously. But in getting back to the idea of a Heavenly Mother, as outlined in Eliza R. Snow's majestic hymn, Brooks notes that:

"The silence around Heavenly Mother is not doctrinal. A far-reaching study published in the journal *BYU Studies* last year located more than six hundred references to Heavenly Mother in the writings and speeches of LDS Church leaders. It's really an important read…. and the authors find that there is *absolutely no doctrinal basis for the prohibition of discussion of Heavenly Mother*. And that's the journal *BYU Studies*, for crying out loud.

The silence around Heavenly Mother, then, is cultural. It's just a human tradition—a habit that fell into place and has become difficult to dislodge. We don't find her as the object of discussion or even mention in General Conference speeches. Little inquiry is made into her attributes, character, or contributions, as if such concerns were marginal or even fringe. And thus for many decades there was a virtual vacuum of substantive reflection on Heavenly Mother."[600]

Brooks considers some of the non-doctrinal, folkloric reasons that she has encountered over the years for maintaining a cone of silence about the Heavenly Mother. First, she mentions growing up in the 1980s when she heard her Mormon seminary teacher state that Heavenly Father himself prohibits discussion of our Heavenly Mother because He wants to protect Her from the abuse of the world—from regular mortals taking Her name in vain, and the like. But Brooks dismisses this as, "a story that always sounded utterly preposterous to me. As if *God Herself* were too fragile!" After all, Catholics have never shied away from proclaiming the glories of Mother Mary, so why should Mormons hesitate to discuss any aspects of our Heavenly Mother in the higher realms?

Second, Brooks explains that she sometimes hears in Mormon circles the hushed speculation that we don't talk about Heavenly Mother because there are in fact plural Heavenly Mothers. This tidbit of theological speculation can be traced to the nineteenth-century Latter-day Saint

---

600 *Ibid.*

theologian Orson Pratt's *The Seer*, which even in its own day was disavowed by church authorities as a speculative rather than a doctrinal text.

Nevertheless, Brooks has also met contemporary polygamous, fundamentalist Mormon women who do believe that Heavenly Father has many exalted wives, i.e. many Heavenly Mothers for the benefit of all humankind. She recently spent a memorable evening with some of these unique women, gathered around a dining room table to discuss the matter of a Heavenly Mother, and took note that, "They were so utterly scandalized by the fact that talking about Heavenly Mother was so scandalized in the mainstream LDS Church."

The Mormon feminist explored the scandalous nature of the Heavenly Mother discourse even further:

"The residual speculative idea that there are plural Heavenly Mothers is substantiated in some mainstream Mormon minds by the polygamous facets of *Doctrine and Covenants* 132, plus current LDS temple sealing policies that permit living husbands to be sealed to more than one wife for the eternities (but not wives to husbands), as well as an ultra-literal projection of human procreation onto Heavenly Parents. Yes, it's true that some LDS people today imagine that our Parents in Heaven create the spirits of humankind in a manner similar to the means through which the bodies of humankind are created on Earth. That's a lot of spiritual procreation, the story goes, hence the need for so many Heavenly Mothers. Again, none of this is doctrine, but it is the kind of storytelling we hear in the absence of doctrine."[601]

When it comes to what is really going on in the heavens, most anyone's guess is probably as good as another's. Many of my friends from the local congregation of Jehovah's Witnesses, for example, frequently deliver pamphlets to my home depicting people out in the Sun building houses, painting these homes or mowing grass on a celestial, post-apocalyptic Earth. If doing hard labor and working up a sweat like that is what the eternities are all about, I'd rather go back to the medieval version of floating on a cloud and strumming a harp with the angels. Thus, in the Mormon folkloric version of the Celestial Kingdom, extending to countless worlds throughout the universe, Brooks comments that, "Just for the record, I'll say it again, *I know plenty of women who would firmly disagree that eternal pregnancy in the company of a gaggle of eternally pregnant wives is no heaven.*" So short of traveling to ultra-dimensional Venus in a flying saucer, or being translated there, one can only speculate about the wonders to be behold and participate in.

The kind of persecution that Annalee Skarin faced from the Mormon Church is still going on, the likes of which Brooks relates in the following account:

"A few weeks ago, I was in a group of LDS women, when one of the women related a story of a friend who had given a talk on Heavenly Mother on Mother's Day in his LDS congregation in the western U.S. He was extremely cautious, crafting his talk only from on-the-record statements by high-ranking LDS leaders. Why not, after all, talk about Heavenly Mother on Mother's Day? But as soon as he finished his talk, he was followed at the pulpit by his bishop, who denounced the talk and shamed the man. Within a few weeks, his Stake Presidency issued a statement asserting that talk of Heavenly Mother was prohibited.

'That was wrong,' I said to the women in the group. 'That's not doctrinal.'

'How do you know?' the woman looked at me with big fearful eyes, stunned.

'Because I know,' I said. 'It's not a mystery. The official statements are available for everyone to study. We need to take responsibility for knowing our own religion, right?'"[602]

601 *Ibid.*
602 *Ibid.*

In this case, the Latter-day Saint bishop was clearly out of line. But the refusal of the congregants to know and act on their own doctrine served to keep the very idea of the Heavenly Mother suppressed. And in exploring that refusal, we find its roots in the gender-conservative Mormon culture that often privileges polite demurral and passivity in women over intellectual curiosity and authority. Declares Brooks, "Perhaps the quiescence we assign to Heavenly Mother is a reflection of what Mormon culture at its most conservative values in women."

Why should it come as any surprise that feminists continue to be ostracized in the Mormon Church? No sooner do they speak out, than the hard, squashing hammer of the priesthood falls down on them. Brooks keeps us posted in her blog site:

"And there was a moment two decades ago when our Mother was once again making a resurgence in Mormon talk and thought, thanks to Mormon feminists like Carol Lynn Pearson, whose marvelous play *Mother Wove the Morning* has given us some of our best imaging of her power and presence. Then, in 1991, President Gordon B. Hinckley gave a talk instructing LDS Church members that it was inappropriate to pray to Heavenly Mother. And Mormon feminist theologian Janice Allred, whose best-known work is a book entitled *God the Mother*, was excommunicated. And in 1996, Professor Gail Houston was fired from Brigham Young University for publicly describing her personal relationship with her Mother in Heaven, including her use of 'meditation' and 'visualization' to deepen that relationship. All of these events, I think, led to a renewed stigma around even talking about our Mother. On a day-to-day basis, she is bracketed in speech, again and again and again."[603]

Only now are Brooks and other Mormon feminists coming to understand what Annalee Skarin did in 1952, that being that all of the Latter-day Saints are responsible for the perpetuation of this silence concerning the Heavenly Mother and the role of women in the modern church. Brooks rhetorically asks, "And who is responsible for the improper value attached to that silence—as if refusing to acknowledge Her or perpetuating some spooky sense of mystery about Her were a sublimely virtuous act? Who is responsible? We are."

While Brooks does not think Mormon Church leaders are plotting to keep Heavenly Mother out of the conversation, she does believe that they are so preoccupied with the many challenges of running a worldwide church that the idea of a Mother in Heaven simply doesn't occur to them, except as a fringe theological speculation. Therefore, it may be up to those Latter-day Saints for whom She is not a fringe concern—*perhaps because She looks like us or someone we love*—to take responsibility for becoming acquainted with the doctrine.

Brooks also thinks that it would behoove us not to blame God for the silence. "After all," she writes, "why would God prohibit discussion of the truth that women are partners in Godhood; that God looks not only like the husbands, brothers, and sons we cherish but also like *us, our sisters, and our daughters*? That She has parts and passions like *ours*, as Mormon doctrine teaches."

The ardent Mormon feminist continues:

"We live in a world where women's bodies are exploited, shamed, abused and distorted beyond recognition in popular culture, with serious spiritual consequences for men, women, boys, and girls. So many women, including- especially Mormon women- have issues with food, size, and embodiment that are tremendously costly to our spiritual lives and the lives of our families. Understanding the embodiment of God in the female form calls us to emancipation from the distorted and distorting relationships (previously held) to our bodies."[604]

603 *Ibid.*
604 *Ibid.*

Women did not always feel so self-conscious and deprecating about their own bodies. Venus figurines formed as statuettes beginning as far back as 35,000 years ago, portrayed women with exaggerated physical features. Most of these have been unearthed in Europe, but others have been found as far away as Siberia, with their distribution extended across most of Eurasia. These Venus figurines were carved from a sundry variety of soft stones, such as steatite, calcite or limestone; bone or ivory, or formed of clay and fired. The clay Venuses are among the oldest ceramics known. In total, there are over a hundred such figurines extant; virtually all of modest size, between 4 cm and 25 cm in height. They are among some of the earliest works of prehistoric art. The majority of these statuettes have small heads, wide hips, and legs that taper to a point, exaggerating the abdomen, hips, breasts, thighs, or vulva. In contrast, arms and feet are often absent, and the head is usually small and faceless. Anthropologists speculate that they may have served a ritual, symbolic, or pornographic function. What is most remarkable is that there are no statuettes of the men, i.e. no Jupiter figurines. Apparently the women, collectively viewed in the role of the *creatrix*, held a higher place in the social strata than the men folk in prehistoric times.

And now in the twenty-first century, that some Latter-day Saint women are developing a deeper relationship with and getting closer to their *creatrix* through meditation and visualization, Annalee Skarin, translated and exalted, looks down from the shining orb of Venus, appreciative of all the Mormon women, and men who continue making an effort to bring Heavenly Mother steadily and politely back into everyday speech and thought among her peoples in the intermountain valleys of the American West. For Annalee Skarin was the seventh of twelve children, born and raised in the rural heart of the gender-conservative Zion. But perhaps it is more than coincidence that she was the seventh child and born on the seventh day of the seventh month. In the Apostle John's *Book of Revelation*, the number seven is imbued with significant prophetic and supernatural meanings. One of Skarin's biographers, Samuel W. Taylor, penned the following:

"Her father was a sturdy Mormon farmer who died when she was nineteen. Annalee was a delicate child but developed into a beautiful young lady. A brief marriage ended in annulment. She then married unhappily again, an ordeal lasting twenty-one years, during which she had two daughters. After a divorce she finally married her true love, Reason Skarin, a police officer in Buffalo, New York. Her oldest child never forgave her for this, and turned against her. Linda, the other girl, remained close to her mother."[605]

Just like Menger and most of the contactees, Skarin had to endure a difficult personal life while making her way in the Earth plane. Regrettably, of the enigmatic Skarin these are the only verifiable facts we have of her controversial life. It would be wonderful if we could acquire additional information; for with each passing year as more become acquainted with her deeply spiritual writings, she continues to gather an ever-expanding entourage willing to proclaim her as a genuine prophetess of the New Age. Skarin herself claimed that as the direct result of a beatific vision, *Ye Are Gods* was "written under the direction and power of God and according to His command."

And while all the controversy swarmed about her, Skarin's youngest daughter Linda was dying of consumption, suffering with the disease over a period of two years. It was at this difficult time when Skarin prayed that Linda would be restored to perfect health; but if meant to die, she would be taken without suffering. But then one night after an unusually long siege,

605   Samuel W. Taylor, "The Puzzle of Annalee Skarin: Was She Translated Correctly?" *Sunstone* magazine, Salt Lake City, Utah, April 1991

she realized that Linda's life force was ebbing out of her body. At that very moment, Skarin dropped to her knees beside Linda's bed, feeling as if her heart would break. But suddenly, in a wild, heartbroken panic, Skarin clung to her, sensing that she could never go on living without this precious little one in her life. Upon holding her tight to her bosom, a long shudder pulsed through Linda's tiny frame. The daughter's body stiffened and then grew limp; but the agony of Skarin's soul was so profound that she found it impossible to express her feelings or even to lessen her grip, albeit letting go. Of this time, Skarin wrote: "I was thinking of myself, not of the little child in my arms- and a wider vision came. It was then that I truly prayed."

And when she looked down for the last time upon that tiny upturned face, Skarin was speechless with gratitude and awe. Her child slept in peace; and all fever was gone. And then, she noted that, "looking up in wonder, *I seemed to see no ceiling in the room -the open dome of heaven shown above. And then, so near that I was startled, I saw the veil of heaven drawn back as the curtains of a stage* - and He stood there - with all the glory, majesty and power of eternity stamped upon His brow, the Savior of the World." Interestingly, this is exactly the description provided by Adamski, Menger and other contactees of their experiences in traveling aboard Venusian spacecraft, where the very walls, ceiling and flooring became transparent, opening the view to outer space. This also occurred while these contactees were on their way to meeting an ascended master. And Carl Sagan borrowed this same motif in describing the view from the inter-dimensional pod that would transport a cosmic voyager to the Vega star system in his best-selling science fiction novel, *Contact*.

The amazing information imparted by Skarin was beginning to change the lives of thousands. However, because Skarin claimed the authorship of *Ye Are Gods* was not hers, "except that I had been called to be the scribe," she "could accept no pay or receive no royalties" for the work. At first, it should be noted that established publishers turned the book down; but so convinced was Skarin of its importance that she borrowed $5,000 to have it published by a vanity press and then went so far as to distribute the first edition gratis. One Salt Lake City book dealer, Eugene Wilson, gave away 500 free copies for her. This was truly a labor of love, if there ever was one.

The Latter-Day Saints and others throughout Utah and the Intermountain West took the book to their bosoms, forming study groups to discuss it. This continued into the late 1980s, with about a dozen individuals meeting each month in the home of Kay Studstrup in Salt Lake City, organizing as a chapter of the Outer Space International Research and Investigations Society (OSIRIS). Not long after the Harmonic Convergence of 16 and 17 April 1987, this chapter, of which I was the director, traveled to Mt. Shasta at the behest of the Rev. Clayton Parker, who promised us that we would meet an ascended master there as we got closer to the summit. The reverend, who organized a church to propagate the teachings of Annalee Skarin and the I Am Presence, said that he would stay behind, so we could have more time, individually, with an enlightened being from the cosmos. Apart from many amazing experiences shared in our caravan's journey to the magic mountain, our physical encounter with a young extraterrestrial woman at the point of a spring spurting from a rock high above the tree line was the decided epiphany of all our lives.

As we sat down at the base of a massive rock to take a sip of the spring water and rest for a while, a thin, young woman with reddish-hair, being about five feet, ten inches in height, and dressed in a white jump suit, appeared seemingly out of nowhere. She had the appearance of being in her late teens or early twenties and identified herself as Lady Encara, stating that she knew why we had come to the mountain and further explained that she was prepared to answer all of our questions. We stayed there for quite some time, taking in accurate knowledge about our universe and the angelic realms, but losing track of the passing of time in the process. Our spiritual eyes were opened as a result of this encounter, and we thanked Lady Encara for her graciousness in visiting us and sharing the information that we would eventually impart to all our readers in the pages of the *New Millennial Star.* Upon bidding farewell to Lady Encara, Kay asked if she could take a photograph of her for a keepsake of the visit, to which she voiced no objections, other than no flash camera was to be used to secure it.

After Kay Studstrup snapped the photograph, we all took turns in embracing and hugging Lady Encara, and then slowly and carefully made our way back down the mountain to thank Rev. Parker for bringing us to this sacred spot and also relating to him the incredible account of our rendezvous with the extraterrestrial. Interestingly enough, about one week later, after Kay had picked up the developed photos of the Shasta trip from her local drug store, it was noted that while all of the OSIRIS chapter members were in the group picture that was taken with Lady Encara, the beautiful lady from the stars was nowhere to be seen in it.

But getting back to the day of the encounter, it was later in the evening that Rev. Parker confided in me that Lady Encara was the name that Annalee Skarin had taken for herself after her permanent ascension to the heavens in 1982. For while she was translated in 1952 following her excommunication from the Mormon Church, she remained on the Earth long enough to write and publish many more books. Rev. Parker was the last one to see Annalee Skarin while she still had a postal address on the Earth. He met with her on the porch of a health food store outside of Redding, California, on her birthday in 1982. Skarin asked him if he could drive her to up to Mt. Shasta, for there were certain points of doctrine that she wanted him to clarify with her followers regarding the true nature of the Celestial Realm; and she could take advantage of the leisurely drive to the mountain in order to accomplish this task.

The Rev. Parker and Annalee Skarin shared a long history. Back in 1952, when Skarin started to preach at fireside chats in Salt Lake City's East Ninth Street Hillcrest Ward (chapel), Parker was one of the first to become enthralled with her message, hanging on to every word that she uttered, as if it were honey from the spiritual honeycomb. But at one ward meeting in the late spring of that year, in the middle of one of Skarin's discourses on the teachings of Joseph Smith regarding the mission of beings from other planets of the solar system, to include Venus, where the translated city of Enoch is located, Elder Mark E. Peterson of the Council of the Twelve Apostles just barged in and confronted her, telling everyone to go home because Skarin's book was "inspired by Satan." The so-called "apostle" then labeled Skarin an "apostate" and told her in loud and not uncertain terms that unless she repented and repudiated her book, *Ye Are Gods,* she would soon find herself on a "runaway train to outer darkness."

Moments after Peterson's outburst, Parker was startled to see a gang of the local congregation's elders seize Skarin from both sides, dragging her by her arms into the office of the bishop. Of course, Parker and some others got up, trying to protect Skarin, but six young men, most likely returning missionaries, blocked the door to the bishop's office. Standing in a row in front of the door, each with their arms folded across their chest, they stood as silent sentinels, not allowing anyone to pass. Of what transpired in the bishop's office, Skarin related that, "I was refused counsel. My efforts to bear witness to what I had written, or even to defend myself, were denied and silenced." In all of these, Parker saw parallels to the New Testament, where first Jesus found himself before the wicked priests of the Sanhedrin before being sent further along to Pontius Pilate for the sentencing. The bishop, however, who knew Skarin and her family well, hesitated to take any immediate actions. He believed that Skarin needed to have time to prepare her defense, and that a matter of this magnitude should really be decided by the General Authorities in Church Administration. Therefore, that is exactly where her case went, coming under the jurisdiction of the Quorum of the Twelve Apostles in June of that year. Truly, both Jesus and Skarin were treated badly, as lambs to the slaughter. And in the meantime, there were local purges, with Parker and other sympathizers trying to defend the problematic Skarin being rewarded with excommunication for their efforts.

Rev. Parker, only one year younger than Skarin,[606] agreed to take the prophetess to the mountain. On the way there, the reverend recalled that the last time he had seen Skarin, many of her teeth were missing, and most of the few remaining were otherwise in terrible shape. But now, even though she was 83 years old, her teeth were not only all present and accounted for, but they looked brand new. Rev. Parker commented on the beautiful teeth, and said, "For store-bought teeth, they sure look real enough to me." To that, Skarin laughed and said, "They're not dentures, but the real thing. One morning a couple of weeks ago, I woke up and they were just there, all grown back in, real and natural." Other matters that Skarin brought up in the car with the reverend were later written down by him in a notebook and shared with members of his local Murray, Utah, congregation as well as those in the Salt Lake City OSIRIS chapter. In 1988, Parker also published a book, *My Will Be Done Through Clayton* (Salt Lake City, Utah: Paragon Press), with 201 pages containing messages channeled to him directly from the I Am Presence.

Once at the stream that pours forth from the rock on the slopes of Mt. Shasta, the two fast friends bid farewell to one another. And then, raising her hand to the square, an orb whose brightness outshined the Sun descended from the sky, engulfing Skarin in what appeared to be a flame of living and sparkling golden light. The reverend would later comment that, "The prophetess was going home to be with the angels and the gods, forevermore to assume her rightful place in the Celestial Kingdom. Now I know what Peter, James and John felt like when they went with Jesus up to the Mount of Transfiguration."

In later life, Annalee Skarin, Sanat Kumara, Lady Venus and other ascended masters would appear to Clayton at unscheduled times and diverse locations. The brilliance of their auras was so intense, that Clayton complained that it was burning out his eyes. But after a few encounters with these exalted beings, he began to carry a special pair of eyeglasses, the lenses of which were darkened but peppered with small holes that he could squint through in order to look at these angels and gods without actually going blind. And after his first encounter with the ascended Annalee, Clayton became the strictest of vegetarians. He always carried a plastic bag full of mixed nuts and raisins with him, however, especially when trekking up and down the mountain trails in Northern California's Trinity County and Mt. Shasta region.

606 Obituary, *Deseret News*, Wednesday, 10 December 1997, Salt Lake City, Utah: "Clayton A. Parker, passed away peacefully in Ogden, Utah, Dec. 8, 1997, at the age of 97. He was born in Joseph, Utah, January 23, 1900, a son of Joseph William and Margaret Jane Neel Parker. He married Irene Gibbs, June 11, 1930. They were later divorced and he married Sylvia D. Mast, August 14, 1975. She died December 5, 1996. He was a veteran of World War I, having served in the US Marine Corps in the invasion of France and Germany. He is survived by two sons: C. Gerald (Helen) Parker, Kaysville; Russell G. (Karen) Parker, Houston, TX; four daughters: Janet (Lincoln) Sorensen, North Ogden; Peggy (Karl) Miller, Sandy; Kathryn (John) Stevens, Bountiful; Colette (Kim) Malan, Ogden; and many grandchildren and great-grandchildren; sisters,....
Funeral services will be held at 12 noon, Friday, December 12, 1997 in the Wasatch Lawn Mortuary Chapel, 3401 South Highland Drive, where family and friends may call on Thursday evening from 6-8 p.m. and on Friday from 10:45-11:45 a.m. prior to services...." He was interred at the North Ogden Cemetery.

As noted previously, Skarin's life experiences were very much in line with those of the contactees. Like Howard Menger in High Bridge, New Jersey, Skarin became a reluctant celebrity in the Buffalo area, once she had moved there to be with her new husband, Reason. Any credit for miracles, she claimed, belonged to God, and not herself. Many in Buffalo and the surrounding area had confused Annalee Skarin and her ministry with that of Kathryn Kuhlman, the Pentacostal evangelist and faith healer operating out of Pittsburgh, Pennsylvania. Besides sharing a similar appearance, it should be noted that Skarin's and Kuhlman's "heart-to-heart" messages proved to be inspirational for thousands. Their abilities to yield the power of the Holy Spirit generated a continued interest and desire from people all around the world to seek out and go deeper into their advanced teachings. After all, both would concur with Kuhlman's motto that, "Nothing is impossible with God!"

And while no doubt many were blessed from the ministries of both Kuhlman and Skarin, it was the latter prophetess who sought to get the farthest away from the crowds. Both she and her husband went into seclusion for a while because, as she so aptly stated, "Too many were seeking to take hold of us, expecting us to do their fulfilling for them. This was impossible; the Kingdom of Heaven dwelt in every bosom. Each individual has the complete path of his own divine progress . . . right within himself." In this regard, Skarin's case closely paralleled Menger's, where many of the contactee's followers made their way up to his High Bridge farm, thinking that they were going to get a god from outer space to personally intervene and solve all of their problems for them. And in response to this pressure, the Mengers quit ufology, selling their farm, packing up and moving their whole family down to Florida. Another interesting similarity in the contact scenario is that of the rock motif. The beautiful Venusian appears to Menger on numerous occasions at the big rock on his farm property; while Lady Encara, the ascended Annalee Skarin, materializes for the benefit of her devotees at the rock spring on the slopes of Mt. Shasta.

Because Skarin rejected the material things of the world, it was her contention that the only reality of any consequence was the mind and spirit. Therefore, one could say that she was an ascetic in the pattern of all the great mystics, down through the ages. And like all explorers of the supernatural realms, Skarin needed a retreat from the "matrix" we ordinary mortals must endure on an everyday basis.

Living in the Salt Lake City of the early 1950s was to breathe, eat, drink and sleep Mormonism. Clearly, one might think that being in such an environment- in the world yet so apart from it- would prove beneficial to Skarin as she sought inspiration to write *Ye Are Gods* and many of the other books that were to follow. Over the ages, authors have employed various devices and methods for courting the muse. One way that I get warmed up is by listening to and watching some of my favorite videos on You Tube: Alesso's *We Could Be Heroes*, Pat Benatar's *We Belong*, the Carpenters' version of Klaatu's *Calling Occupants of Interplanetary Craft*, Joan Osborne's *One of Us*, the closing scenes from the 2012 movie version of *Les Misérables* and Freedom Music's *Dolores Barrios and the Sixth Race of Love*, replete with its chorus of "Venus is rising." But the only inspiration Skarin could find to write came after she had got on her knees to fervently pray. Long before the actual work of creative writing began, Skarin remarked that "the calluses upon my knees bore witness" to the search for inspiration, adding that, "When the book, *Ye Are Gods*, was scheduled to come forth, I spent many anguished hours pleading with God to have someone important write that glorious record." The Mormon prophetess was going to quit until one day she received word that she was chosen as the author because of her strong faith. Thereafter, "under direction of God and according to his command," Skarin related that she wrote with "fire and tears as the Light of God poured through my being and out through my fingertips upon the pages placed in the typewriter." After she found the muse, it only took thirty days for her to write the book.

Meanwhile, back at the East Side Hillcrest Ward, Latter-day Saints under the direction of Clayton Parker formed the first study group for enthusiasts of her book. Word spread like wildfire of the coming excommunication trial throughout the intermountain empire of Mormon wards and missionary districts, so when the verdict of Annalee's trial by a church court was announced in an open meeting in the Hillcrest Ward, James D. Wardle, an observer sent from the local branch of the Reorganized Church of Jesus Christ of Latter-day Saints, reported that, "You can be sure these doings created a lot of excitement." Wardle, a barber in Salt Lake City who maintains what well might be the finest private collection of Latter-day Saints' materials in the world, reported to Taylor that, "I attended the meeting and heard it done. The hall was packed, with not even standing room in the wings." But Wardle, unlike the Latter-day Saints of the Utah church, felt that the only thing wrong with *Ye Are Gods* was that the Salt Lake City church officials, "just could not stand having a mere woman teaching their own doctrine and.... having it accepted as inspiration through her, instead of themselves."

The Utah church was now in a quandary of what to do about Annalee Skarin, for soon after her excommunication, she vanished, "going off the grid," so to speak. There were even numerous eyewitnesses to this, in addition to testifying that she had become a translated being. By late 1956, as news of Skarin gained worldwide attention, an unusual denunciation of her and her ministry appeared in a full page article of the *Church News* on 3 November. Various church priesthood leaders took turns in trying to demolish her image. They referred to her followers as nothing but gullible "cultists," and further stated that her so-called translation was nothing but a "disappearing act" which she had used twice before in the Buffalo, New York, area. According to the article, this was "her stock in trade, especially if the act can be staged with the trappings of the occult." Wardle informed Taylor that the *Deseret News*, which publishes the *Church News* on a weekly basis for the Mormon Church, was supposedly provided the material used to denounce Skarin by her eldest daughter. But then a prophet is rarely accepted, even in her own household.

Skarin came up with eight more books in a twenty-one year span following her translation. Whether she wrote these books while resident on Venus or some other world, or in hiding here on Earth, still remains a mystery. But we do know that she kept busy. The success of her first book, *Ye Are Gods*, guaranteed that the others would also be best sellers. The second book in the Skarin collection was *Sons of God*, written under the ghost name of "Christine Mercie" (1954). This was followed by *To God the Glory* (1956); *The Temple of God* (1958); *Secrets of Eternity* (1960); *Celestial Song of Creation* (1962); *Man Triumphant* (1966); *Beyond Mortal Boundaries* (1969); and *The Book of Books* (1973), with all of them focused on the "how to" of obtaining translation to a higher realm.[607]

Mormon historian Samuel W. Taylor, writing on the life of Annalee Skarin in the Mormon intellectual *Sunstone* magazine of April 1991, notes that:

"With nine books in print after many editions, and with a growing Skarin cult actively promoting her works, she very possibly is the most successful author the Mormon culture has produced. Though officially cast out, she maintained her faith in LDS doctrine. Annalee

---

607 All of Annalee Skarin's books were published by Devorss of Camarillo, California.

claimed that 'I was to have the gift and power of the 'Three Nephites,' that I would be able to go forth…. to serve mankind and help bring the world to light," while the "same promise is yours if you only lay hold of it.' She believed in the literal promise "of overcoming death given in what is known as the 'Word of Wisdom!'…. 'And, I, the Lord, give unto them a promise that the destroying angel shall pass by them'…. She claimed that *'Death is the dreary, backdoor entrance into the other world. It is the servant's entrance. But there is a great front door of glory for those who overcome.'"*

Taylor maintains that he has a Mormon friend that also lays claim to the "Word of Wisdom," but that he does not expect to be translated, nor become immortal, but merely that he will live to be a ripe 500 years old. While he retired at age 65, that would mean that he could be living off Social Security for 435 years, something that even the Obama administration couldn't afford to pay out, let alone budget.

In *Man Triumphant*, written 14 years after her excommunication, Annalee Skarin wrote:

"I was not hanged as a witch. I was not crucified. I was stoned to death …. And the great man who hurled those stones of mockery and falsehood had others hold his cloak while he did the stoning…. In the tragedy of my heartbreak and in the overwhelming grief of my sorrow I went forth an outcast."

But so it is with all the prophets, rejected of their own people, but finding solace and renewed hope in the protective arms and enfolding wings of an angel. There is an "Editor's Note" on the flyleaf of *Ye Are Gods* that reads: "Soon after publishing the first edition of this remarkable book the author, Annalee Skarin, according to Affidavits in our files, underwent a physical change known as "translation," such as did Enoch of Biblical days." Since Skarin could no longer spend a lot of time with the Latter-day Saints, helping them overcome the vicissitude of problems they would continue to encounter on a daily basis, she was moved to follow the admonition of Joseph Smith, who stated in 1834: "I teach them correct principles and they govern themselves" (*Doctrine and Covenants* 58:26).

Lost in "Translation"

The various canonical scriptures of the Church of Jesus Christ of Latter-day Saints refer to a unique class of beings, individuals whom the Lord or some other divine entity has "translated," or changed from a mortal state to one wherein they are temporarily exempt from death; and neither can they experience pain nor sorrow, except for the sins of the world. Mark L. McConkie, a general authority of the church, writes in the *Encyclopedia of Mormonism* that while such beings appear to have much greater power than mortals, "All translated beings will eventually experience death and resurrection." The general authority then explains that translation is a necessary condition in special instances to advance the work of the Lord.

The important distinction made in the *Book of Mormon* is that translated beings are not resurrected beings, albeit that all translated beings either have since been or yet will be resurrected, or "changed in the twinkling of an eye" into a resurrected state (3 *Nephi* 28:8). Besides Enoch and his people, however, Joseph Smith's *Pearl of Great Price* indicates that there may have been many others who were translated before the flood, whereby "they were caught up by the powers of heaven unto Zion" (*Moses* 7:27). And in the generations after the great deluge, it also appears that many righteous ones "were translated and taken up into heaven" (*Inspired Version, Genesis* 14:32-34). In the *New Testament*, it is John the Beloved who is translated (*John* 21:20-23), while in the Americas, there are three Nephites who receive this spiritual boon, for according to 3 *Nephi* 28:7 in the *Book of Mormon*, these were the Western Hemisphere disciples blessed by Jesus to "never taste of death; but ye shall live to behold all the doings of the Father unto the children of men, even until all things shall be fulfilled according to the will of the Father, when I shall come in my glory with the powers of heaven."

Throughout the history of the Latter-day Saints, there have been many reported sightings of one, two or all three of these Nephite ministers. My first wife and I even encountered one in a west side supermarket in Salt Lake City in the spring of 1987. As we approached the register to pay for our groceries, the clerk said there was no need to pay for anything, for the gentleman that was ahead of us took care of the bill. The cashier pointed to the door as the man was leaving. He was about six foot tall, had pure white hair and was dressed in a white suit with white slacks, much as one would wear inside the Mormon temple. I bolted to the door, hoping to catch up with him before he got to his car, so I could thank him for his kindness. But once outside the door, I scanned up and down the sidewalk and all around the parking lot, and he was nowhere to be seen. Another *Hebrews* 13:2 moment had just transpired, to be sure.

Such translated beings are assigned special ministries. While John the Beloved and the Three Nephites carried out their missions on Earth on a continual basis, other translated persons such as Moses and Elijah made appearances on Earth only on rare occasions, and hundreds of years later in the case of the transfiguration[608] of Christ prior to his resurrection. Joseph Smith explained the unique position of translated beings thusly: "Many have supposed that the doctrine of translation was a doctrine whereby men were taken immediately into the presence of God, and into an eternal fullness; but this is a mistaken idea. Their place of habitation is that of the terrestrial order, and a place prepared for such characters He held in reserve to be ministering angels unto many planets, and who as yet have not entered into so great a fullness as those who are resurrected from the dead."[609]

The question entered my mind if the matter of translation was something particular to Mormonism, or does it have some universal applicability? As a historian of Basque history, I delved into my private library in search of answers, going back to the time when the Basque nation (*Euzkadi*), and the whole of the Iberian Peninsula, fell under the administrative jurisdiction of the Roman Empire, with all its myriad of gods. It appears that apart from the main gods, from whom the planets of the solar system and other celestial objects are named, the Roman religion included a plurality of minor deities.

Of these lesser gods, Roman historian Harold Mattingly writes that their "range was as varied as life itself- nymphs of sea, hill and woodland, 'genii' or spirits of persons and places, beneficent powers that found expression in social and personal life- Pax, Pietas, Concordia and the rest- countless little powers and revealed at a flash in isolated acts and vanishing as soon as revealed. The world in fact was full of gods and their forms were many."[610]

Throughout the empire, its citizens and subjects were cognizant that the gods came in many forms, but assumed a human appearance for our benefit. Of this transformative phenomenon, Mattingly continues: "When fully realized, the gods were realized as persons, and, as the only

---

608   A transfiguration is a more temporary spiritual condition that allows a human being to behold spiritual beings or things not usually possible in a mortal condition. The OSIRIS group's encounter with Lady Encara on the slopes of Mt. Shasta is a good example of transfiguration, where our eyes were opened to beings of various kinds, to include insectoids, from other planets and star systems.

609   Joseph Fielding Smith, *Teachings of the Prophet Joseph Smith* (Salt Lake City, Utah: Deseret Book Company, 1989), 170

610   Harold Mattingly, *Man in the Roman Street* (New York, New York: Numismatic Review, 1947), 21

real persons in our experience are human, they were therefore represented in human form. They had their own houses- their temples- and images (idols) that attested their presence there."[611]

On the Iberian Peninsula, the sundry gods that proliferated throughout the Roman Empire found their specific cores of devotees, to include those followers of Jesus, the Christ. But while Christianity arrived on the Peninsula as just another religion, there was a difference. F. J. Wiseman, a noted historian of Spain under Roman occupation, writes that: "First, it (Christianity) was actively and widely preached by the apostles; secondly, it was opposed to all other religions. Its followers were persecuted from time to time, not because it was in itself a subversive religion, but because it was so intolerant of other beliefs. There was sufficient of a religious act associated with emperor-worship to make the Christian reject it and he was, therefore, persecuted on political grounds as a disloyal citizen." We have to keep in mind at this point that the Roman emperors claimed to be the descendants of the goddess Venus in a direct line.

But Wiseman continues that, "Incidentally, *striking proof of the power of the belief in other gods was provided by the fact that the early Christians acknowledged their existence, but thought that they were the creations of the powers of darkness.*" This is important to keep in mind when considering the evolution of magic in the Basque country, and its ties to extraterrestrial interventions.

In seventeenth century Basque society, many had attained powerful influence through ecclesiastical careers. In my book on the development of a Basque culture in the Sur del Lago Maracaibo region of Venezuela, I focus on its transport there from the western Pyrenees Mountains of the Iberian Peninsula by Captain Juan de Chourio from the village of Ascain, that was once the focal point for religious zealots in the burning of suspected witches. In 1610, a priest of approximately 70 years of age by the name of Arguibel was burned at the stake there for his alleged failure to maintain the purity of Roman Catholic doctrine in his speech and writings. He supposedly was a practitioner of varied forms of Basque magic and witchcraft, and mixed these administrations with his local service as a parish cleric. In that old world of beliefs, all things and people, and their respective images, were united by a mystical power known by the Basques as *adur*. If you had sufficient faith in the *adur*, then whatever was done to the image was bound to happen to the thing or person it represented. This was something akin to African and Caribbean Voodoo. And even if an educated Basque had his doubts about this fetish system, he would maintain silence about it. There is an old Basque saying that goes, "*Direnik, es da sinistu behar; ez direla, es da esan behar.*" Translated, that means that, "If you don't believe they exist (dark spiritual forces), don't say they don't exist." So, in essence, you were damned if you did not acknowledge the existence of magic, and equally condemned if you were seen as too eager to believe it. For a Basque to loose title to her or his home and property, all a Spanish occupational authority had to do was declare her or him a practitioner of witchcraft (*sorgin*).

---

611 *Ibid*, 22

Club Venus

In Journey's *Don't Stop Believing* (1981), we find the opening lyrics:
Just a small town girl
Livin' in a lonely world
She took the midnight train
Goin' anywhere
Just a city boy
Born and raised in South Detroit
He took the midnight train
Goin' anywhere...

The time was early October 2012 and I found myself working in the People's Republic of China as an English teacher of middle and high school students at an international school in Wuxi, a large city in southern Jiangsu Province. Located to the south of Long Mountain, on the outskirts of Wuxi's Mashan Town, the 88 meters (289 feet) tall Grand Buddha statue can be seen. This is one of the largest freestanding Buddha statues in China, and the ninth tallest statue of any type in the entire world.

In any event, I was on a school break waiting for classes to resume following the national holidays. So one cool evening around 5 p.m., I took a brisk walk from my apartment to the downtown shopping district, looking to buy some current American DVDs from a Korean video establishment and a Panda AM-FM-SW radio for my room from an appliance store. In addition, I also wanted to get a little exercise in. And as I lived up on the eleventh floor of a massive apartment complex, I figured that the reception for a short wave radio should be outstanding from the heights.

And then, after purchasing the DVDs and radio, I noticed a back street to the shopping area, jam-packed with bars and restaurants. This street was crowded with locals and tourists, and most of the establishments had English names. One large night club particularly caught my attention, the "Club Venus," so named after my favorite goddess and planet. It was then about 6:30 p.m. and I had plenty of time to kill. You entered the club ascending a spiral staircase on the outside of the building up to the second floor. Once inside, the interior was very dark. There were photos of exotic dancers lining the wall; but they wouldn't appear in the show until after 11 p.m. As much I would have loved to see some "Chinese Venusians," I wasn't going to wait that long for their grand entry. Rather, I opted to sit for a spell and down a few Snow beers. Most of the locals preferred the darker Tsingtao beer, but the foreign residents in China went for the lighter brews.

As I slowly sipped my Snow beers and listened to contemporary Asian rock music blaring from a juke box, suddenly the darkness was pierced by the flashing of overhead strobe lights. Also, there was a huge orange-red dance globe representing the planet Venus that lit up and started to rotate on its own accord above the show platform. At first I thought a show was about to start; but there weren't any girls coming out onto the stage area. Nevertheless, a woman about five foot, two inches in height did emerge from the shadows, walking over to me and seating herself in an adjacent stool up at the bar. Much to my surprise, it was Débora Bergara, the mutual Basque friend of I and Gabriel Green from my days as co-editor and publisher of the *New Millennial Star*. Of course, we were so happy to see each other again, as it had been a quarter of a century since we last met back at Gabriel's home in Yucca Valley, California.

We embraced and I asked Débora if there was anything she would like to eat or drink. She replied that she needed something solid in her stomach; so I ordered a small vegetarian pizza pie for the both of us and some Diet Cokes to go with it. I remembered that during our last encounter, Débora mentioned to all of us at Gabriel's home that Venusians do not consume meat or ingest alcoholic beverages.

When I inquired as to what brought her to China, Débora replied that she was on her way to Tibet to meet up with other Venusians gathering there for the arrival of two motherships that would land at separate locations in the Lakes District to the north of Lhasa. This was to take place at the close of the Mayan Calendar's final Venus cycle on 20 December. While the actual date of the Mayan closure to the last Venus round was to take place on 21st of December in the Western Hemisphere, it would transpire on the 20th in China as its calendar is half a day ahead. But, she insisted on paying me a visit once she got word from friends in ufology circles that I was teaching in Wuxi.

Raymond: Débora, I can't thank you enough for coming to see me here in Wuxi.

Débora: No problem, Raymond. Your work with the *New Millennial Star* earned you a lot of points with the Hierarchy of Light. There were so many readers of that publication that gained enlightenment through your words of wisdom.

Raymond: Well, thank you for your kind words. I have to say, you don't look like you've aged a bit. You are still a ravishing beauty, for someone 427 years old. By the way, how did you get to China?

Débora: I sense that you are thinking about the scout craft, like the one you sighted fly over the railroad trestle at Tinker's Creek in Ohio when you were just ten years old. But this time, I took a China Airlines flight from Brazil. I'm temporarily working as a Portuguese-Mandarin translator for a top secret project of the Brazilian government; and I'm attached to the People's Republic of China's interplanetary research program out at Lop Nur in Xinjiang. We Venusians feel that China will become, as is the United States, a beacon of hope to the peoples of Earth as the decades progress.

Raymond: But being so busy, as you are, how were you able to find the time to visit me here in Wuxi?

Débora: I am currently bi-located. My denser being continues at the research lab in Lop Nur. But through the use of Venusian orb technology, I am the lighter body, the transcendent Débora that you are conversing with now. But I can only hold this bi-located form for the space of about five more hours, as it is night; but only for three hours in daylight.

Raymond: What are you permitted to tell me about the meaning of the Mayan calendar?

Débora: As you know, on Earth the clusters of stars along the plane of your ecliptic form the twelve formations of the Zodiac. But on Venus, we too share a roughly equivalent orbital plane; and we, too, commence our new years with our planet's transition into the constellation of Aquarius. The only difference between your Zodiac and ours is that we add another configuration, Ophiuchus (the Healer), squeezed between Scorpio and Sagittarius, with all of our months coming in much shorter durations because of Venus' closer proximity to the Sun itself.

Every fifth Venusian year heralds the farewell to our old queen and the ascension of a new one. It just so happens that this transition will take place on Venus at the same time as the conclusion of the last 52-year Venus cycle on your Mayan calendar. If at all possible, a Venusian woman has the responsibility to be back on the home world to help in the selection of a new queen and to participate in the ascension ceremonies. I say ceremonies, plural, because the retiring queen ascends into the fifth dimension while the newly selected queen ascends to the throne of Venus.

Raymond: That's awesome, Débora, but could you be more specific about the landing zones for the two motherships?

Débora: The first mothership of the Venusian Starfleet, the *Victory* under the command of Valiant Thor, will come down and hover over the northwest quadrant of Namtso Lake, also known as the "Heavenly Lake," nestled in the mountains in the border region between Damxung County of Lhasa Prefecture and Baingoin County of Nagqu Prefecture in Tibet. It's about 70 miles north by northwest of Lhasa.

Raymond: What is the significance of Namtso Lake?

Débora: From the beginnings of life on Earth, Namtso

Starting in the early 1960s, the Chinese government was preparing the children to cohabit other planets with extraterrestrials. Note both the Earth rockets and Venusian saucer in the background. See http://www.neatorama.com/2012/11/21/Chinese-Space-Children-Posters/.

Lake has served as a marker for Venusian spacecraft penetrating your world's atmospheric envelope, recloaking and establishing a flight path and landing pattern for touchdown in Shamballah, a little further north in the Gobi region. The Tibetan monks know all about it. Because of its frequency in being visited by extraterrestrials and their shining craft, the monks consider the entire lake to be a sacred stargate and have built a monastery on one of its islands. It is the highest salt-water lake in the world and those who bathe in its crystal clear waters have been cured of many ailments. Contrary to popular belief, when George Adamski was but ten years old, it was here that his Uncle Sidney took him to learn at the feet of some of the ascended masters, and not the Grand Potala in Lhasa. Namtso is the daughter of the god Indra (one of the kings of Shamballah) and the wife of Nyenchen Tanglha. The goddess of the lake rides a blue dragon and wields a mirror in her left hand, symbolic of her command ship's reflector array. Her hair is raised in a high bun with the other hair falling gracefully down her back. Some of the monks who have met here say that she is, like all Venusian women, "quite charming."

On 15 October 2003, Yang Liwei became the first taikonaut. While America cuts back on its space program, China advances at light speed to all of the planets of the solar system and beyond. See http://blog.rollom.com/2008/09/chinese-space-program.html.

崇尚科学 破除迷信

Raymond: What about the second mothership's landing zone?

Débora: The second mothership, the *Isis*, commanded by Lady Encara, is currently *en route* to our solar system from the planet Belaton in the Sirius Star Sector. The nature of their work there cannot be revealed to you at this time; but Commander Encara looks forward to seeing you again when we rendezvous with the *Isis* at Siling Co, which is the lake south of the Qiangtang Plateau at an elevation over 4,500 meters. It's the largest lake in Tibet. In the remote past, this lake was the site of a great battle. After the Venusian Starfleet, led by Red Sangha and deployed from Shamballah, liberated Lhasa from its Draconian occupiers, they pursued the remnant serpents to this location where they were rounded up and transported back to their respective home worlds. The memory of this battle survives in the collective consciousness of the monks of the region; and hence they have named the lake Siling Co, which signifies the "Lake of Demons."

Raymond: Oh, Débora, thank you, thank you, thank you! Even seeing you, after all these years, is more than I could have ever hoped for; but to actually rendezvous with the *Isis* and her crew at Siling Co would be living the dream.

Débora: Well, "step on down," Raymond, because you're going to Venus!

The Mysterious Débora Bergara

Those Venusians whose missions bring them to Earth primarily come from the fourth dimensional plane of existence. But it may come as a surprise for many readers to learn that a good many of the Venusians at this level were actually born on the Earth's third dimensional plane. They were, in effect, immigrants to the planet Venus, selected by fifth dimensional beings to become "naturalized" citizens of our sister sphere. Here I am referring to the process of "translation," as previously described. And so it was with both Annalee Skarin and Débora Bergara.

Of course, most Venusians, whether indigenous or translated beings, find it necessary to completely change their identities and operating locations every fifteen to twenty years or so, as Earthlings will begin to wonder why one of their friends seems to defy the aging process. For a while, there were a lot of rumors in ufology circles about Dick Clark of *American Bandstand* fame being a Venusian or some other type of extraterrestrial; but as it turned out, he too made "the journey whence no man can return" at the age of 82, thereby proving that even "America's Oldest Teenager" was himself a mortal being. So Déborah Bergara is only a name chosen for convenience. On Venus, she is known as Lady Orda. But on Earth she was born in 1585 as Catalina de Erauso at San Sebastian, Spain, a city in the mountainous Basque province of Gipuzkoa. Then, as now, the Basques maintained their own language completely distinct from all the linguistic groups of Europe; and strove to preserve both their culture and political identity. Nevertheless, they were and continue to be technically subjects of the Spanish Crown.

During the time of Catalina's birth, Spain was in a Catholic frenzy. This was the golden age of the Catholic Counter-Reformation. Her parents, María Pérez de Galarraga y Arce and Captain don Miguel de Erauso were also born in San Sebastian, and ardent practitioners of the Roman Catholic religion, devout members of their local parish. In order to express their devotion and loyalty to the church, Catalina's parents consigned her, at the age of four, to a life of toil in a Dominican convent, just as they had done with her three older sisters. Now, at the age of 60, I still think back in horror at my first day of kindergarten at Dunham Elementary

School in Maple Heights, Ohio, when I was but five years old in 1959. And oh how I cried and wailed! But that was only for a few hours per day, when school was in session. Imagine what it was like for the young Catalina, trapped in a dank, dark medieval structure and being forced to scrub floors and wash habits. Right away Catalina began to mull over a plan of escape.

Moving ahead to 1600, we find Catalina at age 15 unable to endure convent life anymore. It is eight years since the centenary of Columbus' landing in the New World, so beside the business of the Inquisition, the church takes an active role in the propagation of the Christian faith throughout all the acquired realms that are becoming incorporated into the Spanish Empire. Spain needs every young man it can muster to serve the Crown in converting the heathen of these pagan lands, or failing to do so, reducing these unrepentant indigenous inhabitants with the sword. Catalina's only and older brother, Luis, is already serving as a junior officer at a military garrison in Upper Peru (Bolivia, as of 1825). Most Spanish men actually welcomed military service, for life in Spain at the start of the seventeenth century was tedious at best, availing few opportunities. On the other hand, those adventurers going off to the Indies (the Americas), could escape any of the unprofitable and unseemly elements of their past and shape their future in a decidedly positive direction. The Age of the Conquistadores would not last forever, and Catalina was determined to follow in her brother's footsteps, rising to the challenges and taking advantage of every opportunity. But how could she pull it off, being a woman?

Being trapped in a convent, Catalina more than most women, realized that the prospects for a brighter future were growing increasingly dim, at least insofar as she remained where she was. But even if she were to affect an escape, seventeenth century Spanish society was patriarchal in the extreme. What this meant was that freedoms for women, either civil or religious, were extremely rare. But the clever Catalina has passed eleven years pondering this problem, and comes up with a viable solution.

One of her duties in the convent is to sew garments for the nuns and priests, as well as the knighted benefactors of the local congregation. Then on the evening of 25 March 1600, following vespers on the feast day of San Dimas, she musters the fortitude to carry out a bold plan. In the wee morning hours of darkness, she scurries away to a cave in the outskirts of San Sebastian, where she cuts off her hair and fashions for herself a suit of clothes out of her nun's habit. Having stolen some silver candlesticks from the convent chapel, Catalina rationalizes this act of thievery in her mind, if not her soul, assuming that God owes her that much, at least, for the eleven years of her life she's given Him. Catalina then lays low in the cave for a few days, and then on the night of the third day sets out for Bilbao on the western road, whence she sells the candlesticks for a handful of pesos to a blacksmith along the way in the coastal village of Zumaia.

Catalina has an aunt on her mother's side of the family resident in Bilboa whom she suspects will look favorably upon her efforts to liberate herself from the stifling confines of the convent. This aunt was more than once accused by Catholic religious fanatics of being a *sorgin*, so naturally her love for the clerical establishment was waning. Who better to help a fugitive nun, right? Tired out and on the outskirts of Zumaia, however, Catalina finds shelter in the hayloft of a barn and falls soundly asleep there with the setting of the Sun. In the middle of the night she is awakened by a loud humming noise. The very air is crackling with white and colored sparks, waking her up and nearly blinding her in the process. There is an angel standing over her, who identifies himself as Dysmas, otherwise known as San Dimas in Spain and Portugal.

He was the good thief who was crucified on the right side of the Savior Jesus Christ. For the kind words that he spoke to the Savior, Dysmas was granted immortality in Paradise, where he would enter that realm with the Lord himself in but a few days following their crucifixion.

Dysmas shows the wounds in his hands and feet, placed there by the spikes cruelly driven in by Pilate's Roman guards. "Be not afraid, Catalina," announces the angel. "But do not proceed to Bilboa, for there is danger there. The constables are even now searching the whole of the Basque country for you. Go instead by way of the southern route, proceeding only at night, until you have reached Valladolid, the city of the great explorer Columbus. There you will find a gentle priest, Alejandro, who will aid you in your quest." With that, Dysmas laid his hands on Catalina's head, pronounced a blessing, and faded into a cloud of light. The loft became filled with swarming bees. But none touched Catalina, for even they realized that they were now in the presence of an elevated, divine being.

Pope Urban VIII gives Catalina de Erauso special permission to dress as a man and fight for Spain as a conquistador. See http://celarx.deviantart.com/art/Female-Conquistador-374923680.

Catalina, about a week later, arrives in Valladolid and locates Father Alejandro Prieto, of the Augustinian order, in the great cathedral there in the city plaza. They step into a confessional and Catalina tells him what has happened to her of recent days, including her encounter with the angel. Father Prieto might normally think Catalina possessed of a demon, but ponders the fate of his own soul if she is telling the truth and he causes any harm to her.

The priest risks his life in helping Catalina continue her trek on to Madrid, where he enrolls her as a royal page, the first step in becoming a knight of the realm. Catalina is then sent on to the castle of Manzanares el Real, 30 miles to the north of Madrid. It is an imposing example of the military architecture of the fifteenth century, to begin her training. Of the castle, the *Madrid City Guide* states:

"The construction of the castle began in the year 1475, at a time when Madrid was just a little town. The castle has a quadrangular plant with four towers on the corners. Three cylindrical towers and a larger one known as Torre del Homenaje (Homage Tower) with a squared layout. Each of the three cylindrical towers is crowned with smaller towers, and the "Homage Tower" is finished off with another smaller octagonal tower. The body of the castle has sides of 30 meters and the cylindrical towers have a diameter of 6.5 meters at the base. The central courtyard (called Patio de Armas) is surrounded by corridors with arcades as an example of the late Gothic style with Mudejar influence. Finally, the castle is surrounded by a barbican wall with a single entrance through a beautiful gate facing the west side and flanked by two solid towers. All the walls of the barbican have arrow loops in the shape of the cross of Jesusalem.

The castle of Manzanares appears in the movie "El Cid" (1961) featuring Charlton Heston and Sophia Loren."[612]

It is at this spacious fortification that Catalina learns from real knights in the royal court the arts of war, to include proper horsemanship, the use of the two-handed sword, battle axe, mace, dagger and lance. She also undergoes a strict regime of physical fitness and strength building. Catalina becomes adept at the lance, while astride a horse properly holding it, tilting it, and directing its lunge in a manner most lethal to the opponents of Spain. At the level of the page, however, swords and shields are wooden to prevent any serious injuries in the course of training. Catalina also learns and continually improves upon climbing, slingshots, javelins, archery and wrestling. But because she is on the expansive grounds of the castle and afforded her own private quarters, she successfully maintains her guise as the young man "Antonio de Arce." Also, her short height of five feet, two inches, was overlooked because of her unparalleled zeal in defense of the realm.

When Catalina finished her training, she reported back to Father Prieto in Valladolid, who was assigned by the ecclesiastical authorities in Madrid to the building of missions in Panama. The priest's orders also included taking the young Antonio with him as the captain of his military escort. For more than two decades and headquartered in Fort San Lorenzo in Portobelo, Catalina moves with Father Prieto up and down Spanish America setting up mission districts, converting the Native American populations and building chapels. Throughout this time, the two share many exciting adventures and battles with both pirates and rebelling indigenous tribes. Following the death of Father Prieto in 1625, however, Catalina is forced to go it alone, roaming the Western Hemisphere. She decides to take some time to find her brother Luis, and joins up with a contingent of Spanish soldiers in Upper Peru, where she last got rumor that he was stationed. However, it does not take long for one of the soldiers to discover her true identity as a woman, and this one attempts to force himself sexually upon her. In reaction to this violent episode against her person, Catalina wields her sword and thrusts it through the heart of the assailant, instantly killing him. She then runs to the nearest mission chapel, seeking sanctuary, and doesn't give herself up to the local constabulary until such a time as guarantees are presented to her for safe transport back to Europe, where she believes she will be tried fairly.

On her person, however, she carries a sealed ecclesiastical document concerning the case of "Antonio de Arce" from the late Bishop Alejandro Prieto, addressed to and only to be opened by Pope Urban VIII in Rome, whom Catalina's "saintly friend" deemed the only one worthy on the planet Earth to fairly judge her. Catalina is placed under house arrest on three counts. First, it was against the laws of the church for a woman to dress and act like a man. Second, it was against the laws of the Spanish crown for any woman but the "wife" of a colonist to travel and settle in the Indies. And third, she took the life of a Spanish soldier, albeit in self-defense; and the taking of a human life, especially that of a Spaniard, was considered both a grave offense against the crown and a mortal sin to the leadership of the Roman Catholic Church.

Having received such an assurance from the local law enforcement authorities, Catalina agrees to vacate the chapel and place herself under military house arrest, where she remains for two years until she is finally summoned before Pope Urban VIII at the Vatican to be judged. Brought before the pontiff in irons, Urban VIII orders that the chains be removed. Having

---

612 "Castle of Manzanares El Real," 2014, *FeelMadrid.com*, http://www.feelmadrid.com/manzanarescastle.html
(Accessed 15 February 2015)

previously been handed the sealed document from the Vatican's legate at the royal palace in Madrid, the pope is aware of the unique circumstances surrounding Catalina's life. Recognizing that even while pretending to be a man, Catalina had accomplished much on behalf of the church while working with Father Prieto in the Indies, Urban VIII feels compelled to exercise a little more leniency in judging her case. He also concurs with Father Prieto's written assessment that, in cases which concern private revelations, such as the visitation of an angel, it is better to believe than not to believe. The pope opined: "For, if you believe, and it is proven true, you will be happy that you have believed, because our Holy Mother asked it. If you believe, and it should be proven false, you will receive all blessings as if it had been true, because you believed it to be true."

"Enter my chamber, dear Catalina, for we have much to discuss," noted the gracious Florentine pontiff. Left alone with the pope, Catalina was able to assure him that despite being guilty of violating at least two laws of which she was charged, she had always been a true and loyal subject of the Spanish crown and the Roman Catholic Church, and that in spite of everything that had happened to her since her arrival in the Indies, she had managed to retain her virginity all throughout her life. As to the charge of murder, the pope found himself in agreement with Catalina's plea of innocence. It was obviously self defense and the undisciplined soldier was the one who had acted in a manner unbecoming his status as a defender of the Spanish crown. Also, being able to prove the maintenance of her virginity to the satisfaction of Urban VIII, convinced this pope to not only grant Catalina her freedom, but permission to continue dressing as a man and serving in a military capacity, even giving her a papal letter to that effect.

In 1629 Catalina returned to the Basque country, putting all of her legal affairs in order and bequeathing a significant amount of money to the nuns' relief efforts among the poor in exchange for the liberation of her three sisters from the convent. Catalina then returns to Latin America, whence she is never heard from again, either in her own name or that of "Antonio." Nevertheless, rumors persisted through the progress of the centuries throughout Latin America and the Caribbean of a female conquistador that would mysteriously show up when women were being beaten or abused in any way, exacting judgment at the point of her sword and other weapons of warfare.

Of all of the locations on Earth, Catalina feels most comfortable in those regions where the Basque peoples settled as sheep herders, specifically the pleasant valleys of California, Nevada, and the areas that would one day become the states of Idaho and Utah. In 1830 we find Catalina now living outside the mission of San Francisco Solano, north of the Bay Area. Here she is disguised again as a man, but helping the aging and kind Father Buenaventura Fortuny in his outreach program to the indigenous populations of Northern California, as well as working as an agent of the Mexican government in conducting reconnaissance, gathering intelligence on the operations of the Russians to the regions yet further north, especially their coastal settlement at Fort Rus, later called "Ross" when Anglicized.

One day while exploring the northern, mountainous regions of California, Catalina chances upon a Russian "fur trapper," who introduces himself as Ivan. But something is not right. Catalina does not see any pelts or trapping gear anywhere near Ivan or his encampment. She later discovers that this man was Ivan Kuskov, a surveyor staking claims for the Russian-American Company, headquartered at New Archangel (now Sitka) in Alaska, but operating out of Fort Rus. But Ivan, unaccustomed to meeting fellow Europeans in these remote parts of California, invites "José" to spend the next couple of days with him at his campsite, at least until the cold front blew over.

Fortunately for our intrepid José, Ivan speaks fluent Spanish. In his service to the Russian-American Company, he would frequently travel down from Fort Rus to Monterey, where he traded pelts for valuable goods and supplies brought by Spanish cargo ships coming in from the Philippines and other points in the Orient. But in the course of their conversations, José learns that a little further to the north and east there are some *indios* of the Okwanuchu band inhabiting the lands at the base of a mountain they call Shasta. The Okwanuchu have been waiting for quite some time for the arrival of Christian missionaries in their land, and they are eager to hear about the good news of Jesus Christ.

As Ivan and his new friend feed the campfire with some dried twigs, Ivan reveals yet more about the Okwanuchu people, and why it would be worth José's efforts and time to check them out. There are reports of angels of light appearing to the *indios* on the slopes of the mountain. And there is some speculation about angels living inside the mountain as well. In addition, many "cloud ships" are reported both landing and taking off from the entire region on and about the sacred mountain. After retiring to sleep for the evening, Catalina pondered the marvelous stories related by Ivan and decided that she would go to see these things for herself. Perhaps she might find some of the answers she had been diligently looking for over the past 230 years.

Ivan had kindly provided her with a crude map, in case she wanted to go there, and assured her that most of the *indios* encountered along the way would have no problem in pointing out the correct direction to take all along the way, especially if they were cognizant of helping a "religious man" and "seeker of truth." They too, believed as the Christians the world over, that one never knows when they are in the presence of angels, and being tested by them.

At daybreak, she bid farewell to Ivan and made her way back to the Solano mission. There, "he" secured pack animals and provisions for the trek up to Shasta; and three weeks later, arrived in the lands of the Okwanuchu on the vast southern slopes of the holy mountain. Upon entering a village, she is met by the tribal council of elders. Of course, being true shamans, they see right through her disguise, but don't let on. Rather, they direct her to a point above the tree line where she might be able to encounter some of the "mountain spirits." And once arriving at the designated spot, Catalina is not disappointed. It is Ivan who appears seemingly out of nowhere. He hugs Catalina and welcomes her to the holy mountain. He then transforms into an angel of light and reveals himself to be none other than Dysmas, whom she met in the Basque country so long ago. The angel opens an inter-dimensional portal and they both walk through it, hand-in-hand. Soon they will be inside the bowels of Mount Shasta, in the spacecraft hangar and boarding a scout ship to whisk them away to the mothership high in orbit. Their last stop will be the planet Venus.

California, 1946

Now that she was a translated resident on Venus, Catalina was finally comfortable with her feminine sexual identity, in being herself. She enjoyed the unlimited educational opportunities available to her in the Venusian schools, and sitting at the feet of ascended masters, both Ladies and Lords. One of her first impressions of Venus was just how right Dante Alighieri got it when he wrote the *Paradiso* cantos of the *Divine Comedy* back in the fourteenth century.

Venus truly was one of the spheres of Heaven; and there were so many Earthlings there that the self-righteous preachers on Earth didn't ever imagine would make it or even come close to qualifying for residence. "Are they in for a big surprise," she thought.

After all, Dante noted that the only criteria one needed to meet to get into Venus was to have a loving heart. That all Earthlings were sexual beings and subject to their emotions and passions wasn't their fault. That's just how they were created, in the image of God. After all, if God wanted a world of robots, he could have downloaded a far different, yet more compliant programming into our DNA. But against love and kindness there are no laws, and acting on sincere impulse in these directions covers a multitude of sins.

On Venus, one can choose their own name, and Catalina chose "Lady Orda." Through the use of orb technology, one can access the so-called Akashic Records, situated in an ethereal library carved out of a crystal ice cave on Uranus, and discover their direct line of incarnations on Earth and other planets. Catalina came to learn that back in the thirteenth century Eurasian Mongol Kingdom, in her last incarnation she was a princess named Orda who directed an army of elite horsemen, her royal guard known as the "Ordon." But up until Catalina's ascension to Venus, she had already gone through about fifteen aliases. And now, in the Terran year 1946, she was going back to Earth, but this time on a mission of peace in Southern California. Reflective of her Basque origins, and a great grandmother on her mother's side of the family, however, the name that Orda chose to accomplish this new work on Earth was Dolores Barrios.

Just as Catalina had mastered the use of the lance so long ago at the castle outside of Madrid, on Venus she proved more than adept in the deployment of orb technology. Like the comic book hero, the *Green Lantern*, whose ring can do almost anything so long as it is put to the service of the beneficent Lords of the planet Oa, the orbs could only be utilized by Dolores if they assisted the cause and purposes of the Venusian Hierarchy of Light. The descending order of this celestial organization is adequately described in Massimo Cacciari's *Necessary Angel* as "from the gods to the Archangel, from the Archangel to the Angel, from this to the demon, *to the hero, to the archon (in charge of the direction of matter)*, and so on down to the souls most distant from the superior regions, down to the vain apparitions of ghosts, the fatuous fires of deceiving magic, the 'fallacious alterations' of the 'various genera.' *These spaces are extraordinarily animated; they pullulate with entities that are imperceptible to our senses.*"[613] Dolores Barrios, operating as the Venusian manipulator of an orb on Earth, could therefore be considered as nothing less than an archon, for the essential function of the orb is the direction and redirection of matter. Such orbs can be used as a personal transport within planetary atmospheres, or even to bi-locate one's self for brief durations.

Corresponding to the appearance of the mothership over Southern California in early October of 1946, Dolores used her orb to project herself down to the hills to the northwest of San Diego. There, in an open field on the outskirts of the small town of Vista, she materialized in front of a group of Venusians anxiously waiting her arrival. Her mission was to direct the activities of this Venusian contingent already on Earth in establishing contact with select individuals chosen for their communicative ability to promote the message of peace and serve as interplanetary ambassadors. These chosen Earthlings were those that came to be known as the "contactees," to include George Adamski, with whom Orda was already in direct telepathic communications even while she was still onboard the mothership *en route* to Earth.

---

613   Massimo Cacciari, translated by M. E. Vatter, *The Necessary Angel* (Albany, New York: State University of New York Press, 1994), 22

Inasmuch as Orda's plans included the release of information through the contactees about the Venusian presence on Earth, she felt it wise to once again conceal her identity as a woman, and present herself to the world, through Adamski's eyes and descriptions, as a man. Preliminary reports from Venusian cultural anthropologists studying prevailing attitudes toward women in Earth societies following World War II indicated that no one would believe Adamski and the other contactees if they accurately described the leading role that women play on Venus and other planets throughout the solar system and beyond. As women were actually taken seriously on Venus, and ran most of the academic, cultural, political, scientific and spiritual institutions there, no male in any position of authority on Earth was going to accept it. They were going to assume that the whole universe was patriarchal, for how could it be anything else, considering the orderly nature that supposedly reigns throughout the cosmos?

Of this era, an episode titled "The Pill" in the Public Broadcasting Service's *American Experience* series provides the following commentary about the status of the female population in the United States:

"In the 1950s, women felt tremendous societal pressure to focus their aspirations on a wedding ring. The U.S. marriage rate was at an all-time high and couples were tying the knot, on average, younger than ever before. Getting married right out of high school or while in college was considered the norm. A common stereotype was that women went to college to get a 'Mrs.' (pronounced M.R.S.) degree, meaning a husband. Although women had other aspirations in life, the dominant theme promoted in the culture and media at the time was that a husband was far more important for a young woman than a college degree. Despite the fact that employment rates also rose for women during this period, the media tended to focus on a woman's role in the home. If a woman wasn't engaged or married by her early twenties, she was in danger of becoming an 'old maid.'"[614]

By this standard Dolores Barrios, who since her days as Catalina long ago had never married, and even, on occasion, engaged in amorous encounters with other women, was never going to come across as credible in the role of a Venusian cosmonaut. And so it was that when that memorable day of 20 November 1952 arrived, with Adamski feeling so impelled to bring himself and the small party out to Desert Center, California, to encounter a real Venusian, it was not Orda but "Orthon" stepping out of the landed scout craft.

On the historical significance of this encounter, John Mitchell, an authority and author on lost civilizations, writes in the "Foreword" to Colin Bennett's *Searching for Orthon* that perhaps it is not too far-fetched to suggest

This close-up photograph of Dolores Barrios was taken Sunday, 8 August 1954 at the Skyline Lodge at Mt. Palomar, California. See http://www.ceticismoaberto.com/galeria/fotos-de-alienigenas/5532/uma-alienigena-como-dolores-barrios.

---

614 Maria Daniels, Director of New Media, "The Pill," American Experience, originally broadcast 1999, PBS On-line, WGBH Boston affiliate, http://www.pbs.org/wgbh/amex/pill/peopleevents/p_mrs.html (Accessed 14 February 2015).

"that the defining moment of the twentieth century will prove to be 12:30 p.m. on Thursday, 20 November 1952, when George Adamski met Orthon, a long-haired youth from Venus. It happened in the Californian desert in the presence of witnesses. From that moment the cat was out of the bag, the space people were among us, and nothing has ever been the same since.... The effects of this on popular culture are to be seen everywhere.... In the modern imagination the UFO is a constant, not just a space-craft but a reminder that the world is not as rational as our educators pretend.... [Adamski] was an impressive old rogue, like Madame Blavatsky and in the same tradition. Such people, according to Plato are the kind whom the gods choose to enlighten us."[615]

With so many in the ufology community obsessed with finding "Orthon," however, Orda told me at Club Venus that, "Looking back to that space-crazed time in American history, it still amazes me that it took so long for my cover to be blown." As I inquired further, Orda explained that she and her roommates were frequent attendees at flying saucer conventions throughout Southern California, and occasionally in other states; but since they did not have their own car, they relied on fellow travelers in the contactee movement to provide the transportation to these events. Orda, as Dolores, and her roommates as well, knew what a great personal sacrifice that Adamski, Daniel Fry, Truman Bethurum and others were making in behalf of the cause of interplanetary enlightenment and the promotion of peace. They wanted to be there at as many of these flying saucer functions as possible, if for no other reason to show their support and provide encouragement.

Orda as Dolores Barrios was found out nearly two years following her first *physical encounter* with Adamski in the California desert. It was the weekend of 7-8 August 1954 at one of the more curious UFO conferences ever held. Contactee aficionados from all throughout the United States and the world, were massing in front of the Skyline Lodge at the top of Mount Palomar, California, to see and hear Adamski, Fry and Bethurum and learn from them of the true nature of life on other planets in our solar system. Despite the Skyline's remote location, and being situated at an air-thinning altitude of 6,000 feet, management of the lodge counted over 1,000 in attendance. Beside countless flying saucer witnesses, also present were the curiosity seekers, various government agents and a plethora of American and foreign journalists.

All three of the aforementioned contactees had organized the event primarily as an occasion to sell some autographed books; but the turn-out far exceeded any of their expectations. The conference opened at 1 p.m. The temperature was 71 degrees Fahrenheit, with a slight gust of wind coming from the southwest at 12 miles per hour.[616] In other words, it was such a perfect California day that if Katy Perry and Snoop Dogg were around back then, they probably would have made a song about it. Originally, the convention was supposed to be held in the meeting room of the Skyline Lodge; but the huge and growing crowd convinced the management to move the venue outside on the spacious hillside grounds. Each of the contactees took a turn in explaining about their personal experiences with extraterrestrials. When Adamski was up, the "professor" described the Venusians as "very much like human beings, so much so that they had infiltrated our society and were living in the big cities." He also displayed a life-size painting, an artist's depiction of the Venusian Orthon that he first encountered on 20 November

---

615 Bennett, 8, 9

616 "Weather History for San Diego, CA; Saturday, August 7, 1954," *Weather Underground*, http://www.wunderground. com/history/airport/KSAN/1954/8/7/DailyHistory.html?req_city=&req_state=&req_statename= (Accessed 15 February 2015).

1952. A photo of Adamski standing by the side of the painting at the Skyline Lodge appears in the chapter on "Contactees" in this book.

At the time Adamski was presenting the painting of Orthon and talking about life on Venus, Dolores and her friends Bill Jackmart and Donald Morand were still on the road, *en route* to the conference. All three had received a personal invitation from Adamski; and it was the illustrator of Adamski's books, Glenn Passmore, who was driving them there in his own car. Unfortunately, they were delayed a couple of hours in arriving at the Skyline Lodge due to getting a flat tire on the then unpaved and bumpy Palomar Divide Road. While Glenn has since passed over to the other side, his daughter shared some recollections of Dolores and her two male friends in a popular UFO thread:

"I don't know if anyone is still following this thread, but I have personal knowledge of Dolores Barrios and her partners Don and Bill. Dolores was known as "Laurie" to us and she, Don and Bill were close friends of my parents when I was a little girl back in the early 50s.

My parents actually were the ones to take them to Mt Palomar as they didn't drive. They were indeed very, very strange and I have some incredible first hand stories of them. My father was Glenn Passmore, who illustrated one of Adamski's books on flying saucers. I have family photographs of Laurie (Dolores) and the others. What your photographs don't show is how incredibly short she was. My mother is standing next to her in one of the photos. My mother was 5'4" and Laurie looks like a child next to her.

I recorded my father's stories of Don and Laurie on tape before he died and am planning to write a book on the many odd experiences my parents had with them. They were indeed different. I am not speculating on where they were from - I am simply saying they were very, very strange. I met Laurie when I was somewhere between two and three years old.

To my knowledge, I don't know anyone else in my age group who remembers these people, has first-hand knowledge of them or the strange events that occurred. They came to our home on numerous occasions and my parents took them also to a saucer convention out at Giant Rock....."[617]

Toward the end of the first day of the conference, however, there was some commotion when many in the audience noticed the presence of two men and a woman with an exotic appearance. Right away a rumor began circulating that they were Venusians in disguise, just like the ones that Adamski had described a few hours before. All three were Caucasians and one of the men wore glasses. The woman had long blonde hair, but the strangest feature was her huge, black eyes. Dolores was taken aback by all of this undue attention suddenly focused on her, Don and Bill. Don, the gentleman with the glasses, just laughed it off. "Well, Clark Kent is an alien," he jested, "and the glasses seem to do the trick for him."

One of the over-enthused attendees blurted out, without much embarrassment: "Are you or are you not Venusians?" To this, Dolores smiled and calmly replied, "No." This was not a lie, because she was born on Earth, albeit in the year of 1585, C.E.

Then another attendee asked, "Why are you here?" And to this question, Dolores politely replied, "Because we are interested in this subject."

617 Passmore, a.k.a. "UCalien," *Above Top Secret* thread post, 17 March 2013, 4:29 p.m., "Do you remember Dolores Barrios, the woman from Venus," http://www.abovetopsecret.com/forum/thread554264/pg12 (Accessed 14 February 2015).

Then yet another question was shouted from the back of a growing mob: "Do you believe in flying saucers?" Dolores replied with a simple "Yes."

One more up front asked her, "Is it true that, as Mr. Adamski says, that they come from Venus?" And to this Dolores responded, "Yes. They are from Venus."

Also at this conference was the Brazilian journalist João Martins, who specialized in writing about the UFO phenomenon. Upon introducing himself, Dolores replied in Portuguese, stating that it was a pleasure meeting him (*É um prazer conhecé-lo*). Preferring to follow the press-credentialed Martins to a separate room apart from the mob of fanatics, Dolores and her friends agreed to answer some of the Brazilian's questions. From the interview, Martins learned that she went by the name of Dolores Barrios and was a dress designer. She also introduced her friends as Donald Morand and Bill Jackmart, part-time musicians who lived with her up in Manhattan Beach in the Greater Los Angeles area and who also helped her out in her boutique in nearby Hermosa Beach. Even by 1954 standards, however, their type of living arrangement would have been considered "unconventional," at best. Although Dolores explained that her relationship with Don and Bill was platonic, people let their imaginations run away with them, speculating on all sorts of deviant sexual situations that could result from such a threesome. Because of their work with some of the Hollywood movie studios with both music and costume design, they were already suspected of being both communist and homosexual.

And because it was 1954, in the midst of McCarthyism and the Second Great Red Scare (1952-1956), attitudes of tolerance were not exactly prevailing. Federal agents were circulating in the crowd as much to weed out communist sympathizers as they were to learn about flying saucers. After all, Adamski's background was Egyptian and Polish; and despite being resident in the United States since his early youth, Poland, the land of his birth, was a country allied with the Soviet Union. Much of the contactees' explanations of the advanced societal organization on Venus also smacked of "communism," so Adamski, Bethurum and Fry had to exercise some degree of caution when discussing this subject. So naturally, when Martins asked if he could have his photographer take their picture, they all refused. They could sense some of the terrible things that some in the crowd were thinking about them, and said they were, "sick and tired of being called Venusians and everything else under the Sun." But in Martins' estimation and that of many others in attendance that day- and they surmised correctly- Dolores Barrios looked very much like the painting that Adamski had previously shown of Orthon.

For the remainder of the first day of the conference, the three became isolated and rarely spoke with others in attendance. But on the second day, the strange visitors lightened up a little bit and allowed the photographer accompanying Martins from Brazil, Ed Keffel, to snap a few pictures of them, but only on the condition that he did not use flashbulbs. When I asked Orda why the change of heart, she said that, "If attitudes were going to change in this world- as someday they will- then people had to start being honest with themselves and others and opening up to new vistas of reality. We talked it over that Saturday night with George and the other two contactees and came to the conclusion that such a change might as well begin with us."

At the end of the conference, in a grove of trees and down a slope to the west of the Skyline Lodge's main parking lot, Keffel at last took a few photographs of Barrios and her posse. But as word got out that "the Venusians were being photographed" there, people who normally would have been getting into their cars or buses to go back home starting streaming out of the parking area and down the hill with cameras in hand. At that point, Dolores pulled out of her

It is easy to see why so many attendees at the 1954 Mount Palomar contactee conference suspected Dolores Barrios (left) of being Orthon (right). See http://www. ceticismoaberto.com/galeria/fotos-de-alienigenas/5532/uma-alienigena-como-dolores-barrios.

sweater a small circular device, looking something like a shiny metallic tennis ball. As she rubbed her thumb over it, a halo of ionized air suddenly formed over their heads as they disappeared into a cloud of light behind the trees and out of sight. As for the curiosity seekers who had been clamoring down the hill to get a last peek at the Venusians, they were engulfed in a huge swarm of bees that suddenly popped out of nowhere. The fortuitous arrival of the bees facilitated the escape of Dolores, Bill and Don, as well as foiled any attempts by the mob to take any pictures of them with flashbulbs.

Glenn had been in the Skyline bar sipping on an iced Coca-Cola before hitting the road with Dolores and the young men and driving them back to their home in Manhattan Beach. But having the experience of working with George Adamski at his ashram and hanging out with his unusual friends, Glenn came to almost expect these types of occurrences. Upon his return to his home in Los Angeles, however, he did receive a call from Dolores thanking him for the ride to Palomar and courtesies extended to her and the young men. She also wanted Glenn to know that she and her party had arrived back safely in Manhattan Beach. But that is the last anyone had ever heard from Dolores Barrios, Bill or Don.

With the Palomar incident behind them, Dolores, Bill and Don came to the realization that it was time to move again. As they still had some contracts with the boutique to fulfill, however, they had to wait until the end of 1956 before renting a home in Vista, California, to be closer to and assist George Adamski. Dolores herself would later travel out to the East Coast to provide some support for Howard Menger and his outreach; but by the end of 1963, with the assassination of the beloved President John

Ionization cloud forming around cloaked Venusian scout ship hovering over 1954 Giant Rock, Spacecraft Convention in California, to which Dolores Barrios also attended with Glenn Passmore, Adamski's book illustrator. See https://deusnexus.wordpress.com/2013/05/01/history-of-ufo-channelers/.

F. Kennedy, saddened Dolores was residing at Vitoria in southeast Brazil, up the coast about 250 miles north of Rio de Janeiro.

Dolores had returned to her Basque and Latin roots, this time choosing the name of Débora Bergara. Her new first name, "Débora," is of Hebrew origin and designates, "a truly beautiful and charming person who is intelligent and the most fantastic lover. *The name Débora means Queen Bee and the beholder of beauty.* Her intelligence might overwhelm you at first but you'll soon be reeled in by her sophistication and charm. The name Débora is generally given to those who sustain beauty throughout their lives and live life passionately."[618] From the same source, we also learn that, "Déboras are usually sophisticated, witty, intelligent with a great sense of humor. Other women are usually jealous of Déboras and men want her."[619] Bergara is a Basque name surname from a distant matriarchal relationship on her father's side of the family.

Photographs of Dolores, Don and Bill (Left to right) taken in the west grove on the last day of the Skyline conference. See http://www. ceticismoaberto.com/galeria/fotos-de-alienigenas/5532/uma-alienigena-como-dolores-barrios.

But despite Dolores' move to Brazil so long ago, the identity linkages between her and Orthon continue to be a hot topic in UFO circles. A blogger to a popular UFO Internet site posted the following points on a thread concerning some of these connections that he noted between Dolores Barrios and Orthon:

Dolores is Orthon. Here's why:

1. Adamski mentioned in 'Flying Saucers Have Landed' (FSHL) that Orthon had an androgynous look: "In fact, in different clothing he could easily have passed for an unusually beautiful woman; yet he definitely was a man." Also, note that Dolores is flat-chested and has a subtle masculine air in the standing picture.

2. Long tapered fingers typical of extra-terrestrial humans. Again from FSHL: "His [Orthon's] hands were slender, with long tapering fingers like the beautiful hands of an artistic woman." Check out Dolores's right hand carefully in the standing pic: though her fingers are clenched, you can see they're unusually long and spindly, and her thumb is tapered to a point.

3. Orthon's long hair. Adamski mentioned in "Inside the Space Ships" (ISS) that the extra-terrestrial men generally wore their hair short and that "none wore long hair as did Orthon, my Venusian friend of the first meeting. I have since learned that he had a particular reason for wearing his hair in this style." He did not elaborate why Orthon had long hair, but we can assume that the he might have needed it to masquerade as a woman while carrying out his mission on Earth.

4. Their extreme reluctance to be photographed. Adamski explains Orthon's similar reluctance in FSHL: "I could easily understand his desire not to be photographed, because there were a few distinguishing points about his facial features. Normally these would not be noticed. But in a photograph they would be conspicuous and serve as points of identification for his brothers who have come to Earth." One feature could be the vertical central forehead ridge which you can see in the enlarged versions of the photos above of all three ET suspects.

5. Adamski's last contact with Orthon, Ramu and Firkon was on 23rd Aug 1954 (ISS)

618　Deborah lover, entry for "Deborah" (English spelling), 25 August 2009, *Urban Dictionary*, http://www. urbandictionary.com/define.php?term=Deborah (Accessed 15 February 2015)

619　weecheekies, entry for "Deborah" (English spelling), 22 July 2008, *Urban Dictionary*, http://www.urbandictionary. com/define.php?term=Deborah (Accessed 15 February 2015)

after which both Ramu and Firkon returned to their home planets, having completed their Earth mission. The above Palomar conference was held on 7-8th August, 2 weeks earlier, and it stands to reason that not only was Dolores Orthon, Donald Morand and Bill Jackmart were probably Ramu and Firkon in disguise, who were living in California at the time. Adamski's descriptions of Ramu and Firkon in ISS do fit the two men in the photo above.[620]

Bob's analysis seems quite logical and well thought out. My only qualm would be with his presumption in point number three that Orthon was a man who needed to masquerade as a woman. Whereas in point number one, Bob refers to Orthon's "androgynous look," then clearly the entity could just as easily be seen as a woman who can occasionally disguise herself as a man. A woman could easily maintain naturally long, flowing hair at all times and not need to explain herself; whereas a man on Earth might be required to offer an explanation for such a feminine appearance under some circumstances.

As to point number four and the "vertical central forehead ridge," this is definitely a feature of most indigenous Venusians, but also a physical characteristic of the Basque people, who are descended from the Atlanteans, who in turn were descended from the first Venusian colonists on Earth. Mark Kurlansky, an authority on Basque history, takes cognizance that the Basques are well-known to have distinctive body characteristics, stating that, "Ample evidence exists that the Basques are a physically distinct group. There is a Basque type with a long straight nose, thick eyebrows, strong chin, and long earlobes."[621] He also notes that Basque skulls tend to be built on a different pattern. Kurlansky also declares that in the early 1880s, a researcher reported that, "Someone gave me a Basque body and I dissected it, and I assert that the head was not built like that of other men."[622] But while such qualitative differences are indicative, it is really the quantitative evidence, with presence or absence of features, or items being present in different numbers, that has greater weight in deciding whether specimens belong to the same or different species; and such powerful quantitative evidence comes from a consideration of blood factors, such as the presence of Rh-negative blood. Those with this rarer type of blood do share other physical characteristics that include but are not limited to early maturity, large head and eyes, high intelligence quotient, or an extra vertebra (a "tail bone" -- called a "*cauda*"), lower than normal body temperature, lower than normal blood pressure, and higher mental analytical abilities.[623]

Here is a full-length contrast of Dolores Barrios with Orthon. Note the possible orb held in right hand of Dolores and the orb/translation device raised in left hand of Orthon. See www.davidicke.com.

620   Bob, blogger post to thread, "An Alien like Dolores Barrios….," 20 July 2011, 10:30 a.m., *forgetomori*, http://forgetomori.com/2009/aliens/uma-alienigena-como-dolores-barrios/ (Accessed 15 February 2015)

621   Mark Kurlansky. *The Basque History of the World* in Chapter One, "The Basque Myth" (New York, New York: Penguin Books, 2001.

622   *Ibid.*

623   David Noel, "How the Neanderthals Became Basques," 26 August 2002, *Ben Franklin Center for Theoretical Research*, http://www.aoi.com.au/bcw/neanderbasque.htm (Accessed 15 February 2015)

The "vertical central forehead ridge" is more pronounced in this close up photograph of Dolores Barrios. See http://www.abovetopsecret.com/forum/thread554264/pg1.

The New Queen

Pursuant to our conversation at the Club Venus earlier in the month, Débora materialized over the roof of the high rise apartment where I was residing in Wuxi on the evening of Wednesday, 19 December 2012, at precisely 12:01 a.m. She was wearing a white jump suit, similar to that worn by Lady Encara when the OSIRIS chapter of Salt Lake City encountered her above the tree line on Mount Shasta in 1987. She was seemingly levitated about two feet above the roof. She extended her hand to me and said, "Come, do not be afraid. Just touch my hand and we'll be on our way to Siling Co."

In less than a second after putting my hand in Débora's, as well as my trust in her best intentions for me, we were encircled in a bubble of translucent white light, flying high over the Chinese countryside. I could see the bright, crowded cities below giving way to a darkened and sparsely-lit partitioning of farm acreage. The air had been a little on the nippy side that night, and I noticed goose-bumps running up and down my arms. I shivered a little bit, and then the interior of the orb took on a slightly reddish hue, with the temperature rising to a comfortable level. "That's amazing," I remarked to my host, "I didn't even have to mention that I was cold and the orb automatically adjusted the temperature." To this Débora remarked, "The orb is a living appendage to my higher self. As I sensed that the cold was bothering you, the orb did what it could to remedy the situation for you on my behalf."

The feeling generated by the orb flying experience is incredible. I thought that maybe, if there really was a Superman, this is how he would feel. In any event, as we continued our southwesterly route, we were roughly following the course of the Yangtze River. Once over Changsha the mountains below became more pronounced. The orb jumped to a higher altitude and then leveled off, picking up speed, and heading due west. All the while in

Statue of Vitoria greets visitors to the Azure spaceport on Venus. See http://www.hddispatch.net/a-walk-through-the-future/.

motion, the orb made a constant but low humming noise, similar to the planetary resonance that Venus herself emits, like a big bumblebee.

In any event, we soon reached the foothills of the Himalayas and circled over the Tibetan plateau. All of a sudden thin but intense beams of green light could be seen shooting up from an island in the middle of Siling Co, seemingly latching on to other orb fliers as well as Venusian scout craft. The pencil-thin green beams appeared to be acting as tractor rays, guiding the orb fliers and scouts to landing spots all along the northern beaches. Débora explained that the Venusians use stimulated light emissions, something akin to our lasers, in directing flight paths and facilitating non-telepathic communications in order to avoid their interception by Earth authorities, whose intelligence apparatuses are only capable of intercepting and monitoring standard broadband spectrum radio frequencies.

As we hovered over the beach, the intense white light of the orb solidified and unfolded like a lotus. We carefully stepped out onto the damp sand and surveyed the area. From the illumination provided by our orb, we noted that there was a large tent decked out in multicolored Buddhist prayer flags. A group of lamas stood next to the tent, bowing in our direction. One brought over a tray with cups of hot *tsampa,* a local buttery tea. And then, who should step out from behind the folds of the prayer tent but Lady Encara. "Good to see you again, Lady Orda and 'Cosmic Ray.' The mothership is already parked in a mountain vale on the more remote southern side of the lake, in the so-called Forbidden Zone. We received reports from our field agents that the Americans, Russians and others were going to be focusing their satellites intently on the plateau of late, so we wanted to do what we could to hide the mothership as best as possible."

After the final orbs and scouts had landed, a general assembly was convened on the beach about half a mile to the east of the tent site. At the conclave, instructions were given for the order in which the mothership was to be boarded. Lady Encara then activated her orb, with all the other fliers following suit. Those in the scouts waited for all the orb fliers to pass over the lake first and board the *Isis*. Then all of the ground equipment was loaded aboard the scouts, along with their appropriate crews, for docking with the *Isis*, which had already levitated off the ground after all of the orb fliers were safely onboard.

Lady Encara took the command chair and gave the word to launch the *Isis*. The snow-capped Himalayas as far as one hundred miles away were shaking, with avalanches pushing tons of snow down the mountainsides. As passengers lined the port holes on the right side of the *Isis*, they could see Valiant Thor's *Victory* simultaneously ascending in the skies over Namtso Lake. As with the *Isis*, the static charge between the *Victory* and the Earth's surface was generating a massive lightning storm. Lady Encara directed that the ship be rotated so that the passengers on the other side could also sneak a peek at the *Victory*'s ascent before the *Isis* rose above the gray and frosty atmospheric envelope.

Once beyond the Earth's atmosphere, the radiation belts and the La Grange point between our world and the Moon, Lady Encara set a course correction that put the *Isis* into a lunar orbit, where she would then be able to use the natural satellite's gravitational pull to create a slingshot effect, thereby propelling the mothership on a faster trajectory to Venus. Of course, the mothership's neutron pulse engines could supply more than enough power to get us to Venus even without the slingshot effect, but Lady Encara thought those visitors from Earth, such as myself, might enjoy viewing the Venusian colonies on the far side of Terra-Luna, which is the Venusian name for our Moon. It was just as Adamski wrote about in his flying saucer books. There were farms, forests, lakes and modular city complexes built under transparent domes. And there were also "fireflies" dancing everywhere. These, however, were not the result of a natural occurring phenomenon by any means, as some have conjectured. Rather, these are the individual orb fliers either engaging in extravehicular activities or just going about their business, traveling from point A to point B.

Such orbs/"fireflies" have been frequently reported in the vicinity of the International Space

Station (ISS) as well as in orbit by Soviet/Russian cosmonauts. Scott Waring, the editor of the online blog *UFO Sightings Daily*, noted that as recently as 15 January 2015, a mysterious gray orb appeared on an ISS camera as it was rising just above the Earth's horizon, and appeared to be drawing closer to the station's 275-mile high orbit when suddenly the camera went dark and was replaced with a notice declaring "technical difficulties" had disrupted the feed. And ufologist Toby Lundh, who monitors the ISS camera on a regular basis, stated that such orbs "are always showing up, but the picture suspiciously gets disrupted every time."[624]

Something else concerning the orbs occurred with the entire crew of three Soviet cosmonauts in the Salyut 7 while orbiting the Earth on 12 July 1984. On their 155th day aboard the low-orbiting space station, the space farers reported seeing "celestial beings" hovering just outside a porthole of their spacecraft. The three cosmonauts reporting this incident were Commander Leonid Kizim, Vladimir Solevev and Oleg Atkov. According to Salyut 7 Commander Kizim, "What we saw were seven giant figures in the form of humans, but with wings and mist-like halos as in the classic depiction of angels."

As the cosmonauts were in the process of performing medical experiments in Salyut 7, attempting to measure the effects of living and working in a zero-gravity environment on human physiology, their capsule was enveloped by a brilliant orange cloud in the shape of a massive orb. The glow from the orb was so intense that all three of the cosmonauts were temporarily blinded; but when their eyes cleared, they all observed the angels. The heavenly visitors stayed with the Salyut 7 for about ten minutes and then vanished as quickly as they had appeared.

But just twelve days later, on 24 July, cosmonauts Svetlana Savitskaya, Igor Vok and Vladimir Dzhanibevok, were sent up to the Salyut 7 in order to check out the mental health of the initial crew and replace them, if necessary. Following the initial report to Ground Control,

Venusians access ice in the shadowed areas of craters and under the surface of the Moon, converting it into water or air to sustain beautiful habitats on Earth's natural satellite. See http://www.smithsonianmag.com/history/honeymoon-on-the-moon-95565903/?no-ist.

Soviet space program officials thought that Kizim, Atkov and Solovyov had somehow snuck a bottle of vodka onboard the Salyut 7. The cosmonauts' imbibing of this alcohol, they reasoned, must have caused them to hallucinate. All three were now subject to an intensive medical and psychological examination upon their return to Mother Russia. Their report of "celestial beings," an "orange cloud" and "angels" had gone out over an open microphone, causing embarrassment to the atheist state Soviet leadership. *Pravda*, the official publication of the Russian government, 27 years later confirmed that the cosmonauts reported the "group hallucination," which was

---

624 "NASA Blasted for New UFO Cover-Up!" 9 February 2015, *Globe*, Boca Raton, Florida

attributed to "pressure, temperature fluctuations and shortage of oxygen to the brain."[625]

It's interesting how UFOs, angels and other supernatural phenomena, when encountered by average people in the course of their lives, are so quickly dismissed as hallucinations or misinterpretations of astronomical or meteorological events. But when stories about such encounters are related by astronomers, pilots, cosmonauts and astronauts, they become classified almost immediately at the higest echelons of national security. I would have loved to have been there at Ground Control of the Russian Federal Space Agency at Korolyov, near the RKK Energia complex, when en route to the Salyut 7, all of the replacement crew members also reported an encounter with the same, or similar celestial beings. Replacement Cosmonaut Commander Savitskay reported that, "They were glowing," they reported. We were truly overwhelmed. There was a great orange light, and through it, we could see the figures of seven angels. They were smiling as though they shared a glorious secret, but within a few minutes, they were gone, and we never saw them again."

No doubt, there are many wonders awaiting us even in low-orbiting near space. Of the remainder of my trip to Venus, the journey went very much as George Adamski, Howard Menger and Tuesday Lobsang Rampa described it. The highlight of my excursion, however, takes place in the fourth dimension. We are in the Central Temple of Light at Azure, the blue crystalline capital city of Aphrodite Terra, the largest continent in the tropical southern hemisphere of the second planet. It's a beautiful day here on Venus, with a balmy wind and a pleasing temperature of 72 degrees Fahrenheit; but then what day on Venus isn't beautiful? This day, however, stands out more than all of the other beautiful Venusian days, for Queen Mazu will soon enter the sanctuary, whence she will transition into the realm of the gods in the Great Central Sun System of Kolob at the very center of our galaxy.

The vast Cyther Dome at the heart of the temple is rapidly filling up, as representatives from all 51 Venusian republics, to include the territory of Neith, plus all the inhabited planets and moons of our solar system, as well as many dignitaries from throughout our galaxy and beyond are arriving for this most august of proceedings. For it is here where our splendid Queen Mazu will ascend into that region of outer space that transcends all notions of time and space in the higher fifth dimension. With everyone seated comfortably in the Cyther Dome, the thirteen solar portals in the canopy are opened up to the sweet smelling, orange-tinted Venusian air. As the canopy parts, an angelic choir begins to sing Queen Mazu's favorite song, *Ode to Coral*, in the Mandarin language. Besides harkening back to the serenity of ancient China, the *Ode to Coral* is also reflective of the beauty of terraformed Venus in its entire fourth dimensional splendor. The lyrics are as follows:

One tree with red flowers illuminates the jade ocean.

One ball of flame comes out of the water in motion.

The coral red tree, always in the spring

---

625 Margarita Troitsyna Yoki, "Angels in space nothing but top secret hallucinations," 14 June 2011, *Pravda*, Moscow, Russian Federation

The wind and waves grasp the opening flowers it brings.
Clouds come to cover the sky.
Then mist comes over.
Clouds and mist together release splendor.
As the wind blows, the waves hit near.
The open flowers never disappear.

There is then a hush over the assembly as an angel of light descends through each of the thirteen portals, and then one-by-one materializes in a shining human form, sitting in their appropriate thrones on the circumference ring which surrounds the kiva. After the last light being assumes a human form, his wings dissipate into thin air. He raises a gold diadem high above his head with his right hand, and everyone breaks out in a tumultuous applause. Slowly lowering the diadem, this presiding angel then walks down three steps in the form of concentric rings leading into the center of the kiva, and once again silence reigns throughout the Cyther Dome.

Up from the bottom concentric circle emerges a series of nine crystal-like mirrors. And from the center of the cupola suspended overhead, three large crystal discs appear, shaped somewhat in the form of curved lenses. The first crystal to come forth is deep blue in color. The second is ruby red; and the third and last to drop out from the top of the dome is gold. As the discs slowly revolve around an undefined point overhead, the presiding angel speaks:

"On behalf of the Angelic Hierarchy of Light (*Angelikís Ierarchías tou Fotós*), welcome to the Great Central Temple of Light, the Cyther Dome and the Blue Crystal City of Aphrodite Terra. I am your ministering servant Dysmas and today we have come to bid our beloved sister and queen, Mazu, a fond farewell, as she embarks on a journey to the Great Central Sun System of Kolob to dwell in those realms of the Pleroma in divine and perpetual light. But before the queen makes her appearance, we are activating the Cyther timescope to view the highlights of Queen Mazu's life, even as they happen in the third dimensional continuum."

As Dysmas backs away from the center of the kiva, he fades into blackness along with the rest of the Cyther Dome. In the blink of an eye, I find myself as if invisible and suspended in the air, looking down on the birth of a baby girl on a small island off the coast of Fujian Province in China. The date of her birth is transmitted telepathically to everyone's mind in their own language, and we come to understand that it is 23 March 960 by the reckoning of the Common Era on Earth. She came from a large family and she was named Lin Moniang.

As her father and four brothers were fishermen, Lin was always concerned when they went out to sea, as many sailors from the region never returned, presumed to have drowned in the choppy coastal waters. One day while her father and brothers were out fishing, a terrible typhoon kicked up. Lin was sitting at her loom, weaving a garment and trying to keep her mind off of the terrible plight that her father and brothers now found themselves in. As she prayed to whatever gods there be, a bolt of lightning split the air, and a crack of thunder persisted as a rolling rumble for a long duration. Lin suddenly lost consciousness, falling down to the floor and going into a trance. The gods had answered her prayer, for she had bi-located. While her physical body lay limp on the floor, her supernatural being was out at sea and literally walking across the turbulent waves. She spotted her father's capsized fishing boat and immediately went over to it. Lin flipped the still seaworthy craft back over to an upright, floating position.

She then pulled her father out of the raging sea and placed him safely in the boat; and then went on to try and save the three of her older brothers. But in the process of going over to save her one younger brother, back on the mainland Lin's mother was desperately trying to wake her up, but to no avail. Even though her mother's intentions were good, her distraction of Lin caused her daughter to drop her younger brother, who began to drown as a result. Lin struggled to shift her total concentration back out to sea and the task of saving her younger brother, but try as she might could not regain the necessary focus.

Riding on a beam of celestial light high above the clouds, however, the Venusian orb flier known as Guanshiyin heard the telepathic pleading of Lin Moniang as well as the drowning cries of her little brother. Immediately she readjusted her orb and swooped down under the waves, capturing the little boy, Cheng, in her extended aural projection and dropped him off on the nearby island of Nankan in Matsu group, where she left him in the caring custody of some Buddhist monks.

From then on, Guanshiyin kept an eye on Lin Moniang. She was something special, to be sure; and the angels had big plans for her. One day, in 987, C.E., when Lin had reached the age of 28, she was climbing a mountain to visit a temple of Guanshiyin with young Cheng to offer a prayer of thanks and seek celestial guidance. As Guanshiyin was not occupied in performing any acts of mercy at that time, she decided to swoop down and pay a visit with her two ardent devotees. Lin and Cheng had picked a beautiful bouquet of colorful wildflowers down at the beach to bring up the mountain and place them on the altar in in Guanshiyin's temple. When the two Fujians reached the peak of the mountain, Guanshiyin appeared to them, seeming to step out of the heart of a luminous white, unfolding lotus. She was disembarking from her orb. Guanshiyin spoke to Lin and Cheng: "Welcome, dear friends, to my temple. I appreciate your faithfulness and want to reward you."

Both Lin and Cheng bowed down, prostrating themselves at the feet of Guanshiyin, who stated that, "Thank you for your sentiments, but such an act of worship is not required. We all share in the very Eternal Spirit that animates the Buddha." Guanshiyin then embraced and hugged both Lin and Cheng.

Guanshiyin asked Cheng if he would be alright if Lin went away with her to the Land of the Bright Western Star (Sukhavati or Venus), to become an immortal angel and help people. Cheng replied, "Yes, that would make our entire family very proud."

Guanshiyin asked, "Can you make it back down to the beach and your boat safely, Cheng?" To this question he replied, "Oh yes, I will be fine." Cheng cried and hugged his sister Lin; and then he proceeded back down the mountainside to their father's boat that they rowed out to the temple island.

"Come with me now, Lin Moniang. You shall henceforth be known as Mazu, Queen of the Jade Ocean. Take my hand, and we shall fly to Sukhavati." And so it came to pass that Mazu apprenticed with Guanshiyin, patrolling countless planets and saving all of those in distress for any reason whatsoever. Eventually she was elected the Queen of Venus.

There is a tremendous applause that echoes through the Cyther Dome for the space of ten minutes. As the darkness ebbs throughout the temple, the light returns and Dysmas raises his diadem once again, calling Mazu from her seat in the Aquarius chair of the Hierarchy of Light and down into the kiva. Mazu is wearing a jewel-bedecked red robe and holding the ceremonial tablet of the Queen's authority. Her crown is the flat-topped imperial cap with hanging diamond beads in the front and back. When Mazu arrives at the center of the concentric rings at the bottom of the kiva, she hands the tablet to Dysmas to announce the selection of the new Queen of Venus, before she departs in her red crystalline lotus pod for a new life at the Galactic Core.

The accidental apostle announces that, "Our new Queen is Lady Orda. All hail the Queen!"

The Birth of Venus by Botticelli

Aeon

Adamski with Orthon painting

Day the Earth Stood Still

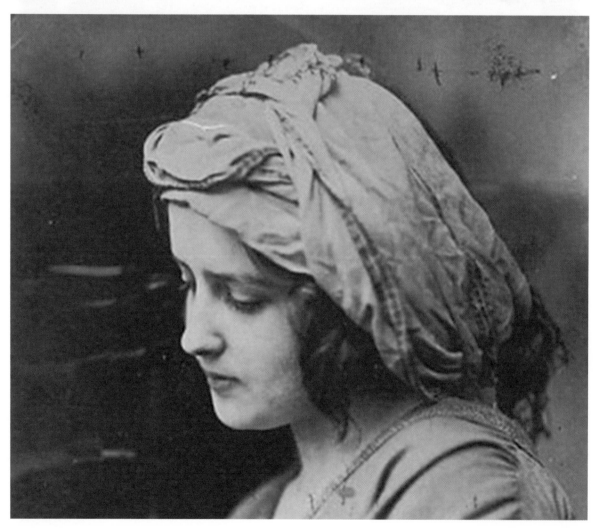

Annalee Skarin

Dolores Barrios

Female Conquistador

Jesus Watching Over the World

299

Omnec Onec, The Woman from Venus

George King

George Van Tassel

300

Superman vs Hitler

Dante Alighieri

Miss Flying Saucer 1959

Nixon and Gleason golfing

Wizard of Oz

Queen of Outer Space

Living Under a Lunar Dome

Venusian City

Last Temptation of Christ

Queen Bee

Mary Binder

303

Zoroaster

War of the Worlds

Space Vixens

Race to Witch Mountain poster

Acknowledgements
Eskertzen Dizut
(Basque/Euskara)

First and foremost, I thank my late Aunt Dolly of Los Angeles, California, who gave me a book about the planets of our solar system for my tenth birthday. This started me on my journey to seek out extraterrestrial life and study the more esoteric realms. It was also out in California that I first became acquainted with the so-called UFO "contactee" community.

Secondly, I credit the famed astronomer, Dr. Carl Sagan, whom I personally met at one of his lectures at the Cleveland Planetarium in 1968, whence he signed an article he wrote about then contemporary discoveries made about the second planet featured in Brian W. Aldiss, ed., *All About Venus* (New York: Dell, 1968). I will never forget Dr. Sagan's profound words that "Somewhere, something incredible is waiting to be known." This sage advice has served as my guiding star.

Third, I am highly appreciative of all the efforts of my associates in the on-going research of the paranormal omniverse. But my particular gratitude is extended to the late Earl J. Neff of the Cleveland Ufology Project, who included me as a cub reporter for the Bedford, Ohio, *Times-Register* newspaper on many of his field investigations; the late Reverend Clayton Parker of Murray, Utah, who introduced me to the real "angels" that share our space-time continuum, living and working among us; *Weekly World News* psychic Andy Reiss, who co-authored my first UFO book, *Extraterrestrials Everywhere* (Hilmar, California: Outer Space International Research and Investigations Society-OSIRIS, 1991); along with my good friends Ballarion Stahr and Michael LaRiche. Ballarion served as my co-director and co-editor of the highly acclaimed and successful Hilmar, California, OSIRIS and *New Millennial Star,* respectively; while Michael and I worked diligently to set up the on-going Coast-to-Coast A.M. Radio Discussion Groups throughout the Northeast Ohio region. An additional and special thanks is extended to Jill Rafter, Director of the Main Library in Clarksburg, Harrison County, West Virginia, and David Houchin, the curator of the Gray Barker collection in the library's Waldomore facility, for their kind assistance rendered in the research phases of this work, and a follow-up book, which is already in the works.

This celestial pilgrim also acknowledges and thanks all of those who have entered and blessed my life with the effulgent light of Venus throughout this and previous incarnations.

Raymond Andrew Keller, II, Ph.D.
April 26, 2015
Morgantown, West Virginia

INDEX

247, 251

Martins, João 217, 286, 287

Mary Marvel 90, 103, 105

Matthews, Arthur 126, 127, 128, 129, 130

Mayan calendar 275, 276

Mazu; see Lin Moniang 294, 295, 296

McDonald, James E. 215

Mehrtens, Susan 80, 81, 82

Menger, Connie, *nee* Weber; see also "Marla,"
   Marla Baxter 58, 59, 146, 149, 159, 170, 176,
   177, 180, 206, 210, 220, 221, 222, 223, 224,
   225, 226, 227, 228, 229, 230, 231, 232, 233,
   234, 235, 254, 255, 265, 266, 269, 288, 293

Menger, Rose 224

Mercury 6, 28, 41, 42, 46, 49, 50, 51, 52, 232

Michael, as archangel 4, 19, 42, 45, 46, 47,
   51, 53, 64, 69, 70, 72, 79, 103, 111, 122, 126,
   139, 141, 156, 158, 186, 194, 238, 240

Milky Way 134, 140, 173, 175, 247

Moniang, Lin 295, 296, 299

Morand, Donald 285, 286, 289

Morning Star 29, 37, 41, 42, 47, 50, 57, 259

Mothership 158, 177, 183, 190

Mutual UFO Network (MUFON) 241

My Saturnian Lover 228

My Visit to Venus 60

My Will Be Done Through Clayton 268

Mystic magazine 99, 100, 150, 151

Nag Hammadi codices 32, 33, 35

Namtso (Heavenly Lake) 276, 292

National Aeronautics and Space Administration
   (NASA) 12, 77, 105, 107, 162, 173, 174, 186,
   187, 188, 189, 190, 192, 195, 202, 212, 214,
   234, 235, 252, 293

National Investigations Committee on Aerial
   Phenomena (NICAP) 72, 190, 214, 215

Natural couples 229

Naval Research Laboratory 189, 190, 251

Neff, Earl J. 4, 241

Neith (cloaked moon of Venus) 171, 253, 294

Nephilim 236, 237

Nephites 139, 271, 272

Neptune 7, 52, 102, 197, 232, 233

New Age 23, 27, 49, 61, 77, 78, 105, 114, 115,
   146, 155, 156, 200, 206, 211, 213, 231, 233,
   238, 261, 265

New Testament 37, 40, 45, 46, 47, 49, 51, 53,

237, 238, 267, 271

Nixon, Richard M. 165, 166, 168, 176, 185

Nogah 38, 39

Norca, Norcans 147

Norman, Ruth 12, 204, 205, 206

North Atlantic Treaty Organization (NATO)
   167

Occult 26, 104, 106, 124

Ode to Coral 294

Olcott, Henry Steel 24, 25, 26

Old Testament 7, 42, 43, 45, 46, 47, 200

Oliver, Francis S. 154, 155, 261

Omnec Onec 210, 211, 212, 213, 216, 227, 253

Ophiuchus (missing astrological sign) 276

Orthon 65, 66, 67, 68, 76, 78, 99, 159, 195,
   284, 285, 287, 289, 290

Outer Limits 87, 88, 138

Outer Space International Research and
   Investigations Society (OSIRIS) 4, 169, 170,
   175, 196, 266, 267, 268, 272, 291

Owens, Ted 83, 84, 86, 87, 89, 97, 103, 104,
   115, 136, 149

Paganism, Pagans 56

Paradiso 53, 54, 55, 282

Parker, Clayton 4, 260, 266, 267, 268, 270

Passmore, Glenn 285, 286, 287

Pearl of Great Price 140, 259, 271

Perelandra 117, 118, 153

Philadelphia Experiment 194

Pioneers of Space 66, 68

Pleroma 30, 32, 50, 51, 52, 77, 141, 145, 249,
   295

Pluto 52, 232, 233

Powder 250, 251

Pratt, Orson 263

Prieto, Alejandro 279, 280

Probert, Mark 158, 159, 160

Project Bluebook 73, 86, 175

Project Grudge 172

Project Sign 172, 173, 247

Project Tic-Toc 192, 193

Quanta, quantum particles 157

Queen(s) 15, 29, 130, 132, 133, 155, 170, 205,
   206, 219, 261, 288, 291, 294, 295, 296

Queen of Outer Space 133, 170

Radar 157

Radiation 12, 189

ABOUT THE AUTHOR

Raymond Andrew Keller, II, was born in Cleveland, Ohio and currently is a lecturer of Greek and Roman Culture and Civilization and Greco-Roman Mythology at West Virginia University in Morgantown, West Virginia. He also serves as an AmeriCorps VISTA (Volunteer in Service to America), attached to In Touch and Concerned, a United Way agency in Monongalia County, West Virginia, where he assists persons with disabilities, seniors and veterans in securing affordable transportation options. He also teaches various social studies classes as an adjunct professor at West Virginia Northern Community College in Wheeling, West Virginia.

Keller has been involved in active UFO research since 1967, when he was a reporter for the *Bedford Times Register* in his hometown of Bedford, Ohio, and a research associate with Earl J. Neff, the founder and director of the Cleveland Ufology Project (CUP). Keller established his own group in 1986, the Outer Space International Research and Investigations Society (OSIRIS) and was the publisher and co-editor with Ballarion Starr of that organization's monthly organ, *The New Millennial Star*. Keller has conducted numerous excursions to UFO hot spots throughout the world and has communicated directly with extraterrestrials on many occasions. *Venus Rising* is his second book; the first being *Emergence of the Afro-Zulians in the Transatlantic World, 1722-1811* (Lewiston, NY: Mellen Press, 2013).

He graduated from Bedford Senior High School in Bedford, Ohio and went on to honorably serve in both the United States Navy, where he was the feature editor of the Miramar Naval Air Station *Jet Journal* in San Diego, California; and in the United States Army, where he worked as a voice intercept operator in the Spanish language throughout Latin America. He received an associate degree in business from the University of Maryland and his bachelor of arts in world history from the University of Maryland, both degrees while on active duty. In 1989 he successfully completed the Multicultural Education Program at the College of Santa Fe in New Mexico, whence he went on to become the Director of English as a Second Language and Bilingual/Multicultural Education programs for secondary education at the Hilmar Unified School District in the San Joaquin Valley in California from 1990-1995.

Keller was employed by VENUSA (Venezuela-United States Academy) in Mérida, Venezuela, in 2001 and 2002 as an ESL instructor and editor of the textbook division. He also was attached to La Universidad Valle del Momboy in Valera, Venezuela, from VENUSA. He returned to the United States in 2002 to accept a scholarship in foreign languages at West Virginia University, receiving his master's degree in Spanish with an emphasis on Latin American literature in May 2004. He enrolled in the doctoral program in the Department of History in the fall of 2004, and mostly taught classes on Africana Studies, with some World History and Latin America.